CW00545823

JENNIFER
BRITTON

RECONNECTING WORKSPACES

Pathways to
Thrive in the Virtual,
Remote, and Hybrid World

RECONNECTING WORKSPACES

Pathways to Thrive in the Virtual, Remote, and Hybrid World

Jennifer J. Britton

Published by
Potentials Realized
Ontario, Canada

Copyright ©2021 by Jennifer J. Britton
All rights reserved.

No part of this book may be reproduced in any form by electronic or mechanical means, including information storage and retrieval systems, without permission in writing from the publisher, except by a reviewer who may quote brief passages in a review. Requests to the Publisher for permission should be addressed to Permissions Department, Potentials Realized, PO Box 93305, Newmarket, Ontario, Canada L3X 1A3.

Limit of Liability/Disclaimer of Warranty: While the publisher and author have used their best efforts in preparing this book, they make no representations or warranties with respect to the accuracy or completeness of the contents of this book and specifically disclaim any implied warranties of merchantability or fitness for a particular purpose. No warranty may be created or extended by sales representatives or written sales materials. The advice and strategies contained herein may not be suitable for your situation. You should consult with a professional where appropriate. Neither the publisher nor author shall be liable for any loss of profit or any other commercial damages, including but not limited to special, incidental, consequential, or other damages.

Copyeditor: Kim Leitch, www.tandemthinkers.ca
Cover and Interior design: Yvonne Parks, www.PearCreative.ca
Proofreader: Lynette Smith, www.AllMyBest.com
Index: Russell Santana, www.e4editorial.com

ISBN: 978-0-9937915-5-0 (paperback)
978-0-9937915-6-7 (eBook)

Quantity discounts are available on bulk purchases of this book for educational, gift purposes, or as premiums for increasing magazine subscriptions or renewals. Special books or book excerpts can also be created to fit specific needs. For information, please contact Potentials Realized, PO Box 93305 Newmarket, Ontario, Canada L3X 1A3.

This book is dedicated to the billions of people around the world who learned to live and work in the virtual space overnight in 2020, and who continue to create exceptional teams and organizations as we navigate our way forward.

CONTENTS

ACKNOWLEDGMENTS

"Great works are performed not by strength, but by perseverance."
—Samuel Johnson

Like any writing project, books evolve over time. This book has been shaped by adventures and conversations over many years. I first put my fingers to keyboard on November 1, 2017, and almost three years later in the midst of the pandemic of 2020, I felt it was time to bring this across the finish line.

As a writer who is ahead of the trends (it's always a gamble to put work out in the world, knowing that it often takes some time for my book to find its place in the time line. My first book, *Effective Group Coaching,* raised eyebrows in the coaching world, and *Effective Virtual Conversations* was years ahead of its time in 2017.

For many years this work was under the project name, VRTWL—Virtual and Remote Teams, Work and Leadership. What was missing from the equation was the focus on the hybrid. It's clear today that the next phase in the work world will be hybrid.

If we do have another unforeseen pivot as we had this last year, then rest assured, you will find this valuable as it relates to the virtual and remote worlds.

Blends have always been part of my world—from where I've worked and lived to the multidisciplinary fusion of my professional work, to the multicultural weave of my own family. To me, hybrids create the space for possibilities. What's possible for you?

A big thank you to so many who helped me move this book forward. As I shared in my 2013 book, *From One to Many: Best Practices for Team and Group Coaching,*

> "If you want to go fast, go alone. If you want to go far, go together." —The African proverb

This work was not birthed in isolation, and has strands across work I've done in all continents, virtually and physically, spanning almost three decades. It's humbling to think about the thousands of conversations which shaped this "tome," as we've called it.

From conversations held under a benab in the jungles of South America to the virtual greenrooms prior to Zoom presentations, these topics are cross-cultural and cross-temporal. Even with so much changing in the virtual world, you'll find this book to be platform agnostic. The principles of each chapter are timeless, regardless of how much changes. The myths have not changed since I first penned them years ago. If anything, the experience of billions of people learning to work in the remote and virtual space has shown just how silly myths can be. Remember, "you'll stay in your pajamas every day"?

I'm once again thankful to those who made lighter work of this project. My team was a great support:

> To Janica Smith. Thank you once again for shepherding this process. Your eye to detail is a keen one, and your steady hand on process is always reassuring.
>
> To Kim Leitch, my editor. Thank you for helping move "the tome" forward. You have been a steady anchor across my involvement in the coaching world for many years, and to find you being on my pathway in the backyard has been amazing!
>
> Thank you to the illustrators who brought to life my ideas—Reza M. Fadhli, Janross Anthony Gutierrez, and Steven Ravensfeller.
>
> To my *Remote Pathways* podcast co-host, Michelle Mullins, I so appreciate your seeing my vision two years ago to breathe to life in the adventures of the Digital Dozen in our podcast. Little would we have know what the future would bring. Thank you for your collaboration and ongoing support!
>
> To Honey Edeque. Thank you for spearheading the graphics and other behind the scenes work. Your smile every Monday morning during our 5:30 a.m. meeting is always a great start to my week!

Thank you to those who have Sprinted with me this year as part of the 21 for 21 Virtual Co-working Sprints. I've loved seeing your commitment to the experimentation and action you have taken every day, bringing to life the *PlanDoTrack* mantra of "Daily Steps + Consistent Action = Momentum."

I also want to thank the organizers of the Muskoka Novel Marathon, who spearhead an annual weekend writing for adult literacy. This book has been flavored by my participation during the July 2019 (in-person) and July 2020 (Quarantine) editions. This will lay the foundation for further offshoot books which will follow the pathways of the Digital Dozen™, so stay tuned.

Finally, to you as readers, thank you for investing time in the process. I hope this book will be a go-to resource for you in your virtual, remote, and hybrid pathways. Whether you are a leader, employee, or business owner, you will find these resources valuable.

Be sure to connect in at ReconnectingWorkspaces.com, to access the additional book resources.
Use access code **4411** when prompted!

WANT TO GET MORE DONE?
JOIN US AT THE VIRTUAL CO-WORKING SPRINTS.

As always, if you have any questions, want to share a story or impact, or want to book me as a speaker, coach or consultant, please reach out to me directly at info@potentialsrealized.com. You will find my other details at the end of the book.

Enjoy the read and your conversations afterwards!

Jennifer Britton | Spring 2021

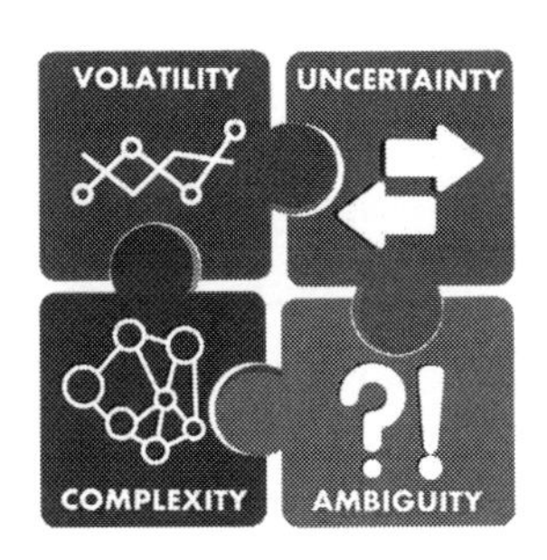

CHAPTER 1

WORKSPACES IN TODAY'S VIRTUAL, DIGITAL, HYBRID, AND REMOTE WORLD

"Digital Darwinism is unkind to those who wait."[1]
– Ray Wang

Principle: Keep it simple.

Myth: We need to physically be present together to get things done, build relationships, have dinner parties, potlucks, or birthday parties, build teams, and achieve business results.

While we have been faced with rapid and ongoing change for many centuries, we are in the midst of another huge wave of change. The pandemic of 2020 literally shifted the way more than three billion people worked, collaborated, and lived.

While pandemic changes have been sudden, they've accelerated some of the major shifts we've seen in recent years. The last few years have seen massive changes, from artificial intelligence (AI) coming to our homes, to booksellers becoming grocers. Disruption is everywhere and is changing the context of leadership, teamwork, business, and life in general. Workplaces have become workspaces, with the boundaries of work and life blurring for many.

As we move into this era where virtual, remote, and hybrid ways of working are the norm, a key requirement to help everyone thrive, and not just survive, is reconnecting workspaces. Professionals of all kinds are hungry for connection. Paradigms have shifted, and in this space everyone needs skills to do their best work. This book is geared for you.

The term VUCA—volatility, uncertainty, complexity, and ambiguity—is commonly bandied around as the descriptor for the forces rocking the business context and shaping our world of teamwork and leadership today. It was ironic that as I started to write this book back in 2017, I was en route to New York, the morning after a Halloween terror attack at the World Trade Center, wondering, could I not just undertake this engagement virtually?

The world of business has changed, and groups are becoming more accustomed to all things virtual, yet there still is a premium placed on having people "in person" or what many refer to as "real." Is building relationships in person any different than collaborating via video with a colleague halfway across the world?

Remote doesn't mean disconnected. The last few years have seen many changes in the workplace and workspace which have been transformed by people "working remote," full time, or once or twice a month. The shift to work-from-home arrangements in the 2020 pandemic has created an even stronger sense of "workspace" where work can take place from multiple locations.

Worldwide, these shifts in business place topics, never seen before, front and center on the radar screens of professionals. These changes are influencing the way leaders lead and team members operate, from having contingencies in place when crises arise and the unthinkable happens, to leading and operating in a way that empowers others.

This book is about creating a vibrant and engaged virtual, remote, and hybrid working environment. It is essential to reconnect people in ways where everyone can contribute, learn, and grow.

It is geared for leaders, team members, and business owners alike, given the tremendous diversity of today's virtual and remote workspaces. From one-person global storefronts of the solopreneur to virtual organizations which operate only remotely, the forces of digitization are reshaping consumer behavior, financial institutions, and even how surgeries are being undertaken.

As much as the outcomes have changed, how are we equipping both our leaders and teams in this new world? As I wrote in my last book, *Effective Virtual Conversations*, virtual doesn't have to be about the "Death by Conference Call" mindset, a frenetic multitasking context of focusing on a multitude of tasks, yet never being present. Virtual doesn't need to mean ongoing disruption. In fact, the digital space can be a leveraged, focused workspace, rich with continuous learning and deep relationships.

This book will explore the vibrant and practical world of virtual and remote leadership and teamwork in today's digitally disrupted era. Whether we are being called upon to change our leadership, conversations, and teamwork due to a global pandemic, changes in technology, new borders that did not exist before, or a merger and acquisition, this book is geared to help you, as a **leader**, **business owner**, or **team member**, to have the necessary **conversations**, **equip** yourselves and your team, and **lead** more confidently through the challenges immediately in front of you and even those not yet on the radar screen.

This book is not just about leadership, it is also about teamwork. It is grounded in the philosophy and recognition that leadership and teamwork go hand in hand in today's business context, especially for virtual, hybrid, and remote teams. Our team members are our experts on the ground. Unlike former models and approaches of leadership, our team members also need the same skills and abilities that leaders do. As such, we will be exploring a range of skills for all professionals in today's workspace—leaders, team members, and business owners.

We'll be looking at more mainstream topics such as time management and personal productivity, key for harnessing the best of a distributed workforce, as well as areas which are still new to some, including emotional intelligence (EI), with its focus on knowing ourselves, understanding others, and building and managing relationships.

We'll also explore topics that are impacting leaders like never before and reshaping what we do, from Agile's influence on project management to digitization, Design Thinking, and AI.

The context in which we lead and the skills needed for leadership today are also rapidly changing. Consider this factoid from Google: the amount of information available from the start of writing/industrial revolution to 2003, is now doubling in two days.[2] Wow! Talk about change at such a pace that we can't see what is needed in the time ahead of us. Skills like **patterning**—being able to see themes in complexity—are also important.

While expert status in the past has been something to aspire to, today many aspire to become a "specialized generalist" in order to thrive in the rapidly changing context. Emerging out of the Agile world, a "specialized generalist" is someone who is talented in cross-functional ways and can contribute across projects. With today's pace of change comes the need to be fluid and flexible, with the ability to pivot and change our behavior. How adept have your organization's behaviors become?

Take a moment and think about the changes you have seen in your business context in the last three years (if you have been at the same job or with the same organization for that amount of time, that is). Think back to a specific moment in time so you can get granular about what your work and leadership was like then.

Now think about the last quarter. What are the conversations you have been having? What are the top three skills you have needed to lead from? What is on the horizon? What was on the horizon three months ago? How has this changed? What was your business context then, and now? What did you use to do your work three years ago? A year ago? Where did you spend your time? Where were your business conversations? My guess is that many of these factors have changed significantly.

Today, most teams are dynamic, breathing, living entities. Today's team composition may not be tomorrow's. The term **teaming** emerged to represent the notion that teams are not only a noun but a verb—a living, shifting entity. Think about the stability of the team you were part of at that earlier touch point. How stable and firm were things like team roles (what different people did)? How stable was the team composition? How different was the role of team leader to the role of team member? Where and how were conversations taking place? Again, my guess is that this has probably shifted.

According to Klaus Schwab and the World Economic Forum, we are in the Fourth Revolution, one that "is characterized by a range of new technologies that are fusing the physical, digital and biological worlds, impacting all disciplines, economies and industries, and even challenging ideas about what it means to be human."[3]

Think about how self-driving cars (and trucks) may change your world and how the growth of AI could reshape your role and work. It's an exciting time and a time during which many are challenged and afraid. Carol Dweck's research around growth mindset is taking root in many organizations to support staff in embracing these changes. Stepping into a growth mindset allows us to see the importance of always learning and that we have not yet finished growing.

These workplace shifts call for the need for skills across industries and for the ability to cross-collaborate. Amy Edmondson, who coined word *teaming*, explores the theory behind successful cross-disciplinary collaboration. Her research has identified four leadership practices essential for navigating the choppy waters of change.

Key skills she identified for team interaction involve "asking questions, seeking feedback, experimenting, reflecting on results, and discussing errors or unexpected outcomes of actions."[4]

What implications does that have for your work? Your role? Your leadership?

For the better part of the last three decades I have been involved in facilitating conversations across boundaries. This work included creating global education programming for a Canadian NGO (non-government organization) in the early 1990s, supporting anti-racism and social justice training in Toronto in the mid-1990s, and bringing together, supporting, and leading a United Nations team of multisectoral professionals from different cultural roots to undertake work in rebuilding countries devastated by natural disaster.

To some of us, the changes we see today are not surprising. **They do require a need for a different way of thinking, of working, and of seeing the world.** The ability to bridge differences, facilitate conversations across cultures, and raise the difficult conversations which require candor and honesty, are now central leadership and teamwork issues for industries of all kinds, including health care, financial services, education, and government.

This book is about how full-time virtual organizations, remote teams, and hybrid workplaces can find a more effective way to communicate, work, collaborate, and problem solve. It is imperative that we reconnect people, to harness the diverse talents of today's workforce. I am hopeful that this book will be of benefit to all in the workspace today, including team members, leaders, and even entrepreneurs and solopreneurs.

An earlier working title of this book was VRTWL, which stands for Virtual and Remote Teamwork, Work, and Leadership. We'll be covering all of these areas.

This book is written with the practitioner in mind, whether you are a team member, leader, coach, or business owner. As such, each chapter will explore the myths and practices needed for the virtual, remote, and hybrid workforce today. We'll explore what science, particularly neuroscience, is discovering to help us excel and thrive. This book also has exercises, checklists, and tools for you to use right away, encapsulated in each chapter's Team Tools. The book will focus on ideas that bring to life the tremendous diversity which exists in teamwork and leadership today.

My hope is that this book provokes you to think about your own impact and how you can contribute to the conversations that your organization, team, and people need. Some of these conversations will be difficult, but many will be positive. I hope this book will equip you to facilitate conversions more comfortably across your team, your stakeholders, and other partners.

One benefit of the workspace today is that we can jet around the world in a very fast way without ever leaving our office. It's not uncommon for me to have had several hours of conversation by 9:00 a.m. with clients scattered across Asia, Africa, Europe, and North America. Globally, I hear across the board how much time pressure there is and how, despite our differences, we are all striving for similar things in our work as leaders, business owners, and team members.

Many business and team challenges cross cultural boundaries, while others are very distinct according to where we operate, and what context we operate from. Chapter 4 explores the unique diversity that exists on our teams. From varying generational differences to understanding the cultural nuances when your team of 10 comes from 10 different cultures, team leadership and teamwork have never been more exciting or diverse.

In my book, *Effective Virtual Conversations,* I had a series of illustrations created. In them, we met Jane and Jo. Jane was a talented virtual facilitator, and Jo a new virtual team leader. Their adventures reflect many of the same challenges and opportunities other team leaders and virtual conversationalists face. We'll be meeting them and some other characters in this book, bringing to life the trials and tribulations of virtual workers everywhere.

Consider how much has changed in your world of work and teams in the last decade:

- It's likely that ten years ago teams were more co-located than they are today.
- Even in regular offices, people had walls rather than the world of "hotelling": rotational meeting spaces to work in, where all you might have is a little ledge to work from.
- Smart phones were still fun and new and not something we felt tethered to.
- Commute times were likely shorter.
- Your local team may have been more closely located than it is today.
- We travelled to grocery stores to buy food rather than ordering online.

Many system changes are creating a remote, hybrid, and virtual workplace today, changing the way we work and the identity we have in organizations.

THE CONTEXT OF A DIGITALLY DISRUPTED WORLD

As we start this book, let's look at the current context.

The facts and figures we can conjure up in today's *Encyclopedia Britannica*, i.e., Google, is quite astounding. While at one point in time non-traditional publishers were looked down upon, alternative presses such as the *Huffington Post* continue to thrive while many of the traditional publishers have withered away. Cable TV has been replaced by Netflix in many homes, and work can literally happen all around the world, 24/7. When I first started working globally and the internet came in, our email had to sit overnight on a server in Trinidad before being released. This provided at least a few hours of being offline.

Here's a snapshot of virtual, remote, and global business. Did you know that,

"One in three executives agrees that virtual teams are badly managed. This is probably a result of virtual working simply evolving into being rather than being planned in advance, but it is also to do with the difficulty of leading people from a distance."[5]

"More than two out of three survey respondents believe that the advantages of working in a virtual team outweigh the disadvantages."[6]

"Virtual working is not always detrimental to a work-life balance. Fully 45% of respondents disagree that virtual working blurs the lines between work and life and a further 21% are undecided. Three out of every four respondents also state that they travel less because of working virtually."[7]

"The single most common challenge, selected by 56% of executives polled, relates to the misunderstandings that emerge because of cultural and language differences from teams operating globally."[8]

Face-to-face meetings are still needed. Jasmine Whitbread of Save the Children notes, "Working in virtual teams can lose the spontaneity of a face-to-face meeting in which you're required to use your full range of sensual perceptions."[9]

Pre-pandemic, a local municipality questioned whether their council meetings should shift to videophone. The concern raised was not whether they could connect, but whether they would be calling in from the outdoors. Rather than pointing fingers, they will remain nameless, and reading this was a push for why more books debunking the myths and challenges of virtual work need to be written. As an update, that municipality, like thousands of others, has made the shift to remote work, with several others feeling the growth and authenticity of this new way of working.

MOBILITY AND WHAT MOBILE LEARNING MEANS

Mobility, along with virtual and remote work, has not been embraced with wide-open arms. Consider IBM who co-located many of their teams after years of remote work, in 2017. One of their earlier internal studies, "The Mobile Working Experience," in 2005 by IBM Europe, surveyed 351 remote workers from 29 European countries. The study made the following observations (quoted verbatim):

There was a rise in the number of individuals who had recently begun working in a mobile environment.

Mobile workers face several difficulties in communicating and collaborating with colleagues.

There is a danger that mobile workers can become disconnected from the informal networks traditionally used to share knowledge and identify opportunities within the organization.

Mobile workers face many challenges in balancing the demands of work and home life.

A reliable, easy-to-use technological structure was essential to the success of the mobile work environment.[10]

Note how similar these earlier concerns around mobile work are aligned with today's challenges with virtual and remote work.

While many of these earlier concerns are still present around collaboration, connection, communication, and work-life, this book explores how professionals can proactively address these issues.

Mobile Learning

Let's look back at the early days of mobile learning and at three definitions:

1. Mobile learning is "any sort of learning that happens when the learner is not at a fixed, predetermined location or learning that happens when the learner takes advantage of learning opportunities offered by mobile technologies."[11]
2. "Mobile learning should be restricted to learning devices which a lady can carry in her handbag or a gentleman can carry in his pocket."[12]
3. Geddes defined mobile learning in 2004 as "the acquisition of any knowledge and skill through using mobile technology, anywhere, anytime, that results in an alteration in behaviour."[13]

Today, mobility means a lot of different things. It's about the ability to move between locations, as well as access information from multiple locations. The freedom afforded through more location-independent work, is appealing to many. It has roots in the mobile world.

As many workspaces shift to a hybrid model, rather than one all-virtual, mobility issues will regain in importance. What are you doing to make sure people can connect from devices of all kinds?

THE DIGITAL DOZEN™

The Remote Pathways podcast explores the adventures of the Digital Dozen and the people, places and pathways to remote work

Ned
New Remote Worker

Jo Virtual
Team Leader

Serge
Serial Remote Entrepreneur

Mel
Coach

Sujit
Project Manager

Sally
Salesperson

Mo
Creative Solopreneur

Jane
Virtual Facilitator

Malcom
Mentor

Alex
Work From Anywhere (WFA)

Victor
Volunteer

Sam
Selling Start-up

In my *Remote Pathways* writing, I speak to 12 different mobile types of work, bringing these to life via the Digital Dozen. As we move through the book, you'll hear more about their world of work. They range from digital nomadism, where freelancers work around the world, to remote workers who are attached to a larger company, to project managers and start-ups leading a completely virtual enterprise. Listen in to the *Remote Pathways* podcast to learn more about their adventures.[14]

New iterations of mobile learning are likely, with predictions of moving to a screenless environment and working in a voice-activated space.

So what else is important?

Complexity, change, community, and conversations are all topics which have relevance in today's business world. Many leaders today realize that what worked last year may not guarantee a home run again. This is changing how we look at time and resourcing. It's also impacting our memory and what we retain.

Today's business context demands continuous learning and collapsing longer training into bite-sized pieces in microlearning. The incorporation of brain-based science continues to get cultivated, as reflected in each chapter's focus on a brain-based, neuroscience tip.

The cost of digital disruption—what impact does this have on engagement?

Carson Tate's May 2016 article in the *Huffington Post* entitled, "Pay Attention: Because It Impacts Your Productivity," indicated that the cost of digital distraction is $10 million.[15]

BENEFITS TO WORKING REMOTE

There are a range of experiences and working relationships in the remote and virtual workspace. There are teams which operate virtually across major urban centers and teams that physically don't ever connect. The Digital Dozen I speak to in *Remote Pathways* bring to life the experiences and adventures of those working in the remote and hybrid space today.

What makes this so compelling and a sector which continues to grow? These following four benefits continue to surface as compelling benefits:

1. **Cutting down on commute time**. As someone who lives in the Greater Toronto Area (GTA), a city with one of the longest commute times in North America, I often wonder how many of my neighbors sustain it day in and day out. Imagine commuting for an hour-plus each way, each day. That translates to almost 10 to 12 hours of commute time a week. During an early revision of this book, a 1.5-hour trip into the city for me became a 3.5-hour adventure due to train malfunction. Thankfully, I had this manuscript to work on! The toll on people's health, well-being, and mindset can be huge. **What would you do with an extra 10 hours of time in your week?** I know for me, it allows me to fit in a couple of swims a week and time to care for my parents and my son.

2. **Reducing Footprints**. For the environmentally minded, remote work may mean less travel, commute, and carbon cost. For an organization, it means reducing the footprint and cost of physical office space. In many urban centers, the cost of physical rent is astronomical. Smarter office design, along with remote working arrangements for some or all employees, can reduce the footprint of many organizations. As a recent study found, "part-time remote work in the U.S. could slow carbon emissions by more than 51 million metric tonnes annually."[16] **What changes has your office made in the last decade around work space and design?**

   At an organizational level, there is usually a reduced cost for office space. While earlier studies found that the cost to support one telecommuter was estimated at $4,000, Firstbase estimated the cost was $18,400 per workspace, including 520 hours commuting, and 5,443 pounds of CO_2 emitted per person, every year.[17]

   The shift to digital workspaces has been significant. The pandemic created a global laboratory to see the pros and cons of working remotely.

   As WSP posits, "in a knowledge economy, an organization's success will still depend on face-to-face interaction, collaboration and serendipity."[18]

These are in addition to employee retention and environmental issues. An Open University study found that e-learning consumes 90% less energy than traditional courses. They found that the amount of CO_2 emissions (per student) is also reduced by up to 85%.[19]

A 2020 study by Crow and Millot found that, "if everybody able to work from home worldwide were to do so for just one day a week, it would save around 1% of global oil consumption for road passenger transport per year."[20]

3. **Leveraging the best of the best regardless of location.** Remote work arrangements also allow employers to tap into the best talent, regardless of location. For most top talent, the ability to be able to work autonomously with minimal supervision is the norm. Top talent is able to identify when collaboration and face-to-face time will benefit their work.

4. **Productivity without all the interruptions.** The cost of interruptions within the context of a day is staggering. Research by Gloria Mark found that it takes approximately 22 minutes to return to focus after disruption.[21] The *Huffington Post* found that the 100-odd interruptions a day converted to approximately "2 hours of dead time" from disruptions.[22]

Even if working remotely is only an option several days a week, employees may notice higher rates of productivity and getting things done from their own remote location, as long as they are not facing regular interruptions. When working from home, interruptions can include emails, meetings, or even children demanding attention.

What is the impact and cost of interruptions in your workplace?

YEARNINGS OF TODAY'S WORKER—FROM ENGAGEMENT TO MEANING TO ACCOUNTABILITY TO DEMAND FOR FLEXIBILITY

The notion of what constitutes an engaged workforce continues to change. The advent of the gig economy signals that not everyone is happy with or aspires to work with others.

David Ulrich writes in *HR, Interrupted*, "In engagement literature, there's been an evolution. It used to be, 'Do you like your job?' Satisfaction. Then it became engagement. 'Does your boss give you the tools to do your job?' Now, engagement literature is about meaning and purpose. 'Do you find meaning and purpose in your job?' 'Is it linked to your identity?'" said Ulrich. "And the other piece that goes along with that is to focus the accountability of this on the employee. This is active engagement."[23]

What are you noticing about what engagement means in your organization?

DEMAND FOR FLEXIBILITY

What are workers yearning for?

According to a global survey of 13,961 workers by the Manpower Group, workplace flexibility is crucial for candidates in the job search process:

- 63% believe they don't need to be sitting at their desk to get work done
- 40% say schedule flexibility is a top-three factor when making career decisions
- 26% say their top preference is flexible work arrival and departure times[24]

THE REALM OF VIRTUAL WORK—FROM TELECOMMUTING TO STREAMING TO TELEPRESENCE

Gary Woodill, in *The Mobile Learning Edge: Tools and Technologies for Developing Your Teams,* quotes Marshall McLuhan as saying, "We look at the present through a rear-view mirror. We march backwards into the future."[25]

We've come a long way since Jack Nilles, known as the grandfather of telecommuting, first wrote about telecommuting in 1973. He defined Teleworking as "any form of substitution of information technologies for work and related travel."[26]

Think about how your virtual work has shifted over time. Three decades ago, my own experience of remote work and telecommuting involved three-times-a-day "sit-reps" (an old army term for a situation report) with a team scattered across a South American nation. It was these thrice-daily conversations which ensured health and safety, troubleshooting, and project success. The radio was a lifeline to those groups, where physical travel could take several days, and the nearest phone was a day or more journey away.

Today, technology has shrunken the world. With several former colleagues, I can now call them up on Facebook Messenger and have a conversation. Technology changes are the norm, not the exception any more. Where once people were petrified to do virtual work because of the challenges, many now embrace the notion that "it's not going to work as I thought it would."

As we look ahead, it's important to also use history as a foundation. Let's look at what has happened in the realm of telecommuting, one of the first precursors of virtual and remote work.

Telecommuting:

According to Nilles, telecommuting means, "Moving the work to the workers instead of moving the workers to work."[27]

In 1990, there were 3.4 million teleworkers, growing to 19.6 million in 1996. By 2015, the latest US census found that 6.5 million workers were working full time from home.[28]

"A majority of teleworkers at AT&T report increased productivity due to telecommuting, listing fewer meetings and interruptions as reason."[29]

By late 2020, CNBC had estimated that in 2021, one in four Americans would be working remotely.[30]

TRAITS OF SUCCESSFUL REMOTE WORKERS AND MANAGERS

Early studies found that successful telecommuters, according to Grensing-Pophal, "stay connected with coworkers and boss, are well organized, get out of the house, separate work from home, make tech a friend, and know when to take a break."[31]

The same study notes that remote work is not for:

- Employees who have a high need for social interaction
- Employees who are easily distracted by outside demands and interruptions
- Employees who need the office setting to provide an environment conducive to work

Schilling noted the following characteristics as foundational for success with early telecommuters or early remote workers: self-motivated, high level of job knowledge and skills, high performance, independence and confidence, comfort with solitude, time management and organization, strong communication skills, and trustworthiness.[32]

How do these compare to what you see as being needed in today's workspace? In some ways, as much as things have changed, they have remained the same.

Tom Joseph, founder and Chief Executive Officer of Bookminders, says, "Developing a results-oriented system for managing performance is fundamental to successful supervision of a home worker."[33]

Contrast this to the 2020 experience which heralded a results-orientation,[34] as well as other indicators such as resilience in predicting Work From Home Success.[35]

KEY TIPS TO MAKING VIRTUAL WORK

In my book, *Effective Virtual Conversations*, I explored what it took to make virtual work. This includes:

- Co-creating expectations
- Placing an emphasis on building trust and connection with the team, and taking the pulse of this regularly
- Clarity (of communication, goals, process, purpose, tools, roles, and end results)
- Ensuring fit by the employee
- Flexibility on the part of the team member

In an earlier study, TeleCommute Solutions asked which attributes of management were most important. More than 50% of these managers identified adequate planning skills as a critical requirement to achieve success in this environment.[36]

The second critical skill identified by these managers was leadership. Stephen Schilling noted, "This skill was seen as the ability to motivate, facilitate and inspire telecommuters as effectively as if they were traditional office workers."[37]

As Lin Grensing-Pophal noted,[38] some of these earlier studies found that managers of telecommuters need the following qualities:

- Comfort with supervising a remote workforce (people you cannot see)
- Understanding of what is required of the position
- Ability to clearly articulate goal and objectives
- Effective interpersonal communication
- Ability to provide clear and consistent feedback

Motivating factors found in that study indicate that excellent leaders were able to:

- Listen to concerns
- Be available
- Share information
- Give ample recognition
- Treat everyone as individuals
- Provide opportunities for professional growth
- Have fun

Mark J. Wallace identified four downfalls that emerge over time in virtual work:[39]

1. Lack of quality face time with people, particularly where high interaction was required by the work process or the nature of the work itself
2. Absence of the workplace
3. Lost creativity
4. Unmet expectations

Anecdotally, many of these factors have been experienced during the 2020–2021 pandemic by some employees. Some organizations have lamented the loss of the "social fabric" while others have made an intentional point in formally and informally building connections across their team.

Our recent experience of remote working has mirrored many of the earlier studies which found the pros and cons of the virtual workspace. With this in mind, it brings us back to the basics around work, performance, and clarifying expectations around work, regardless of whether we are face-to-face, virtual, remote, or hybrid.

Another key factor for success is ensuring appropriate leadership styles are followed.

What hats are you going to wear as a virtual leader? A shift to more of a coaching and mentoring style helps to facilitate autonomy on the part of the remote team member. It's important to cultivate a culture where all employees can bring their expertise to the table, problem solve, and harness the expertise they may have, given their location or context. We'll explore these in Chapter 8.

Blanchard's Situational Leadership Model[40] is one way to adjust leadership style and support, providing different types of support according to the task at hand and the person's abilities, not just their seniority.

Increased collaboration and community, dynamism, personalization, and time savings are some of the many factors which shape today's evolving workspace.

How are these factors influencing your workspaces today?

"Working together, apart" has been part of the pandemic workspace legacy. It has reinforced the tensions in our workspace for individualization and collaboration, structure and flow, and change and consistency.

As we wrap up this chapter, what are you noticing about your workspace?

OUR ROADMAP—AN OVERVIEW

Where are we going in this book? Similar to the shifts we are seeing in the learning space, attention spans have changed. Like my other books, you may not want to read this book cover to cover, but may want to dip into the chapters which are most relevant to you at this time. Each chapter has a different focus.

Along with the chapter title, each chapter will have a chapter icon to anchor learning. Visuals have been found to be more than 60,000 times more powerful than words. Each chapter also includes a principle and myth around virtual, remote, and hybrid teamwork, leadership, and workspaces.

You'll see the following elements, along with the icons, included in each chapter:

A team tool. Use these and share them with your team.

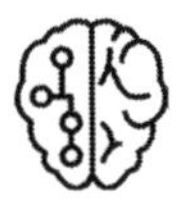

A brain tip. With a tip of the hat to empirical research, we turn to the continued advances of neuroscience.

Six questions to get you into dialogue. You are encouraged to share these with your team to spark conversations.

A reconnection tip to help you thrive in the remote, virtual, or hybrid workspace.

Are you ready to get started? Let's go!

TEAM TOOL—MIND MAP

Mind Mapping is one of many visual mapping techniques. Whether you choose to annotate by hand, Post-it notes, annotation, or one of the many software programs, Mind Mapping is a powerful way to generate, capture, and visualize new ideas.

For several decades now I have seen the power of introducing Mind Mapping to individuals and team members as a process to unlock new ideas and possibilities.

There is a growing variety of different approaches to visualizing ideas and capturing them.

As Sunni Brown shares in her book, *The Doodle Revolution*, there are several types of infodoodling, including Personal, Performance, and Group Infodoodling. She describes the latter as an event where groups can "work together to solve a specific challenge using a sequence of activities inside a visual-thinking process."[41]

> What are the current challenges and opportunities facing you as a business, organization, team, or group? How might approaching this from a new angle help you?

SIX TEAMWORK QUESTIONS FOR VIRTUAL AND REMOTE TEAMS[42]

1. What's going to help you be most productive?
2. What support do you need to do your best work?
3. How do you want to stay connected with the team?
4. What support do you need from me?
5. What information/accessibility do you need to get your work done?
6. What feedback loops should we set up?

SIX QUESTIONS FOR VIRTUAL AND REMOTE TEAM LEADERS[43]

1. When was the last time you held a one-on-one with each of your team members?
2. What are the current support needs you have for your remote team members?
3. When are your next face-to-face meetings scheduled?

4. What type of support does each team member value?
5. Does everyone have the tools they need in order to do their most effective work?
6. Shared vision is critical for success, especially in a remote team. On a scale of 1 to 10, how clear and shared would everyone say the vision is?

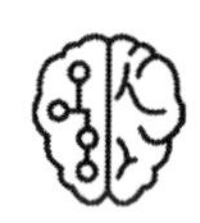

BRAIN TIP: MAKE IT VISUAL/FOCUS

Visuals are powerful. While commonly debated as a point of potential "fake news," a 1982 IBM brochure indicated that our brains process images 60,000 times faster than text.[44]

A study by Crocket found that "people can remember the content of 2500 pictures with over 90 percent accuracy 72 hours after looking at them for only 10 seconds. A year later participants had 63 percent recall of those same images. With traditional lecture format delivery, students only remember 10 percent of the material 72 hours later."[45]

Think about how metaphor, and how visual metaphors, i.e., pictures, can capture and encode ideas in a much different way than just words.

It's one of the reasons why we're exploring this here, and you'll notice across this book that each chapter has icons to signify some of the key tips of the chapter, along with other illustrations.

A LOOK BACK AT OUR DIGITAL WORKSPACES

RECONNECTING THE WORKSPACE TIP

There are many fundamental elements to exceptional virtual, remote, and hybrid work. Regardless of the changes, our principles become anchor points. The foundational anchor points which ground our work at Potentials Realized includes:

- Digital delivery
- Less is more
- Team connections
- Learning always
- Engage regularly
- Trust and connection
- Digital dialogue
- Virtual first
- Strong process

These principles and foundational elements are important to our work with organizations and businesses, whether we are working with a solopreneur, leader, or coach.

What are your principles and foundational elements which help you stand out virtually?

END OF CHAPTER QUESTIONS

- What are the changes you have noticed in your workspace?
- What are the elements which will help people thrive?
- What is important so people can do their best work?
- What are the principles and foundational elements which help you stand out virtually?

CHAPTER 2

TODAY'S WORKSPACE—THE DIGITAL WORLD

"After you've done a thing the same way for two years, look at it carefully. After five years look at it with suspicion. After ten years, throw it away and start over."
– Alfred Edward Perlman

Principle: Virtual work has a life of its own. Expect the unexpected and embrace the chaos. From connections not working, to certain parts of the world being blocked, it is likely that ingenuity, resourcefulness, and patience will serve you well as a virtual professional.

Myth: It's all the same. There's a myth that managing a remote, virtual, or hybrid team is just like managing an in-person team. As we will see in this chapter, there are some very fundamental differences. One of the myths that is greatest to note is, "I need to micromanage." Micromanagement is hard to do in the remote space!

In this chapter we are exploring all things virtual or remote, and the many nuances and things that make today's workspace more complex and different from leading and teamwork in the in-person domain.

In this chapter we are going to explore:

- Roles of team leader and team members
- The CV CAME with FETA, or What's Different with Virtual Work
- Sidekicks for virtual teamwork (cartoon)
- Challenges virtual teams face and where virtual teams struggle
- Tips for supercharging performance on virtual teams

- Mistakes made by virtual team leaders
- Mistakes made by virtual team members
- Success factors
- Motivation and your team
- Team Tool: Ladder of Inference

THE ROLES OF VIRTUAL TEAM LEADERS AND TEAM MEMBERS

You will have noticed that this book is not just about team leadership but it is also about teamwork and business leadership. One of the most significant shifts when moving to the virtual, hybrid, and remote space is that teamwork becomes even more important for everyone.

As indicated in the first chapter, *all virtual and remote team members* need similar skill sets as leaders, given the levels of autonomy and independent work undertaken. While roles may be different—leader and team member—we want to equip all team members with skills needed to excel. Chapters 7 and 8 follow up on team leader practices and team work practices. More about skills can be found in both of these chapters.

A key success factor in virtual, hybrid, and remote teams is being clear on what the different roles are:

ROLE OF THE LEADER	ROLE OF THE TEAM MEMBER
• Work with team to co-create agreements and shape team culture—how we operate and do things here • Shape vision • Share information about the big picture • Provide clarity around process • Clarify assumptions • Troubleshoot • Help keep projects moving • Empower the team, both collectively and individually • Coach and mentor • Connect people with people, people with resources, and people with information	• Share information about what they are doing (with peers, boss, and others) • Ask for support when needed • Proactively make decisions around their work • Manage matrix management relationships • Prioritize work • Communicate regularly (via voice, text, instant messaging, email, etc.) • Build relationships with others (internally and externally, with peers, and those above and below in the organizational chart) • Liaise with others

• Share information across the team about successes and best practices • Ensure everyone has the authority and responsibility needed to complete their work • Feed information forward to their boss from the team, and feed organizational and strategic issues from their boss to the team • Share information with the team and feed information upwards to higher level bosses to ensure adequate resource, authority, and time	• Be self-directed • Proactively flag issues that need attention • Problem solve • Set goals • Follow through on what I say I will do • Proactively flag issues

THE CV CAME WITH FETA, OR WHAT'S DIFFERENT WITH VIRTUAL WORK

There are a number of key differences as we shift our attention and work to the virtual and remote space. These include engagement, autonomy, cross-cultural issues, communication, and the need to act more proactively. It is likely that things may also take more time, given the need for a stronger focus on process to guide the conversations, decisions, and information flow across a team that is not co-located.

Acronyms are a powerful tool for remembering things. As we go to explore the differences with virtual, remote, and hybrid teams, I often speak about the metaphor of the CV CAME with FETA. Earlier derivatives of this acronym were MEATLF CVEC and TEAM/CEC/LVF. Not quite as memorable, is it?

When we move to working in the remote space and with virtual teams, it can be useful to zoom into ten main areas of focus:

Collaboration

Visual

Culture is king

Autonomy

Matrix relationships

Engagement is key

Fluidity

Everyone

Timeframes

Assumptions

Let's look at each one of these areas:

Collaboration: Collaboration is at the heart of working remote. Our stakeholders, both internal and external, become essential partners so that we can do the work. In collaboration we often say, "the sum is more, where 1 + 1 = 3." This doesn't happen naturally. In fact, remote and virtual collaboration need to be undertaken proactively. Take a look at Chapter 10 for more on collaboration.

Visual: Making It Visual and visual cues. As discussed in Chapter 1's brain tip, what is the metaphor or image you want to use to make ideas visual?

Culture: It is often said that culture eats strategy for breakfast. Team culture and identity is critical in the remote space. It keeps us connected to others, and signals our belonging. It's "how we do things here" and what is "acceptable and not acceptable" as a team.

Autonomy: Autonomy is central to virtual and remote work, given that team members are usually working in isolation and become the "expert" in their own right. This turns traditional leadership models on their head, where "leader is expert."

Matrix relationships: Remote workers become adept at navigating matrix relationships, where we may be part of multiple teams at any given time. While I am part of the Toronto team, I may also be part of a special projects team, and a technical team. Learning to navigate the different ways of working, the team cultures, and who is who, is a critical part of any remote team worker's onboarding.

Engagement preferences: Styles, strengths, and preferences for working are part of today's more individualized workspace. Knowing our team members, their preferences, and motivations leads to engagement.

Fluidity: Buffeted by different forces, being fluid and flexible is key to sustainable and long-term satisfaction on the part of remote workers.

Everyone: In the virtual workspace, everyone needs to be equipped with tools, as we explore in Episode 15 of the *Remote Pathways* podcast, "Everyone Needs to Be a Leader."[46]

Timeframes: Many global teams operate 24/7. Creating systems to facilitate flow across the workday for all, is as important as individuals being able to create boundaries so they know when they are "ON and OFF." A growth of asynchronous approaches to leadership and teamwork is a key trend.

Assumptions: Assumptions can be rampant within a virtual team when they are not checked. With people managing different projects, and being part of many different teams, the reality for one team member may not be the reality for another. What assumptions are you holding as a team?

Some of the key issues teams face revolve around:

- Engagement
- Autonomy
- Proactivity
- Process issues
- Cross-cultural issues

Most of these will be explored further in the book.

In terms of cross-cultural issues, even if a team is located in one country, cross-cultural issues may abound. Consider the cross-cultural issues which may exist in your team. Are there differences between how things are done, values, and priorities urban and rural? West or East? North or South? Being aware of how intercultural issues shape communication, priorities, and what's valued, is important for virtual, hybrid, and remote teams of all kinds.

SIDEKICKS FOR VIRTUAL WORK

Effective virtual and hybrid work and teams have several key accomplices, including:

GPS = where you are; where are you wanting to go? GPS becomes our tracker providing information about the context, time zones, and connections.

Map = your context; knowledge of the bigger map. The context includes our tools and resources, our interface, the local context, and the global context.

Radar = vision; where are we ultimately heading? This includes the bigger picture of our work and how it intersects with others we may know, or not know.

Underpinning these key accomplices are:

Compass = our values; what is important to you? To others on the team? For the team itself?

Interconnectivity between communication devices, from phones to laptops to wrist phones. Virtual teams are connected in many different ways.

Parachute cord: pull when needed, jet around without having to jet around.

Phones: staying connected is the mantra of the remote worker.

Small laptop: size and weight are absolute essentials when it can be another appendage.

What are the essential elements you would pack in your go-to kit?

TIPS FOR SUPERCHARGING PERFORMANCE ON VIRTUAL TEAMS

From the field of Team Effectiveness, we know that teams excel when they have great **relationships** and are focused on **results**. We'll explore this more in Chapter 3 on Team Effectiveness.

> Results + Relationships = High Performance
> is a central tenet to this book.

Many remote workers find that remote work can be even more productive because they don't experience some of the distractions an in-person environment may have. If you are looking to enhance *focus*, here are some tips for "supercharging" performance:

- **Minimize meetings:** In addition to impacting focus, meetings are not always led effectively. Chapter 19 deals with meetings.
- **Minimize distractions.**
- **Connect others:** Spend time bringing people together (virtually or physically) so that they know each other, what they do, and how they can act as a resource
- **Clarify goals and roles** in order to create alignment and reduce duplication of tasks.
- **Information is power in the digital age.** Watch for version control! Consider how you are filing things so you don't spend too much time trying to find things. Make tracking and information sharing easy: provide team members with updates on where they should put things.
- **Communicate regularly:** Virtual meetings can range from real-time streaming sessions to virtual work sessions and status meetings.
- **Equip your team:** Coach, mentor, and set up job shadowing to help avoid the pitfalls.
- **Consider matching talents to what you are great at.** If you have one team member who is really good at something, match tasks to their needs.
- **Simplify and anchor things.** Complexity is rampant in the workspace today. Distill things to their core and always ask, "What is the anchor"?
- **Pareto Principle:** The Pareto Principle states that we get 80% of our impact from 20% of our efforts. What activities give you the most impact? What is getting in the way of this?

MISTAKES MADE BY LEADERS, TEAM MEMBERS, AND BUSINESS OWNERS

Mistakes Made by Virtual Team Leaders[47]

There are six common areas where team leaders and team members may slip in a virtual, remote, and hybrid context. These include:

One-on-ones	Learning on feet	Clarity with goals
Connections	Responsibility/ Authority	Context

Not enough one-on-ones: Being out of sight is not the same as being out of mind. Not spending enough time in one-on-ones can be detrimental to the levels of trust team members feel and the connection they feel with others, which will have an impact on levels of engagement. What is an appropriate frequency of meeting time with team members? What does it look like: phone calls, video streaming, onsite visits, or bringing staff into the office regularly?

Not learning on your feet: Part of being an effective virtual and remote team leader is your ability to shift, learn, and adapt. Given that there are much fewer levels of control and greater span, the ability to learn on your feet and expecting change rather than feeling you have all the answers, can make a big difference with team members.

Not being clear with goals: Goals can be a little different with virtual and remote teams. Whether people are matrixed and reporting into different areas, or whether goals can become competitive, providing opportunities to be clear with goals is important.

Not helping people see connections: Because virtual and remote team members are working with different levels of autonomy and independently, helping team members connect with the bigger picture is essential. Trina Hoefling writes, "Myopia is disengaging."[48] Helping teams see the big picture could include helping them understand more about corporate and departmental goals, giving them more access to strategic or corporate plans, and making goals and achievements more visible. Making goals more visible might include making the reporting structures more shared and visually appealing, or mapping out team goals on a weekly or other basis.

Not providing team members with the necessary responsibility and authority: A another mistake virtual and remote team leaders can make is not providing the necessary responsibility and authority to their team members so they can make the decisions they need to autonomously.

Not understanding the context: Understanding the context of our work becomes an area where many pitfalls can emerge. In the remote space, we may need to be even more proactive with helping people understand the bigger picture. In the remote space we often only see the edges of the screen. What can you do to help people understand the bigger picture of their work? Who does what, and how does their work intersect with others?

Mistakes Made by Virtual Team Members[49]

Trust and connection are critical for any team, especially those which operate across distance.

The following section explores some of the more common virtual team faux pas or mistakes. These are things that, when overlooked, can lead to missed opportunities, and sometimes a reduction of trust and connection.

Consider how you might, as a team, be able to avoid these mistakes and what solutions make most sense for you:

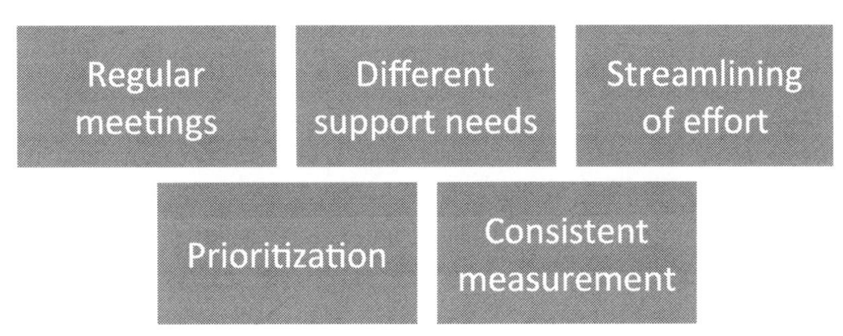

Not trying to meet regularly: Regular meetings are important in the virtual domain *and* an important corollary is that meetings should meet the needs of the group in terms of efficiency. What can be shared before or after the meeting rather than during the meeting? "Out of sight does not always equal out of mind."

Not thinking that different team members need support: Being on a virtual team can be isolating. While many of us love the autonomy this provides, it does not mean that we don't need support. Be clear with support needs across the team. Regular one-on-ones can be important in the virtual/remote world.

Not considering what type of support different team members need: Given that teams are diverse and complementary, it is likely that team members will need different types of support. Spend time inquiring what type of support is most useful if you don't know.

Duplication of effort: Watch for how much duplication of effort occurs. This can be a signal that some changes are required around roles and responsibilities, priorities and/or communication.

Priorities that become competitive: Having a line of sight across the team around priorities is important for avoiding or minimizing this mistake.

Not having consistent measurement across the team: What does success look like from each team member's perspective around their current priorities and initiatives? Be careful to note what consistent measurement means and looks like.

What other faux pas are you aware of or want to take note of for your team?

Things That Can Go Wrong

There are several other pitfall areas which include:

- Assumptions: The lack of contextual cues of the remote, virtual, and hybrid landscape can lead to many assumptions being made and not checked. This can lead to disastrous results, including miscommunication, projects' not being delivered, and conflict and the erosion of trust.
- Misinterpretations of what is being said: The skills of listening and questioning are paramount with communication in the remote space. What needs to be clarified?
- Duplication of effort
- Lack of clarity around outcomes
- Team members' not feeling heard or valued
- Burnout on the part of team members because they never get to rest or "be off"
- One team member's constantly being the one who is the odd person out. This could be the one person who is always calling in super-early, or super-late, or is the only one dialing in and can't be seen. What can you do to create more equity across the team?
- The team leader's micromanaging and not empowering the team itself
- Information from each location not being shared and/or scaled upwards
- Lack of effective collaboration
- Conflicts not getting addressed
- People being too polite due to different cultural approaches to conflict
- Successes not being captured and ignoring what didn't work
- Not being aware of the different priorities which exist across the team
- Saying yes to everything rather than being selective
- Not getting together ever because there is no time or can't all get on one platform

Tricky Issues Faced by Remote Teams

There are several issues that virtual teams can face, from engagement and non-engagement issues through to technology issues and connecting.

Here's a list of typical challenges virtual teams face:

- Motivation (see text box on next page)
- Lack of connection
- Lack of information being shared, which leads to gaps
- Differences in how issues are presented and shared

- Weak, or no, team culture bonding people together
- Lack of team identity
- Issues not surfacing as quickly as you would like
- Not feeling connected with each other, which leads to a sense of disconnection, disengagement, and isolation
- According to Gallup, "an actively disengaged employee costs their organization $3,400 for every $10,000 of salary, or 34 percent."[50]

TYPE	VIRTUAL WORK CHALLENGES	MYTHS	OPPORTUNITIES
VIRTUAL WORK	Technology needed Can't see each other Need to be intentional in developing relationships A different leadership style	You can't collaborate as well You need to be "on" 24/7 You never get a break	Less travel time Ability to draw on global talent pool Team empowerment Learning more about other cultures and ways of working Ability to create work-life solutions
IN-PERSON WORK	Proximity doesn't always equal connection Commute time Environmental footprint cost Cost for maintaining physical facilities	It's easier to work face to face It's more collaborative—a reminder that in-person work spaces are not always conducive to meetings or conversation. Consider the co-worker who plugs into their music at the start of the morning with noise-cancelling headphones, who you don't see until the end of the day. Just because you sit on the other side of a cubicle does not mean it's a collaborative relationship.	Collaboration Body cues Boundaries

MOTIVATION AND YOUR TEAM

- Antoine de Saint-Exupéry wrote, "If you want to build a ship, don't drum up people together to collect wood and don't assign them tasks and work, but rather teach them to long for the endless immensity of the sea."
- Given the isolation and self-directedness of virtual and remote teams, it is important to address the topic of motivation early on. Self-motivation and self-direction are important factors of success as team leaders look to motivate their team members.
- It is important to recognize that team members are likely motivated by both internal and external factors.

- Intrinsic factors are elements internal to us. Intrinsic factors include things such as challenge, curiosity, control, fantasy, competition, cooperation, and recognition.[51] Our internal motivations can vary widely from person to person. Consider those who are driven by challenge, versus those who are driven by exploration and a quest to learn. Being aware of these internal motivation levers are key to learning and performance in the virtual and remote space. Given that we work in isolation, intrinsic factors may play a stronger role in motivation than others.

We are also driven by extrinsic factors external to us, including:

- The ability to be promoted or advance career
- The opportunity to learn something new
- Connecting with people from around the world
- Having a larger impact

There may also be perceived benefits in working remote, such as more flexible working arrangements and the ability to have more control over our time and workflow.

Three Questions about Motivating Your Team[52]

At a team level it can be important to explore the following areas:

What motivates each individual team member? Team members can be motivated by both internal and external factors. For some team members it may be pay that really gets them going, while others may be motivated by doing a good job. Spending time getting to know your team and what makes them perform at their best is a key part of stellar team leadership.

What does each team member find important? Our values shape what we deem as important. Whether our values are security or adventure, these are the things that become our drivers and what we often seek out. Each team will also have its own set of values. As team leaders it can be important to have dialogue around values at two levels: the individual level and the team level. See how value alignment works with motivation for each team member.

What are levels of trust and connection like on the team? Team motivation is often tied at a much deeper level to the amount of trust in a team and how connected people feel. We often look to the surface level of the question, what motivates each team member, without asking ourselves about the status of trust on the team. If trust levels are low, or if toxic behaviors are present, it's unlikely that team members are going to be motivated to bring their best to work each and every day.

SIX TEAMWORK QUESTIONS ON MOTIVATION[53]

1. What should the team know about you and what is unique about your context?
2. What support do you need from me? (explore time of day, type of support)
3. What connection with other team members would benefit you?
4. Where does your work overlap with others? What do you need from them in order to be successful? How does your work feed into overall team success?
5. How would you like to stay connected and share your results?
6. What are the current priorities for you this week? month? quarter? year?

Conversation Sparker

Have a discussion with your team about what they find motivating. What helps them do their best work?

As part of a team meeting, have team members share an example of what they find motivating and when they were at their best. What was the situation? What was it like? How did they feel? What were the elements which were present helping them be at their best?

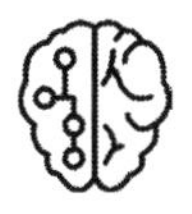

BRAIN TIP: COLOR AND MOTIVATION

The Impact of Color

The impact of isolation continued to take on greater importance during the 2020 pandemic lockdowns. There is some interesting research behind motivation and color use. Did you know that several studies from the University of Essex in 2012 found that viewing the color green created a spike in creativity?[54]

This, coupled with the indoor nature of remote work, can have implications for what you want to view. There was a study done using a green filter which was found to have a greater boost to creativity.[55] What are you looking at, digitally and physically?

There is a whole science behind color which many marketers leverage via branding and advertisement. At the same time, in the remote space, this can be an interesting area to explore based on what you can control in your environment, and with your messaging.

Consider these core colors and how they invoke emotion:

Red—Passion

Blue—Trust

Purple—Loyalty

Yellow—Optimism

Green—Nature, growth

The Impact of Motivation[56]

Motivation goes hand-in-hand with the topic of recognition and rewards. Did you know:

- 41% of companies that use peer-to-peer recognition have seen marked positive increases in customer satisfaction.
- In the virtual space, peer interaction may be as frequent or more frequent than that with the leader. Across this book we will be exploring topics related to peer dialogue, including Chapter 15's focus on Peer Coaching, and Chapter 8's Teamwork Practices. Intranets provide important connectors for the team, as do external social networks around interest areas such as Mighty Networks and Facebook Groups.
- In these environments (where opportunity and well-being are part of the culture), strong manager performance in recognizing employee performance increases engagement by almost 60%.
- Praise and commendation from managers was rated the top motivator for performance, beating out other non-cash and financial incentives, by a majority of workers (67%).

Rewards and recognition is an area where "one size does not fit all." Linked to motivation and other factors, each person will want different elements. Several questions you will want to consider in this area are:

1. What does each team member value in terms of being rewarded? Is it time off? A promotion? Being assigned a special project?
2. What does each team member value in being recognized? Is it public praise? An email acknowledgement? A gift card?
3. Think about what your team members are motivated by. This will help you consider appropriate rewards and recognition for each person.
4. Check out your assumptions around rewards and recognition. We are not always right!
5. What types of rewards and recognition are appropriate in our organizational culture?

THE LADDER OF INFERENCE

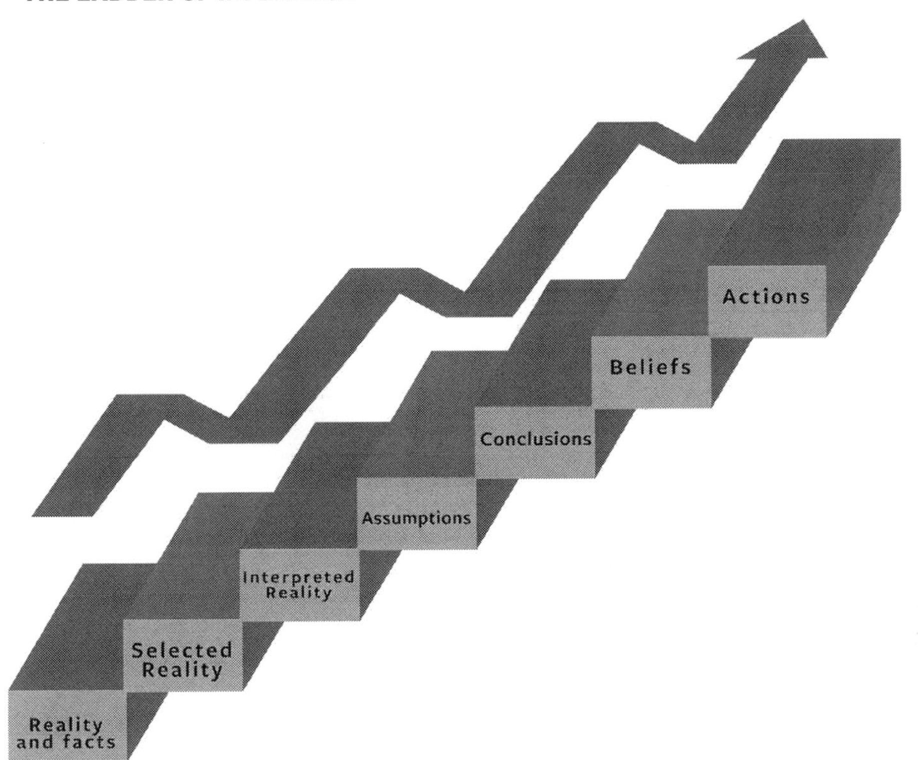

With teams today not always having a shared context, it can be important to be more intentional about the different steps along the journey to action. Chris Argyris created the ladder of inference. It is a powerful tool you can use to check the different stages team members move through to ensure alignment at each stage.

In a virtual team there may be several steps along the way that diverge between reality and facts and the action undertaken. It is important to identify what some of the differences are along the way to support synergy and alignment across the team.

Exploring this tool together helps to shape understanding across the team, as well as alignment. It is significant as inferences can lead to conflict, duplication of effort, and misunderstanding.

The first step is **reality and facts**. At this stage it is about our assessment of what we see.

As individuals we will see only a part of the **selected reality**, and through the lenses we wear will **interpret reality** in different ways, influenced by geography, culture, socialization, and values. This then, shapes our **assumptions**, which then lead to our **conclusions**. Our **beliefs**, for example, of whether this is easy or hard, will then shape our **actions** undertaken.

Part of the role of the team leader as coach can be to support the team in becoming more aware of these various steps along the way and what the lenses are at each stage. These different "rungs" of the ladder can lead to conflict, different perspectives, and differences that exist across the team. It can be a useful tool for "unpacking" the differences which exist. A challenge for team members is that they may be at different stages and have access to different perspectives.

RECONNECTING THE WORKSPACE TIP—BE INTENTIONAL

Being intentional is a key principle for remote and virtual work. We need to be intentional in building in pauses between meetings so we can get out of our chair. We need to be intentional and proactive in forming relationships. We need to be intentional about outcomes, as "winging it" is much harder in the virtual, remote, and hybrid space.

Intentionality is also about thinking about the environment you want to create. Part of the workspace transition can be about reimagining in the workspace and what's possible.

What do you want to be intentional around?

END OF CHAPTER QUESTIONS

- What is important to note about the roles of the leader and team members in your team?
- Which elements of the CV CAME with FETA are important to leverage and move the needle on?
- What challenges does the team struggle with?
- What motivates our team?
- What can the ladder of inference do for support?

CHAPTER 3

TEAM EFFECTIVENESS

"No member of a crew is praised for the rugged individuality of his rowing."
—Ralph Waldo Emerson

Principle: Keep things simple and take time to co-create with the team. In a team or group context, the complexity is with the group. When we are able to input our ideas, we feel a sense of ownership. Teams get activated when they are empowered.

Myth: I can do it all alone.

Regardless of how much has changed, and how different working virtually can be, team fundamentals remain the same. In this chapter, we will be exploring the following areas of team effectiveness:

- The ever-changing landscape of teams—from stable static teams to self-led teams, teaming to holacracy
- Core ingredients for virtual teams
- Why teams struggle
- Components for organizational (and team) excellence
- The Six Factors of High Performing Teams—creating a team that excels
- Team roles
- The science behind teams—oxytocin and social contagion
- Matrix management—making it work
- Creating a strong team culture

THE EVER-CHANGING LANDSCAPE OF TEAMS

Often in teams, the only certainty is that there will be change. It's not just team members who may change but also approaches.

Flash back twenty years ago. It was unusual for teams to change rapidly (other than perhaps for project or programmatic work). Today, the rapid pace of change and impact on teams of all kinds is the norm. This impacts team members coming and going, to global changes influencing the way teams operate, to teams who adopt Agile's rapid iteration and may only exist for a few weeks. We see a range of team lifecycles, from the traditional stable team to Agile's teams who work in frequent sprints for a two-week period, to self-led teams which form organically, and the more recent holacracy.

The landscape of teams continues to shift dramatically, from stable and static teams which were together for years, to teams that are now agile and have shorter life expectancies, and need to leverage the power of teaming.

In this section we are going to explore two key shifts in the world of teams which have been occurring: Teaming and Agile.

TEAMING

Teaming is a term coined by Amy Edmondson which she uses to describe how leaders need to focus on "actively building and developing teams even as a project is in process, while realizing that a team's composition may change at any given moment."[57]

This is a norm for most virtual teams. In her book, she explores the three pillars of teaming, which include helping everyone on the team become more curious, passionate, and empathetic.

In the 2013 Harvard Business Review article, *The Three Pillars of a Teaming Culture*, curiosity, passion, and empathy were identified as key elements for supporting a team culture. These are all essential for a virtual and remote team experience. Edmondson writes:

> Curiosity drives people to find out what others know, what they bring to the table, what they can add. Passion fuels enthusiasm and effort. It makes people care enough to stretch, to go all out. Empathy is the ability to see another's perspective, which is absolutely critical to effective collaboration under pressure.[58]

Curiosity is critical for the success of virtual teams. When we cannot see each other, we need to be open to experiencing each other's reality. The ability to put ourselves in each other's shoes is another important element of empathy, and passion is required for drive and self-motivation.

In addition to these skills, there are four behaviors which support Teaming success, according to Edmondson:

- Speaking up
- Collaboration

- Experimentation
- Reflection

What opportunities are you building in to ensure that individuals have the opportunity and skills to speak up, collaborate, experiment, and reflect?

Teaming provides us with useful advice for teams that form and disband. Edmondson writes, "Teaming is about identifying essential collaborators and quickly getting up to speed on what they know so you can work together to get things done."[59]

Another major contribution from Amy Edmondson's research to understanding the world of teams is the notion of psychological safety, which she defines as, "a shared belief that the team is safe for interpersonal risk taking."[60]

Chapter 5 on trust will explore practical and tactical things teams can do to build trust. Creating a culture where risk taking is encouraged helps to build an environment where experimentation is encouraged and failure is embraced as one more step to learning and getting it right. In today's VUCA context, this is essential.

AGILE'S SPRINTS AND HACKS

Another philosophy profoundly influencing the virtual and remote space of teams is Agile. Originating in the world of software design, Agile's approach to teamwork is now embraced by many industries, including financial services.

Excellent resources can be found at the Agile Alliance, including this definition: "Agile Development is a set of methods and practices where solutions evolve through collaboration between self-organizing, cross-functional teams."[61]

Agile is grounded in several team principles:

- Rapid iteration
- Sprints
- Hacks
- Failing fast, failing forward
- Retrospectives and ongoing reflection

All of these have a tremendous value.

CORE INGREDIENTS FOR VIRTUAL TEAMS

Regardless of the philosophies embraced, virtual teams will excel when certain elements are in place.

These are expanded upon in future chapters:

- Trust among team members
- The safety to raise issues that are uncomfortable
- The feeling that others understand their work
- Understanding of context and the bigger whole
- Clear process on how to get things done
- The ability to create connections with other projects/work being undertaken by others.

WHY TEAMS STRUGGLE

There are several areas virtual and hybrid teams may struggle around, including:

- Lack of clarity around processes
- Not knowing what their other team members are working on
- Not being aware of the different priorities and ways of working of team members
- Not feeling connected
- Not having clarity around key tasks and activities (ambiguity)

Throughout this chapter and the next, we'll be exploring practical things to help teams thrive.

COMPONENTS FOR ORGANIZATIONAL (AND TEAM) EXCELLENCE

Practically and tactically, certain elements need to be in place for teams and organizations to survive and thrive.

The Jamieson model includes four elements of any organization:

1. Strategy
2. Structure
3. Systems
4. Culture

The first element of **Strategy** is described as an organization's approach to reaching its objectives. Many books focus on this as a key area, which is beyond the scope of this book. With the rapid changes in today's workspace, anchoring our work in strategies can be valuable.

The Center for Management & Organization Effectiveness (CMOE), differentiates between a strategy and a plan with the following: "A strategy, on the other hand, is a blueprint, layout, design, or idea used to accomplish a specific goal. A strategy is very flexible and open for adaptation and change when needed."[62]

They define a plan as "very concrete in nature and doesn't allow for deviation."[63]

Part of success in today's virtual environment asks virtual team leaders (and team members) to become more proficient in thinking along contingency lines around plans, while keeping strategy in mind. In other words, if Plan A doesn't work, I'll move to Plan B, then C, then D. Today's VUCA context invites us to become masterful contingency planners.

The second element for organizational excellence is **Structure**. Teaming, holacracy, and Agile are all elements of organizational structure. Ask the following questions about structure for your situation:

- How are teams in your organization structured?
- What are the reporting lines which exist?
- What are the structural elements which help your teams thrive?
- What might get in the way?
- In terms of structure, you may also consider process issues: How are people compensated? Who reports to whom? How do jobs interface?
- Is there any role or job redesign needed?
- How has virtual and remote team structure shifted over time?

The third area is **Systems** which help us do things effectively. Systems help us replicate things, scale, and ensure consistency across the team. When our team is spread across the world or distanced, systems are critical for success. Systems create clarity and a mechanism for things to be shared across a team. We will explore this topic in greater depth throughout the book in various chapters.

Team leaders and team members will want to consider some of these systems:

- Performance management systems
- Information management systems: platforms, repositories
- People management
- Development systems/entities: one-on-ones, training
- Rewards and recognition

The fourth area Jamieson notes is **Culture**. In today's virtual space, team culture or "how we do things" is probably one of the most important definers and shapers of team identity and results. It also one of the most challenging areas. Let's look at this next.

Note: in order to effect change you need to align strategy with organizational structure, and with the systems and culture. As you consider the changes required in your organization or team, what do you need to align?

IN FOCUS: TEAM CULTURE

The term *team culture* is bandied around. So what is it? Team culture is its values, beliefs, attitudes, and behaviors. Simply said, "It's how we do things here."

Having a strong team culture is imperative in the remote space for a variety of reasons, including identity. Our team identity creates a knowledge that we are part of a bigger whole. It creates a sense of belonging. In addition to team identity, the team's agreements, culture, and values are key. The culture of a team is shaped by the beliefs the team holds, both individually and collectively. Also shaping team culture are its values.

The following team culture elements get shared and made explicit through:

- Our mantras—what we say to ourselves
- Our mottos—how we operate
- Our team identity—I am part of the Toronto Ops team, or the special task force on collaboration

Our team culture is exhibited through our behaviors. What we look like and how we do our work. For example, do we value speed over accuracy? Think about a hospital team who will value accuracy versus a financial services team who might value quality first.

WHAT AND WHY OF TEAM CULTURE

In exploring team culture, we are often exploring the *What* and the *Why* of culture.

The **What** gets us to think: Who are we? What do we do?

The **Why** takes us to the bigger picture and gets us thinking about questions such as: Why do we do things? What impact will it have if I do X? What's important for us to consider?

A final doorway into exploring team culture is to ask ourselves: What are the three adjectives which describe our team?

Before moving on, consider how you would describe the different elements of your team culture. This will be built upon in the next chapter.

THE ICEBERG OF CULTURE

For many years the metaphor of an iceberg has been used in intercultural work to explore the things that shape an experience across geographies. It can be useful in terms of exploring team culture as well. Let's take a look.

As I share in *PlanDoTrack*, culture is shaped by our values, beliefs, and actions. It also includes mindset, habits, perspectives and assumptions. Culture is further explored in the next chapter. Belief systems are an important part of virtual teams.

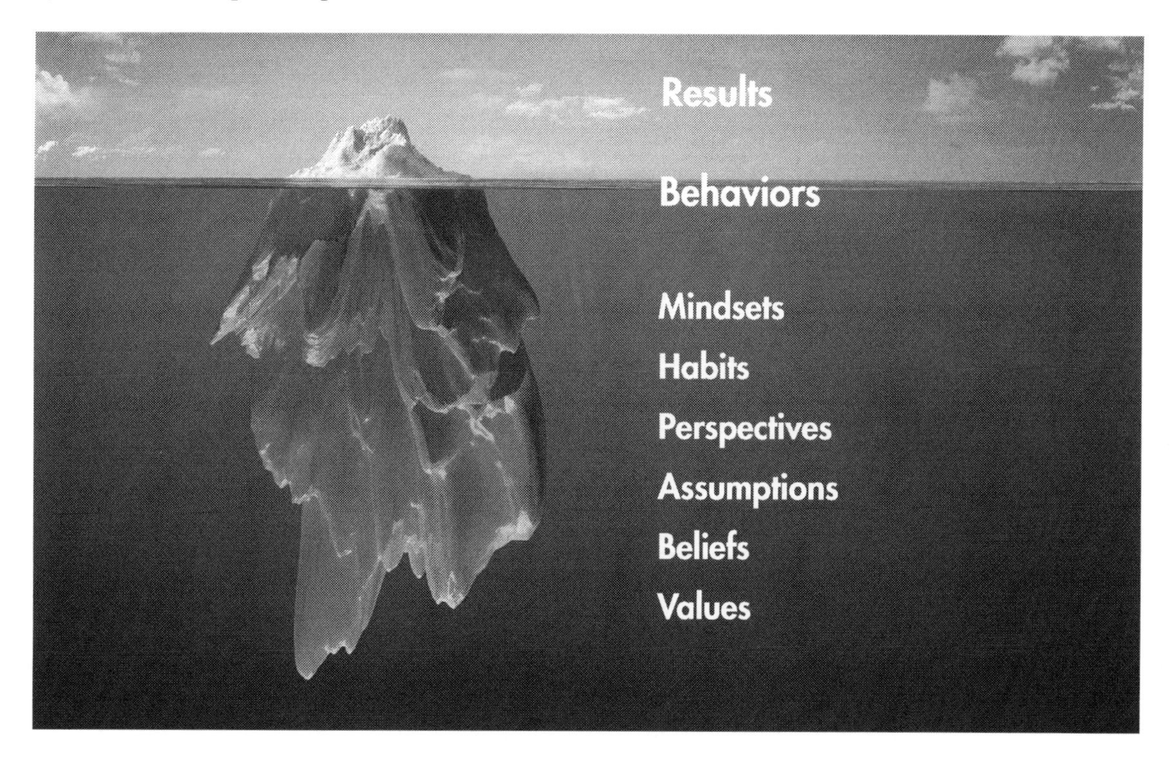

Source of image: The Iceberg from PlanDoTrack, *Britton, 2018. Used with permission.*

WHAT'S DIFFERENT WITH VIRTUAL TEAMS?

To bring to life some of the differences which are the reality of virtual and remote teams, I thought it would be interesting to travel "below the waterline" of things we see on the surface of teamwork. In *PlanDoTrack* and *Coaching Business Builder*, I share the Iceberg model as seen previously.

There are many elements which exist below the waterline, including our assumptions and beliefs. A profound influencer on **behaviors** and **results** are the **beliefs** virtual teams and their members may hold. While these beliefs are not always explicit or shared, they are the drivers and motivators of behaviors, and the shapers of results for virtual teams.

Beliefs a virtual team may hold which help them excel:

1. It's more efficient to work virtually than in person, considering commute times, etc.
2. I enjoy movement and the flexibility of being able to work from anywhere.
3. I love learning and need to be constantly learning, given the changes that occur regularly with technology.
4. I love being able to work autonomously.
5. I love being on my own.
6. I am comfortable in not having all the details around the context of my work.
7. I am able to contribute to my team.
8. I have an equal voice; I may know more about things than my boss or others on my team.
9. Give and take is part of the way we work.
10. My own cultural preferences are respected and there is a TEAM way we do things.
11. I can grow and learn every day in my work.
12. I can connect with others in the team (formally and informally) in ways that work for our schedules, locations, and time zones.
13. We all lead as team members, not just our leader.
14. My team leader knows me and values my work. I hear from them regularly. They do not micromanage.
15. I have the resources needed to do my work most effectively.
16. We meet in a way that respects time zones, accessibility, etc.
17. I have a way to contribute my unique skills and abilities for the betterment of the team.
18. There are opportunities for me to share my priorities with others. This is taken into account with work planning.
19. We meet regularly as a team to share priorities, revisit goals, and identify obstacles, as well as opportunities.

20. Meetings are important to keep connected.
21. We have opportunities to network and meet each other.

Consider how each of these beliefs shapes behaviors which then shape different results in your team.

> What are the beliefs shaping your virtual team?

THE SIX FACTORS OF HIGH PERFORMING TEAMS— CREATING A TEAM THAT EXCELS

There are many factors which help teams excel today. Seminal research including that of Hackman and Wageman, and Katzenbach and Smith, uncovered elements which makes teams excel. In my work I commonly call these the **Six Factors**. As a practitioner, I've observed that teams who can dialogue through these, find it easier to create alignment and focus with each other when distributed.

Key to any successful team is alignment. Alignment around process, alignment around roles, alignment around reporting.

Team members may be a part of one or many teams, especially in a virtual and hybrid workspace. As members of virtual teams, they are likely moving in and out of many different teams at any given time. Some they meet and connect with, and some form and disband too quickly to do so. As such, it can be very useful to be proactive in working through the six factors with each and every team they are part of.

The first of the six factors that really helps our team gel and get more done and have better relationships is, of course, having a **shared vision**.

The second factor is about creating **shared performance goals.** What are we doing? What does success look like?

Factor number three is about creating **shared behavioral norms**. How do we do things on our team? How is this team different from others I am a part of? Values are an important part of this process. Is this important to us?

Factor number four is about clarifying or creating **clear roles**.

Number five is creating **shared team practices**.

Number six is **creating shared commitment**. What are we going to do, by when, and why?

Later in the chapter you will find a table which explores how these are different in the virtual space than the in-person realm.

Like levers, each one of these can be adjusted to help a team get on track. Let's look at each one.

FACTOR #1: CREATING SHARED VISION

> "To the person who does not know where he wants to go, there is no favorable wind."
> —Seneca

The first of the six factors is creating a shared vision, mission, and purpose. It's important that we do understand our purpose, why we exist, and have a vision for where we want to go.

Having a shared vision is important because it:

- Provides an end point for everyone to aim towards. Even with different roles and perspectives, having the shared end point is critical.
- Helps everyone row in the same direction, even if they are rowing in different lanes.
- Allows for the opportunity to identify and notice where you are on the path of moving towards your vision.
- Helps the team focus on possibilities. Research has shown that working around vision (personally or organizationally) widens the number of possibilities seen. Cognitively it activates the Positive Emotional Attractor (PEA network) which helps them be more open to behavioral change, be more altruistic, and make better decisions.[64]

THIS FIRST FACTOR EXPLORES WHAT THE SHARED VISION AND MISSION IS FOR OUR TEAM.

Questions teams may be asking themselves are: What is important for us? What is our team vision? What do we take a stand for? What are the top three adjectives which describe our work?

When these factors are not present, we see behaviors like:

- Lack of alignment (team members in location A are doing things differently than team members in location B)
- Lack of buy-in
- Not sure why we are doing things
- Not feeling connected or contributing to a bigger picture

WHAT MAY BE DIFFERENT WHEN WORKING IN A VIRTUAL TEAM

Each team member may be holding multiple visions at once. They may have a vision that is in support of Team A where they are member, or, also have a different vision for Team B.

Imperative: Be sure to check in regularly around vision, particularly during times of disruption. While tactical elements may change, vision remains relatively static.

IN FOCUS: FOUR WAYS TO WORK WITH YOUR TEAM AROUND VISION

Working with a team around creating a shared vision is a foundational team activity. It is likely something you will facilitate multiple times throughout your career for project teams or longer-term teams. There are several different ways we can work with teams on creating vision, including these four ways:

1. Craft a vision through reflecting on a series of **visualization questions**.

   Questions you might ask are:

   a) As a team, what makes us unique?

   b) One year from now, we want to be able to look back and see . . .

   c) What are we known for?

   Check my Teams365 #891 Blog on visualization.[65]

   Create a model of your vision out of materials such as aluminum foil. Go to Teams365 #1071 for a post about this.[66]

2. Select **visual cards or icons** to represent the vision. Visual anchors play an important role in creating shared understanding. An interesting tool to bring into your visual meetings is visual cards (our deck, Conversation Sparker, or other decks such as Visual Explorer). Have team members select the photos that represent their vision for the team. From the collective series, the team can choose to make their own storyboard or timeline of these photos.

3. Create a **team drawing** of the vision. Depending on the team size, break the team into groups of three or four. Provide each team with a pen and flipchart and 15 minutes to draw their vision for the team (at the end of the year, three years from now). Provide them with some prompting questions such as: What will you look like? What are you known for?

   In my own work as a Certified Facilitator of the Draw Your Future™ process originally created by Patti Dobrowolski, I have seen how impactful it can be to create a visual map of the future.

4. Create a **team storyboard** with photos/collage and a blank easel. If the team already has a "big picture" vision, have them plot out their storyboard or story line for the year. Get them to do this on a blank easel or a big piece of butcher block paper.[67]

How else might you work with teams around vision?

Activity

Facilitate a discussion about your vision for the next quarter or the next year.

FACTOR #2: SHARED PERFORMANCE MEASURES

The second of the six factors is creating shared performance goals and measures. What are the goals and measures that define success for your team?

Teams exist to get results, to make thing happen for the business. Spending time as a team in creating shared performance goals and measures is critical to success. For virtual teams, support dialogue around goals and what performance measures will be used to determine success. For example, in creating a report, what's expected? How long should it be? By when?

> A question to always be asking is this: What will success look like?

When this is not clear:

- Everyone does their own thing
- There is overlap and duplication
- There are gaps between effort
- The exact results we are wanting are not achieved

In looking at creating shared performance goals, we want to make sure our goals are:

Clear and visible to everyone. How are goals codified? In addition to having a goal report, you may also want to include a goal visual which everyone can have, and/or print off at their own location. It could include a visual map of key goals and timelines.

Succinct: The one tool I subscribe to, is having people complete a One-Page Plan which contains the top three to five goals you are working on. As a virtual team, have each person share them on Slack. Project management software or a benchmarking tool can provide a visual around key goals for the team, or at the individual level. For those who have a copy of *PlanDoTrack*, my workbook planner for virtual and remote professionals, you will know how valuable it can be to have your top five goals visible in a One-Page Plan. You'll find it here on the next page.

Common: A challenge for many teams is to have a common understanding of how goals are measured. In a virtual team, each member may be working on different goals and performance measures. Part of a team meeting may include discussion on this.

SMART-E: Many teams benefit from using the SMART-E framework. If you're not familiar with the SMART-E framework, it's about creating goals that are **S**pecific, **M**easurable, **A**chievable, **R**ealistic, **T**imely and **E**xciting. SMART-E goals allow us to move from very broad-stroke goals into something that's more tangible, so we will know when we reach them.

CONSIDER THIS GOAL:

We want to improve customer service. That's quite generic. How would you make that goal more SMART-E? What would be the specifics, the things that you can measure, and the things that you can achieve as a team?

Activity

Take a minute before moving on to think about what are some of the SMART-E goals facing you and your team now. Write out the top three SMART-E goals for the next quarter in a One-Page Plan.

One-Page Plan

Goal	Description	Key Timelines	Resources (Who and What)	Enablers/Derailers

FACTOR #3: SHARED BEHAVIORAL NORMS: HOW WE DO THINGS

Shared behavioral norms are "how we do things." It is our belief systems and the behaviors that represent and comprise who we are as a team. These behavioral norms are sometimes explicit and other times implicit. Part of moving to a high performing team is the ability to be clear and aligned around how we do things. Being able to communicate this from one part of the team to another creates a seamless experience when you are working with team members from Asia to Canada to Italy.

With this factor, the question is: How do we do things? This is particularly important for virtual teams, and when members are part of multiple matrix teams.

When this factor is not present:

- Everyone does their own thing
- There is lack of consistency across the team
- There is no shared identity or team experience

WORKING WITH A TEAM ON CREATING SHARED BEHAVIORAL NORMS:

Another key activity is in enshrining Shared Behavioral Norms. Many teams create their own Standard Operating Procedures (SOPs) or Team Charter or WOW (Ways of Working). In a virtual team it is extremely important to do, as team members may not see each other in action every day. Behaviorally, what does excellent customer service look like? What does it mean? Taking time for the team to spell out key behaviors which align with the team values helps identify assumptions and ensures a constituent experience across the team.

Creating a shared experience has been found to lead to high performance, as seen in the Google Team Aristotle Experience.[68]

Five factors were found to lead to team effectiveness in Google's research experience, including:

1. Psychological safety
2. Dependability
3. Structures and clarity
4. Meaning
5. Impact

Activity

Spend time as a team creating your Ways of Working, Terms of Engagement, or Team Charter. What are the behaviors you are all agreeing to?

FACTOR #4: TEAM ROLES

Across a virtual or hybrid team, team members may wear a variety of hats or fulfill a number of roles. They also may be part of multiple teams, given matrix relationships.

In a typical team there will be a web of relationships, and within these relationships there may be a number of roles that get filled. Consider these roles which show up regularly within teams and some of these informal titles:

- "Get it done" person
- Catalyst
- Social coordinator
- Initiator
- Project incubator
- Evaluator
- Quartermaster/logistician
- Planner
- Pantster (someone who flies by the seat of their pants)
- Innovator
- Cheerleader
- Detail/quality
- Inspirer
- Devil's advocate

Role clarity is critical for success in virtual teams. It:

- Facilitates sharing across the team
- Ensures that boundaries and processes are clear
- Facilitates matrix relationships

At the level of virtual teams when team roles are not clear, we see:

- Lack of understanding of how my work impacts your work
- Duplication
- Gaps
- Conflict

Note that our roles may not be the same as our position. One team member may be a business analyst, but they may also be the best social coordinator on the block.

Note that establishing a role does not mean that the person understands how roles fit together. In a virtual team, it's impotant to help team members understand their roles and where there is overlap and gaps. Peers should be equipped to reach out and step up when needed. It can be useful to spend time sharing what you do.

Another note of caution is around role fatigue. If we are constantly being asked to take on a role within the team, over time this can become tiring. Sharing the roles and keeping them fluid may be a better approach over time.

Some of the best-known work around team roles has been done by Belbin, which you can explore in the Nine Belbin Team Roles.[69] Also common is Parker's work around 12 Roles.[70]

Key questions to be asking around roles include the questions:

- What roles exist?
- Who does what?
- How do our work processes overlap? For example, does the same document get multiple reviews? Do similar projects and reviews happen at the same time?
- How do our roles and work intersect?
- Given our individual strengths, what roles are best suited for each team member?
- If there was another role you could inhabit, what would it be?

Activity

Discuss roles which exist in your team using the questions listed here and/or explore the resources listed.

To learn more about this often under-explored area, do some web research to learn more about:

- Belbin's roles
- The Six Thinking Hats from Debono
- Roles and Systems Theory from the Centre for Right Relationship
- Parker's 12 Roles

FACTOR #5: SHARED TEAM PRACTICES

Shared team practices are all about getting together to share information or to learn more about each other. Whether it's getting together once a year or quarterly for face-to-face meetings, or for weekly team meetings, daily huddles, shared team practices, or other activities that the team does regularly, it is essential in order to build relationships and focus on results.

Teams which excel focus their practices on both results and relationships. For more on this, refer to Chapter 8 on Teamwork Practices and Chapter 19 on Meetings.

Some of the typical team practices for virtual teams can look like this:

- Fifteen-minute daily or weekly huddles. The focus may be on these questions: What are you doing? What's a priority? Who needs support? What else should we know?
- Quarterly virtual retreats for virtual planning sessions to support prioritization, alignment, and goal setting, as well as harvesting lessons learned.
- Get It Done hours: Procrastination is something that team members may struggle with. Dedicate one or two hours a month, or every quarter, to virtually work together to "get things done" and get those often overlooked items off your list.

When team practices are not present and undertaken on regular basis there can be:

- Conflict
- Challenges with communication, alignment, and motivation
- Assumptions
- Power struggles

Meetings are often the doorway into the work. If you are not already having regular discussion around topics like this, consider incorporating them.

Potential topics for team meetings:

- Our vision for this year
- Key goals for this quarter
- Priority setting for the quarter/year
- Exploring key success factors
- Post-mortem or debrief on key projects: What worked? What didn't? What do you want to do more of?

Connection Tools for Teams

Technology can serve as an enabler or derailer for team practices. Some of the current technologies which are being used are:

Slack: Used by many virtual teams, Slack is an important channel for project updates, photos, filesharing, and other projects.

Zoom: As most of the world discovered in 2020, Zoom is the platform for many activities including team meetings, quarantinis, and also team development sessions. Zoom creates quick work with recording and transcription of meetings (with the integrated Otter.ai app), as well as breakouts for smaller group discussion.

Microsoft Teams: The meeting place for many organizations, continuing to adapt to create as many similar types of experiences as Zoom.

Asana: Popular in the entrepreneurial sector for managing projects and related communication.

These point to the need for relationships and skills, the focus of systems, which will be explored in Chapter 7, Making It Scalable—Systems, Platforms, and Tools.

Activity

Consider what types of team practices you currently have, and aspire to create to support both building relationships and results.

FACTOR #6: CREATING SHARED COMMITMENT

The final factor for teams which excel is about creating shared commitment. The question here is: How do we have each other's backs?

Just like the knot, teams are as strong as their weakest link. If we have some faulty threads, if we have some areas that need attention, if we have some members pulling more than others, it's not going to be a balanced team.

As it relates to commitment, teams dialogue around:

- How do we spend time as a team?
- How do we really pull equally?

- How do we support people who need extra support?
- What are the things we can put in place to make sure that we have a shared commitment?

Another way of looking at shared commitment is asking yourself: What are you committed to doing no matter what? Regardless of what happens, at the end of the day, what are we sure we're going to do or make sure happens?

SUMMARY OF THE SIX FACTORS

FACTOR	IMPACTS	WHAT'S IMPORTANT ABOUT IT IN THE VIRTUAL REALM	WHAT'S DIFFERENT ABOUT THIS VS. THE IN-PERSON APPROACH	WHAT QUESTIONS CAN TEAM LEADERS ASK OR USE TO SUPPORT?
1: Shared Vision, Purpose, and Values (WHY)	Direction Alignment Possibility What we do Focus Goals Priorities	Keep it visible Incorporates different people in different locations. Is vision different? Team members may work on different visions	Matrix Different locations Cultural layer of values	What is our vision? What's possible? What do we want to be known for? Three years from now . . . What is exciting about our vision? What are we all pulling towards? How can you contribute to the vision?
2: Shared Performance Goals (WHAT)	Results How things are done Priorities Quality of work	Shared measurement Who does what? How does it feed into one another? What are our checkpoints?	Priorities may be different in matrix Visible Part of different teams	One-Page Plan Different platforms for goal sharing What will success look like around this goal? Plans
3: Behavioral Norms (HOW)	Action Behavior	Clarify expectations at the start Remind along the way Visibility	Behaviors are not always visible Make it intentional Be proactive in shaping team identity WOW—Keep it visible	Who are we? How do WE do things? What do behaviors around ____ look like? How does what we do differ from other teams?

4: Clear Roles (WHO)	Results Relationships Conflict	Roles and responsibilities Reporting Make connections How do things fit together (how A fits with B)?	Matrix Overlap	Who does what? Who else?
5: Shared Team Practices (HOW)	Relationships Communication Connection Sharing Alignment	Make it intentional Make it regular Provide team roles	Needs to be proactive Easier to put off Meet regularly What other players/people should be involved? Body language? Watch time zones and/or who is inconvenienced on a regular basis	When are we getting together? When will we meet? What can we do to connect?
6: Shared Commitment (WHAT)	Follow through Accountability Sharing	What is our commitment? How do we have each other's backs? How connected do we feel to each other?	Be intentional Job shadowing Who will back up?	How do we have each other's backs? Who is going to do what? By when? What if we don't follow through?

AND WHAT ELSE?

In addition to the Six Factors, there are some other characteristics that we want to be cultivating. We want to ensure that there are high levels of trust and collaboration on our team. Partnering should be the norm rather than the exception. We also know that high performing teams have complimentary skill sets. They aren't all the same. High functioning teams really leverage the strengths of each other, so they look for and they use each other's strengths.

High performing teams also have constructive and transparent communication even when it's difficult. They're not afraid to surface the difficult issues, and high performing teams are the ones who really show innovation, are more engaged, demonstrate confidence, and, of course, are very respectful of each other and have incredible levels of loyalty.

TEAM TOOL: SIX FACTORS WHICH HELP TEAMS EXCEL

As a team, work through this worksheet, grading yourself on 1 to 10 in each of the areas. Note what needs attention and how you can behaviorally "move the needle" higher.

SIX FACTORS	VIRTUAL TEAM CONSIDERATIONS AND DISCUSSION POINTS	OUR RATING 1 TO 10
Shared Vision	What are the different visions team members are supporting?	
Performance Measures	What are the metrics that each person is measured by? Is this clear to everyone? Is performance measured consistently?	
Behavioral Norms—WOW	How do we do things? For each team member, how does each team they are part of do things differently?	
Roles	What are the roles of the different team members? How does this intersect with other team members? What is the role of matrix management?	
Team Practices	When do we meet so that it is regular and proactive? What are the best mechanisms for sharing information? Communicating? Connecting?	
Shared Commitment	What is the shared commitment across the team to get things done? How does the team communicate needs (support needs, resourcing needs, etc.) across the team? How do team members ask for support? How do team members offer support? How does the team have each other's backs?	

BRAIN TIP: THE SCIENCE BEHIND TEAMS—OXYTOCIN (BONDING) AND SOCIAL CONTAGION

There is an increasing focus on the science behind team work. There are both scientific factors as well as other elements which help teams thrive, including these neuroscience elements:

Emotional Contagion: Emotional contagion brings to life the notion that "one rotten apple spoils the bunch." Research continues to demonstrate how our emotions, particularly as leaders, spread to those around us. What do you notice about the tone of the team?

Oxytocin: A second element which has been seen in high performing teams is a higher rate of oxytocin, also known as the bonding element. Within in-person environments it can be stimulated through touch, like high-fives and physical team huddles. Virtually it is stimulated by:

- Virtual high fives or, as a participant in a recent meeting I spoke at demonstrated, a Butterfly Hug!
- Bonding and feeling connected in the remote space is critical, especially when physical distancing measures are in effect. What can you do to get people bonding?

RECONNECTING THE WORKSPACE TIP—REIMAGINING WORKSPACE CULTURE

If your organization is shifting to a hybrid workspace, what is the culture you want to create?

Culture is not a static entity, and taking time to intentionally reimagine as a workspace evolves, is an important issue. Like an umbrella, it will frame out WHAT you do, and HOW you do things.

What's possible for you as a workplace right now? In the future?

How will this shift what's important to you as an organization? What impact will this have on your systems, processes, and practices, such as feedback, compensation, or connection?

A valuable activity can be to take time to dialogue around what your workspace culture can look like.

A key part of creating a vibrant virtual, remote and hybrid workspace culture is to make sure we are activating the 7 Remote Enablers[tm]. These are: Communication, Clarity, Connection, Culture, Consistency, Community and Collaboration. Each of the 7 Remote Enablers[tm] helps to boost relationships, and focus the results needed for exceptional work. Each one can be activated individually, or together.

On a scale of 1-10, how strong are you in each of the enablers? What is important for you to focus on as you move forward?

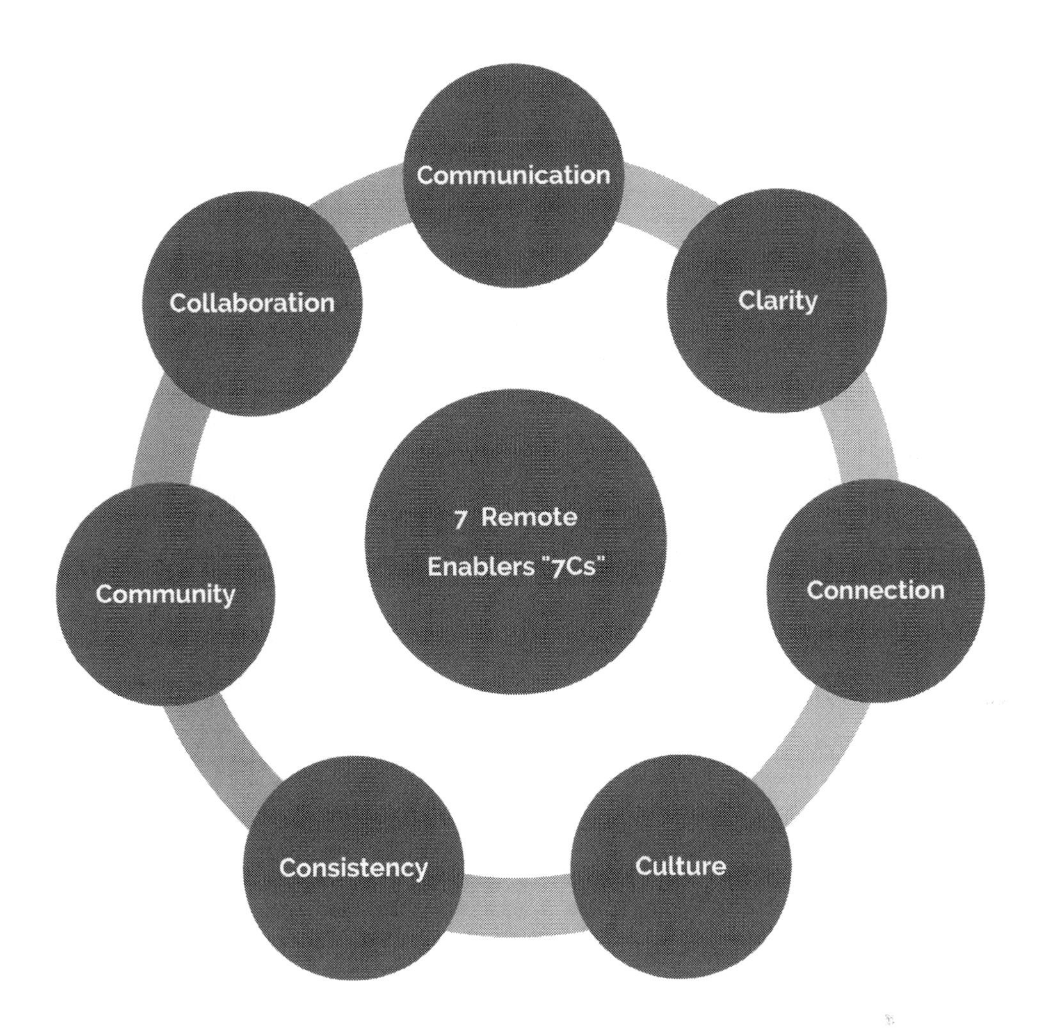

6 SIX TEAMWORK QUESTIONS: SIX FACTORS

1. What's our vision? (Vision)
2. What does success look like? (Performance measures)
3. How do we do things? (Shared behavioral norms)
4. What are our roles? (Team roles)
5. What are our team practices (Team practices)
6. How do we have each other's backs? (Shared commitment)

END OF CHAPTER QUESTIONS

- What is the team culture you want to create?
- What do you notice about your Iceberg of Culture?
- What are the elements you need to note?
- Where are you as a team with each of the Six Factors?

CHAPTER 4

THE TAPESTRY OF TEAMS—A VIRTUAL TEAM OF INDIVIDUALS

"Teamwork is the ability to work together toward a common vision. The ability to direct individual accomplishments toward organizational objectives. It is the fuel that allows common people to achieve uncommon results."
– Andrew Carnegie[71]

Principle: Meet people where they are at. Everyone on the team is going to have different preferences in terms of how they like to work, team, and operate. Prioritize relationships and the ability to know each other and adapt for us.

Myth: Everyone is the same. In fact, a team is a diverse collection of individuals. Treat everyone as unique. Each team member will bring different strengths, styles, and socialization. One brush cannot work for all!

Regardless of the many changes there have been to the space of remote and virtual teamwork, the fundamentals of teams remain the same. Building onto our last chapter of team effectiveness, this chapter explores the core foundations of teamwork, and how the unique individuals of each team shape the team culture. In this chapter we are going to explore:

- The context of teams today: keys for harnessing the best of teams today
- Team culture
- Harnessing individual abilities/characteristics for collective strengths
- An antidote to group think

- The things that make us unique:
    - Generations
    - Culture
    - Styles
- Tricky issues
- The ongoing evolution of teams—Tuckman's model
- Team Tool: Styles work
- Brain Tip: Synchrony

This chapter connects into Chapter 2: The Digital World, Chapter 8: Teamwork Practices, and Chapter 16: Strengths.

THE CONTEXT OF TEAMS TODAY: KEYS FOR HARNESSING THE BEST OF TEAMS TODAY

Teams today are buffeted by several factors, from ongoing change and increasing complexity, to teaming and ongoing change across members of the team. Taking time to build a strong culture is absolutely essential for team effectiveness. As much as things change, it is important to go back to the basics around teams as well.

Tuckman's model[72] informs us about the stages teams move through as they evolve. His research found that teams move through the stages of forming, storming, norming, performing, and adjourning. While remote teams may feel more like a collection of individuals, highly efficient virtual team leaders ensure that they are able to create a solid culture with their team. Taking time to help teams understand where they are in the journey of developing into a team is an important element. Tuckman's model is viewed in depth later in this chapter.

While we may not be able to control or influence the pace of change and/or how much complexity there is, we can influence having a strong team culture, easy ways to communicate and share, and clarity around expectations.

As John Coleman writes in his article *Six Components of a Great Corporate Culture*,[73] six elements of corporate culture include shared vision, values, practices, people, narrative, and place. Let's look at each one of these in turn.

1. **Vision**: Where is the team going—collectively, individually, and as members of matrix organizations?
2. **Values**: What's important to the team? What are the collective values which guide the team and help individuals prioritize?

3. **Practices**: Coleman writes, "values are of little importance unless they are enshrined in a company's practice." Practices say a lot about *who* a team is. Do we ensure Monday meetings happen, regardless of who can attend or what is "on the go?"

4. **People**: Who are the people that make up this team? Helping team members connect and get to know each other through one of the many assessments available (e.g., Myers-Briggs Type Indicator (MBTI), Herrmann Brian Dominance Instrument (HBDI), DiSC), we are able to help team members understand more of their unique style, the styles of their teammates, and what adjustments may be needed for team success. Do we ensure those who are not at meetings are kept on track?

5. **Narrative**: The unique history and story of the team. Team identity is as important for virtual teams as it is for in-person teams. What is the story of your team? One activity to get to this is for established teams to think of a "time when you were at your best." Identify these moments of learning and exceptional performance. Consider how they are enshrined and referred to.

6. **Place**: What is the virtual housing of the team? Is there a Slack Portal? Basecamp site? Is there a social media time which has photos/videos/artifacts of the team? (Artifacts are things that are usually created by the team, e.g., a sculpture, a vision board, or a collage.)

These six elements combined create a unique team experience and fabric. This goes hand in hand with creating a shared team identity. Elements of a team identity might include:

- Who are we?
- What do we value?
- What are the symbols of our team?
- What makes us unique?
- What is the bond that brings us together?
- As a virtual team, what are the artifacts/external representations that define us (i.e., mascot, saying, logo, etc.)?

Virtual team leaders will want to support the team to find their common bond, visuals, and metaphors, and help to facilitate this sense of "connection" in a virtual space. One activity which will support this is using visual cards to create a library of metaphors which team members can pull from. Another activity is to have the team draw icons and share what they see as representing the team.

A reminder from Chapter 3 is that the Six Factors of High Performing Teams provides us with a focus on six areas we always want to make sure we are in alignment around, including the foundations of creating shared agreements and creating a clear vision.

The vision question brings us to the questions of Who are we? Why do we exist? What's important for us as a team? What are the things we aspire to reach for? We know that in that place of aspiration it opens up possibilities and allow us as a team to activate the PEA part of the brain.

TEAM CULTURE: HOW DO WE DO THINGS HERE–PRACTICES AND TEAM HABITS

Our culture is shaped by our habits, those things we do repeatedly. Part of team identity is the culture, artifacts, and habits which make us unique. Let's explore culture first.

Team Culture

The culture of a team or organization is much more than a few words. It's the way things are done here. It encompasses team behaviors, values, mission, practices, priorities, and the motivational factors of a team.

In building strong teams, it is important for teams to become aware of and focus on their team culture, including the good, the bad, and sometimes the ugly. It's about *how we do things*. It is also important to note when team culture is distinct from, or aligned with, an organizational culture.

For example, a team of project managers may value **agility**, **speed**, and **problem solving**, whereas the organizational context may value **quality**, **specificity**, and **thoroughness**. In this instance, there can be conflicts between the team culture and organizational culture. The team culture may have an influence on the organizational culture over time, shifting it to be more agile or responsive. We are seeing this today in many organizational contexts (i.e., teams in one location) which are rethinking how they operate and the roles their teams play.

One micro-team may have a different team culture than another micro-team in your group. Consider a regional team, with one leader responsible for Toronto and New York. While technically they are one department, the culture of the team in Toronto may vary dramatically from that in New York.

A useful activity for a team is to consider what their team culture is. Consider your values, and what you prioritize. You may also want to ask yourselves the questions:

- What are the actions and behaviors which define us?
- What are the three adjectives we would use to describe our culture?
- What is acceptable on this team? What is not?
- What are the three adjectives other teams would use to describe our culture?
- How do our other stakeholders describe our culture?
- What do you notice about culture in your team?
- What's important to keep an eye on?

Team Habits ultimately shape our team culture, an area many authors write about. Since this is an area I find myself working in with teams as well, I thought it would be useful to share what I had written on **Team Culture** a few years ago.

Three key areas which make up any organizational, or team culture, are your values, practices, and habits. Our values form the foundation of any team. Whether explicit or not, they shape what we value and prioritize and how we make decisions. Consider these questions:

- What are the values of your team?
- How do these align with the organization?
- As you consider recent decisions and priorities, what values did those demonstrate?

Values are often under the waterline, invisible, and not necessarily seen. High performing teams are well aware of their values and lead and act from these, making them as visible as possible. Part of my work as a leadership and team coach is to help teams identify what their core values are, and make these explicit in their decisions, actions, and communications.

Team Practices

What is above the waterline, and what is visible to the team and others external to the team, are our practices as a team. This may be a Thursday evening post-work hangout, acknowledging others in a particular way, undertaking a debrief/post-mortem after any project, or some other actions which are done consistently, and specifically, by you as a team. Our practices are an important part of how we operate and communicate as a team. They are often a **visible part of team culture**. Once again, high performing teams are intentional with the practices they undertake as a team, and they are aware of how these connect to their values. In some respects, practices are values in action."[74]

Practices may include developing ourselves, discovery, and improving to get better.

Examples of team practices could include:

1. Making sure everyone has wrapped up key projects by the end of the week by doing a Friday morning check-in/status update and pitching in where needed.
2. Scheduling a year-end retreat to support team development and team planning.
3. Being ready to start work with computers on and coffee in hand at 8:30 a.m. (and not in the coffee room until 9:00 a.m.).
4. Making a point of job shadowing for half a day each quarter with a different team member.
5. Dedicating time to participate in ongoing learning and discovery, such as individual learning or team coaching.

As with these examples, most, except item 3, work in favor of the team. What happens over time is that teams can slip into habits that really don't benefit the entire team or its performance.

Consider:

- What are the current practices of the team?
- What is getting in the way?

Team Habits

Hand in hand with practices are habits. Habits are things that we do unconsciously which support us in today's frenetic business context. In the virtual and hybrid space, there are many habits which we can cultivate to support a team.

These include:

- Always shutting off notifications during team meetings
- Making sure that other windows are closed during Zoom or Teams calls
- Doing a check-in at a certain time of day to see how progress is coming
- Starting our meetings by inviting those working remotely to speak first
- Checking in with remote team members and asking them for input

In fact, you might ask: When does a practice become a habit? It is these ongoing habits which really kick teams into high performance. Whether it is the habit of closing the door for half an hour or making sure a team huddle happens each Friday afternoon to review the week and prep for the next one, habits shape who we are.

Consider:

- What are the habits your of your team?
- How are these supporting excellence and high performance?
- How do these connect to your values and what you prioritize?
- What habits are getting the way?

In her TEDx Talk and writing, Jan Stanley[75,76] talks about how routines help us in that they:

- Constrain choices which helps us focus and reduce distraction
- Enable action. Routines often become a narrative of "What we do," and so a routine around exercise every day becomes part of how I work
- Offer coherence and help us to see that our actions serve a greater purpose
- Provide stability and mutability; and as our environment changes, routines can adapt.

This was illustrated as routines adapted quickly during the pandemic.

In times of uncertainty, flux, and change, routines are invaluable for providing some perceived stability as well as momentum.

One activity you might want to undertake as a team is to identify the habits and routines your team has developed. Think about those things you consistently do. Which ones help? Which ones hinder? How are these habits automatic? What do they allow you to do?

> "Culture is unspoken, but powerful. It develops over time."[77]
> —Mark Fields

6 SIX QUESTIONS FOR THE TEAM: TEAM CULTURE

1. What are the three words that describe the culture of the team?
2. What do you value?
3. What are the behaviors that are acceptable and not acceptable on the team? (These can often point to values)
4. What are we known for?
5. What are the practices that help define us?
6. What artifacts have we created which are important parts of our identity?

OUR TAPESTRY—THE UNIQUE INDIVIDUALS THAT MAKE UP A TEAM

Every team is uniquely shaped by the individuals that make up the team. There may be different generations, cultures, and working preferences. This chapter sheds a light on these to help leaders, and team members, navigate the murky waters of working across differences.

Each one of us is uniquely different according to our

- Culture: geographic culture
- Generation
- Styles
- Strengths
- Workplace preferences

To learn more about the unique tapestry of the team, it can be useful to proactively build in time to get to know each other. As a team leader, you can find it very useful to host a regular series of one-on-ones for team members. As team members, undertaking structured networking time to get to know your peers is also critical.

Key to engagement is knowing WIIFM (What's in it for me?), and helping individuals connect with their own WIIFM.

A large part of team development should focus on helping individual team members articulate:

- Who they are
- What's important for others to know about them
- The values which are important to them as a professional (i.e., accuracy, speed, collaboration, group work, individual decision); these are shaped by our culture, our socialization, and our professional role (i.e., accountant vs. creative designer)

Activities for Helping Teams Identify What's Unique

There are a number of activities we can undertake to help team members identify what they bring that's unique to the team. Rather than disintegrating the team, knowing our differences helps us to adjust our behaviors. Here are a number of activities which can help team members identify what makes them unique, including:

- Visual cards
- Icons
- Personal logos
- Miniature metaphors
- Individual value lines

AN ANTIDOTE TO GROUPTHINK

The strength of a team is its diversity. Unfortunately, when trust levels are low, it's unlikely that different opinions will be raised.

Groupthink was a term coined by Irving Janis and describes the group phenomenon where "like-minded people make bad decisions without seriously examining them."[78]

What is common in teams is that one person says, "Yes, that's a great idea," and the rest follow, without critically exploring whether it is true or not. Boosting trust in a team can help to create the safety needed where you can have spirited debate with each other, rather than everyone saying *Yes!*

There are several areas which we can cultivate to avoid groupthink, including encouraging structured decision making and different perspectives using processes such as De Bono's Six Thinking Hats. Build skills and strengths in the area of productive discourse, where a "Devil's Advocate" perspective may be brought forward intentionally. Research has also found that "creating thought diversity" is also an antidote to groupthink.[79]

Foundations of Geographic Culture

For the better part of the last three decades, I have been involved in intercultural training, helping individuals understand their uniqueness that they bring as they step into the global workplace.

Understanding more about cultures and the differences which exist is essential for a virtual team. While this section is not intended to replace a deeper dive into the understanding of culture, exploring our own social identity is an important part of effective team membership. We need to understand our own cultural bias and recognize how we have been shaped by our socialization, life, and work experiences.

There are several different intercultural models, including that of Geert Hofstede, who is famous for his book title, "Culture is like the software of the mind."

Hofstede is well known for his research around geographic culture, having identified how one country can vary from another on six distinct lines, including Power Distance (how equally power is distributed), Individualism vs. Collectivism (whether we look at issues from an *I* or *We* lens), Masculinity vs. Femininity (how competitive or cooperative are we), Uncertainty Avoidance (our tolerance for ambiguity), Long-Term Orientation (how focused we are on tradition), and Indulgence (how focused we are on immediate gratification). For more on this, check out his research, and the country comparison, at Hofstede Insights.[80]

Global Dexterity

A key part of virtual work is that it widens our reach in the world. With this in mind, it can be valuable to cultivate skills in intercultural effectiveness, or what is also called "Global Dexterity." Author Andy Molinsky describes the term *global dexterity* as, "the capacity to adapt your behavior, where necessary, in a foreign cultural environment to accommodate new and different expectations that vary from those of your own native cultural setting."[81] He goes on to write that "Global dexterity is a critical skill for anyone from any culture attempting to function successfully in today's global environment."[82]

We no longer need to travel in order to benefit from building skills in global dexterity. Any time we are part of a global or regional team, we can benefit from pausing to think about the different layers of culture.

Molinsky also identifies three core challenges when learning to adapt our behavior:

1. The competence challenge or, as he writes, "feeling that knowledge and skill is not up to the task of adapting behavior."[83]
2. Authenticity challenge, experiencing new behavior as being in conflict with your accustomed way of behaving and with pre-existing cultural values and behaviors.
3. Resentment challenge, feeling that the very act of adapting cultural behaviors is a burden and an imposition.

He modifies Hofstede's work and talks about these six culture dimensions:

1. Directness
2. Enthusiasm
3. Functionality

4. Assertiveness
5. Self-promotion
6. Personal disclosure

These are all elements which can vary dramatically across the different members of the team. Think about the team members you work with. How do they differ across each of these areas?

Key to expanding your cultural dexterity is moving into the stretch zone and being able to identify topics, decide how to engage, and adjust your approach.

What are the layers of global culture which are important to explore on your team?

TRICKY ISSUES

The title for this chapter is The Tapestry of Teams, to acknowledge that every team is different and every team's fabric is uniquely made up by its members.

Tricky issues emerge in the virtual space for many reasons. In general, they occur because people do not feel:

- Heard
- Valued
- Connected
- Safe
- Trusted

When team members do not feel safe, valued, or heard, some of the strengths can become augmented and turn into weaknesses.

Individual team members may:

- Not feel like they are connected to other team members
- Not see how they need to be connected to each other
- Not feel like they are part of a whole
- Feel cut off from others
- Feel resentment when they are the ones who always have to meet at the one time that works for others

It is important to have regular one-on-ones to take the pulse of the group and identify tricky issues.

DIFFICULT PERSONALITIES ON TEAMS

Issues can become quickly augmented and magnified on virtual teams, given that we connect for only short periods of time. The "window of the screen" captures people at only one given moment, and if each time they come to the call they are rushed, we may automatically assume that they are always like that, without unpacking the assumption to realize that the reason they are rushing is because in order to connect to the team call they have to commute through rush-hour to reach home in time.

There are several principles which are key to harnessing the best of teams and ensuring their diversity:

- Each voice is important
- Each voice provides valuable insight
- All voices are equal

At the same time, teams are dynamic, living, breathing entities. Our fellow team members may not be ones we choose on any given day, yet we need to learn how to work with them. Some of the more common team members we may see in a team who are tricky to deal with:

- Are super-performers
- Do not show up
- Do not share information
- Are not confident
- Are gossips
- Do not keep you updated
- Are backstabbers or saboteurs
- Engage in self-promotion
- Do not have each other's backs
- Waste time or slack off
- Do not follow through with work
- Are inappropriate cross-culturally
- Are anti-team members; these are the lone wolves—the people who do it all on their own. An anti-team member may try to disrupt virtual team progress with:
    - passive-aggressive behavior; rather than dealing with conflict, they don't show up
    - always being late or holding people back by not being ready; for these people, note to always start meetings on time.
- Are pessimists; these people have an important voice for the team to listen to. They can flag things that other team members may not see.

Let's zoom into a number of these personality types and explore a little more about their world and how they can be supported.

TEAM MEMBER	WHAT IT LOOKS LIKE VIRTUALLY	WHAT DO THEY NEED? WHAT'S THE REQUEST BEHIND THE COMPLAINT?	WHAT SUPPORT MIGHT BE PROVIDED
Anti-team member	Lone wolf or fearless individual	Feels like doesn't need to be part of the team	Finding ways to bring strengths into special projects
Passive-aggressive behavior	Not addressing conflict as it arises by sidestepping it, such as double booking meetings, not showing up Making snide remarks but not taking action	To be heard To have someone help them raise and address the conflict	Provide tools for all team members to raise and address conflict Provide space and support for conflict issues to be addressed Modeling of appropriate ways for conflict to be addressed Group/team agreements around modeling of conflict Being clear with how conflict should be addressed productively
Pessimist	This isn't going to work	Listening	Encouragement to bring this perspective, as it can have great value, but not to get mired in it or too sure of it
Is always late	Doesn't show up on time, is not ready	A watch!	Be clear about expectations around time and what is needed behaviorally Be honest in dialogue about what is expected, when, and consequences if it is not ready Start meetings on time; do not punish other team members by waiting
Super-performer	Does everything perfectly, super fast Always gets results and goes beyond what is expected	Recognition To be able to go quickly	Mentor others Lead processes

Does not show up	We don't know them They are never there	To be reached out to One-on-one time	Is this a performance issue? What needs to be adjusted? What assumptions am I making?
Does not share information	Does their own thing Doesn't collaborate Hoards information	Knowledge and power	Support by helping them to: • Look at how jobs are interconnected • Mapping information flows • Get them to think about the impact of not sharing the information As a leader, be direct in expectations about sharing information
Not confident	Lots of emails, phone calls, and questions Not sure of what to do	Provide support and feedback Get them to job shadow others Get them to teach other team members so they know how much they know	Regular check ins Mentor and teach others to recognize what they do know
Does not keep you updated	Does their own thing May be working on a different tangent than other team members	They want to get it done They want to be autonomous	Clarify expectations around communication and end results
Self-promotion	I did this . . . Did you know . . .	Wants to get ahead Wants to be seen Wants validation	Provide them with a strong mentor who can share more appropriate strategies for self-promotion Have them mentor others
Does not have each other's backs/sabotages	Gossip Badmouthing	Low trust Lack of respect Lack of understanding of each other	Clarify rules of the road regarding communication and raising issues Focus on building relationships and interdependence

Wastes time/slacks off	Social media and surfing Does not follow through	Lack of focus—needs direction on job requirements Clarification of what's expected and what's a priority Modeling of getting things done	Regular check ins Clarify roles and responsibilities Shadow and work with others
Does not follow through	No results or fewer than expected Blaming others	May not understand the bigger picture and how their role interacts/ connects with others	Make accountability part of the work Reporting Follow up with them Create a habit of check-ins and updates
Inappropriate cross-culturally	Assumptions Bad mouthing Inappropriate cultural word Lack of sensitivity	Training Exposure to other ways of working Exploring unconscious bias Understanding their own cultural biases	Mentoring and training Firm agreements around what is and is not appropriate cross-culturally
Other:			

What other issues do you see at play? Some of the more common ones can be:

- Lack of follow-through and accountability
- Gossip
- Finger pointing
- Hoarding—information/resources/contacts

These are all signals of low or no trust. Without addressing these issues, it is unlikely that the team will be able to be productive.

What about Me?

By their nature, virtual teams may be much more driven by individuals, given that members operate on their own. Team members may lead with the mindset, "What about me?" given people are working separate from their leader and/or team members when working remotely.

Keeping this in mind, it can be very important to start the conversation from the individual experience and then roll it up to the collective or team experience which is common across the virtual or remote team.

Helping individual team members learn more about themselves, their style, and their preferences is an essential step in developing self-awareness. Given that individual team members may need to be more personally focused, providing them with tools and ideas around **productivity**, **goal setting**, and **evaluation** can be important. They are the "boots on the ground" or the local level Subject Matter Expert (SME).

Cultivating a team member's emotional intelligence can be an important starting point for capacity building in the team. We will be exploring this topic in Chapter 17.

Revisiting the Six Factors: Under Chapter 3 on team effectiveness, we explored six factors that help teams excel. One that is very significant is team roles. Do they understand their role? Do they know what is required of them? Does each team member know where to go for support? How their role intersects with others?

GENERATIONS IN REVIEW

While not intended to stereotype, the value of exploring and learning more about our different generations is that we have all had different societal experiences that have shaped who we are, how we were educated, and our level of comfort with technology. In today's workplace we have at least four, if not sometimes five generations in the workplace.

In the workplace today, we see:

- Generation Z (sometimes also described as iGen)
- Millennials
- Generation X
- Baby Boomers
- The Silent Veterans

With current workplace demographics, most employees may be either Baby Boomers or Millennials. There are fewer Generation X professionals by numbers, and Generation Z or iGen is just starting to enter the workplace. Each group has different approaches and comfort levels with technology, approaches to communication, and different values around what is important. Let's look at each of these.

GENERATION	VALUES AND PRIORITIES AT WORK	LEVEL OF COMFORT WITH TECHNOLOGY
iGen or Gen Z (2000 onwards) By 2020 one-third of the US population	92% have a digital footprint Sharing Actions speak louder than words Value feedback, ongoing training, and 39% want to work independently[84]	Digital natives. Used to being "always on" Streaming before everything
Millennials Old Mills (1980–1990) Young Mills (1990–2000)	Quick, fast feedback and movement Ongoing learning	Older Millennials may be more like Gen X and internet was not always there vs. Younger Millennials who grew up with the Internet
Gen X (1965–1980) Smallest generation overshadowed by Boomers and Millennials	Independence Work/life balanced	Quite comfortable
Baby Boomers (1946–1964)	Meetings and communication (high touch)	May not be as comfortable with all the technology changes

ENGAGING ACROSS GENERATIONS[85]

In our work as virtual facilitators, it is likely that we are engaging across generations, each of which has different aptitudes and comfort levels for technology and virtual learning. Additionally, in any group, you may find that some people are more comfortable than others. As we lead virtual calls, it is important to consider the experiences of different generations, not to spotlight differences, but to better understand each generation's comfort level with different types of technology. These shape our preferences for virtual conversations.

Let's take a closer look at each generation.

Baby Boomers (1946–1964)

While this generation is starting to retire out of the work force, you may still be working with Boomers as Subject Matter Experts (SMEs) and mentors, if not as leaders. Keep in mind that Boomers have historically valued teamwork and meetings in ways that others do not. This can lead to preferences on their part for meetings which are not shared by others. The Boomers have seen technology emerge in the workplace from Rolodexes to the first satellite phones, which were often housed in a briefcase.

Gen Xers (1965–1979)

Enshrined in Douglas Coupland's book *Gen X*, Xers have a smaller demographic footprint in the workplace than both Boomers and Gen Yers, due to their size. They bring a variance in their technological savvy. As a member of this generation, I explored DOS programming in Grade Six computer science camp and marvelled at Atari's pixelated games. I wrote my high school papers on a computer, although I had to save them on floppy disks. When I led programming and teams of more than a hundred in South America, we were connected by short-range radio, while my communication with the head office was through the fax, or an email that sat in Trinidad overnight. The need to take immediate action led to high degrees of autonomy in my work as a leader. Gen Xers may be comfortable in the virtual realm, as many of us started engaging in "distance learning," as it was called in the 1990s. Not all of us may be as comfortable in navigating the ever-changing platforms, even though we will enjoy the real-time nature of virtual events and focus—as long as it is during work time.

Millennials (1980s–early 2000s)

The Millennials are the first digital natives. They value group work and collaboration, influenced by an educational process that was often more group oriented than earlier generations. One of the biggest distinctions seen with Millennials is their fluidity around different forms of digital communication. For many, texting is as common as a verbal conversation. Real-time/just-in-time communication, or instantaneous communication, is often expected. Millennials are positioned to offer an important voice around innovation and creativity.

Gen Z (those born after 2000)

Gen Z are truly the digital natives. They have grown up with smart phones and tablets in their hands, and global connectivity. iPads are part of everyday life in classrooms, and for many are a toy from infancy. Skype and Face Time have replaced phone calls, and video streaming is their norm. YouTube is their TV. Gamification is an extension of their learning process. The ability to connect immediately with people around the world, getting real-time data and seeing inside each other's households and businesses in a way that no other generation has experienced will no doubt shape what is possible with virtual learning.

IN FOCUS—GENERATION Z

Gen Z has been found to be the most entrepreneurial generation according to many studies.[86] They prefer traditional methods of conversation, and need frequent feedback. Surprisingly, many studies indicate interest in more face-to-face communication than digital communication.[87] Frequent feedback has also been indicated as a preference. This may reflect the just-in-time and real-time learning experiences they were socialized with, for example, marks being posted immediately online.

Did you know:

- According to Gen Z expert, David Stillman, 90.6% of Gen Z said, "a company's technological sophistication would impact their decision to work there."[88]
- Two-thirds of Gen Zers value "open, curious mindsets over skillsets."[89]
- 40% say working Wi-Fi is as important as a functioning bathroom.[90]

Understanding the unique perspectives, values, and desires of each generation, and appreciating the life stage of which they are at, is another important component of understanding your unique team tapestry.

TOOLS FOR GETTING TO KNOW YOUR TEAM BETTER

Creating trust and connection in your team is critical. It usually starts with the leader, and virtual and remote team leaders will want to take a proactive role in making sure that they are creating trust and connection.

There are a number of tools we can use for getting to know our team better. These include such assessments as:

- MBTI
- DiSC
- Hogan Personality Inventory
- Herrmann Brain Dominance Instrument
- Enneagram

Use the table below to explore what the focus is for each of these.

ASSESSMENT TOOL	FOCUS
MBTI	Based on Carl Jung's theory of personality types, the MBTI provides a window into a person's personality type, strengths, and preferences. Also referred to as 16 personalities it explores.
DiSC	The DiSC (and different iterations) provides a common language for individuals around four areas. When used in teams, it can provide enhanced insights around how people prefer to work, communicate, and interrelate.
Hogan	Hogan assessment looks at "bright-side personality"—qualities that describe how we relate to others when we are at our "best." In contrast, the Hogan Development Survey explores the "dark side" of personality which occurs when things get disrupted. Note, an understanding of what I term our "underbelly" can be valuable, especially when we are working independently.
Hermann Brain Dominance Instrument	It helps to "decode and harness the cognitive diversity of individuals, teams and organizations."[91]
Enneagram	The Enneagram is another assessment which is used to provide insights into both the personal development and business development realms.

The key to having people participate in any assessment is that it provides a "doorway" to learn more about themselves. Having a common framework will help a team to create a shared mental model so they can speak and work across differences more effectively. As we get to know ourselves better, we are able to:

- Identify our strengths to know what we uniquely bring to the table
- Understand what is more challenging to adjust to and/or blind spots that could derail us
- Know our "go-tos" during times of stress and pressure
- Consider how our strengths and styles impact others positively and negatively
- Consider how we may need to adjust our conversation to be in connection with others

Taking an Appreciative, Strengths-Based Approach to Leadership

The Gallup organization has undertaken decades of research around the benefits of managers supporting their staff's strengths. The business case for strengths-based leadership is quite compelling. Gallup has found that employees who are encouraged to lead from strengths by their managers are six times more engaged and demonstrate 8.9% greater profitability and 12.5% greater productivity.

We will be exploring the topic of strengths to a greater extent in Chapter 16.

STYLES

Our style preferences impact how we:

- Communicate
- Make decisions
- Approach innovation
- Provide and receive feedback
- Approach change

Within a team there will be a range of styles. It is important to understand our own style, as well as know what we might need to do to adjust our style to be effective in working with others.

As seen in the table around assessments, there are many different frameworks where people may have varying preferences. They may be:

- Introverted/extroverted
- Big picture/granular detail
- People/facts
- Start/finish

Understanding how each person best works is valuable in exploring stressors, enablers, and how people naturally work. Most assessments can provide a springboard to understand how people on a team may prefer to communicate, prioritize, and make decisions. For example, if I have a preference to get things done rather than do things for accuracy, I may find tasks such as reviewing financial details much more laborious than launching a new product. Understanding styles and preferences on multiple levels is valuable personally and as a team.

IN FOCUS—THE DISC

The DiSC emerged out of the work and writing of Dr. Moulton Marston and his book, *Emotions Of Normal People*. It was one of the first books which explored human emotion. This research found that there were four main personality types:

D: Dominance (Marston) or sometimes called Driver. People with a D preference value speed, results, and getting things done. Feedback may be blunt and not diplomatic. D's benefit from the opportunity to learn more about themselves and slow down the pace.

I: Inducement (Marston) or Influence. Influence is the term used by many DiSC assessments today. People with an I preference love relationships and spending time with others. I's often energize a room or are the "social butterfly." There is an opportunity to harness this in team development opportunities.

S: Submission (Marston) or referred to as Steadiness in many of today's assessments. People with an S preference focus on details and are very methodological. They value support and collaboration. Feedback can be provided in a more collaborative way, and should be sensitive to how feelings might get involved. S's can sometimes be overly trusting.

C: Compliance (Marston) or Conscientious in some of today's frameworks. People with a C preference value accuracy. They may also work at a slower pace. When providing feedback to C's, provide factual examples and provide them with time to reflect, think, and respond. There is an opportunity for C's to grow more in the area of risk taking.

Stakeholder Analysis

Given that many remote team members are working on their own, it can be useful to introduce them to a series of team-based tools. Many, or some of these, may only have been privy to team leaders. Given the more interdependent and autonomous role of the team member, equipping them with team tools is also important.

TEAM TOOL: WORKING WITH STYLES
TEAMWORK SKILL: WORKING ACROSS DIFFERENCES

It can be very useful to help teams of all kinds, including virtual teams, understand the unique style of each team member. Whether you do opt to use an Everything DiSC®,[92] or you use an MBTI or other assessment, what is often most important is the discussion which ensues.

Here is a quick activity to help team members expand their thinking about styles, and also boost connection.

Time: 20–30 minutes

Materials needed: A slide with icons which team members can speak to.

Pre-preparation: Identify what the topic is with the team and how you want to explore styles. Do you want to look at it through the lens of how you like to approach communication? Working styles? Decision making? Conflict? Feedback? Make sure you have alignment around this.

Show the team the slide and ask the team to share what their preference is around about how they would approach the topic area. For example, if you are looking at how you make decisions, there might be a round of questions where you go around the table and hear from each person. Sharing could include each person's response on these areas.

1. Which icon represents your natural approach to___________ (decision making or _____)?
2. Which icon represents how you would like to be supported in _______?
3. As a team, which icon represents how you think the team in general needs to approach ______?
4. At our best as a team, we would approach decisions by _____________________.
5. What was important for me about this conversation was _________________.

Depending on the size of the team, you may need to select certain questions to discuss. It can be a very powerful activity.

THE ONGOING EVOLUTION OF TEAMS

A final area to be aware of is that of Tuckman's model (as adapted from *Effective Virtual Conversations*). Like a staircase, teams move up and down the staircase of development. They move through a series of stages from forming to storming to norming to performing and to adjourning. At each stage they are placing emphasis on different areas, with different virtual nuances and considerations. Hybrid, remote, and virtual teams will be aware of the things that they want to be doing at different stages, as well as build in specific activities at certain stages.

STAGE	WHAT'S IMPORTANT	VIRTUAL NUANCES	CONSIDERATIONS	THINGS TO MAKE SURE YOU ARE DOING	ACTIVITIES YOU MAY WANT TO USE
Forming In this stage, we are helping the group explore the What?	Creating Safety within the team, shared expectations—what is expected around communication, roles, flagging, and escalating issues Roles and responsibilities Matrix management arrangements Creating agreements on how you want to operate Creating shared vision, mission, and purpose Getting people to connect and/or share their WIIFM	Group/team members can't see each other Geographically dispersed Different realities and priorities Notice how people are engaged in the virtual realm—video versus text-only interaction Creating of a shared group portal or "go-to place" for resources can be important	WOW—Ways of Working Focusing on connecting the group Choosing platforms and considering synchronous and asynchronous* connections. How do people want to connect? How do you ensure privacy? Confidentiality agreements	Clarifying what is expected Creating team agreements and team norms (what are our values and what do these look like in value? What's acceptable and not acceptable?) Creating connection Reviewing goals at corporate level Creating shared team goals Checking in around individual team accessibility Meeting with team members one-on-one	Activities to create trust and connection such as: What do you bring that is unique to the team? Vision/values Assessments Goal setting

* Synchronous conversations happen real-time. For example, I can be conversing real-time with someone in London right now through text, chat, or voice from my desk in Toronto. In Asynchronous Learning, there is a lag—so, for example, I might post a comment on a shared thread tonight that can be read tomorrow by someone else, somewhere else.

Storming In this stage, we are helping the group explore the What? So, who are we? What's this all about?	Continued discussion around roles, purpose/ agreements How do we want to work across conflict? Creating shared approaches to how we want to operate and how this connects with me What are/ could be the major sources of conflict? Clarifying of boundaries Distinction between individual and collective	Greater likelihood of disengagement on the part of team members	Different cultural approaches to conflict Notice differences in how people approach, and are comfortable with, conflict	Normalizing conflict (this is a natural part of the process of team agreement) Reinforcing the team agreements Helping team create common frameworks for navigating conflict Providing an opportunity for team members to identify and share their approaches to conflict	Normalize functions, tasks, decisions Appreciation Best team Aspirations—what do we want? Connecting to the vision of the organization and team What's holding the team back? How to have difficult conversations or working across differences—prioritization Style assessments—MBTI and DiSC
Norming In this stage we are exploring Who we are? What's acceptable? What can we do?	Matrix management roles and responsibilities figured out Planning, roles, figuring out how you really want to work Continuing to help the team learn about each other, their strengths and capabilities How do we synergize? What else do we need?	Individual and team norms Making explicit different roles, ways of working, norms Is there an evolution of new shared group/ team culture?	How do we want to operate together? What do we need to know about your reality?	Continuing to build trust Getting people into deeper dialogue with each other Strengths-based work—how can you bring your skills to work? What are we great at? What else do we need? Clarifying roles and responsibilities of matrix Deepening identity of the team	Values and behaviors Strengths-based work Values Culture work at the team level

Performing In this stage we are exploring acceleration. What's working? What will keep momentum going?	Getting things done Making sure the team and its members have all that they need to excel	There may be competing demands and priorities at times which can impact performance Who else needs to be part of the discussion?	Resourcing, roadblocks, enablers Systems and structures that will sustain the work Involvement of other matrix	Creating opportunities for reflective pause Noticing energy and renewal as people get the work done Provide ample feedback cycles—what's working and what's not	Resourcing Helping the team excel Revisiting team agreements Revisiting the six factors as needed Involvement of matrix managers as needed Learning captured for next time Troubleshooting Planning for celebration Regular feedback rounds and iteration/ adjustment Sprints and hacks Rewards and reinforcement Use the work (and structures) they are undertaking
Adjourning In this stage we are helping the team learn from experience and consider Now what?	Debrief or evaluation of the project or team experience. What worked? What didn't? What learning did we have? How can this be applied to future projects or team situations? Wrap up Sustainability Evaluation	Last time together Application to local context	Feedback Evaluation, lessons learned Celebration	What do you want to take from this experience? What has been the key learning? How do you want to stay connected?	Celebration Spider's web Acknowledgment Action planning: One-Page Plan and commitments Evaluation, learning, takeaways

BRAIN TIP: SYNCHRONY

As we have explored in this chapter, teams are made up of a collection of individuals. Key to creating a team is helping the team get aligned, as well as synchronized. There is a scientific concept called Synchrony.

Have you seen the Synchrony videos on YouTube, bringing to life the concept of how we synchronize with others?

As Blount and Leroy write, "The synchrony preference captures the degree to which a person tracks the pace of other people's behavior and is willing to adapt his or her own behavior to match it, in terms of both speeding up and slowing down."[93]

Our ability to adjust our dials up and down is significant in a team context. Just like being a part of an orchestra, we need to be able to amplify certain facets of ourselves when working with some, and mute the same items when working with others. In a remote team, our ability to read others and get feedback is core to success. Synchrony and emotional intelligence go hand in hand as our social awareness skills and self-awareness play a key part of the feedback loop for adjusting.

RECONNECTING THE WORKSPACE TIP—PURPOSEFULLY BUILDING TEAMS

Things don't "just happen" in the remote space. It's hard to have spontaneous moments. Reconnecting the workspace needs to be purposefully planned.

This chapter's reconnection tip gets you to think about *how* you want to reconnect people. What is important for you as a team? An individual? An organization?

When are you are going to build teams? When teams are distributed across distance and time, being purposeful about building in time to reconnect is important. Unless time is scheduled, it's unlikely to happen.

On an ongoing basis, strategically build in time to allow teams to get to know each other and focus on results. This might include facilitating an icebreaker at each meeting, such as:

- What's outside your window?
- What's on your desk?
- What pathway are you working on?
- What doorway do you want to go into?

Each one of these activities provides us with a better understanding of what the context is for our colleagues and team members.

As you consider reconnecting your workspace, what does intentionality look like?

END OF CHAPTER QUESTIONS

- What is important to note about the different styles and preferences of your team?
- What can you do to harness the best of everyone on the team?
- What stage are they at? What do they need in order to thrive?

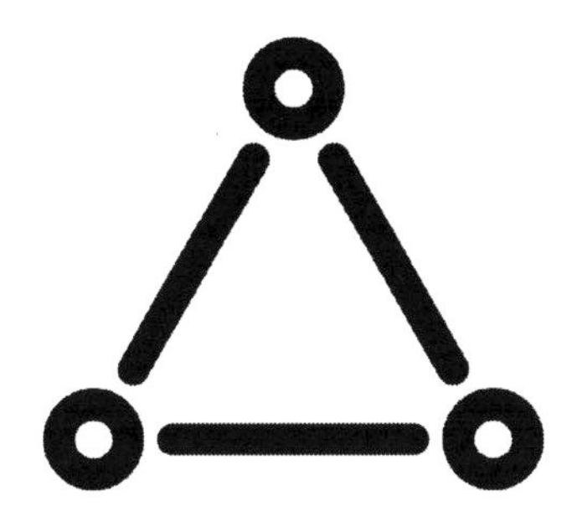

CHAPTER 5

THE TRIAD OF TRUST, SAFETY, AND CONNECTION

"Trust each other again and again. When the trust level gets high enough, people transcend apparent limits, discovering new and awesome abilities of which they were previously unaware."
– David Armistead

Principle: It's reciprocal. As Newton's Law states, "For every action, there is an equal and opposite reaction." Trust, safety, and connection are recipocal. As Stephen Covey wrote, "Trust begets trust."

Myth: Leader as Driver (it's all about the team). Whether it's been due to a top-down model of leadership, limited resources, or other factors, one of the myths which gets shattered in the virtual space is that it's "***all about the formal leader***." In the virtual space it is important to equip everyone as leaders with the necessary skills, authority, and resources, given the solo nature of their work.

An increasing amount of research has pointed to the critical virtual team foundation of trust, safety, and connection. Without trust, it is likely that a team will remain a collection of individuals, rather than morphing into the cohesive entity of a team.

In this chapter we explore:

- What's the difference? Team versus group
- Trust as the foundation for any virtual team
- What builds trust and what depletes trust

- The TRI (Trust/Respect/Influence)
- Essential elements for creating a team that excels
- Team Tool: Trust indicator
- Brain Tip: Psychological safety and amygdala hijack

WHAT'S THE DIFFERENCE? TEAM VERSUS GROUP

"A team is not a group of people who work together. A team is a group of people who trust each other."[94] —Simon Sinek

Many teams today think they are a team but are merely a collection of individuals.

Key to team success in the virtual space is ensuring that we are focused on the Triad of Trust, Safety, and Connection.

Let's explore these.

TRUST AS THE FOUNDATION FOR ANY VIRTUAL TEAM

Trust, and lack of trust, starts on day one of any team. Likened to a bank account, Stephen Covey notes in his book, *The Speed of Trust*, that trust accounts can be built up over time, and they can be depleted. Trust is the foundation of any team, especially one that is virtual. As Armistead notes, trust is the ingredient "allowing virtual teams to transcend limit" and move from being individual contributors to a team.

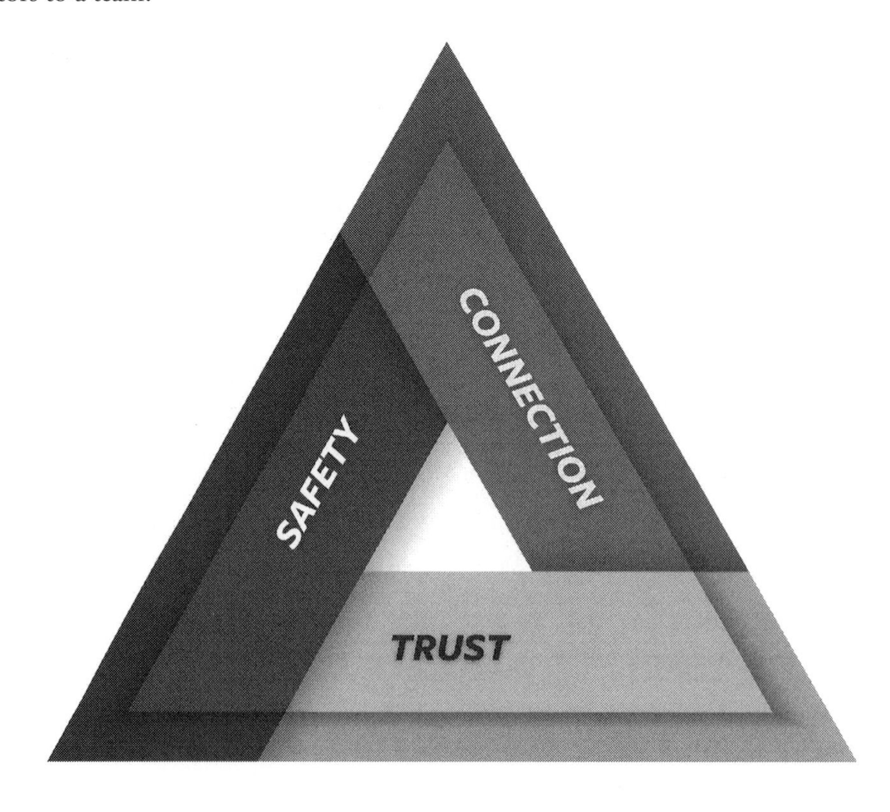

Trust is a behavioral activity. It involves all team members—both team leader and team members. Everyone is responsible for building trust.

As a starting point, as team leaders and team members, are you:

- Taking time to get to know each other—who you are, what you offer, what you bring to the team?
- Clarifying what's expected of you?
- Creating shared agreements around how you will operate?
- Identifying the things that can erode trust?
- Naming and identifying actions and behaviors that minimize trust?
- Clarifying the behaviors that lead to the results you want?
- Ensuring that your actions are in alignment with your values? If you say you value teamwork, but your systems, i.e., compensation, benefits, etc., reward and recognize individual performance, how does that help with trust?

These are all issues that are part of the context of trust.

THE BUSINESS CASE FOR TRUST

There is a compelling business case for trust. Trust is no longer a "soft skill" or something that is nice to have. It is imperative.

As Stephen Covey notes, a 2002 Watson Wyatt study found high-trust organizations outperformed low-trust organizations in total return to shareholders by **286%**.[95]

Trust is the foundation of many teams and can lead to exceptional results or lead to tremendous downfall.

Disengagement—Today's Biggest Virus?

The cost of engagement:

70% of employees are disengaged or actively disengaged:

- Costing the US $350 million, one of the most important factors to engagement is having connection with your manager
- Only 41% say their manager creates dialogue with them

Gallup reports that engaged employees are more productive, more profitable, more customer focused, safer, and less likely to leave their employer. Most recent engagement statistics include the following business case:

A Towers Perrin study[96] found that the most critical components affecting employee engagement were:

- A company that offers its employees challenging work and the resources to get that work done
- Employees who have a clear vision of the business from senior management but the authority to make decisions on their own, within management's guidelines

WHAT TRUST LOOKS LIKE

Having each other's backs, going the extra mile, reframing conflicts as opportunities, leveraging strengths, and working across differences: these are all essential for team members to be able to show up every day and do their own work.

What other behaviors are helping to build trust? Erode trust on your team?

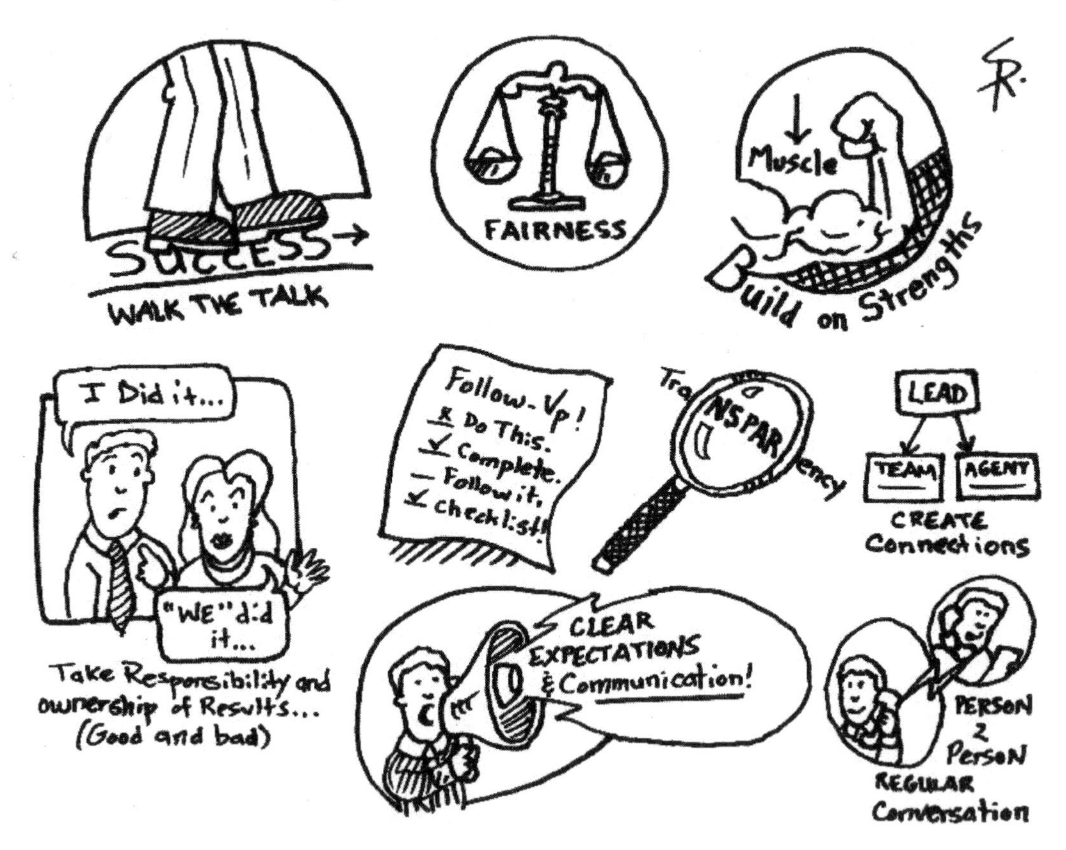

Specific Behaviors That Build Trust in Virtual Teams

As leaders and team members, we can model a number of behaviors.

What Builds Trust:

- Walking the talk
- Being fair
- Building on strengths

- Taking ownership (for what works and what doesn't)
- Being transparent
- Creating connections
- Having clear expectations and communication
- Having regular one-on-ones/communication

What Erodes Trust

When trust gets eroded, we see a variety of impacts, from turnover and illness to lower levels of motivation and engagement to a shift to more territorial behavior and move to silos.

Specifically in virtual, remote, and hybrid teams you may see the following issues, which have these impacts (what happens) and solutions:

ISSUE—TRUST EROSION	IMPACT—WHAT HAPPENS	SOLUTION
Lack of follow through	No improvement Mistakes are not corrected or learned from	Keeping responsibilities top of mind Making goals and milestones visible.
Favoritism	Cliques form Lack of cohesion and alignment	Ensuring people are valued as individuals and not being compared to each other Ensuring fairness Bringing all voices into the room as a practice
Not calling out issues as they emerge	Results are not achieved Bad behavior is permitted Conflicts grow and fester	Having a clear process to address
Not addressing conflict	Sweep things under the rug Issues fester and grow	Having agreements as to how you want to address conflict Having difficult conversations as needed
Not feeling safe to bring issues	Turnover Low morale Poor performance	Team agreements and norms Intentional focus on behavior and impact

THE TRI (TRUST/RESPECT/INFLUENCE) OF LEADERSHIP AND TEAMWORK

In my work around leadership development with new supervisors and leaders over the last few decades, we have naturally gravitated to discussion around what we would commonly refer to as the TRI of Leadership: Trust, Respect, and Influence. In *Effective Virtual Conversations*, I write about the triad of creating trust, safety, and connection.

Trust is the foundation for any work in today's context. It's what sets the foundation for respect, safety, and connection. It allows for team members to strive for their best.

ACTIONS THAT BUILD TRUST AS LEADERS	ACTIONS THAT BUILD TRUST AS TEAM MEMBERS
Follow through—doing what you say you will Addressing issues as you see them Fairness Holding people accountable for their results Ensuring a respectful and inclusive environment free from discrimination Positive and constructive feedback Taking swift action when the workplace is not seen as respectful or inclusive	Follow through Addressing issues as you see them Being prepared and present—ready to engage and ready to check ego Positive feedback—acknowledging what's working Constructive feedback—pointing out mistakes Having each other's backs Sharing information Sharing resources Mentoring each other Sharing ideas and experiences Taking responsibility for mistakes Creating a respectful and inclusive workplace
ACTIONS THAT ERODE TRUST AS LEADERS	**ACTIONS THAT ERODE TRUST AS TEAM MEMBERS**
Lack of follow through Inadequate or no feedback Playing favorites—favoritism (perceived or real) Lack of transparency Lack of accountability Not being seen as going the extra mile Little, infrequent, or no communication Infrequent touch points	Gossip Not pointing out mistakes Talking behind each other's backs Not connecting or communicating Language that is defamatory, discriminatory, or not inclusive Passive-aggressive behavior Not taking ownership for mistakes

In the virtual space there are several things we can do to build trust. It's based on the skills we bring, what we say, and what we do.

The skills we bring: Many trust models, including those of Reina and Reina, Covey, and others, indicate that part of the trust-building process is skill based.

The skills we bring, and the trust we create through doing a job well, are important in today's virtual and hybrid context. Subsequent chapters explore what skills are essential for today's virtual space.

What we say: It's also about walking our talk. How are you, as a leader or team member, following through with what you say?

Our words also cultivate trust. This includes how we say things—our tone of voice. It is also about using language that is appropriate and inclusive. With the multi-languages that may be the reality of a virtual team, it is important to clarify what language is and is not appropriate. Language should always be free from discrimination and retribution.

What we do: Without trust it is unlikely that virtual team members will engage. Our actions speak volumes in a virtual team environment, and it is important to note:

- *What is being perceived?* In the virtual space we are seen through our actions on the screen, our follow through, our emails, and any other engagements. A lot of what people are judging trust on are these infrequent, imperfect touchpoints. It's very different than the time we have around the watercooler.
- *Our touchpoints are not as frequent.* Things get magnified in the remote and hybrid space. What do your behaviors communicate? Consider the more subtle cues like your body language, eye contact (are your eyes to the camera or the screen?), and also, your pace of speaking.

What are the behaviors you want to model in your calls?

DIFFERENT MODELS OF TRUST

In their writing, *Trust and Betrayal in the Workplace,* Reina and Reina's model of trust is grounded in character, competency, and commitment.

As team leaders we are not always with our team members, and using the skill of influence is critical.

What does the skill of influence mean to you?

The skill of influence is related to the Triad of Trust, Safety, and Connection. Trust alone in a virtual team is not enough. Great teams need to feel connected and also feel safe.

Our attention now turns to Safety.

Psychological Safety

The foundation for trust is safety, and Amy Edmondson defines psychological safety as "shared belief that the team is safe for interpersonal risk taking."[97]

Without psychological safety, team members may be unwilling to:

- Take risks
- Raise issues which need to be addressed; when issues are not raised, they can fester or become "an elephant in the room"
- Provide direct feedback to peers and upwards

Google has explored this topic and was spotlighted in a 2017 article by Laura Delizonna in the *Harvard Business Review*.[98] In the article, they identify these six things that Paul Santagata, Head of Industry at Google, did to build psychological safety with their team:

1. Approach conflict as a collaborator, not an adversary
2. Speak human to human
3. Anticipate reactions and plan countermoves
4. Replace blame with curiosity
5. Ask for feedback
6. Measure psychological safety

As Delizonna notes, Google questionnaires includes questions such as "How confident are you that you won't receive retaliation or criticism if you admit an error or make a mistake?"

Two additional notes to these practical things we can do to build psychological safety.

First, what is the environment we are creating? As we look back to the conflict management research, including *Getting to Yes: Negotiating Agreement Without Giving In*, by Roger Fisher, we know that collaboration is, as one of my clients says, "a game to win . . . ." As soon as we place people in a win-lose dynamic, a number of things occur, including activation of the amygdala and the intuitive fight-or-flight mechanism.

Another component of psychological safety is about creating an enabling, connected environment. Researchers such as Barbara Frederickson have found something called the "broaden-and-build theory of positive emotion." The broaden-and-build theory is grounded in the notion that positive emotions help us "look for creative, flexible, and unpredictable new ways of thinking and acting."[99] Experimentation, collaboration, and exploration are all important mindsets when approaching conflict.

As you approach psychological safety in your organization, what are you doing to build in these elements?

Connection

Connection is another important element of trust. We see this especially in virtual teams where casual relationships and touchpoints are not as frequent. We can't meet up in the lunchroom unless it's planned *or* our workspace allows for streaming 24/7.

It helps people go the extra mile and bring their best selves to work.

As part of supporting trust, we also need to feel connected. Many chapters of this book focus on building connection in the virtual, remote, and hybrid space. As we know, high performing teams are not only results oriented, they also have positive relationships.

Things to do to boost connection in the virtual space:

- Take time to connect people
- Explore technologies which will allow people to meet with each other
- Create peer partners
- Use a coaching approach

SIX LEADERSHIP QUESTIONS ON TRUST[100]

- What's the current level of trust in our team right now?
- What's helping to boost trust?
- What's breaking down trust?
- What behaviors have the biggest impact on trust in this team right now?
- What do you know you can count on each other for?
- What is one thing we could do to boost trust levels in our team?

TEAM TOOL: TRUST INDICATOR

Use the following to assess your current level of trust in your team. What does it look like behaviorally? Where are you on a scale of 1 to 10, and what can you do to improve it?

AREA	WHAT IT LOOKS LIKE BEHAVIORALLY (THINK ABOUT THE OBSERVABLE THINGS OTHERS CAN SEE)	WHERE AM I WITH THIS? MY RATING ON A SCALE OF 1 TO 10 (1 BEING LOW, 10 BEING HIGH)	WHAT CAN I DO TO IMPROVE IT?
Walk the talk			
Be fair			
Build on strengths			
Take ownership			
Be transparent			
Create connection			
Set clear expectations			
Communicate			
Hold regular one-on-ones			

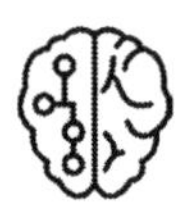

BRAIN TIP: GROWTH MINDSET AND AMYGDALA HIJACK

The work of Carol Dweck has gained attention in recent years. Her research shows that there are behaviors which shift leadership and teamwork "above and below the waterline" (reference the Iceberg).

We are naturally hardwired for the amygdala hijack, where we want to either flee, fight, or freeze when facing a threat. Threats in the virtual space can be activated by not feeling sure, as well as by feeling that people are threatening you or your ideas. When trust levels are higher, an oppositional comment may not be perceived as a threat.

Building trust and safety helps to minimize the impact of the amygdala hijack.

RECONNECTING THE WORKSPACE TIP—CREATING CONNECTION

Reconnecting workspaces requires regular attention and focus. Dedicating time to build, and check in around trust, safety, and connection, is important. What time are you earmarking for regular check-ins?

Activities you may want to incorporate include:

- Time earmarked in the team for discussion about how the team is doing, not just business.
- Using breakouts where possible to move conversation to smaller, more intimate groups.
- Create peer learning partners to keep conversations flowing and boost connection.

Consider how you want to build connection on a community level. Building community in the virtual space involves creating a shared sense of purpose (Why are we here?), a common identity, along with a sense of belongingness (Do I belong here?), and safety (Do I feel safe and that I can contribute and will be respected?)

END OF CHAPTER QUESTIONS

- What are the things that are building trust in your team right now?
- What are you doing to boost psychological safety?
- What are you doing to be proactive with connection?

CHAPTER 6

COMMUNICATION AND CONVERSATIONS

"Two monologues do not make a dialogue."
—Jeff Daly

Principle: It's all about the conversation—which takes time and scheduling!

Myth: We all want to communicate in the same way. There are many different styles and preferences which exist on a team. There will be team members who want to verbalize everything and tell their story, and there will be others on the team who prefer a reflective pause before sharing their ideas. Some team members will want to share their ideas in writing, rather than verbally. Others just want to get on with their job, finding verbal communication a waste of time and preferring a text.

What do you notice about how different team members want to communicate?

There are a myriad of conversations which happen every day in today's teams, from the conversations that we dive into, to the ones we avoid at all costs. This chapter explores the range of conversations which are needed to accelerate teamwork and results.

It's an important reminder that fostering skills across the team is essential in building a more collaborative, autonomous team. In the remote, virtual, and hybrid team, a team's weakest link can be any team member.

This chapter explores the range of conversations and skills required, including:

- The ecosystem of virtual conversations
- What's different in the virtual and remote world

- Communication breakdowns—fails!
- When to use what channel
- Essential communication skills
- Listening
- Reframing/attention
- Questioning
- Identifying your own style
- Conversations and the brain
- Email and other communication etiquette

Subsequent chapters take a deeper look at three more distinct types of conversations which accelerate team results every day. Be sure to explore these topics as well:

- Performance conversations, i.e., feedback
- Difficult or courageous conversations
- Peer coaching

THE CONTEXT OF COMMUNICATION—THE ECOSYSTEM

The context of communication in today's virtual and remote teams ranges from live, verbal, and real-time to on-demand, asynchronous conversations.

- How much time do virtual teams spend communicating?
- How many emails?
- What's most important?
- What is voice? Text? Email?

Some of the biggest challenges in communication today are:

- We think we have been understood. Really?
- Make it a one-way passage of information

THE VIRTUAL CONVERSATION ECOSYSTEM

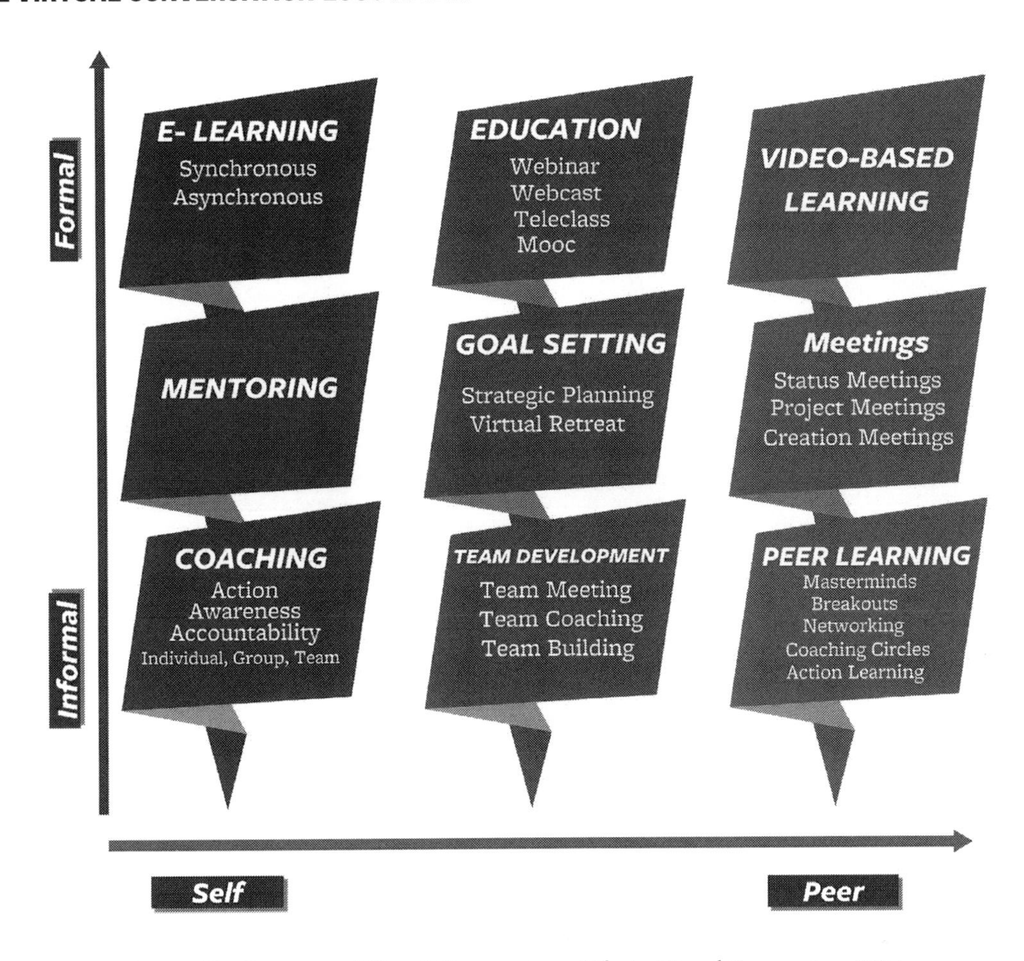

Figure: The Ecosystem of Virtual Conversations, *Effective Virtual Conversations*, 2017.

In the span of any given day there will be a range of conversations which are taking place across the virtual ecosystem, some formal conversations including meetings and team development, while others are informal like a mentoring conversation or peer sharing. Some of these conversations are more focused on the self: what I want to learn, and others more focused on the peer experience: what I can learn or co-create with others in dialogue.

In my book *Effective Virtual Conversations* I lay out nine different types of virtual conversations across the continua of formal and informal, as well as peer and self.[101] I ask people to circle the types of communication their team engages in, notice the different platforms they use for each conversation, and consider how effective they are.

What's Different with Virtual Conversation?

Communication is one of the areas where we see some of the biggest differences across teams with virtual and remote communication. There may be no, or fewer, visual cues in communication with virtual teams. Have you seen everyone on your team?

Another significant difference is the potential for different first languages, which can have significant impact on the understanding of words, meaning, and how ideas are communicated. What is the working first language of the team? How proficient is everyone in this?

Cross-culturally, we may also carry a different lens. Consider the meaning of the word "chips." For me as a Canadian it can mean potato chips or French fries. When I worked in the UK, chips were French fries, while crisps were potato chips. Likewise, consider football. Are we talking American football, or soccer (which is called football in many parts of the world).

Frequently, in a virtual team we do not have all of the information or knowledge of the context, making the communication and coaching skills of **listening**, **questioning**, and **inquiry** even more important. Coaching takes on a new priority in the virtual realm, as we usually are having to work through others and help them solve their own issues.

Listeners may also not have pieces of the context, making it even more important to identify, name, and challenge assumptions.

Different communication channels may be available for meetings across the team, with some members joining on one platform and others on another. Keys for making this work include:

- Work to the lowest common denominator so you meet all needs
- Think about what supports will anchor the conversation, i.e., any visuals, or a warm-up to start the conversation
- Note where you are listening: are you listening to understand what the person is saying, or are you listening to figure out what you are going to say next?

Finally, we need to listen to learn and be curious. The individuals in each location may be the expert.

FRAMING THE CONVERSATION: PURPOSE, CHANNEL, AND AUDIENCE

In communicating effectively and framing the conversation, we want to think about several components:

- Purpose
- Channel
- Audience

The Purpose of Communication

Along with the channel we select, we will also want to consider what is the purpose of communication. It may be to:

- Inform
- Make a decision
- Provide context

- Share information
- Educate
- Influence

SIX QUESTIONS TO ASK AT EACH CONVERSATION TOUCHPOINT

To avoid the trap of thinking we're communicating and setting everyone up for success, it is useful to ask:

1. Is it clear?
2. Is it sent to the right people?
3. What is the request I have made?
4. What is the receiver's preference?
5. What is the purpose of the communication?
6. Is this the right channel?

Channels for Virtual Communication

The channel for virtual communication or, **how communication is being undertaken**, has a strong influence on the conversation. Most virtual professionals will find themselves bouncing in between conference calls, video streaming calls such as Teams and Zoom, and/or telepresence meetings where they are in a board room and connected with other teams all over the world.

Currently, we have a range of different vehicles from low touch to high touch, including text, email, voice, and teleconference.

There are several communication channels that virtual teams will find themselves interacting with each and every day.

LOW DETAIL	HIGH DETAIL
Instant Message	360 Interactive events
Chat	Conference call
Annotation	Webinar
Text	Video streaming
Email	Telepresence

Each platform brings advantages and disadvantages, and the need for a slightly different facilitation approach. Let's take a look at each one of these in turn:

Conference Calls

Conference calls have historically been the standard approach to virtual calls and may be the one you are most accustomed to. While they have been the tried-and-true standard, are they the most efficient? Given the vast amount of Zoom fatigue people have experienced, some organizations have reverted to conference calls to create an easier flow.

Facilitation Tips

Ensure that you are firm with process. Be specific about what people can expect; let people know where you are in the course of the conversation, what's been covered, and where you are still going to go.

Keep it moving. Given that people can't see each other, a quicker pace can be important, as are frequent check-ins and different pace changes.

Conference calls are useful when there is a lot of information. Consider you might support this with additional visual supports like a handout or download you can send via email.

No visual cues mean that you can't see what is connecting and what is sending people into multitasking. It's important to check in frequently to confirm changes needed.

Tips for Engagement

Connect people to their WIIFM (What's in it for me?) early on. Call on people. Have them create a virtual table so they have a sense of who is on the call. Recap regularly (here's where we are, what we've looked at). Encourage note taking.

Advantages:

- Cheap and fast
- Ease of access, including accessibility from mobile
- Good for getting high volumes of information back

Disadvantages:

- Lack of visual cues
- Lower engagement rates
- Disconnection
- Not always able to do breakouts
- Not sure if your message really got through

Video Streaming—Zoom/Teams/WebEx/Go To Meeting

In recent years video streaming has become more commonplace for many workplaces today. While not everyone is comfortable being seen on the screen, video streaming offers many benefits, including higher engagements and the capability to build trust and connection. See what happens the first time your team or group goes to video.

Challenges

Not everyone may want to be "seen," and video streaming should be flagged to ensure there is no confidential data as well. There may be more need to set up, and/or have cameras and mikes activated.

Facilitation Style

Host, welcoming, use engagement, invite participation. Consider balance of sharing information and facilitating discussion.

Tips for Engagement

- Use breakouts where possible to bring people together from different sites.
- Use whiteboards so you can have them capture their thinking/ideas and share it.
- Like all virtual calls, change the pace regularly.
- Use visuals as much as possible.
- Use the equalizer—everyone has a voice.

Advantages:

- Can see each other
- Easily built into your system
- More mobile friendly
- Screen sharing
- Recording

Disadvantages:

- Bandwidth speed
- Need to be in front of a system or have loaded the app onto your computer

Telepresence

Telepresence was used quite a bit prior to the pandemic within larger organizations, especially if they were linking people in different hubs or conference rooms together. It is different than a Zoom or Teams call, given that you can see everyone.

Facilitation Style

More formal, able to write (but may not be seen), equalizer—ensuring all voices are being heard.

Advantages:

- Able to use this in the main conference room
- Ability to clearly hear and see everyone
- Can set up breakouts so the groups can have discussion

Disadvantages:

- May be cost prohibitive and difficult to set up in smaller satellite offices
- As a facilitator, you have more things to be aware of: any slides you are sharing, the people in your room, and the people in other rooms; the ability to take in information from all of these different sources at one time can be challenging for facilitators
- For participants it may feel like you are part of a crowd rather than being an individual contributor
- Sound capture from one room to the other may not be good
- Harder for room one to share with room two compared to if everyone were logging in via their own system
- Can silo teams rather than equal the playing field
- How are you capturing the information? Is it on the screen (which would be captured for all to see) vs. on a flipchart?

ENGAGEMENT IS KEY IN THE VIRTUAL CONVERSATION SPACE!

- In virtual conversations we may think that it's all about the conversation, when in fact, we want to use a number of different engagement strategies. I call these the Five Engagement Levers™.

Power Up
Stand Out Virtually
5-Day Challenge

5 Engagement Levers™

Effective Virtual Conversations

©Jennifer Britton. All Rights Reserved. 2020

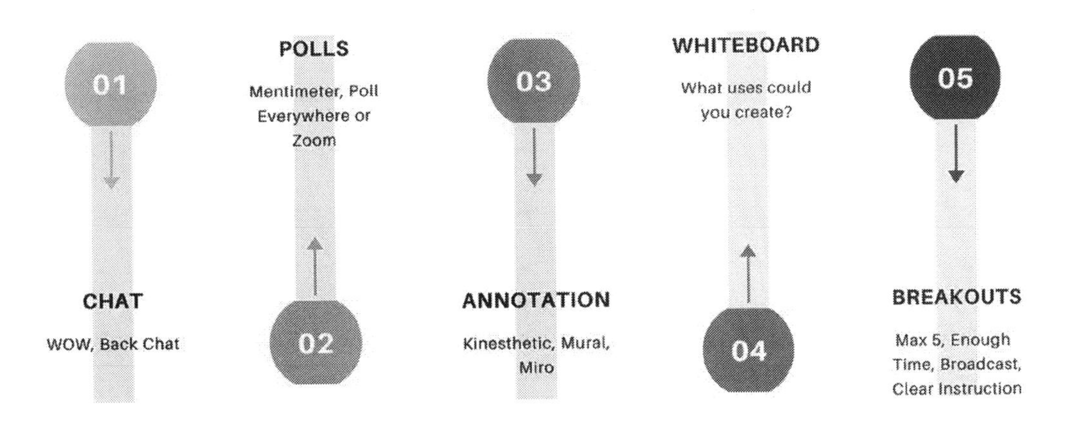

ENGAGEMENT STRATEGY	WHEN TO USE IT	TIPS
Breakouts Similar to in-person environments, virtual breakouts put people in smaller groups	When group size is large When you want smaller groups to have the opportunity to be in dialogue with each other For problem solving	Keep group size small, i.e., 3 to 5 Assign roles to involve everyone Leave enough time. Make sure people know what to do if they have technical questions Consider how you can broadcast messages to each group Remember that what you have on the screen will likely not go into the room with each group Provide clear instructions regarding what you want people to do when they return Make sure that bodies are synched with voices
Annotation	Annotation is available on most platforms and, when enabled, gives participants the opportunity to note and write ideas on the screen. Valuable for those who are more kinesthetic or body centered	Provide instructions on how to use this and practice opportunities Leave white space so people can note it
Polls Polls allow for a pulse check and input around key questions	Whether your group is small or large, it can be useful to get a poll for what people want	Consider polls like Kahoot.it, Poll Everywhere, or MentiMeter Polling function in Zoom, WebEx or other Remember that you may need to set this up in order to activate it

Chats	Chat can be valuable in larger groups. For very large groups, use of the "Back Chat" is a great way to harness the wisdom of the group; for example, each person can share a tip, resource, or idea, thereby leading to a list of options	Don't just rely on chat, also consider how you can bring voices into the room; the overuse of chat may shut the conversation down
Whiteboard	Use whiteboards to visually map out your process, or co-create learning together; whiteboards can be used in both the main room or in smaller breakouts	Every platform has a different set up for whiteboards; check what is possible

THE AUDIENCE: THEIR PREFERENCES FOR COMMUNICATION STYLE

The audience, or who you are speaking to, is going to influence the conversation. What are their preferences? What are they listening for?

Sending the message is only one half of the equation. How is your message being interpreted? Keep in mind that in any group you may have people who have a preference for different types of input—Visual, Auditory or Kinesthetic.

Also consider what you can do to integrate more visual cues. This could include boosting the graphics in a call.

Finally, the pace and level of interactivity of a call will also help to bolster against Zoom fatigue. Consider changing your pace every 7 to 10 minutes by activating one of the 5 Engagement Levers™.

IS IT A MONOLOGUE OR A DIALOGUE? COMMUNICATION ENABLERS

Regardless of the channels you are utilizing, several things help to facilitate effective virtual conversations, including:

- Trust
- Connection
- Knowledge of each other
- A common framework around styles and strengths to provide knowledge and understanding; even though we have a preference, we are able to adjust our approach/style to be with others
- Knowing what works and what doesn't

Key to successful virtual conversations is leaving time to:

- Breakout and connect with others in a smaller group setting in meaningful dialogue.
- Incorporate silence and a reflective pause so that people can think and capture ideas. If you are incorporating silence, be specific as to how long you will be silent for. Consider setting a chime or alarm on your phone so everyone can relax into the experience.

- Get things done. Virtual retreats, or virtual co-working sprints like the 21 for 21 Virtual Co-working Sprints, are a powerful way to work in real-time.
- Clarify what's been agreed to and what next steps are.
- Write things down. We continue to see that the act of writing creates new neural pathways in the brain, reinforcing learning in a way typing does not. This might involve having people keep a journal or take notes by hand on a worksheet. To a lesser extent, annotation also helps to make the conversation more kinesthetic.
- Get people moving. Many new virtual team members and leaders are able to move around. With "sitting becoming the new smoking," it's essential that in the shift to virtual work, we are also encouraging a healthy workplace. This could involve building in more kinesthetic and activity-based virtual exercises, i.e., sending materials to be printed and having team members post these, standing up and moving to different sheets as they go (consider a SWOT).

COMMUNICATION BREAKDOWNS: KISS OF DEATH— SEVEN MISTAKES OF VIRTUAL MEETINGS

Whether it is in person or virtual, there are many potential areas for communication breakdown and poor communication etiquette, including these seven areas:

1. **Overwhelm of communication**. Too many emails, no differentiation between what is important vs. what needs attention. Lack of prioritization. All things are deemed urgent and important.
2. **Not enough attention to process**. Process is important. How much time will it really take?
3. **Too many distractions**. Distractions can be created from a variety of factors, from too much visual stimuli to too much on a slide. Consider what will provide focus and what will provide distraction.
4. **Using the right medium for the conversation**. While email and text are great, they are not always the most effective, especially when issues are *urgent*, complex, or require a talk-through. Make sure you match the right type of issue to the right mode. What can benefit from an eye-to-eye conversation? What could be done quickly and with little misunderstanding?
5. **Lack of visual cues.** In the face-to-face world, it is asserted that 55% of the message is communicated through body language. Once we shift to virtual messages without streaming, we lose that ability.
6. **No, or minimal, preparation**. Consider Conversational Intent. What do you hope will happen as a result of this conversation?
7. **Too much or too long**. Reinforce, reinforce, reinforce. For many years it was asserted that we could only remember seven, plus or minus two, items. In the world of virtual presentations it can be useful to speak in sound bites. Conciseness and brevity are essential so you can hear from everyone. Also it can be useful to get people to use more metaphors or share photos to bring ideas to life. Another way to say this is distill it down to three bullet points. What are the main topic areas? What's important?

THE FOUNDATIONS OF COMMUNICATION: LISTENING, ATTENTION, QUESTIONING

At the core of virtual communication are three skills: listening, attention, and questioning.

Skill #1: Building Your Listening Muscle

"Listening looks easy, but it's not simple. Every head is a world."[102] —Cuban Proverb

In today's digitally distracted world, we may not be listening as deeply as we could. We may be listening with "half an ear" while actually doing one or two other things. Moving to a video streaming platform means that we are "on the spot" and may need to pay more attention.

Listening has become a lost art form, and employees today surveyed said they just wanted to be listened to. That means listening without being told what to do. In the virtual context, it is critical for the team members to have someone who can listen to them, without judgment or criticism. This is where peer coaching comes in. Sometimes our peers need an opportunity to "talk it through," and they just want to be heard. Chapter 15 addresses the topic of peer coaching.

According to salesforce.com, employees who feel their voice is heard at work are 4.6 times more likely to feel empowered to perform their best work.

Here are four things we want to notice when we listen:

1. **Pace**: What is the rate at which people are speaking? Fast? Slow? What does this signify?
2. **Pitch**: What is the pitch at which the person is speaking? High or low? What about the volume? Was it loud or soft? What might that signify?
3. **Word Choice**: What do you notice about the word choice? Does anything need clarification? What lingo are you using?
4. **Candence**: Is the person speaking with a variety of energy in their voice, or are they speaking in a monotone?

We listen through our own lens—BIAS

Each conversion we engage in is influenced by our own lens and bias. Are we listening to hear the person, or are we listening to figure it out? There's a big difference between these two. To really be present in virtual conversations so that you can coach someone who is the expert in their area, the former listening, listening to hear the person, is the stance which is important to adopt.

Peter Senge wrote, "To listen fully means to pay close attention to what is being said beneath the words. You listen not only to the 'music,' but to the essence of the person speaking. You listen not only for what someone knows, but for what he or she is. Ears operate at the speed of sound, which is far slower than the speed of light the eyes take in. Generative listening is the art of developing deeper silences in yourself, so you can slow your mind's hearing to your ears' natural speed, and hear beneath the words to their meaning."[103]

What are the assumptions you are making?

What is the lens we are listening through—our socialization, our exposure, our range? What aren't we hearing?

As Lizet Pollen writes in her Pulse Post, *6 Ways to Improve the Leadership Skill of Active Listening*, "Listening is a verb that describes an action. It's not just about passively hearing words. The Chinese character that means 'to listen' is made up of the characters that mean 'you', 'eyes', 'ear', 'undivided attention', 'king' and 'heart'."[104]

With these characters in mind, consider these elements next time you go to listen:

You: What are you noticing about your own listening? Are you listening for what is being said or for what your response will be?

Eyes: How are you using your eyes to take in information? If you are using a conference call only, are there any visual cues or anchor points for the conversation, e.g., handouts or slides people can connect with? Can you move to streaming where you can see each other, especially for important conversations or when teams or groups are new or don't feel connected?

Ear: What are you hearing? What do you notice about the pace, pitch, and word choice?

Undivided attention: The business context today is full of things that can disrupt, distract, and get in the way. What are you doing to demonstrate your undivided attention? How are you leveraging the skill of self-management to ensure that you are focused on the topic? What distractions do you need to silence?

King: How do you demonstrate respect for those you are speaking with?

Heart: What are you hearing on a heart level? What are you connecting to? What emotions are emerging?

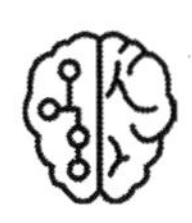

BRAIN TIP: PRIMING FOR LISTENING

Throughout the day we are part of a myriad of conversations. In some, we actively listen, and in many, we don't. In teaching coaching training skills, I share a framework of three questions to encourage people to become more active listeners, or prime them to be an active listener. Next time you observe a conversation (e.g., conference call, team meeting), rather than listening passively, note these for yourself:

1. Listen to what speaker #1 says or asks.
2. Notice the impact.
3. Notice for yourself, what's important about that?

Leave time at the end of the conversation to discuss what you notice.

Building the Skill of Listening: the Bus Listening Exercise

Some of my favorite activities in the training room (virtually and in person) revolve around the *aha's* created with communication. In the virtual space, communication takes on new meaning. One activity I use is called the Bus Route activity. It brings to light several of the nuances we've been exploring in this chapter. Take a few minutes to listen into the bus listening exercise here: plandotrack.com/bus. What did you listen for? What happened? Did you hear the instructions clearly?

What do you notice about what you are listening for in terms of:

- Detail
- The big picture
- Connection
- Context
- Results
- Outcome

We all listen for different things. The challenge on the team is to better understand what the other person(s) we are talking to value and are listening for. What changes do we want to make to the conversation?

Stepping into the place of not knowing

Part of leading today is learning to become comfortable in being in the place of not knowing and understanding what we may not know. We need to ask questions we do not know the answers to. We need to listen and check the assumptions we have been making. How comfortable are you in stepping into the place of not knowing?

Skill #2: The Science of Attention

There's compelling scientific research which continues to show that our brain cannot handle two tasks at once (also known as "cognitive switching"). There is a cost involved in having to switch rapidly between tasks.

To illustrate our inability to focus on two things at once, take a look at the Stroop Task. In this we hear different words describing the color, printed in colors that do not match the word. For example, the word purple might be printed in green, and the word blue might be printed in pink. If you ask people to name the color of the word, it is very hard to do, as most people focus on the color of the ink. This exercise divides your attention, making it very difficult to focus.

Some of the strategic questions for team's today are:

- What can we do to reduce distractions and increase attention?
- What can we do to allow people to focus on one thing at a time?
- What can we do to help people become more intentional with their focus, i.e., notice things around them, notice connections, etc.?

Skill #3: Questioning

"Effective questioning brings insight, which fuels curiosity, which cultivates wisdom."[105] —Chip Bell

Questions truly form the backbone to any conversation, including meetings, coaching conversations, difficult conversations, feedback, and team development sessions.

Questions shape the frame of our conversations. Questions may:

- Expand awareness around an issue
- Help create clarity around different perspectives at play
- Prioritize
- Reframe an issue, or refocus how someone sees something
- Help connect the dots
- Identify next steps

The most effective questions are usually short, only five or six words. Questions should be open and not leading. For example, rather than asking, Do you think you should do x ? (which would solicit a yes/no response) ask, What steps could lead to those results?

A shift in the virtual space is in moving from asking questions to advising or figuring it out yourself, to asking questions to help your team member figure it out themselves.

Questions in the virtual space are often used to build capability, coming from a place of curiosity for you, and coming from a place of learning for them.

For many leaders, coaches, and team members, developing a cadre of questions is important. These are often highlighted as a growth edge. In the coaching skills training I have led virtually and in organizations, questions were one of the areas. Having a variety of questions to pull on at any given time can create the space and confidence to relax into listening and dialogue.

Questions that start with *What* open up the space for more discussion, elaboration, and expansion.

How questions typically take people into process (think about the question, How will you do this?).

Why questions should be used sparingly, especially if there is a history of distrust or there are low levels of trust and connection. *Why* questions may put people on the defense, making them feel like they must justify something.

TEAM TOOL: ASK BETTER QUESTIONS, HAVE A BETTER CONVERSATION AND RESULTS

Questions can be used for different purposes: to expand awareness, prioritize, create clarity, make a decision, identify actions, or support accountability. Questions are an area we can all get better at. Consider how you might use these types of questions:

QUESTIONS TO:	EXAMPLES:
Expand Awareness	What's important about that? What are your assumptions? What perspective are you looking at this from? What's another approach? What impact would that have? What's the big picture *or* how does it fit in the big picture? What's at the core? What else?
Prioritize	What's important? What's urgent? What needs to get done first so that other things can get done? In the big picture, what's needed? What could get deferred? If there was only one thing that could get done, what would that be? What's the number one priority? What could get delegated? What can you say no to?
Create Clarity	What do you see as connected? If you could do only one thing, what would that be? What's clear to you? What is important? What's the priority? What's possible in terms of outcome?

Make a Decision	What results are you aiming for? What's most important? What's a priority? What will success look like? What will work best in the short term? What will work best in the long term?
Identify Actions and Accountability	What support do you need? What will you do in the next 24 hours? What are your next steps? What else? When will you check back in? Who will you check in with? What will you do by next week? What else do you need? What's next?

Notice the overlap of some questions like "What else?" or "What's the possibility?" These are stock questions which are really broad and open up the conversation in a variety of different ways.

WHAT'S NEXT? CREATING ACCOUNTABILITY AROUND "WHAT'S NEXT?"

With work in the remote space being fluid and often self-directed, it's important to create structure and clarity around what's next and what's important. This is where coaching's focus on accountability can be valuable.

What I Wrote in a Teams365 Blog Post[106]

A critical part of the coaching conversation is having dialogue around What's Next? What are you going to do now? In the virtual space, having a conversation without talking about the What's Next is like leaving a conversation half done.

A major challenge of many organizations today is that people are not clear on what accountability means or what it can look like. We often leave meetings with a long laundry list of things to do. Accountability provides the specificity of what's going to be done, and when and how you will report back. This is essential for virtual teams.

It can be useful to ask, What does accountability look like? What does accountaility sound like?

When exploring accountability, we will want to consider incorporating these tips into your team conversations and meetings this week:

1. **Get specific**: Accountability is enhanced when everyone leaves the table with a shared understanding about what next steps are. Make a focused effort to be specific in meetings

you attend and lead, around who is going to do what, by when, and how this will be tracked. Given the amount of meetings we attend, send a quick follow-up note highlighting key action steps, timelines, and those responsible. This should be brief.

2. **Micro-monitor, don't micromanage**: At your team meeting this week or during your one-on-one sessions, ask the questions, "What are you focusing on this week? What results are you accountable for this week?" Being aware of what your team members are focusing on helps you to track all that is happening in the team. Note that it is to micro-monitor, not micromanage.
3. **Partner team members together**: Consider the idea of creating accountability partners on the team. This involves pairing team members together and having them meet on a weekly or bi-weekly basis to support each other in checking in around their major tasks and milestones.
4. **Get clear**: Make sure everyone is clear about "what success looks like" with the major tasks and activities being focused on this week. When we aren't clear about the end result, it is hard to be accountable.
5. **Make check-ins a habit**: Experiment with starting meetings with a check-in or status update on key activities and tasks different team members are working on. Again, check-ins should be brief. Avoid the trap of their becoming the entire meeting!
6. **Be curious and helpful**: If follow-through is not happening, have a discussion with those involved. Adopt a coach's stance of "curiosity" using questions to help "tease out" or explore what is happening or why follow-through has stalled. As leaders we may automatically move to a more punishing approach, shutting people down rather than exploring what's at the root cause.

What do we need to have in place to boost a culture of accountability within our team?

1. **Focus on the end game**: What are the goals you are working on? What does success look like?
2. **Ask "What if?"**: What are the consequences if something is not done? For you? How does it impact the work and results of others? When we don't provide the big picture of how different tasks are connected, it can detract from why follow-through is important.
3. **Share the *Why?***: Helping people understand the *What if?* along with *why* these tasks and results are important, also helps to boost accountability. Help team members understand how their activities connect to each other, and to those you support.
4. **Give feedback**: We need to provide feedback on what's working, and what's not. Without a feedback loop, team members will be unclear as to how things are progressing.
5. **Offer space for check-in**: We know it's important to check-in but we don't leave time, or create time, to do so. What will it take this week to dedicate time for these activities: providing clarity, making sure the team understands the *What if?* and *Why?* creating time for feedback?

6. **Offer resources**: Finally, decide who needs to be involved and what resources are needed to boost accountability within your team.

> What else is important for you with respect to accountability, both individually and collectively?

IN FOCUS: EMAIL ETIQUETTE

Recent statistics have shown that professionals spend almost six hours of their time managing work and personal email a week.[107] The average employee receives 120 emails per day.[108] In 2019 it was estimated that they also send 40 emails a day.[109] This does not count the time spent on Slack or other messaging channels.

Email etiquette is an important topic for virtual, remote and hybrid teams when this may be the main vehicle for a team's communication. As teams, you will want to come to agreement around topics such as:

- How to flag things as important (and not overuse)
- Indicating when replies are needed
- Bringing people into the loop
- Indicating that an email has been read/actioned

It's important enough to warrant these best practices around email:

- Be aware of subject lines: Is it specific—do you want action?
- Watch for exclamation marks
- Watch for abbreviations
- Out of Office—who is covering for you if you are going to be away
- Be aware of how the tone may be interpreted
- Do a reread
- Avoid overly cc'ing people
- Consider what needs to be communicated in other ways

BUSINESS ETIQUETTE ITEMS FOR REMOTE TEAMS

There are several etiquette items for remote teams to take into consideration:

1. **Starting and ending meetings on time**. It is absolutely essential to start and end meetings on time, given the possibility that people are participating at different times of their day. It has become more common practice in recent months to have meetings wrap up five to

ten minutes before the end of the hour to allow for people to prepare for, stretch, or take a "bio-break" before their next meeting.

2. **Use subject lines appropriately**. Here is an example of what not to say, and what to say:

   Do not say: **Feedback please**. This is unclear as to what the email is about, who needs to be involved, and when a reply is needed.

   Do say: **KPI Priorities—Response needed—11/15, 5 pm GMT**

   Let people know when a response is needed, and give enough time. If you need a response quickly, will end of business today be enough time given that several team members may be five to twelve hours ahead of you?

   Watch for the acronyms you use, i.e., KPI—Key performance indicator (agree within the team on key words which you will shorten).

3. **Send materials well in advance**. How much time will people need to read, review, action, and prepare?

4. **Be clear** on any pre-work, time involved, and what the expectations are in terms of pre-preparation (reading, prioritization, pre-discussions, and decisions).

5. **Consider the impact of language**. While many global teams may have one working language, it is likely that some team members may have that working language as a second or third language. Consider the impact of:

   a. Excessive acronyms. Does everyone understand what it means?

   b. Idioms such as "speak of the devil," "a piece of cake," "rubber hits the road." What are the slangs or colloquialisms used commonly that may not translate as you intended?

6. **Video and conference call etiquette**. Use your name when speaking, (i.e., "This is Jennifer.") Let people know if you are not able to stay and how you will catch up and follow up and be sure to do this. Avoid overbooking where possible, as this sends a negative message. Use headsets to avoid echoes and feedback. Mute when needed. Notice the background and be sure to show up in professional clothing.

7. **Be aware of your surroundings**. Consider any other ambient noise which might be picked up. In video streaming, be aware of your background and how others can hear your call/see your call. Do not move around with video on. This can be very disruptive and distracting to other group members. If you need to move, be sure to turn off your video feed.

What else is important to note?

Keys for Clarity

Here are six keys to help ensure you are clearly heard and understood:

1. Check in with people to ensure that they do understand what you are saying. Have them repeat back and/or share what their interpretation is, as it relate to their own work context.

2. Use word choice that works, given that your working language (English or other) may be a second, third, or fourth language to others.
3. Put it in writing as well as saying it verbally for important issues. Do a further follow-up in writing. We may be moving so fast that it is hard to read through everything. Be clear (or bullet out) main points and deadlines.
4. Be brief and use bold, underline, and italics to draw attention.
5. Avoid the "!"

6 SIX TEAMWORK QUESTIONS: COMMUNICATION

For this chapter's teamwork questions, let's return to the essential questions we want to be asking ourselves around communication each time:

1. What is the purpose of this communication?
2. Is this the right channel?
3. Is it clear?
4. Is it sent to the right people?
5. Have I made a request?
6. What is the receiver's preference?

Several other chapters touch on this foundational skillset of communication, including:

- Chapter 13: Performance Management and Feedback
- Chapter 15: Coaching and Mentoring

RECONNECTING THE WORKSPACE TIP– ACTIVATE GREAT CONVERSATIONS

Great conversations are at the heart of reconnecting the workspace. A key part of this is "bringing all voices into the room" or making sure that we have used a variety of approaches to activate the different learning styles and ways people engage with the world.

The virtual space is not unidimensional. The hybrid world merges the virtual space and the 3D world of in-person events. With this in mind, to reconnect the workspace, we want to use a variety of approaches for conversations large and small.

Consider these approaches:

- Use whiteboard to get people to work on the screen real time and input
- Use images to speak to those who are more visual learners
- Use pauses and reflection time before people speak for those who need more time to process
- Activate your body through movement
- Incorporate sound to shift emotion

What can you do to activate great conversations?

END OF CHAPTER QUESTIONS

- Which of the Five Engagement Levers™ do you want to activate?
- What can you do to listen better?
- What questions do you want to incorporate into upcoming conversations?
- What will create more effective virtual conversations?

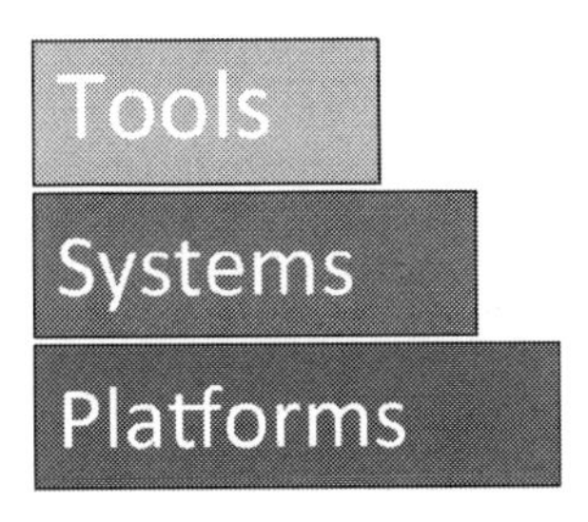

CHAPTER 7

MAKING IT SCALABLE—SYSTEMS, PLATFORMS, TOOLS

"Organize around business functions, not people. Build systems within each business function. Let systems run the business and people run the systems. People come and go but the systems remain constant."[110]
– Michael Gerber

Principle: Lowest Common Denominator.
Everyone needs to know.

Myth: I need to have all the answers.
I shouldn't share what I know.

Part of the challenge and opportunity of remote work is the fact that we are all working apart. This requires that we build and equip each other with platforms, systems, and tools. Hybrid work also benefits from systems we can access from in the office, at home, or on the road.

When work becomes asynchronous and location independent, platforms, systems, and tools become the glue that ensures teams are aligned and working similarly.

One of the most powerful things a team can do for itself is to systematize. It's important for teams to always be thinking about "How can I share what I know?" Given the around-the-clock nature of virtual and remote work, we may not be available, but team members may need to know where to go in order to find what we know and what we create. In this chapter we look at many of the systems which help a team to excel.

Whether team members are fully virtual and remote, or working some days mobile, having systems for performance is key.

In this chapter we explore these main areas:

- Systems
- Why systems and why systematize?
- Ten systems every virtual team needs
- Tools and the remote workforce
- Ten systems for virtual team leadership
- Enablers for the mobile and virtual space
- Tools: Ten tools for virtual teams
- Platforms: different options for different purposes

There are a number of systems you will want to put in place to be at your peak, productivity-wise. For more on this topic, check out Chapter 18, which covers Personal Productivity and Time Management.

WHAT'S DIFFERENT WITH VIRTUAL AND REMOTE TEAMS

Systems take on even greater importance with virtual teams. Given the 24/7 nature of our work, different team members may be accessing information at different times of the day and night. The rise in asynchronous work has been tracked during the pandemic.

Asynchronous work is nothing new, and it has enabled remote team members to work together, while apart. As Cross, Rebele, and Grant wrote in 2016, "At many companies people now spend about 80% of their time in meetings or answering colleagues' requests."[111]

Even if work is undertaken asynchronously, work is still interdependent. Teams and organizations excel when systems exist that help facilitate passing off tasks at the end of the day from one team member to another. Think, perhaps, of a team member in India who might pass off to a team member in North America at the start of their day.

Asynchronous work also provides us with the opportunity to work independently and autonomously. It provides windows for focus and attention.

In teams and organizations, being able to present a uniform experience with one team member in the Ukraine and one in Canada is possible, in part, due to systems. Systems help us do things in a similar way.

Why Systematize?

With the potential to "run all the time," much of a virtual team's work is interconnected. It is important to make sure that team members can access resources just-in-time when they need them. This is where systems come in.

In addition to materials and information needing to be available, we also want to make sure that we make things visual and visible. Visuals become even more important and create shared meaning when teams are not meeting each other in a streaming fashion.

Tools for the Remote Workforce

In addition to regular tools needed in the workplace (reports, budgets, etc.), virtual and remote teams benefit from additional shared tools to make things more visible. In assessing any tool or platform for the remote workforce, we want to consider how they:

- Are accessible to all
- Add value (not time) to the work
- Make things visual
- Connect with other ways of working across the organization

Note the team tool in each of the chapters. Tools allow us to do things quickly while leading to a tangible outcome.

Systems should:

- Be easy to be understood
- Be easy to update
- Be easy to access
- Not use a lot of bandwidth
- Support for evolution
- Support the team

The key to any system is having discussion around:

- Filing of materials
- Version codes around materials
- Contacts

Activity

Consider the tools you are currently using. How do these stack up to the characteristics listed here?

TEN SYSTEMS FOR VIRTUAL TEAM LEADERSHIP

Systems help us get things done on a repeated basis. Systems span a range of functions from communication to collaboration, project management, team development, and meetings.

Systems allows team members to share resources, information, and knowledge over time and distance, and to make things available when people need them. Key to efficiency in today's remote, virtual, and hybrid workspace is having things streamlined and available from different locations. Systems that help us work from anywhere the cloud connects us to, or we have access to, is essential.

In general, systems include:

- Communication systems including email, Slack, instant messaging, Voxer, other apps
- Project systems such as Asana, Trello, Monday.com, Project
- Meeting systems
- Performance management systems
- Reward and recognition systems
- Resourcing systems
- Information management systems—platforms, repositories
- People management systems
- Learning and coaching systems/entities including one-on-ones, training, coaching logs, performance logs
- Learning management systems
- Relationship management systems

With remote work there are several systems we can employ to support all team members. Systems support you in streamlining and not having to reinvent the wheel all the time.

Key notes around systems include:

- When there is breakdown
- When the system is not used consistently
- When things are not updated
- Build into your time window who should update these

Consider ten areas leaders usually have in place. In general, virtual team leaders may find that they need to develop skills in the following areas:[112]

System #1: Communications

Consider how the team communicates with each other, for example, by email, text, face to face. Ask yourself:

- What's working?
- What's not?
- What are the shared agreements you want to have about how and when to communicate?
- What's the accepted norm? What's not?

Email: Consider how email is used (for all messages, subject lines), boundaries around this, and how you want to track and file your email. Email management can take up to 40% of a leader's time.

System #2: Projects

Project systems include tracking systems such as Asana, Slack, and Monday.com. Using a consistent platform where dashboards can be updated is key.

System #3: Goals, Progress, and Accountabilities

These systems include annual plans, project reports, corporate goals, or even the very simple but powerful One-Page Plan.

System #4: Meetings

With meetings having the potential to take up a significant proportion of the day, what are the systems which are going to help you thrive, regardless of the platform you use? Consider what's going to create interactivity as well as connection with people.

How are your meetings facilitated? Face to face? Where could your meetings be tweaked? What works? Where do things get stuck? Review Teams365 #211: Meeting Management Faux Pas to avoid these traps.[113]

System #5: Performance Management

Performance management systems are key to helping people thrive. What is the culture of performance management? Hopefully, feedback is not once a year but an ongoing series of conversations with each of your team members.

Performance management systems may include exploration around such things as:

- How do we create goals?
- How do we track goals?
- How do my goals align with yours?
- Teams may use scorecards or dashboards
- Take a look at one-on-one conversations

System #6: Rewards and Recognition

What do you do to reward and recognize your team members? How does each person want to be recognized and rewarded?

While platforms and apps will continue to change, the principles of mobile work have remained somewhat the same over time. Key systems virtual and remote team leaders will want to develop are:

- A system for keeping notes on key resources needed by team members
- A system for noticing and tracking goals—the One-Page Plan is a useful frame where each person can have their own for each month or quarter; this can be shared on Slack or the learning management system

System #7: Learning Management

In the virtual, remote, and hybrid world, learning is ongoing. Having a solid skeleton to share learning is key. The ecosystem of learning management systems is varied across corporate, small business, and individual worlds. What will enable your people to keep learning, sharing, and tapping into resources that exist which can help them thrive?

System #8: Relationship Management

Business is done through relationships, even in the virtual space. Relationship management systems may include contacts, stakeholders, and other contact systems, including emails and phone numbers. Note that data security is essential, and some devices may need to be checked at international border points. How are you able to ensure consistent focus on this?

System #9: Financial/Budget

Finances are the lifeblood of any organization. Clear instructions and processes around financial and budgetary frameworks need to be accessible to all, especially if people are running a home office. What systems are in place in your workspace?

System #10: Administration

Administrative systems may include everything from email to meeting management and reporting tools.

SIX TEAMWORK QUESTIONS: SYSTEMS

1. What systems will help you do things faster, quicker, or more streamlined?
2. What current tasks are done repeatedly that could benefit from systems?
3. What are the key activities which different team members need to track?
4. What else might need to be passed on to others (think information, data, contacts, etc.)
5. What are the systems/information everyone needs access to?
6. When do we need to flag issues immediately?

TOOLS AND TEMPLATES FOR TEAMS

In addition to systems, there may be several tools and templates which can help teams be more efficient. When onboarding new team members, it is important to share and walk through these resources so that members across the team are using them consistently.

Attention should also be given to how to complete and share the materials with others on, or outside of, the team.

Some of the more common tools and templates you will want to evolve as a team are:

1. Templates for goal setting action
2. Administrative forms for budgets, expenses, reporting, vacation
3. Performance management:
    - Coaching logs
    - Mentoring logs
    - Development plans, e.g., One-Page Plan or other
    - Evaluation forms
    - Retreat checklist/team development
    - Performance management checklist

4. Planning:
    - Meeting plan
    - Feedback sheet
    - Project planning, status meetings, mid-project reviews, end-of-program debriefs, or retrospectives
5. Two strategic planning tools: SWOT, strategic issues mapping
6. Key activities to accelerate performance results: meetings, communication, ability to provide iterative feedback, ability to change on course

Many of these tools and templates are included throughout this book.

CHECKLISTS FOR VIRTUAL TEAMS

One more granular step down from tools are checklists. Checklists provide a common framework for everyone to follow. They can be embedded in other areas. Consider what tools you have and make them available:

- Goals
- Action
- Strategic planning
- Project log
- Status update
- Milestone checkpoint: where are we and where do we want to be?
- Vision/mission/mandate meetings: What's our vision for our work?
- Three-way midpoint meeting
- Goals, accomplishments, resources
- Matrix management checklist:
- What do we need to cover (reporting, goals, priorities)?
- What issues need to be surfaced, when, and how?
- What are the things we need to know about each other? What are our preferences for knowledge—lots of info, less info, when to surface issues?
- How do we communicate in between issues? To what level?

SELECTING PLATFORMS TO SUPPORT VIRTUAL CONVERSATIONS AND VIRTUAL TEAM WORK

I often get asked the question, "What do I consider when selecting a platform for a virtual or online conversation?"

From WebEx to Zoom to Skype to Teachable to GoToMeeting, how do you choose a virtual platform for your programming? There are a myriad of different platforms to choose from, as we saw in the ecosystem of virtual conversation in Chapter 6.

First, ask yourself: **is this for a live or on-demand virtual program**? On-demand programs may range from short video-based courses taken at an individual pace, to entire programs which can be listened to, versus conversations participated in real time. If you are looking at on-demand programs, which people can take at their own pace, you will be looking at more of a Learning Management System (LMS) where materials can be housed and accessed (recordings/print/video).

Here are other questions you will want to consider as you make a platform selection.

Purpose of the call: What is the type of call you are hosting? Is this a coaching, training, or facilitation conversation? Different types of platforms are more amenable to different types of conversations. Think Zoom for coaching and highly interactive calls; WebEx for more one-way webinar presentations.

Formal versus informal: How important are things like quizzes, checking knowledge, or having participation tracked (i.e., SCORM)?

Is this more of an **Individual** or **Peer Learning** Process? This can help you make selections such as the importance of breakouts.

Is recording required? Who has access to it?

Along these lines, it is also important to consider how important some of these other elements are: What **level of interactivity** are we looking for? What can we do to **leverage interactivity** in the call, including:

- Annotation
- Chat
- Recording
- Video streaming
- Screen sharing
- Breakouts

IN FOCUS: URGENT/IMPORTANT MATRIX

One of the most important tools all team members can use regularly is the Urgent/Important Matrix.

As you think about your work this month, what tasks are urgent? These are the tasks that *have* to get done, at least from the perspective of yourself, your boss, customers, or other key stakeholders. These are often known as the *fires*.

Which of your tasks are important? Important tasks are key to longer-term business sustainability, customer, and team satisfaction and growth. Consider which of these important tasks are *urgent* and which ones aren't. Tasks which are important and urgent may be key meetings for you to attend for your boss, crises/accidents/incidents, and things that really do need attention and can't wait, at least without a significant business impact.

Stephen Covey asserts we should spend our time in Quadrant Two, or those areas which are important and are not urgent. Important and not urgent issues are things like building relationships, planning, and team development time. Over time these fundamental important and not urgent issues build our base.

If we spend our time always working on important and *urgent* issues (the fires) we may find that we burn out or, even worse, will not be addressing important issues.

You can read more about Covey's Urgent/Important Matrix online. As an activity, you and/or your team may want to consider all activities in the Urgent/Important Matrix.[114]

Making Remote Work for You[115]

Sometimes we are remote by choice, sometimes remote by change. Here are tactical things you can do as a remote worker to make it work for you and your employer:

1. **Create a dedicated workspace**. Just as in a typical office space, create a dedicated office space. Depending on the type of work you do, it may be a standalone desk or table with access to internet and/or phone. Consider if you need doors, a filing cabinet that locks, and/or other things to do your work. It can be tempting to spread everything out, but boundaries in remote work arrangements help you to create balance and focus. Consider what space will be dedicated to working, and what you want to put away at the end of the day. A final consideration is how you ensure privacy and secure your data.
2. **Set regular office hours and break times too**. Just as in any office, it is important to set regular office hours and break times. We can only be productive for so long, so build in breaks (some say every 50 minutes) as well as start and end times. You may find that without the commute, you can start even earlier and end earlier in the day, or perhaps you want to fit in a swim (as I do) or work out at lunchtime to clear the cobwebs and create space for thinking.
3. **Consider what pieces of work are done best remote, and what you will need to be able to access.** It's important to have everything at hand in order to do your work. What needs to be accessible remotely on Dropbox, via a VPN, or other? How will you keep documents secure? What pieces need to be completed when you are in the office?
4. **If you are working remote for long periods of time, it is important to consider how you will stay connected with the office**. Consider how you can integrate face-to-face time and/or video streaming calls with your team members and boss. Just because you are not physically

there doesn't mean you aren't part of the team. Schedule in time to connect with the office. As I shared back in Teams365 #1810, "What doesn't get scheduled, doesn't get done."[116]

5. **Be proactive in communication with your team and your boss.** As in this last point, consider how you can best stay connected with your boss and the team. What updates are important to provide, what meetings do you want to schedule? You may find that you are more intentional and deliberative in your communication. This might actually set a nice precedent for others in the office as well!

Creating Focus as You Get Back to Work[117]

It's easy to get on the flywheel of doing, doing, doing, which creates its own momentum. Building in time for daily planning bursts can help create laser-like focus.

Create pockets of digital downtime. Research is starting to identify the dark side of ongoing digital connectivity. We all need time to digitally disconnect. What pockets of digital downtown do you want to create for yourself? What conversations do you need to have in order to create these disconnection points? Digital detox was made popular via Cal Newport's book, *Digital Minimalism.* What are you doing to create pockets of downtime? Spending time offline and outside has been seen to be a valuable health benefit. As of February 22, 2021, doctors in Ontario, Canada, are now able to prescribe time spent in nature as a prescription.

Consider what routines are going to support you to be at your peak. Each one of us has an internal clock which adjusts our energy levels. There is increasing research which shows that our own circadian rhythm influences whether we are a morning or night person. In Daniel Pink's book, *When: The Scientific Secrets of Perfect Timing,* he shares the compelling research around the chronotypes of the owl and the lark (or early bird). Till Roenneberg mapped the circadian rhythms of 220,000 people and found that people generally fall into these two chronotypes.

Given that it is possible to work around the clock, when can you leverage your most productive work? More productivity tips are given in Chapter 18.

What routines will allow you to run at your peak? Are you best when you get your most important work completed first? What routines will help you be most successful? What activities are going to help you renew, blow off steam, etc.?

Consider what those around you need from you. Work is not the primary focus for many workers today, and it's important to consider the other roles we inhabit. Spouse, parent, caretaker, friend. What support are those around you looking for? How do you ensure that there is time for their needs?

There has been a shift in recent years away from a once-a-year performance process to having more regular conversations.

PLATFORMS FOR VIRTUAL AND REMOTE TEAMS

In addition to having systems that facilitate work, results, and relationships, we also need the vehicles that will help us do this. This takes us into the realm of platforms.

Information management wise, we need to think about the different platforms we can use to help people:

1. Communicate
2. Make decisions
3. Hold meetings
4. Share information
5. Build and share the knowledge-base platforms to do these things

1. Communicate	Teams Zoom What'sApp Messenger Voxer Slack
2. Make decisions	Google Poll Kahoot MentiMeter Poll Everywhere Poll on Zoom
3. Hold meetings	Zoom Teams WebEx GoToMeeting

4. Share information	Slack Asana Teachable Google Drive Dropbox
5. Build a knowledge base—Learning Portals	Teachable Kajabi Xperiencify Intranet Resource portals
6. Manage projects	Basecamp Asana Monday.com
7. Collaborate	Slack Basecamp Asana
8. Make changes to documents	Word Zoom
9. Network	LinkedIn Virtual communities of practice Professional associations (virtual events)

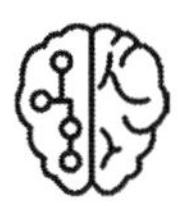

BRAIN TIP: THE IMPORTANCE OF A SOCIAL NETWORK

Connection is a critical part of thriving in any workspace.

Matthew Lieberman explores this topic in *Social: Why Our Brains Are Wired to Connect.*

In addition to having systems and being able to work asychronously, there is value in a social network and connection.

Back in the 1970s, Arthur Bandura created Social Learning Theory, grounded in four main areas:

- Observation (environmental)—observing and learning from the context in which we operate.
- Retention (cognitive)—how do I remember this?
- Reproduction (cognitive)—how do I reproduce this? Use this?
- Motivation (both cognitive and environmental)—noticing what is motivational and what is not

In order for learning to occur, we need to create opportunities for learning on all four layers. What are you doing in your organization to focus on these four areas?

6 SIX QUESTIONS FOR MORE REMOTE WORK

1. What's going to help you be more productive?
2. What support do you need to do your best work?
3. How do you want to/need to stay connected to the team?
4. What information/accountability do you need to get your work moving?
5. What feedback loops are needed?
6. What is important to share with others?

TEAM TOOL: RELATIONSHIP MAPPING

Part of success in the remote, virtual, and hybrid space involves working through others. With this in mind, we need to understand the context in which we operate. If we are not clear on who we connect with and how things flow, it can be challenging. The Team Tool for this section may seem a little counterintuitive—a focus on relationships as we look at systems. The key to having a connected workspace is being sure we understand how relationships operate.

The team tool is that of relationship mapping, which can be done on an individual or team level. Part of this process helps us understand how things work beyond the systems.

When people start their role, help them map out the different contact people they may work with. With a map in hand (global for global teams, regional for smaller remote teams), walk people through who some of their main contacts will be. In a face-to-face environment, we may distinguish between internal and external stakeholders. In the virtual space we want to do that as well, although building relationships with people you are in contact with internally and externally may feel somewhat the same due to lack of proximity. Virtual team leaders will want to help team members map out key relationships they wish to foster.

On a team level, you can map out key relationships (internally and externally). Have discussions around what you notice is important about these relationships. Also, flag issues which need attention. Having a visual map can be useful to contextualize your work, as well as provide an overview for the team, and key conversations you are having.

RECONNECTING THE WORKSPACE TIP—SYSTEMS

Systems ensure consistency in the hybrid and remote world so that we can be location independent. What systems are going to help people reconnect and collaborate with each other?

Systems bring fluidity regardless of what time or day we are working on it, or where we are engaging on it from. Systems range from customer service to communication, onboarding, administration to marketing.

What are the systems which are going to create consistency and connection across your organization?

END OF CHAPTER QUESTIONS

- Which tools are going to help you do your best work?
- What systems are going to ensure consistency?
- What do you notice about the relationship webs and systems that exist across the organization?
- Which areas need more attention?

CHAPTER 8

TEAMWORK PRACTICES AND SKILLS FOR RESULTS AND RELATIONSHIPS

"When you meet your workmates by the water cooler or photocopier every day, you know instinctively who you can and cannot trust. In a geographically distributed team, trust is measured almost exclusively in terms of reliability."
– Erin Meyer

Principle: Ensure all voices are in the room. Teams are strong because of their diversity. Having a variety of strategies to harness the talents and approaches of everyone in the room is key. This might involve using Post-its in the physical space or apps like Miro and Mural in the remote world. Dotmocracy and using annotation to vote are other ways to surface interests.

Myth: There is a myth that everyone is the same. That we have the same needs, wants and preferences. We know that socialization, education, and upbringing shape what we value, how we operate, how we work, make decisions, involve others, and address conflict. Remote teams by nature are more diverse.

This chapter explores teamwork practices. Practices are things that we repeatedly do so that they become habits. Practices are the consistent anchor when things are fast, uncertain, unknown, or complex. It is these practices which support teams through the ebbs and flows of work, and the unknown waters typical in today's workplace.

Within the context of teamwork, virtual teams excel when there is both a focus on **results** and **relationships**. Too much focus on relationships leads to a "feel good experience" and having fun, but not moving the needle on getting things done. Too much focus on results can lead to lower morale and burnout.

This chapter explores these topics:

- Why practices? The values of habits and go-tos
- Size matters
- The Two Rs: teams which excel, focus on results and relationships
- The One-Page Plan
- Habits for highly effective teams: things teams want to do regularly
- Keeping connected as a virtual team member
- Evaluation and pulse checks
- Knowing and not knowing
- Busting assumptions
- The umbrella of team culture—harnessing the best of teams today
- Essential teamwork skills
- Tricky issues

We will also be exploring the Team Tool entitled At Your Best, and Six Questions for Collaboration and Partnership.

Why Practices?

Practices provide team members with a way to regularly focus on the critical areas for team success (see text box on page 141), while also building the core flywheels of any team—a focus on results and relationships.

From the research we know that teams which excel focus on both results and relationships. We'll be delving into this in this chapter. There are a number of areas virtual teams may struggle around, including:

- Lack of clarity around processes
- Not knowing what their other team members are working on
- Not being aware of the different priorities and ways of working of team members
- Not feeling connected
- Not having clarity around key tasks and activities

WHAT'S UNIQUE (OR THE SAME) WITH VIRTUAL TEAMS?

In a virtual team, thinking about team practices may feel contradictory, particularly if team leaders are approaching each team member one at a time, rather than thinking about team members collectively. Because team members are not visually present, the old adage of "out of sight equals out of mind" may hold true. This requires that we make team touchpoints a priority and regularly focus on outreach to others.

A unique challenge for virtual teams is that team members may be members of multiple teams. They may sit with a local team that houses their office space (i.e., part of the Toronto team in Canada), but direct work may in fact be global in nature. With these type of matrix relationships, it is important to create a sense of belonging and identity. In fact, Druskat and Wolff[118] say team success is based on three conditions:

1. Trust
2. Sense of group identity
3. Sense of group efficacy—belief that they can work better together than apart

Cultivating #2 and #3 is essential in helping the team feel like a team.

A Reminder: Essential Elements for Team Success

- Compelling vision
- Time to meet, connect, and be in dialogue with each other
- Focus on results *and* relationships
- Clear sense of purpose
- Ability to surface the hard issues and have courageous conversations
- Understanding of the different types of virtual events

SIZE MATTERS

What's the best size for a team? Team Genius authors have found that the best size team is somewhere between five and nine. As a team work practitioner, I usually assert that each person added to a team adds an exponential layer of relationships, conversations, and perspectives.

As I shared in *Effective Virtual Conversations*, Richard Hackman found that as team size grew from 5 to 13, the number of communication touchpoints needed grew from 10 conversations when the team was five people, to 73 conversations when the team grew to 13.[119]

As teams grow in size, there is a tendency to develop nested teams within the larger team. Within these larger groups, there are smaller teams, each with their own culture and focus.

Virtual and Remote Team Practices—Three Principles

In general, when thinking about practices, it can be important to follow these three virtual foundations:

1. Keep it **simple**
2. Make it **visible**

3. Make it **accessible**

Keeping it simple is critical when there may be different team members who might interpret things differently. Simplicity is key for remote work, especially when different languages are at play. Complexity is the kiss of death!

Making things visible helps to keep things clear and top of mind. Examples of making things visible range from using streaming where possible, to using visual dashboards like the Red, Yellow, and Green Stoplight, to sending out visual reminders.

Another important part of making things visible is unearthing assumptions. Assumptions are inevitable in virtual teams and serve to weaken the foundation.

Keeping things visual and visible is key to remote work success. This can be achieved with the use of Kanban boards, slide design, visual dashboards, and videos, to name a few.

Kanban boards help us to lay out and visualize workflows, with the tracking columns, "To Do," "In Progress," and "Done." As Kim Scott writes, "A Kanban board is different from a dashboard because it focuses activities and work in progress. It gives your team time to identify and resolve issues before they hurt the results."[120]

What can you do to visualize your workflows, both as a team and individually?

Another important tool is the One-Page Plan, which is explored later in this chapter.

Making things accessible so that people can access things 24/7 on different platforms, connections, and ways is also critical. Virtual and remote teams will want to get into the practice of thinking through how they are going to file things, and where and how they are going to update versions. These small issues can become a critical issue when files are not updated and saved and team members work off of old versions.

TEAMWORK PRACTICES

In virtual teams, teamwork practices are just as important as leadership practices. Teamwork practices can be distinguished between those activities that focus on results and those that focus on relationships.

From years of research with teams we know that:
High performance = Relationships + Results

Activities That Focus on Relationships and Results

PRACTICES FOCUSING ON RESULTS	PRACTICES FOCUSING ON RELATIONSHIPS
Regular team meetings: For some teams this may be a daily huddle at a shared time of day to provide updates. For others, it may be a once a week streaming session	Getting together regularly and spending quality time together helps to boost relationships
Ongoing communication through Instant Messaging such as Slack	Face-to-face meetings when possible
Spending time weekly to upload core documents to shared services	Proactively outreaching with other team members
Sharing priorities: It's likely that some of your priorities may overlap with others on the team	Having a learning buddy: Pair team members together for discussion
Making a regular practice to share practices to reduce isolation	Peer coaching
Job shadowing	Job shadowing and peer mentoring
	Facilitating a culture of play

As we explored in some of the first chapters, teams excel when they have strong relationships and are clear on their results. Before you go on, read through these team practices one more time, and identify which ones build relationships and which ones focus on building results.

Teams That Excel Focus on Both Results and Relationships

Team development focuses on results and relationships:

1. Results include the categories of goals, actions, leadership, metrics (KPIs, organizational goals, team goals).
2. Relationships include a focus on topics such as teamwork, navigating conflict, addressing tricky issues, team culture and camaraderie, candor, styles.

Teams which excel focus on both results and relationships. Focus areas in these domains include:

RESULTS	RELATIONSHIPS
Key performance indicators (KPIs) Strategic goals Organizational goals Team goals Performance objectives and constraints Things we are exploring are: goals leadership solutions priorities expectations	Knowing each other Trusting each other Feeling safe to take risks, make mistakes, take responsibility, and own mistakes Feeling safe to surface issues that are not working Candor Empathy Emotional Intelligence Working across differences Conflict management Relationship building

Many companies like Netflix and Google have been putting an intentional focus on cultivating relationships while driving for results. We know from practice that both are required and a balance between results and relationships is needed.

Consider a **team that prioritizes results**. This may be the team known as the super performer, the golden team, or the A Team. While this team may be terrific at getting and surpassing results for a period of time, fatigue, burnout, and exhaustion will set in over time. Experience from the field of high performance sports has shown that teams need to cycle and recharge, and that while intervals are important in providing a sprint, sprints can't be sustained forever.

Topics such as renewal and building in "down cycles," where team members focus on momentum and special projects, help team members to renew. A team which is "always on" will likely burn out, which could result in taking medical leave, movement to new teams, and/or low levels of morale.

Now, consider a team that prioritizes relationships. This may be the dream team that gets along and has fun. While their relationships may be infallible, if they spend all their time socializing and having fun, it's unlikely that things are getting done, leading to low results.

In his book, *Extreme Teams*, author Robert Bruce Shaw writes that Netflix is reported to encourage a focus on results by having teams consider, and be in dialogue, around these questions:[121]

1. What is it your team will be accomplishing six months from now?
2. What specific results do you want to see?
3. How is that different from what your team is doing today?
4. What is needed to make these results happen?

TEAM TOOL: RESULTS—THE ONE-PAGE PLAN

One of the most important team alignment tools is the One-Page Plan. Simple in its format, this framework is powerful as a tool to share information across the team, enabling individual team members to both zoom in on what's important and quickly update others.

One-Page Plan

Goal	Description	Key Timelines	Resources (Who and What)	Enablers/Derailers

As I shared first in *Coaching Business Builder* and *PlanDoTrack*, One-Page Plan is a one-page planning template. It includes five different columns:[122]

1. Goals
2. Description
3. Key Timelines (who and what)
4. Resources
5. Enablers and Derailers

Let's walk through an example of this.

Imagine that Jane is sitting down with Ned, the new remote worker. The **Goal** section in the first column allows you to note the main goal that he's working on.

The team goal is to grow business revenue by 50% this quarter. A second goal is to "enhance communication." This is not very specific. I'm going to use this as an example because we can get SMART-E about this. As I shared in *Effective Virtual Conversations*, SMART-E stands for Specific, Measurable, Achievable, Realistic, Timebound, and Exciting.

One way the team can enhance their communication is by increasing social media presence. So, under my description I'm going to make sure that it's specific.

Specifically, "increase" means posting to Facebook three times a week. It might also include twice-a week Instagram posting and blogging daily, just as I do here at the Teams365 blog.

The next column, **Description**, allows us to get a little bit more specific. Specificity is good. Measurement is good. It's good that I know that, "yes, I've done three posts this week on Facebook or I've included a daily blog post."

The third column allows you to capture **Key Timelines**. When are you going to do this? This might be a weekly task as I've just mentioned, or maybe there is a different goal to hit a certain revenue mark and with a key timeline that is the end of Q1. We also want to make sure that we include resources that are appropriate.

The final column looks at **Enablers and Derailers**. Who and what will help you be successful with this goal?

We want to look at the key activities that are going to help or hinder you. There may be things that you can do, or people you can enlist to help you, or "Enable" you. Derailers are the things that are going to take you off the path.

Here's how some teams use the One-Page Plan:

- Have each team member complete it and bring it to their one-on-ones with team leaders *or* peer coaching sessions.

- Have each team member complete it and share it across the team.
- Have a shared One Page Plan portal online.

RELATIONSHIPS: BONDING, BUILDING, OR BELIEVING?

On the relationship front, in his book *Bowling Alone: The Collapse and Revival of American Community*, author Robert D. Putnam differentiates between two types of social capital, Bonding with the Group, and Building. Robert Bruce Shaw, author of *Extreme Teams,* adds one more layer of social capital: Believing.

In order to thrive, teams need time to bond, build relationships, and believe in themselves and their mandate. The vehicle to this is team meetings, one of the most important team practices.

A critical part of virtual team success is team meetings. This is often one of the first practices that gets abandoned when things get busy. There may be an assumption that they are not important when, in fact, there may be a lot of synergy across a system. For teams that are interdependent, it's critical to provide teams with time to meet. These help to clarify what people are doing, as well as build connection. Meetings are an important opportunity to bond people together and build a sense of connection.

As Jeff Sutherland indicates in *Scrum*, a success factor was daily meetings, capped at 15 minutes. Meetings have gotten a bad rap due to their length of time. It's estimated that often 35% of a leader's time is spent in meetings. Meeting management is further explored in Chapter 19.

Team meetings should be brief and to the point. Technology can serve as a platform to do some of the granular sharing. In order to make team updates flow quickly, it can be important to leverage the visual tools available—from video streaming to whiteboards, work on the screen and in the call. This keeps work visible. Many systems now offer the opportunity to have local dial-in if broadband is not reliable. At least on a recording, the team members may be able to "see others" and any information shared during the call.

Consider these meeting items through the lens of results and relationships:

RESULTS	RELATIONSHIPS—MEETING ITEMS
Project updates Successes Lessons learned Goals Planning Resource sharing Identifying synergies	Celebration of personal milestones Connecting with each other—what are you doing for . . . Learning more about each other's priorities Values Vision

In their book, *Extreme Teaming: Lessons in Complex, Cross-Sector Leadership*, Edmondson and Harvey found that two critical characteristics for teams to thrive in complex environments are their ability to work across differences and their openness to learning.

HABITS FOR TEAM PERFORMANCE

Habits are things we do unconsciously which support us in today's frenetic business context. In the virtual space, there are many habits which we can cultivate to support a team. These include:

- Keeping connected as a virtual team member
- Evaluation and pulse checks
- Knowing and not knowing
- Busting assumptions

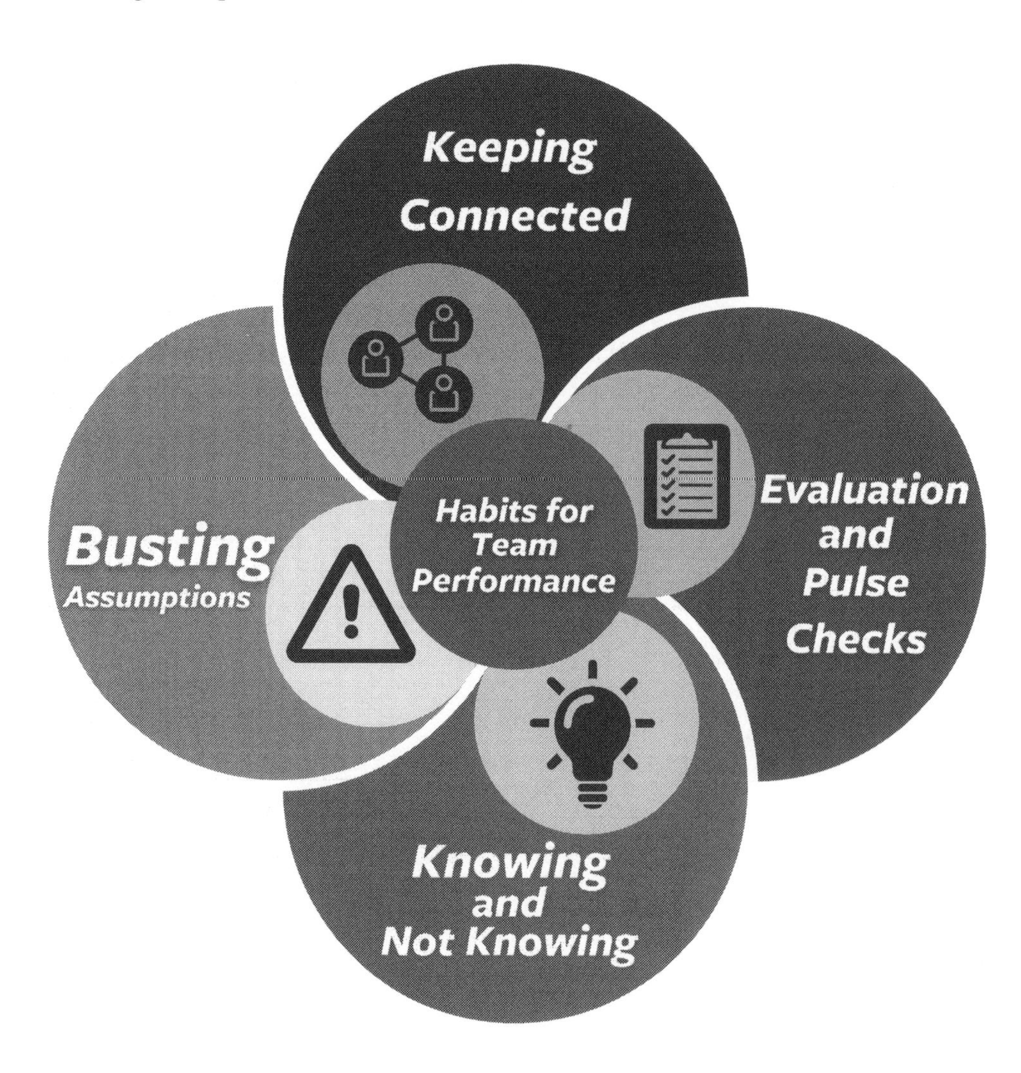

Habit #1: Keeping Connected as a Virtual Team Member

Keeping connected as a virtual team member is critical. Team members should feel that they can do it themselves and not have to "wait for their leader" to connect with others. The notion that "teams are as strong as their weakest link" is pertinent to remote teams.

In addition to the relationships you have with your own team (or teams, if you are in a matrix relationship), it is important to build relationships with other stakeholders.

Here are three ways to keep connected about how things are going:

Post information on an intranet. Many teams may use Slack or Basecamp to house searchable information about current tasks and priorities. Create shared agreements of how frequently people on the team will do this. Is it daily, weekly, biweekly, monthly?

Create team buddies or peer partners. Leaders will want to work to create links among the team. Many virtual teams pair people together so that they are building relationships and networks across the team. This helps with information flow as well as building trust and connection. Providing team members with the opportunity to get to know others on the team is critical. Buddies might meet once a month for a virtual call to:

- Share detail and more about the projects they are working on
- Identify some of the best practices in their results/projects/relationships
- Compare notes
- Identify opportunities and challenges

What could peer partners on your team focus on?

Building skills in peer coaching is an essential part of this process. At the foundation are seven skills required for effective peer coaches, as I shared in an article entitled, "Peer Coaching: An opportunity for capacity development."[123]

1. **Listening**: We listen at multiple levels in the coaching conversation. Listening is not about what am I going to say next. Rather, listening as a coach puts the emphasis on hearing the client and the context you are in. What do you notice about the pace and pitch of the speaker? What is being said, and what is not being said? What is being said between the lines? What do you notice about the words and the tone? What is the energy behind the conversation?

2. **Questioning**: In coaching we want to use questions that are open-ended and are not inviting a yes/no response. In any coaching conversation (peer coaching, team coaching, leader as coach) it is important to use questions that expand **awareness**, prompt a new **perspective**, invite **discovery**, or support **action**. Powerful coaching questions often start with *What* and are only five to six words in length. We also want to use language that is consistent with, and is impactful for, the person being coached.

3. **Curiosity**: Throughout the coaching process, the person being coached is the expert. This can be a 180-degree shift from our typical process where the leader is the expert. Fostering curiosity and a comfort in "not knowing" or not having all of the answers is important. A central philosophy in coaching is that the client has the answers that they need. The process of coaching will help them distill, clarify, and find focus.

4. **Assumption busting and perspective shifting**: Throughout the coaching conversation, it is likely that you will be exploring and "busting" assumptions as well as shifting perspectives. Helping peer coaches gain skills in this area is important for all kinds of conversations needing to take place in organizations today.

5. **Mirroring**: The skill of mirroring is similar to paraphrasing, but it is reflecting back what you have heard verbatim (word for word). In mirroring, it is important to reflect the words back exactly as you heard them. Mirroring often creates new insights for the speaker as they hear themselves in stereo.

6. **Support for goal setting and achievement**: Coaching is grounded in the core goals as set by the person. A starting place for any coaching process is to identify goals and the focus of the conversations. The peer coaching conversation should provide an opportunity to move towards those goals, as well as identify blockages.

7. **Creating accountability supports**: Creating support for accountability is essential. As John Whitmore wrote in his seminal *Coaching for Performance,* accountability is about getting people to specify, "What will you do? By When? and How will I know?" Holding people accountable for taking the action they have identified is foundational to the coaching approach. As peers, we know that accountability plays an even bigger role.

The *Harvard Business Review* article by Joseph Grenny, "The Best Teams Hold Themselves Accountable," highlights that "in high performing teams most performance issues are managed amongst themselves. As we move to mediocre teams, bosses hold the space for accountability, and in poor teams there is no accountability. Being intentional in the remote space to create accountability frameworks amongst peers, like peer partners, while strengthening the skill set for teams, is a win-win."[124]

Teams should also discuss how they want to share information.

Habit #2: Evaluation and Pulse Checks

A second habit to activate is that of evaluation and pulse checks.

It is important for virtual teams to pause regularly and invite comments on how things are going. As research has shown, some teams will move into a Groupthink where "everything is okay." We know from research that teams can suffer from confirmation bias. Simply put, confirmation bias occurs when we search for, or find data that supports our point of view. As remote and hybrid teams, we want to make sure that we are cultivating diverse perspectives and undertaking multiple opportunities for feedback and pulse checks.

Feedback loops can take a number of different shapes, from retrospectives done as a team to formal meetings, peer coaching, and regular input to rotational roles where different team members take the lead with questions.

Questions you may want to use to check in or undertake what is often called a "retrospective" are:

- Which things are working for us as a team?
- What's not working?
- What processes could be reshaped?
- What's one thing we could be doing differently to improve results or relationships?
- What could we stop doing? What needs an immediate change right now?

Reminder: Onboarding Team Members

As you will see in Chapter 12, onboarding is a key part of the team development process. Onboarding describes the initial orientation and months of work of new team members. It's these first few weeks that lay the foundations for success.

Key items to be reviewing in the onboarding process with new virtual team members include:

- What team agreements exist?
- What issues need to be surfaced and when?
- Team identity
- Six Factors of High Performing Teams

Habit #3: Knowing and Not Knowing

Habit three is the habit of being comfortable with knowing and not knowing.

Hal Gregersen of MIT, and author of *Questions Are the Answer*, talks about the importance of being comfortable in not knowing what we don't know. As we become more experienced and senior in a role, it may be an instance where issues are not being raised with us. Learning to cultivate questioning within our teams is an important part of breaking this cycle. Refer to Chapter 6 on questions.

Part of the challenge of the remote space is learning to be comfortable with not knowing. It is not possible to know everything in the remote space, given that we can only see what is on our screen. Questions provide a pathway into the coaching conversation so we can empower those we are in dialogue with to glean insights. It is often through the collective collaboration that we get the details and resources we need in order to solve problems.

Habit #4: Busting Assumptions

The final habit virtual, remote, and hybrid teams will want to be aware of is that of busting assumptions. There are many assumptions we can hold as both leaders and team members. Assumptions are important to identify, as not everyone sees the world with the same eyes. In a remote team, our context and what's outside our window can look completely different. Busting through assumptions is critical for global teams today.

Henry Winkler writes, "Assumptions are the termites of relationships." Assumptions quickly erode the foundation of any team. It is important to regularly revisit what assumptions are being made by the team, and by individual team members.

A big assumption team members may hold is that because someone is of a certain global background, they are going to be a certain way. With educational opportunities abounding, it is possible that someone may bring years of experience living and working in another county. This may make them outside of the norm.

Other assumptions team members may make:

- Everyone is going to love working remotely
- Working as a virtual leader is just like a face-to-face leader
- The way I work is how everyone else will want to work
- It's not important that we meet face to face
- It will be convenient for them
- They will want to do the travel to see us
- Everyone wants to collaborate like I do

What are the assumptions you notice in your team? Which ones need to be explored?

THE UMBRELLA OF TEAM CULTURE: KEYS FOR HARNESSING THE BEST OF TEAMS TODAY

Teams today are buffeted by a number of factors, from ongoing change and increasing complexity to teaming and change across members of the team. Taking time to build a strong culture is absolutely essential for team effectiveness. As much as things change, it is important to return to the basics around teams.

Tuckman's model informs us about the stages teams move through as a collective. These stages include forming, storming, norming, performing, and adjourning. While virtual teams may feel more like a collection of individuals, highly efficient virtual team leaders ensure that they are able to create a solid culture with their team. Taking time to help teams understand where they are in the journey of being a team is an important element.

While we may not be able to control or influence the pace of change and/or how much complexity there is to having a strong team culture, finding easy ways to communicate and share, and co-creating clarity around expectations, are critical for success.

Team Culture—the Umbrella

These elements combined create a unique team experience and fabric. This goes hand in hand with creating a shared team identity. Elements of a team identity might include:

- Who are we?
- What do we value?
- What are the symbols of our team?
- What makes us unique?
- What is the bond that brings us together?

Common bonds, including visuals and metaphors, help to facilitate this sense of "connection" in a virtual space. Leaders will want to help team members find their common themes or threads by asking, on a regular basis, the question, "What's common across the team?"

Another activity which will support the creation of shared metaphors is to incorporate visual cards to create a library of metaphors which team members can pull from. For example, through dialogue we may see that our team members are like members of a crew on a boat. Or we may use a metaphor around a butterfly and its journey.

ESSENTIAL TEAMWORK SKILLS

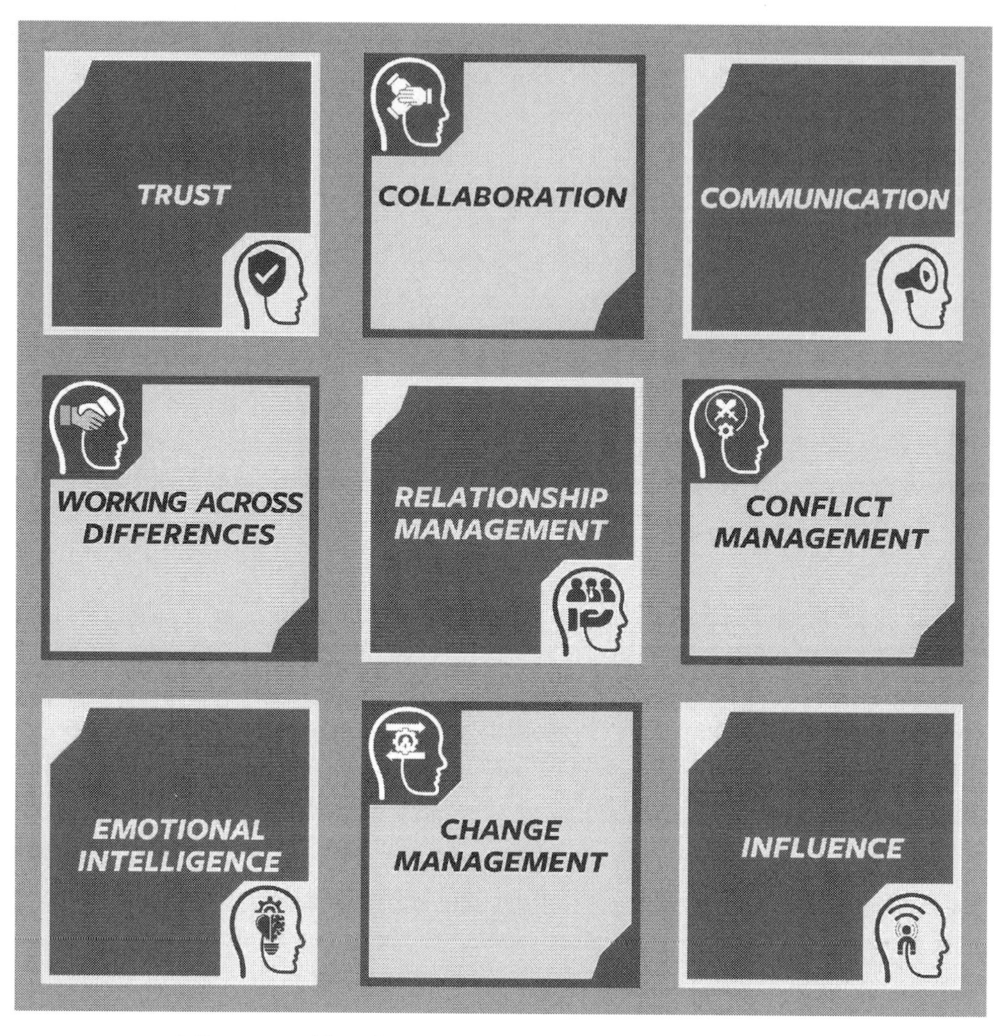

There are nine core skills required by all team members (virtual, in-person, or hybrid), including:

1. Trust
2. Collaboration
3. Communication
4. Working across differences
5. Relationship management
6. Conflict management
7. Emotional intelligence
8. Change management
9. Influence

Specific to the virtual space, additional skills for team members include:

1. Global mindset
2. Openness to learning and exploration of new ideas
3. Self-awareness and ability to work across differences
4. Autonomy and initiative
5. Flexibility, adaptability, and agility

Many of these skills are further addressed in upcoming chapters with three being more cross-cutting:

1. Authenticity/candor
2. The ability to work across differences
3. The skill of influence

Authenticity

If we are not authentic, it's not likely that we will be trusted. Authenticity is about showing up as we are. It's about being real. Part of the shift in the virtual, remote, and hybrid space means that we are showing up the same way in all facets of our life and work.

Dr. Carl Robinson writes, "Authentic leaders create communities ***at*** work; communities ***that*** work. They foster friendships among and between coworkers to link humans to one another so they have something else and someone else to work for other than themselves."[125]

Candor

At the heart of remote work is the ability to raise issues as we need to. Without a proactive approach to feedback and improvement, progress is unlikely to be made. Many organizations, large and small, are looking to foster more candor in their organizations.

As Kim Scott writes in *Radical Candor*, "Radical candor happens when you put 'Care Personally' and 'Challenge Directly' together. Without caring personally and challenging directly, team members may find themselves in the realm of Obnoxious Aggression, Ruinous Empathy or Manipulative Insincerity. Radical candor builds trust and opens the door for the kind of communication that helps you achieve the results you are aiming for."[126]

She continues, "When people trust you and believe you care about them, they are much more likely to:

1. Accept and act on your praise and criticism;
2. Tell you what they really think about what you are doing well, and more importantly, not doing well;
3. Engage in the same behavior with one another, meaning less pushing the rock up the hill again and again;

4. Embrace their role on the team;
5. Focus on getting results.

These are all essential elements in supporting teams to do their best work."[127]

Influence

Another key skill in the remote space is that of influence. We get our results through others, and our ability to persuade and influence is critical. In a virtual team it is likely that we are getting our work completed through other members. This might include our teammates, our leader, other matrix relationships (local level/regional level or technical) as well as through other internal and external stakeholders.

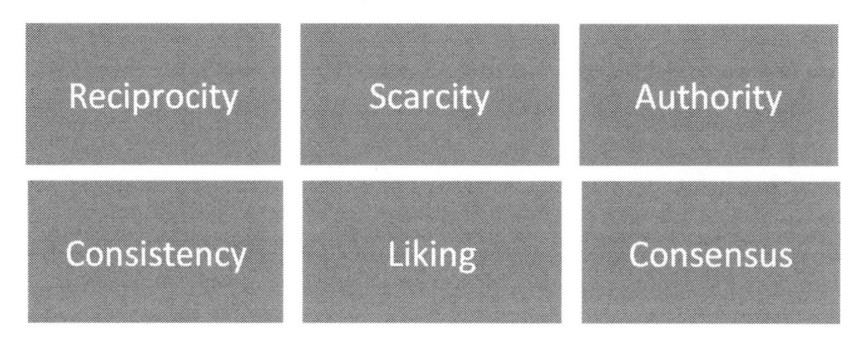

There are many different ways we can cultivate influence in a team. Influence comes from respect, trust, connection, and good intent.

Within the virtual space we are always having to work *through* people. Many remote workers have found this to be a multiplier effect. In his YouTube video, "Secrets from the Science of Persuasion,"[128] Robert Cialdini outlines six universal guides that shape our behaviors. They are each a lever for motivation.

Let's look at each of them:

Reciprocity: Humans are guided by give and take. We give back the behavior we have received. If you help me, I will help you. If you have been given a favor, you will return it. As a consumer or in a relationship we are more likely to say yes to those we owe. Be sure to be the first to give and that what you give is something unexpected.

Scarcity: This principle notes that we want more of what we can't get. When something is scarce, we tend to want it more.

Authority: People follow those who are credible and have expertise. Signal to others what makes you a credible expert. What have others said about your work? What track record do you bring to make you an authority?

Consistency: Be consistent with the things your customers and teams are looking for. Ask for small commitments that can be made regularly.

Liking: People will say yes to those they like. We like people who are similar to us, who pay us compliments, and who cooperate towards mutual goals. To employ these factors in online negotiations, share a snippet of personal information with each other before you begin negotiating. In one study, 90% were able to come to agreement.

Consensus: When we feel uncertain, we look to the actions and behaviors of others.

As you think about your team experience, what are the things you need to influence? Which of these six principles could be a lever or something you could cultivate so that you can work more effectively through others? If you don't know, consider starting with reciprocity, by reaching out first to a colleague to share information, or explore the liking principle by finding some common ground with another team member.

RELATIONSHIP BUILDING

Building relationships is critical in today's virtual world of work, and it's not always as easy as dropping in and out of locations. Finding your virtual networks or neighborhoods is critical. This might include arenas such as:

- Professional associations or communities of practice who meet
- Virtual groups
- Virtual Meetups

The topic of relationship building is explored more fully in Chapter 10.

MOTIVATORS IN THE VIRTUAL SPACE

We are all motivated by different things. Everyone on the team will have different drivers (motivators) as well as recognition needs. Styles become such a critical part of what we do as team members.

Virtual team members may be motivated by a range of internal and external factors, including drivers such as autonomy. This section also includes more information about frameworks which come from neuroscience, including David Rock's SCARF model, and Daniel Pink's *Drive*.

Daniel Pink shares in his book, *Drive*, that there are three main factors that lead to motivation, including:

1. **Autonomy:** Our desire to be self-directed. We want engagement, not compliance—self-direction is better. In a remote working context, mastery may be an important influence in terms of how we may be able to shape our working hours, place of work, etc.
2. **Mastery:** This refers to our ability to be good at what we do, to learn regularly, and feel competent in what we do. Support for ongoing learning can be an important part of the workplace culture.
3. **Purpose:** Often referred to as our *Why*, our purpose, or the bigger picture. In the remote work space, helping others connect to this can be another important motivation lever.

With more complex, creative tasks, it can be valuable to figure out which of these drivers is important. It is likely that each employee will be motivated by something different. Knowing the primary levers for each person can help the employee in the following areas:

AUTONOMY: GETTING THINGS DONE	MASTERY: WE ARE SKILLED AND CAN DO THINGS	PURPOSE: WE ARE ATTRACTED TO A HIGHER PURPOSE
• Doing a good job • Being able to have a global impact (or an impact bigger than their own) • Flexible schedule • Being able to "control" the work • Working from home	• Being able to serve a micro-niche and really master a specific set of skills which is valuable to a global audience • Having job responsibilities tied to skills	• Connecting into our *Why* • What impact they want to make • Get better talent

In addition to the intrinsic/extrinsic factors discussed in Chapter 2, motivation is a key part of the remote work experience. New neuro-research on what motivates us has found that motivation is somewhat counterintuitive. It doesn't always mean the higher the reward, the better the performance.

For example, studies have found that with cognitively difficult skills, like conceptual or creative thinking, more reward led to poorer performance. In contrast to simple, straightforward tasks, such as "do this, then get that", with cognitively challenging tasks, if/then rewards work more effectively than the traditional "carrot and stick" approach.

TEAMS THAT THRIVE

Research today is starting to explore the notion of moving beyond the concept of just doing, to flourishing and thriving. As we think about teams which excel, it can be useful to consider how to cultivate practices that support what the research is showing leads to thriving.

This takes us back into the neighborhood of **strengths** and **styles**, as discussed previously.

Let's look at five different studies which point to five different factors:

- Positive feedback to each other
- Flourishing
- Cultivating happiness
- Connection
- Mindfulness

Positive Feedback to Each Other

Several studies have found that teams which provide both constructive and positive feedback to each other tend to be higher performing. Gallup's studies found that 67% of employees have managers who focus on their strengths. Zenger and Folkman's 2013 research also found a 6:1 ratio around positive feedback to negative feedback with teams that thrive.[129]

What are you doing to create a conversational space around positivity? It might be framed as "I see one of your strengths as . . . " or " I appreciate," and "I would like to see more of . . . ." I personally have used this framework with thousands of coaches and team members who have worked remotely to each other. It's always proven to be a powerful connector and way to open up a conversation for both positive and constructive feedback.

Flourishing

First, work around flourishing comes from the realm of positive psychology. Seligman created the PERMA model, focusing on:

- Positive emotions
- Engagement
- Relationships
- Meaning
- Accomplishments[130]

Many authors from John Gottman to Chester Elton have noted that teams which excel, have what's often known as the "positivity ratio" of 5:1 or 7:1, where they provide positive feedback 7 times versus the 1 negative feedback.

Gretchen Spreitzer and Christine Porath found that thriving staff:

- Performed 16% better than peers
- Experienced 125% less burnout
- Were 32% more committed
- Felt 46% more satisfied
- Had fewer sick days and were more likely to get promoted[131]

Sutherland notes that these employees are "vital, passionate, trying to perfect their craft."

Cultivating Happiness

"What are the things that actually make people happy? They are actually the same things that make great teams: Autonomy, Mastery and Purpose."[132]

Many studies have been done that point to cultivating happiness.

A meta study in 2005 found that "Happiness leads to success in nearly every domain of our lives, including marriage, health, community involvement, creativity, and in particular, our jobs, careers and business."[133]

Connection

Other studies point to intentionally focusing on connection, including Zappos, who has embraced a principle that people thrive through connection. "The more connected people are to each other, the happier they are and apparently the more productive and innovative as well."[134] They host apprenticeships and boot camps and have even designed their building's doors to promote "chance encounters." A challenge in the virtual space is this: how do we create conditions for "chance encounters?" It is not a surprise that virtual networking became a popular business add-on during the pandemic, framed by speed-rounds; meeting others in breakout rooms.

Mindfulness

What can you do to help people become more aware of themselves and the world around them? This is an increasingly important area.

PRACTICAL THINGS VIRTUAL TEAMS NEED TO THRIVE

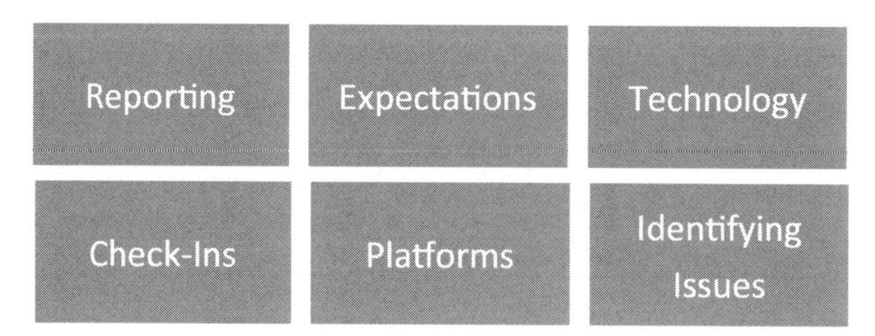

New virtual teams require the following ingredients to thrive:

1. **Clarity regarding reporting relationships.** Who are they to report to on what issues? When is reporting required? If matrix reporting relationships exist, what do they report to whom? What issues need to be co-reported?
2. **Clarity regarding expectations regarding working.** Hours, approaches, breaks, how to log and share work, etc.
3. **The technology and ability to connect with others** in the team and across the organization. Working remote can be a lonely endeavor; and just as social time is important for face-to-face teams, so is face-to-face for virtual teams.
4. **Regular check-ins and feedback**. Regular check-ins and feedback may revolve around the questions:

- How's it going?
- What's working? What's not?
- What support do you need?
- What are your current priorities?
- What resources do you need in order to get the results you need?

5. **Platforms to see each other and connect with their team.** This could include regular virtual potlucks where the team actually connects for a meal from each of their locations. It could also include face-to-face time, such as quarterly or on another regular basis.
6. **Clarity regarding how to flag issues.** What issues should be raised and when? Who should they be flagging issues to? When is the team leader available and how?

HELPING OUR TEAM MEMBERS BECOME COMFORTABLE

While *we* may be comfortable in the team context, it's important that others feel comfortable, particularly if you have some team members who perceive themselves to be more remote than others. We don't learn well when we are uncomfortable, and the paradox is that learning makes us uncomfortable.

Taking time to brainstorm with them solutions for connection is an important part of the process. Likewise, we also want to be sure that we work with them to find solutions. Taking some extra time to work this through as a team is very important.

As a team leader, you are likely to have team members with different levels of comfort with technology. It can help to hold meetings on the platform you are going to be hosting calls on, so that people can get a handle on the platform in terms of accessibility, what they need to do, and what they also look like. Not everyone is comfortable at first in the virtual space. Helping people troubleshoot before the call can help to maximize team time together.

TRICKY ISSUES WHICH CAN EXIST IN A VIRTUAL TEAM

No chapter on team practices would be complete without a focus on some of the tricky issues which can exist on a team. These include:

- The different personalities and team members which exist
- Technical issues

Different Personalities/Team Members

Different personas and personalities can make team life more challenging. The strength of a team is its diversity, and this can be the most challenging part of being a member of a team. In this section we are going to explore several personas who may show up in any team context.

It's interesting that regardless of gender, nationality, and team location, these personas may be present. As you read through this section, consider how you would positively support these individual team members:

- The Verbose
- The Joker
- The Challenger
- The Super-Performer
- The Know-It-All

Within every group there exists a tremendous variety of personalities. As facilitators, we may find that some of them are easier to support than others. As I shared in the Teams365 blog several years ago,[135] different types of personalities can be part of a virtual call. These may become difficult issues for facilitators to manage. Let's look at four styles and some potential ways to mitigate and support, while maintaining respect and a positive learning environment for everyone involved.

1. **Challenger**: The challenger challenges everything, and it may include why you're meeting, who is at the table, and outcomes. In the virtual realm, the challenger can quickly turn everyone off. Being clear prior to the start of the meeting with process—outcomes and agenda items—is one of the ways to mitigate against this. In the virtual realm, clarity of communication and process is key.

   The challenger's vantage point is usually one of great value. Typically there is always value, and something to be learned, from the perspective of the Devil's Advocate. What is the request behind the challenger's complaint?

2. **Avoider**: The avoider may be a more passive group member who is disengaged and does not take responsibility for outcomes, participation, or next steps. While we can only influence, as a facilitator our role is to make sure there is agreement around what next steps are, who is responsible and what is expected. It may be important to talk about "what happens if these are not followed through?" Let the group and/or systems in place also address the impact of the avoider.

   Creating opportunities for work and dialogue in smaller groups, such as virtual breakouts, often encourages and necessitates that the avoider becomes a more actively engaged participant around the virtual table. What is behind this avoidance? Lack of knowledge, skill, understanding, or confidence? If you are working with this person for a longer time, helping the person become aware of the impact they are having in the virtual space can be an important series of conversations to have.

3. **Dominator**: The dominator wants to take charge and probably wants to be leading the meeting. They usually hog air time and dominate the call virtually through speaking, sounds (grunts), or even over-annotating with tools they have.

   Consider providing this person a structured role so they can positively channel their focus. Perhaps they become a time keeper or minute taker for the process.

4. **Multitasker**: The multitasker is a very common and difficult participant, who can be present in most virtual calls. Their multitasking may be very visible through typing, background noise, etc. Creating shared expectations as a group with respect to what focus and engagement is expected can provide encouragement. When you do have rapport with group members, letting them know that you can see their multitasking online may prompt them.

   What will help this person focus? What do they need in order to stop multitasking? What are they aware of in terms of their impact?

While there are many more difficult issues, these are four common ones that show up in different virtual calls. As the facilitator, you play a key role in ensuring that it is a safe and positive learning environment for everyone, grounded in respect.

Reframing and refocusing are key skills to help people bring their best to calls.

ASKING FOR SUPPORT IN THE VIRTUAL SPACE

We all need support at different times. It can be beneficial to give team members practice in asking for support.

It can be as simple as asking people to make their requests direct. For example:

- I need _____ in order to _____, *or*
- I would like support in _____ so that I can _____, *or*
- What would really help me right now is _____.

Even though we may not be in the other person's shoes, we can likely empathize, and there may be some group members who have a consistent experience.

Each team member may have a different preference and comfort level with asking for help. It can be useful to get into a team practice of going around the "room" and having each person share one challenge or area they are looking for support around. That helps to normalize that business is full of ups and downs and that every team member may need differing levels of support.

6 SIX TEAMWORK QUESTIONS: TEAMWORK

1. What do we both bring to the table as strengths? How are they complementary? Similar?
2. What is important for us individually? How do these values align? How are they similar? How are they different? How do we define these values? Where are they illustrated?
3. What is our shared vision for our work together?
4. What can we count on from each other?
5. What will we do if things go off the rails?
6. When and how will we check in around our progress? Provide feedback to each other?

TEAM TOOL: APPRECIATION—AT YOUR BEST

Team Activity: Appreciation/Strengths[136]

Helping team members understand their strengths helps teams leverage their skills and harness their capabilities. Gallup has also found very compelling results when team members are able to bring their strengths to work every day. This includes enhanced quality of life.

Common strengths surveys include StrengthsFinder 2.0 from Gallup, as well as the VIA (Values in Action) Strengths Survey.

The following team tool is a short warm-up activity to more detailed discussion as a team around your strengths.

When I've Seen You at Your Best

Time: 15 minutes

Materials Needed: None

Instructions: Virtual team members need acknowledgement as well, particularly as they may receive less feedback than teams who can see each other face to face.

Ask team members to think about one person on the team who they have liaised with, or worked closely with (virtually) in the last quarter. At one of your team meetings you will give people the opportunity to share with that colleague responses to the following questions:

1. I see one of your strengths as _____.
2. I appreciate _____.
3. Going forward, as we work together, I'd like to ask you _____.
4. You bring _____ to our team.

This is an activity which will cultivate positive emotion and will bring team members closer together. Teams need positive reinforcement as well as constructive feedback. For more on the concept of constructive feedback, check out the Foundations of Feedback[137] series I did. It will be of interest to teams of all kinds who are hoping to build more of a feedback culture.

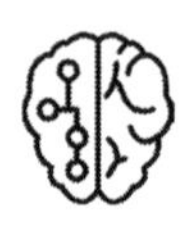

BRAIN TIP: ZOOM FATIGUE IS REAL

In February 2021, Stanford researchers, led by Jeremy Bailenson, noted that their research uncovered four cases of Zoom fatigue. Zoom fatigue is real!

They identified these four factors leading to Zoom fatigue, making the following recommendations to mitigate against it:

1. Excessive amounts of close-up eye contact is highly intense. When faces are seen so large, "our brains interpret it as an intense situation that is either going to lead to mating or to conflict."[138] Bailenson and his team recommended minimizing face size by coming out of full-screen mode. Personally, I take off my glasses!
2. Seeing yourself during video chats constantly in real time is fatiguing. Adjust your settings to "hide self view."
3. Mobility is reduced. Bailenson notes that "when people are moving, they're performing better cognitively."[139] Researchers suggest turning video off periodically, or doodling to get activated. Personally, I incorporate a lot of annotation where people can work on the screen, or build in activity breaks to get people, and their brains, moving!
4. Cognitive load is much higher in video chats. Researchers suggest going to audio-only at times, and also turning your body away from the screen. As I like to note, activate the 20/20/20 rule to video meetings: every 20 minutes, take 20 seconds to raise your eyes from the screen, to look ahead 20 feet.

RECONNECTING THE WORKSPACE TIP

Connection is at the heart of a reconnected workspace. We want to connect people on multiple levels—to each other, to their work and results, to their purpose and passion, and to their vision.

As a team, there are several things you can do practically to boost connection:

- Regular meetings focusing on both building relationships and achieving results.
- Feedback between peers, and formally and informally with the leader and other stakeholders.
- Acknowledgements and appreciations.

END OF CHAPTER QUESTIONS

- Which of the four habits do you want to cultivate?
- Which areas could your team benefit from?
- What are the motivations for each person on the team?
- What strengths does each team member bring?
- What can you do to cultivate team strengths?

CHAPTER 9
LEADERSHIP PRACTICES

"Your foremost job as a leader is to take charge of your own energy, and then orchestrate the energy of others."
– Peter Drucker

Principle: Empower others. A virtual team leader's role is to empower and enable others. Consider what's going to help your team and others be successful.

Myth: A myth in the virtual space is that it's all about the leader, when in fact, it's usually all about the efforts of the entire team. While not to minimize the role of the leader who plays a key role in coordinating, and, as Drucker says, "orchestrating," a large part of the virtual leader's role is to ensure that the team has the resources, skills, tools, and direction to do their best work.

In this chapter we turn our attention to leadership.

Initially in writing this book, I had thought that I would not include a chapter on leadership practices, given the importance all team members play. Yet this would have done a disservice to the fundamental role of the leader in creating an **enabling** environment for **action**, **focus**, **relationships**, and **results**. The leader may be a team leader or a business owner. At times, team members may be "stepping in" and "acting up" for their team leader who is away. As such, it will be important for readers in all roles to explore this chapter.

Leaders play a key role in shaping team identity and creating team culture, as well as supporting and developing their team members, resourcing, and troubleshooting. This chapter explores many of the leadership practices virtual and remote team leaders will want to engage in regularly. Whether you are a small business owner or part of a multinational team, these leadership practices will be valuable.

Building the skills of our team members is a key part of the team leader role, and this is covered in chapters 8, 9, and 12. Part of this capacity development may involve coaching, training, mentoring, and supporting peer coaching, which is the focus of Chapter 15.

This chapter explores:

- Elements of virtual, remote, and hybrid team leadership
- The role of the team leader
- The hats team leaders wear
- Skills needed by team leaders
- Essential virtual team leader practices
- Creating shared expectations
- Providing clear direction
- Rewards and recognition
- One-on-ones
- Managing uncertainty
- Maintaining perspective
- Learning from seasoned leaders
- Leadership Tool—Providing Clear Direction(Is/Is Not)

Our six questions come in the area of one-on-ones, and this chapter's team tool is the Is/Is Not Framework.

ELEMENTS OF VIRTUAL, REMOTE, AND HYBRID TEAM LEADERSHIP

What's on a typical team leader's desk or on their desktop?

- Files for each team member with templates, status reports, meeting reports, financial reports, performance management reports, onboarding materials
- Contact details: email, addresses
- Phone which carries back-ups, particularly of meeting room codes, team members. The phone doubles as a mobile hot spot as needed
- Multiple laptops, including smaller ones for travel with voice-activated note functionality
- Nightly synching with the elements

What Is a Superhero Virtual Team Leader?

As we can see from the cartoon, the world of today's virtual and remote leader can be quite Zen, quite compact, or quite creative.

What does the superhero virtual team leader look like? While "super virtual leaders" could not fit one mold, given the diversity that exists with this work, they do bring specific qualities to the table, including:

- Empathy
- Comfort with not knowing
- Open ears
- The ability to go the extra mile
- Clarity in creating expectations
- Skill at building relationships
- A focus on both results and relationships
- Super hosting skills
- Humility
- A knack for creating identity and fun for a team
- Expertise in navigating the tension of being coach and leader

THE ROLE OF THE VIRTUAL TEAM LEADER

Leaders play a key role in shaping team identity, creating team culture, supporting and developing their team members, resourcing, and troubleshooting.

Aligned with the focus of this book, the virtual team leader spends their time focusing on both result and relationship functions. These can include:

RESULTS	RELATIONSHIPS
Resourcing	Creating team identity
Goal setting	Supporting peer coaching and mentoring
Troubleshooting	Working with matrix managers
Connecting people with others	Networking

FOCUS AREAS OF TEAM LEADERS IN THE CONNECTED WORKSPACE

What are the focus areas and practices of team leaders? Here are four core leadership best practices team leaders will want to cultivate.

Team Process:

- Co-creating shared agreements
- Regular team meetings
- Frequent one-on-ones

Boosting the Skills of a Team:

- Cultivating a peer coaching environment
- Building the skills of listening, decision making, influence, relationship building
- Building/instilling confidence in others

Managing the Team:

- Focusing in on rewards and recognition
- Providing clear direction (see Tool: Is/Is Not)
- Supporting action towards key goals by troubleshooting with team members and providing the necessary resourcing

Coaching the Team:

- Working with the team to create shared vision and goals
- Helping team members in the virtual, remote, and hybrid workspace to uncover or discover their own answers
- Creating an enabling environment so the team can problem solve on their own and/or with support from peers and their leaders
- Creating "pause points" for the team to reflect on what's working and what's not
- Creating accountability for the team around what they said they would do

- Connecting team members to what motivates them
- Connecting team members with others on the team

Virtual team leaders successfully navigate the tension of being expert and coach. This can be an initial stretch point for many, as virtual team leaders are hired because they are very good technically and are technical experts. At the same time, they may not be experienced or bring expertise in "people management."

When you're a virtual team leader, your ability to people-manage and work through others is just as important as being a technical expert. Developing your team is covered further in chapters 11 and 12.

HATS VIRTUAL TEAM LEADERS WEAR

Virtual team leaders need to fill multiple roles. In this section we are going to explore five roles of a virtual team leader:

- Leader as Coach
- Leader as Mentor
- Leader as Logistician
- Leader as Teacher
- Leader as Liaison

Leader as Coach

The leader as coach helps the person being coached tap into their own knowledge base, insights, and thinking. The leader as coach:

- Draws on the expertise of the team members
- Witnesses changes being made
- Acts as a sounding board so that the other person can talk it through
- Serves as a creativity sparker by providing questions which help to connect the dots, expand thinking, or provide a different perspective
- Serves as a "cheerleader"
- Acts as the bottom line around accountability by "holding feet to the fire" so that people are getting things done, and making sure that there is a loop back to the things people have said they would do

Skills the leader as coach is leading from include:

- Questioning
- Listening
- Acknowledgement

Leader as Mentor

The leader as mentor helps the person being mentored to:

- Navigate the informal rules and political currents of an organization or industry
- Pass on what's worked and what hasn't, from their experience
- Highlight pitfalls and traps for team members, spotlighting things that aren't always talked about
- Provide feedback in ways that peers and supervisors may not

Typical mentoring conversations may revolve around how things are done.

Skills a leader as mentor will draw upon include:

- Listening
- Questioning
- Relationship management
- Storytelling
- Liaison

Leader as Logistician

Team leaders may also act as a logistician. Equipping our virtual teams with the skills, resources, and authority to do their work is critical. With this hat on, leaders are focusing on:

- Resourcing: providing physical resources and the natural autonomy required
- Acting as liaison: connecting people with the resources they need
- Planning: supporting goal achievement and lessons learned
- Troubleshooting: identifying resource issues, communication channels, and other things that might get in the way of success.

Leader as Teacher

Sometimes the virtual team leader will act as a teacher, helping team members master skills, create shared mental models, or access resources.

Skills a leader as teacher will draw upon include:

- Educating: helping people equip themselves with the skills they need, through providing training or connection to educational resources (coaching, training, e-learning, other resources)
- Communicating

- Mentoring: passing skills on in an experiential way
- Applying: supporting the integration and application of skills

Leader as Liaison

One of the most significant roles the virtual team leader may serve is that of liaison. Given the lack of proximity, it is likely that the leader as liaison is a good:

- Troubleshooter, working with the staff member to identify and remove any blockages
- Liaison in terms of connecting the person with other resources
- Expander of networks
- Liaison with people needed
- Connector with resources needed
- Clearer: Helping to remove obstacles, providing the necessary authority and responsibility

Skills a leader as liaison will draw from include:

- Networking
- Relationship managing
- Decision making
- Problem solving
- Implementing/executing
- Managing logistics, connecting people with the resources they need

As you think of your own work, what hats are you wearing with different team members?

SKILLS FOR EXCEPTIONAL TEAM LEADERS

There are three skills we want to cultivate in the team leader:

- Managing uncertainty
- Building intrapreneurial skills
- Navigating matrix relationships

Tips for Managing Uncertainty

"In an uncertain world, almost by definition, you can't figure it out—that's the whole problem," said Jim Whitehurst. "So the management problem needs to be less about 'let me be a smart strategist' and much more about 'how do I build the capabilities in my organization to be able to react quickly when things happen?'"[140]

The year 2020 was one of learning to lead through uncertainty. Three core skills for navigating uncertainty are:

- Curiosity
- Experimentation
- Building intrapreneurial skills

Curiosity

Curiosity is a key skill to helping us become comfortable with learning and not knowing. When we are stuck in an expert mindset, we may feel we "know everything." There is a danger in this, especially when contexts change. Cultivating more curiosity for learning, exploration, and trial and error, gives team members permission to try things out which may not work.

How do we cultivate curiosity? Encourage people to ask questions such as:

- *What else?* This question helps us see alternative paths and solutions.
- *Why not?* This question gives permission for us to explore another angle around things.

Encourage trial and error. Get team members to explore what failure means and does not mean.

Provide opportunities for growing skills in new areas through job shadowing, mentoring, and/or special projects.

Experimentation

Experimentation is key for business leaders and teams today. When the context changes so quickly, we don't have time to complete an entire roll-out before having to make a final decision. That can lead to a mindset of experimentation, of "trying things out" to see what works and what doesn't, and these activities are encouraged. Squarely rooted in the notion of "growth mindset," this can be a shift for many professionals.

In supporting experimentation in our team, we want to:

- Encourage and reward trial and error
- Create safety around not "getting things right"
- Provide team members with time and resources to experiment, beyond their everyday team responsibilities
- Facilitate an evaluation of projects or "experiments" that are completed or are even at the midpoint.

Questions we may ask at project reviews include:

- What's working?
- What's not?

- What are the things that need to be abandoned or tweaked?
- What additional resources do we need?
- What unknown obstacles have become visible?
- What is the big learning we are taking?
- What is the one thing or the many things we are going to do differently going forward?
- Who else can we learn from (including our own past projects)?

What are you doing to build capability in this area?

Building Intrapreneurial Skills[141]

The term *intrapreneur* is becoming more mainstream these days as many larger companies are looking to leverage the skills and strengths intrapreneurs have to offer. Rubbermaid, 3M, and HP are all known for fostering an intrapreneurial climate. The year 2020 was an important one to build more intrapreneurial skills in organizations.

The term *intrapreneur* was first coined in the late 1970s by husband and wife team, Gifford and Elizabeth Pinchot, while undertaking studies at the School for Entrepreneurs in Tarrytown, New York. Originally coined *intra-corporate entrepreneur*, the term *intrapreneur* evolved throughout the 1980s, being added to the *American Heritage Dictionary of the English Language* (3rd Ed.) in 1992.

An intrapreneur can be defined as: "in-tra-pre-neur (intrəprəˈnər) n. A person within a large corporation who takes direct responsibility for turning an idea into a profitable finished product through assertive risk-taking and innovation [intra(corporate) + (ENTRE)PRENEUR.] -intrapre-nouri-al adj. -intra-pre-neuri-al-ism n. -in'trapre-neuri-al-ly adv."[142]

Intrapreneurs exhibit certain characteristics in the workplace, including risk taking and innovation.

Many writers liken intrapreneurs to the corporate world, as entrepreneurs are to the small business sector.

These ideas have led to offshoots of intrapreneurs in a range of sectors, namely, ecopreneurs who work for environmental sustainability through the introduction of green technology, intrapreneurs in the governmental sector, and many others. While intrapreneurism originally got its start in organizations like Xerox and EMB, many larger organizations have continued to see these skills as necessary for their ongoing evolution.

Negotiating Matrix Management Relationships

A key area for remote team leaders to be aware of is the need to navigate matrix management relationships, where you are supporting team members from several different teams. In a matrix relationship, team members may have two or more bosses and be part of two or more teams. For example, even though I am in Toronto, I may have a boss in Toronto supporting me and one in London who is also supporting components of my work. Just like hybrid work, it's important that we are clear on how communication flows, who has what responsibility, and what goals and work take priority. Holding regular meetings with other matrix leaders who support members of your team can go a long way in avoiding duplication and also conflict.

For more on matrix management tips, check out the Teams365 blog I have hosted since 2014 at PotentialsRealized.com.

STEPPING INTO THE ROLE: FIRST 90 DAYS AS A NEW TEAM LEADER

The first 90 days of any role is usually deemed instrumental for success. It's often what is seen as making or breaking a leader's experience as it creates the foundations for relationships and results of their tenure. While entire books are dedicated to this topic, including an upcoming one by me, I would be remiss not to address some of the key issues for supporting team leaders in the first 90 days.

Immediate issues to explore as a new team leader:

- Who do I need to connect with? (difficult to ask if you don't get any handoff)
- Technical issues
- Who is on the team?
- Who are your other internal stakeholders?
- Who else do you need to connect with?
- What is the mark you want to leave on the team and program you are working with?

Tools in the Team Leader Toolkit

Team Development	Hackman and Wageman—Team Coaching Lencioni—Five Dysfunctions of a Cohesive Team Tuckman's model
Team Meetings	Agendas Virtual Facilitation
Team Support	One-on-ones Mentoring Coaching Job shadowing
Project Management and Tracking	Asana—project management software
Knowledge Generation	Bloomfire ZohoDesk
Systems Development	Key systems, including reporting, projects, communication

Helping the Team Get Things Done—FOCUS	Another tool you will want to explore is Getting Things Done. Having real-time virtual work settings to support the team in getting things done. Virtual co-working has made a significant resurgence. Check out Chapter 18 on Productivity later on, as well as the 4 D Tool to productivity.

COMMON MISTAKES NEW VIRTUAL TEAM LEADERS MAKE AND HOW TO MITIGATE

There are several mistakes new team leaders can find themselves facing which can be avoided or mitigated against. Common mistakes include:

Not enough one-on-ones: The quality of your relationship with your team members is paramount. Make scheduling of one-on-ones a priority! Create a culture where team members are initiating one-on-one time with you as well.

Not learning on their feet: Team leaders expecting things to always be the same. In the virtual space it is likely that team leaders will be learning every day. It is critical for team leaders to be able to synthesize information and build in short pause points to reflect, evaluate, pivot, and then react.

Not being comfortable working in the unknown or knowing and not knowing: As shared in an earlier chapter, learning to be comfortable in working in the unknown is a core skill for the 21st century.

Not helping team members connect with the big picture: Not every team member will see, or will know, the big picture. Helping our team members connect with and understand the bigger picture is essential in supporting team members to make decisions with the context in mind. If we don't communicate the bigger picture, it is impossible to think that they will know it. In this virtual context you will want to share items like:

- What are the current strategic directions of the organization/department/team?
- What does the strategic plan indicate?
- What are the organizational KPIs? Team goals?
- What are the priorities for your region?

Not providing the necessary responsibility or authority: This is a really big pitfall faced by virtual teams. When we assign a task, are we sure that the person has the requisite responsibility or authority needed to get the job done?

Not checking in frequently enough: When team members are working separately, it can feel isolating. Keeping check-ins consistent through different channels such as voice, text, and email can help team members feel connected.

LEARNING FROM SEASONED LEADERS

Research and practice show that the most successful team leaders are those who have been in the role before. Seeing masterful virtual team leadership modeled effectively is important. Some sage words of advice from seasoned leaders include:

- Try it out
- Relationships are key
- Always have a back-up
- Don't lose sight of what's important
- Take time to cultivate relationships
- Consider what will work for your team
- Create boundaries

WHAT'S DIFFERENT: SKILLS NEEDED BY VIRTUAL TEAM LEADERS

While this book goes into many of the nuances needed for virtual and remote work, some of the main differences with virtual work are:

- Clarity around community, roles/responsibilities (matrix as well), and goals
- Being explicit and intentional in developing relationships, creating boundaries, and clarifying expectations
- Building trust and connection in the virtual space
- Global competencies
- More developed communication
- Working through others and the skill of influence
- Building relationships virtually

While the technology platforms have changed, many of the basics of great virtual team management have not. Here's what Joyce A. Thompsen wrote in *Quality Digest*:

"There are five core categories of effective leadership skills in virtual project team or distance-management situations:

- Communicating effectively and using technology that fits the situation
- Building community among project team members, based on mutual trust, respect, fairness, and affiliation
- Establishing clear and inspiring shared goals, expectations, purpose, and vision
- Leading by example with a focus on visible, measurable results
- Coordinating/collaborating across organizational boundaries"[143]

In addition to these skills, there are four key leadership practices which will benefit virtual team leaders, specifically:

1. Creating shared expectations
2. Providing clear direction
3. Rewards and recognition
4. One-on-ones

Leadership Practice #1: Creating Shared Expectations

Troubles often emerge when expectations are not clear. In a remote team, it's important that expectations are co-created and shared across the team. Creating shared expectations involves:

- Creating Ways of Working (WOW): What things are acceptable and unacceptable on the team?
- Being clear with leadership expectations—Here's what you can expect from me; what can I expect from you?
- Ask the team to consider: What can you count on me for? What can you provide to others?
- Creating shared expectations can be done in team meetings, as well as one-on-ones with team members. Ask team members to specify how these agreements may be different than with other team members.

Leadership Practice #2: Providing Clear Instruction—Is/Is Not

One of the most important roles a team leader can fulfill is to provide clear instruction.

> Lack of clarity = Lack of results.

What happens in a virtual team is that we may not all have alignment or clarity around instructions. A common task assigned is, "I'd like you to write a report."

TEAM TOOL: IS/IS NOT

While it might sound clear, the person hearing this may have a very different idea of what's needed. To avoid assumptions, create clarity. This can be assisted by what Steve Robbins calls the Is/Is Not tool. In an Is/Is Not tool, we want to have people articulate what the report is and is not.

Let's look at the report writing example more in depth. To really leverage the Is/Is Not tool, you would want to get even more granular. For example,

The report is:

- Detailed
- Geared for our customers
- Showcasing at least six examples
- Including _(quantity)_ photos of the work in action
- Including _(quantity)_ stakeholders' voices

The report is not:

- Video based
- Future focused
- Geared for staff
- Focused on what didn't work

In any projects you have coming up, consider how you might be able to use an Is/Is Not framework to help create clarity around the results. This helps to make things very specific and avoid assumptions. A key virtual tip is to name assumptions.

Leadership Practice #3: Rewards and Recognition

Rewards and recognition in the virtual space are critical for motivation and team performance. While we may not be able to undertake all the same things we could in an in-person environment, recognize others through things like:

- An email to the person
- A formal award during your team activities
- A gift card
- A mention in the team newsletter or function

Remember that we are all motivated by different things, so working with your team/knowing your team can be very useful. Some questions you will want to ask regularly in a one-on-one might include:

- What are your current projects?
- What are the things that are most important right now?
- How do you want support?
- What's a way you would like to be recognized?
- Are there any conversations you want to have?

Five quick tips around praise:

1. Make it **specific**. Be specific with your examples of what you are providing positive feedback around.
2. Make it **regular**. Don't wait for performance review time. Provide positive (and constructive) feedback regularly.
3. As several leading businesses say today, "**Catch people doing it right!**" Don't always be looking to find people doing it wrong. Notice when people are doing things right. This ties into our focus on strengths.
4. Be **authentic and real** in your feedback. Authenticity is key. We can probably all think of times when false praise has been given.
5. Look to build a **feedback culture** where it's not just the leader giving positive feedback, but peers are giving each other feedback as well. A quick and easy practice is to spend five minutes at your regular team meetings on acknowledging positive events/actions that week, whether it is done collectively or individually.

Leadership Practice #4: One-On-Ones

> "Have a structure for one-on-ones; and take the time to prepare for them, as they are the best way to help people be more effective and to grow."
>
> – Bill Campbell, CEO, Intuit

A fourth fundamental leadership practice, which some might argue is the most important, is the art of a one-on-one. One-on-ones are an opportunity to coach each team member and help the person pinpoint what is going on.

Essential elements of a one-on-one conversation

There are several elements which are critical in any one-on-one, and team leaders will want to schedule regular team meetings with their team. Questions you may use to frame it include:

- What have your successes been this week?
- What are you most proud of accomplishing?
- What's the one thing you've been putting off (or putting on the side burner)?
- What feedback are you getting from those around you?
- What support do you need?

One-on-ones provide an opportunity to be in dialogue around what the team member needs. Perhaps they need to:

- Expand their ideas/brainstorm on one of the projects they are working on
- Clarify their activities and tasks
- Focus in on making a decision
- Prioritize what is important
- Focus on goals

These different lenses are going to frame a different type of conversation.

SIX LEADERSHIP QUESTIONS FOR ONE-ON-ONES AROUND GOALS

1. What are our top three to five goals this month?
2. Are the goals SMART-E? Specific? Measurable? Achievable? Realistic? Timely? Exciting?
3. What does success look like for each major goal? Do we all share the same vision of success?
4. What does each one of us do to contribute to the achievement of that goal?
5. What are the things that could get in the way, or derail, the goal? What will help, or enable, the goal?
6. What are the measures we will use to know that we have reached the goal?

As a starting point, ask the team member what they want to get out of the conversation. This serves as a frame and an orientation point. As a virtual team leader, it is important to encourage your team members to prepare for, and set the pace of, the conversation.

Questions form the backbone of the conversation. Here are more questions you might want to use at different stages of the virtual conversation:[144]

Questions to Open Up the Conversation

What's most important for us to focus on today?

What end results do we want for this meeting?

What are you bringing to the call?

What's the most important thing for you to get out of the call?

How engaged do you plan to be? (Note you may not ask for a response on this but only pose it to get people thinking about their focus.)

Wrap Up

What are you committed to doing after this call?

What are you going to take action on?

What's the one most important thing to recall from our conversation today?

What new ideas around process are you going to take?

What resources are needed to put your action steps into action?

What are you committed to doing in the next 24 hours, no matter what?

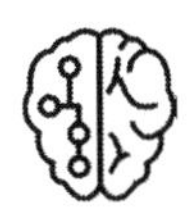

BRAIN TIP: NEURAL PATHWAYS AND HABITS

In the field of neuroscience it's often said that when things are repeatedly done, new habits are formed. You may have also heard Hebb's Law, which states, "Things that wire together, fire together." When we undertake an action, we create new neural pathways in the brain. Each time we do this, we create another groove in that pathway. As one of my cognitive psychology professors shared years ago, habit formation is like a track in the brain. Each time we do something the track in our brain gets more and more pronounced. As we repeat it, that connection becomes stronger and stronger. This is a plus for both positive and negative pathways.

As I wrote in *Coaching Business Builder*, "Habits are things that we do consistently and often subconsciously. Habits become automatic ways of doing things, often without much thought. Habits can be in service to our work, and also can get in the way of our success."

In the virtual and remote space, habits are an important part of getting things done. As we develop habits, we create more "room" for getting things done because the decision-making part of our brain doesn't have to work so hard.

Habits require three things to create new neural pathways: attention, focus, and reinforcement. What can you do to create new pathways? What are the things you want to reinforce? What can you do to create new patterns and habits around that?

RECONNECTING THE WORKSPACE TIP—LISTENING AND QUESTIONS

In reconnecting workspaces, it's critical for leaders to leverage the skills of listening and asking great questions that invite input and expansion. Questions asked can either expand awareness for our team members or focus their attention or drive to a point.

Curiosity is key to an open mindset. Asking questions from a place of curiosity helps to surface possibilities and explore options. In the virtual, hybrid, and remote space, we often are not aware of "what's beyond the screen" of our team members. We can't see their context, or know what's on their desk, other than what systems can inform us.

Great questions are informed by great listening. Take note of what you are listening for. What are you noticing about your team member's voice? Body language? Facial expressions?

The best questions are short (usually 5–7 words in length) and start with *What*.

Create opportunities to connect people with each other and the resources, information, authority, and autonomy they need to do their best work. Refer to the multiple questions included here.

END OF CHAPTER QUESTIONS

- What can you do to create shared expectations?
- What application do you have for the Is/Is Not Tool?
- What can you do to incorporate more praise and rewards and recognition?
- What will you do differently in your one-on-ones?

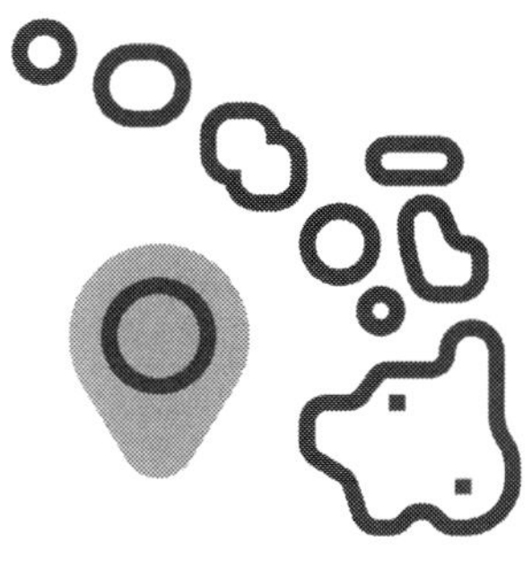

CHAPTER 10

NO PERSON IS AN ISLAND—RELATIONSHIP MANAGEMENT AND COLLABORATION

"You can't build an adaptable organization without adaptable people, and individuals change only when they have to, or when they want to."
—Gary Hamel[145]

Principle: Relationships are an important part of high performance. Work is not just about getting results. In today's VUCA world, change is effected through many. As we consider the mantra of High Performance = Relationships + Results, note that one half of the equation for exceptional performance is relationships.

Myth: I work in isolation. There is a myth that even in the virtual space we work in isolation. In fact, most work today is interconnected. Even if I don't see you, my work may be dependent on you. In virtual and remote work relationships, the web of connections may be greater than we realize, either enabling or hindering our efforts.

No person is an island. In this chapter, we explore the important topic of relationship management. In the virtual space, work is done through, and with, others. Work in virtual and remote teams can feel siloed as well as more complex if our relationships are not strong. Leaders and all team members need to excel in the area of building, maintaining, and cultivating relationships, both internal and external to the team. In this chapter we are going to explore:

- The foundations of collaboration and partnering including the acronym of LEAN IN WELL
- General principles for relationship management
- Key sets of relationships:

- Your boss—managing up—developing powerful relationships with your boss
- Expanding connection with your peers
- Matrix relationships
- Fostering relationships with internal and external stakeholders (further built upon in the project management chapter, Chapter 20)

There are several team tools related to relationship management which we'll explore in this chapter including:

- Relationship mapping
- Networking mapping
- Managing-Up worksheet

WHAT'S DIFFERENT WITH COLLABORATION IN THE VIRTUAL SPACE

As we step into this chapter think about your world of work in the last month. What were the key relationships which helped you get the results you were looking for? My guess is that some of the relationships on your list were virtual relationships, people you have never met before in person. Consider which results you got by working alone, and which you accomplished with others.

In the virtual sphere we have a myriad of relationships. Some are acquaintances, some are collaborative relationships, and others are partnerships. In this chapter we will explore not only relationship building but also collaboration.

What's different about collaboration and virtual relationships?

- Out of sight does not equal out of mind.
- In the remote space it is important to be proactive and more intentional in building relationships.
- We need to be more focused. From scheduling time to make things a priority, to how we approach the calls, focus is key in the virtual world where we are operating over differences.
- There is less differentiation between internal and external stakeholders. In the remote world it can feel like all partners are external to us.
- What do you need to surface, when? Timing is everything in relationships. Know as much about the other's context, so you know what to surface and when not to.

FOUNDATIONS OF RELATIONSHIP MANAGEMENT

"Relationships are the currency of business," wrote Marc Effron in *Leading the Way*.[146] They open doors and get in the way of results.

In the virtual and remote space, relationship-building skills can be even more essential, given the need to intentionally reach out and be more proactive in building relationships.

Relationship management is critical in getting work done through others. Even if you haven't met people, you will want to focus in on getting to know them virtually.

Key to building solid relationships are these steps, captured in the acronym of **LEAN IN WELL:**

L—Listen

E—Expectations

A—Alignment/aspirations/assumptions

N—Noise reduction (focus)

I—Intent

N—Needs

W—WIIFM

E—Execution—get it done!

L—Loop back

L—Learning

Let's look at each one of the LEAN IN WELL acronym steps:

Listen: Listening is key to the partnership you want to form. Notice what's important to the person you are speaking with. How do they speak? What do you notice about their word choices? Do they use words like "like" or "feel"? Or "I think," which may signal more of a cerebral focus. What signals does this provide for you? Are their preferences more cerebral? Emotional? Kinesthetic?

Expectations: The clearer you can be in creating shared expectations, the smoother the partnership is likely to become.

Where expectations aren't aligned, the likelihood of conflict is greater. When expectations diverge, the chance is greater that the relationship will not gel.

Partnership questions are included in this chapter to help you to frame expectations. In designing partnerships, you will want to explore:

- What is important for you?
- What end results do we want from this conversation?
- How will we know we have been successful?
- What roles can we play which leverage our strengths?
- What feedback loops (formal and informal) would be useful?

Refer to the partnership questions located later in the chapter.

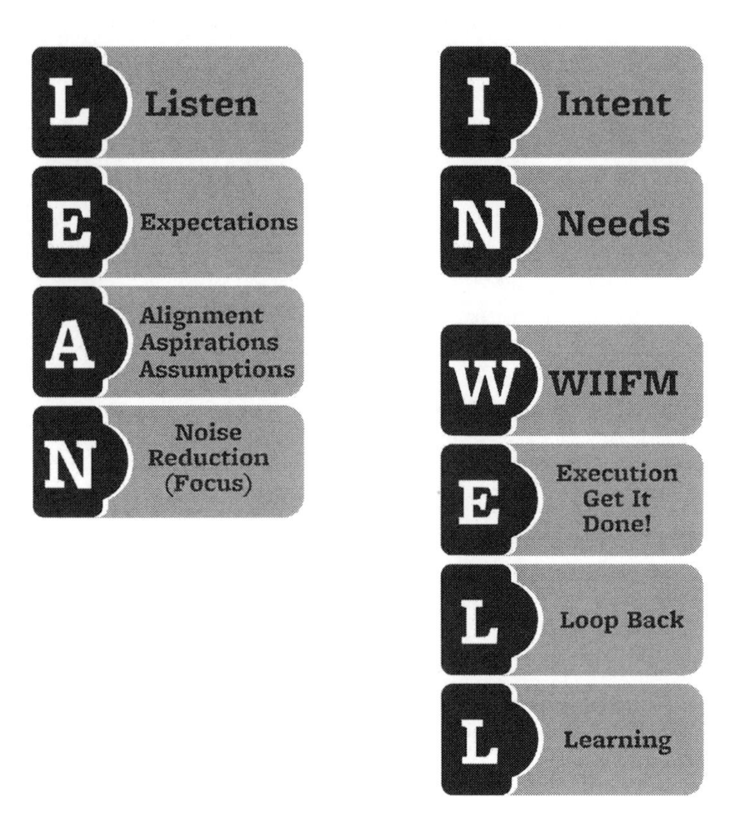

The **A** in LEAN IN WELL encourages you to consider your alignment, aspirations, and assumptions.

- **Alignment**: What is the common ground we share?
- **Aspirations**: What are our hopes?
- **Assumptions**: What assumptions are you making? What assumptions need to be clarified? What assumptions are others making?

Noise reduction: Creating a conversational space in which to focus is critical in building relationships. There is a lot of noise. What's the focus both parties want to have? In partnering and collaborating, it's important to reduce the noise and focus in on what is most important.

Intent: What is your intent? In partnering and collaboration, it is important to assume good intent, and that your partner is leading from a positive place. What is your intention? Is it to make it fun? Have greater impact? Focus on relationships?

Needs: The varying needs of partners make collaboration a challenge and an opportunity. What are your needs? What are your partner's needs? What feedback will you provide? What feedback do you need? How do you want to work with details? What support do you want in different areas? How will you address conflict? Make a list of needs and discuss how you are going to meet these.

WIIFM: What's in it for me? This involves helping people connect in with "What's in it for me?" and prioritize time for focusing on building the relationship. When we lose sight of the value of what's in it for me, people are likely to disengage.

Execution: Relationships often falter because of lack of follow through. Get things done. Get things scheduled and execute. In collaboration, it is important to remember that someone else is relying on you.

Loop back: (Check-in/accountability). Partnerships thrive when there is an accountability factor. What feedback loops have you built in? What are you committed to doing? What check-ins are you creating? What do you do when things are not getting done? How do you agree to address this?

Learning: Create multiple checkpoints to identify key learning as a relationship. What's working and what's not. Iterate and adjust as needed based on the learning you have created together.

SIX QUESTIONS FOR PARTNERING

Once you have people together, what can you ask to get the conversation going? Consider these Six Conversation Sparkers when partnering:

1. Tell me a little about your work.
2. What do you find most interesting?
3. What are your priorities this year?
4. Where do you see our work overlapping?
5. Where might we have an opportunity to collaborate?
6. What support do you need in order to get your work done?

KEY SKILLS FOR VIRTUAL RELATIONSHIPS: BEYOND LEAN IN WELL

Beyond the elements enshrined in LEAN IN WELL, virtual relationships thrive when:

- You are clear on what you are able to offer to others.
- You know your Line in the Sand—What's important to you?
- You reframe the situation. The skill of reframing in coaching is about helping to reorient how you look at issues. The skill can be very important when you are looking at working across differences and values. What are the values at play? What are the core "come-from elements" you have?

In *The Art of Connection*, Michael Gelb focuses on seven key relationship-building skills every leader needs. Many of these are woven into greater detail throughout the book.

CORE RELATIONSHIPS FOR VIRTUAL WORKERS

In the virtual space, we are navigating a wide variety of relationships including our peers, our bosses, and internal and external relationships. A great starting point is to figure out what relationships you have and focus on them.

TEAM TOOL: RELATIONSHIP MAPPING

Given that building relationships is critical for all team members, this chapter focuses on relationship mapping and also getting clear on what's important about relationships.

In today's interconnected world, virtual workers interface with a wide variety of both internal and external partners. This extends from members of other teams to our customers/clients to other agencies and organizations. Given that teams, not just leaders, are responsible for relationship development, it can be useful to get the team attuned to what their key relationships are internally and externally.

Relationship mapping is an activity you might consider doing as part of your next team meeting.

Instructions

On a whiteboard, draw a circle on the board first, with the name of your team. Make a list of all the potential people you partner with. Select one color marker for internal team partners and one for external team members. One at a time, map out how close you are to each of these internal and external relationships. If it is a close relationship place them closer towards your circle. If it is a more distant relationship, place them further away.

Ask people to indicate what is important about that relationship. Is it a relationship which enables you to do things? Do you get important information from them? Do they provide resources, etc.? Also note for each relationship, what needs attention.

Seeing these interconnections visually can bring to life the relationships, helping people understand how much they are part of a web and dependent on others.

Part 1: Map out your relationships

Part 2: Look at each relationship and consider the following questions:

- Who do you want to connect with?
- What does it mean to connect? What would it look like?
- Who can help you build your network?
- Who is the most important internal stakeholder to connect with?
- What do you have to offer?
- What are the top three to five issues you want to connect around?

- If you would like to have one takeaway from the conversation, what is it?
- Ideally, what is the outcome to the conversation?

NAVIGATING THE WEB OF RELATIONSHIPS

For virtual workers of all kinds, there are four different relationships which are critical to navigate, including:

1. Your boss, managing up—developing powerful relationships with your boss
2. Your peers
3. Matrix relationships
4. Fostering relationships with internal and external stakeholders (built on in Chapter 20)

#1: Managing Up—Tips for Creating a Positive Experience with Your Boss

Our bosses are one of our most important relationships. In the virtual and remote space, it may mean that we are supported by one or more leaders. Skillfully navigating and influencing these relationships are critical for success.

Almost every job I held involved reporting to my boss who was located in a different country. Whether we were connected by fax (in the early days), phone, or email, knowing your boss and managing up was then, and is now, a critical skill. Here are some tips to consider:

- What do they value? What's important to them? How do they like to be communicated with? What's important?
- Remember that they too, keep you visible and will open up doors for you.
- Keep them apprised—how do they prefer to receive information?
- Involve them in important decisions—keep them apprised of issues as they emerge, at a level of detail they appreciate.
- Bring the solution along with the challenge.
- Knowing what your boss values is key. What are their priorities, and how does this fit in their world?

As a virtual team leader, you play a key role as liaison/role in the middle.

Bosses are people too. Consider how they want to be communicated to; what their priorities are; what will help them fulfill their mandate.

As you prepare for a conversation with your boss, these are questions to consider:

- What does your team want you to communicate upwards?
- What do you need to prioritize?
- What do you need to ensure your boss understands about your work?

- What's the complaint behind the request? What's the opportunity for the team to be focusing on?

As you reflect back on Chapter 4, consider the different styles and strength of your boss.

Activity/Journal

Take a few minutes to consider the different styles and strengths of your boss(es). Work through these questions above.

Not addressing issues will lead to more challenges down the road, so stretch and reach out to your leader(s) for a conversation. Be proactive with any topics which need to be addressed.

6 MANAGING UP—SIX QUESTIONS

1. What are the priorities of my boss?
2. How do they prefer to be communicated to?
3. What information do they need to be successful with their work?
4. What information do they want you to feed to them?
5. What needs to be surfaced? When?
6. What do I need to ask for them to feed back to my team?

#2: Developing Relationships with Your Peers

Developing a relationship with your peers is critical for virtual and remote team success. In fact, many studies point to how important these relationships can be.

The cost of social loneliness. Over the last decade, several research studies have pointed to the cost of social loneliness. From being compared to having the same health impact as smoking 15 cigarettes a day, to the UK's focus on combatting this issue, social loneliness is seen to have a cost.[147] This can get even more magnified in the remote space, as recently evidenced with the impact of the pandemic. Long-term remote, virtual, and hybrid working arrangements may work for some but won't work for all, especially those who are extraverted and thrive with social connection.

Dr. Julianne Hold-Lunstad, as cited in Dr. Nasreen Khathi's article in *Lifespeak*, indicates that there are three types of loneliness: structural, functional, and relational. As Dr. Khathi indicates, "In other words, relationships need to exist (structural), fulfill an appropriate role (functional), and be mostly positive (quality) to keep loneliness at bay."[148]

Remote work has proven to be isolating in nature for many, devoid of boundaries unless proactively encouraged.

What to do if you are feeling lonely:

- Develop peer relationships, so critical when working remote, as isolation can set in.
- Make sure the boundaries in your work and life are clear. Are you leaving enough time for other pursuits?
- Consider a new hobby or returning back to something you enjoy doing.

In becoming more effective with the relationships:

- Understand the other person's styles, needs, and priorities.
- Make a point to go out of the way to get to know each other.
- Create social activities, e.g., virtual book club, lunch time meetings, virtual co-working sprints

#3: Another Set of Key Relationships—Matrix

One of the most important relationships you will want to foster in virtual teams, especially if your team is global, is the matrix management relationship. Your matrix manager may be someone who is local, or from the same technical background.

Following are four keys to making matrix management work.[149]

1. **Creating shared expectations:** given that your staff member will be managed by two or more sets of people, creating shared expectations among the three (or more) of you is key. Who do you report to on what? What does success look like to all the parties involved? What are everyone's various expectations and priorities? How do these align? Conflict?

2. **Clarity:** clarity around roles and responsibilities, reporting relationships, goals, and who does what is key in successful matrix management. Taking time to be extremely clear is key to success. Having a plan and process in place to address lack of clarity issues can also be important.

3. **Checking assumptions:** given that matrix management relationships often occur at a distance, it is important to check the various assumptions. Assumptions about priorities, flow, pace, and quality may be a starting point for discussion on a regular basis.

4. **Frequent touch points and adjustments:** Regular and frequent touch points amongst the three parties can be especially useful, along with an understanding that regular adjustments will need to be made. In my former world of work, I usually tried to aim for quarterly or semi-annual three-way meetings (both supervisors and employee). While this took some planning time, it was often identified as a critical success factor.

6 MATRIX MANAGEMENT–SIX QUESTIONS

1. What's important for each team/leader?
2. What's a priority for each team/leader?
3. What is the most important approach?
4. What are key priorities?
5. What needs to be shared? With whom?
6. How do we check in and make sure all parties are on the same page?

Empathy—A Core Skill

What would it be like to walk in someone else's shoes?

One of the many emotional intelligence skills is empathy.

Oxford languages defines empathy as "the ability to understand and share the feelings of another."

What is important about being empathetic?

A 2020 study completed by the Workforce Institute of Ultimate Kronos Group (UKG) found that a top priority during the pandemic was the organization's ability to balance workload to prevent fatigue and burnout. This study found an equal impact of burnout for employees working both remotely and in-person (43%). Among employees surveyed, 29% indicated that they would like their organization to act with more empathy.[150]

Deloitte's 2020 guide had "the ability to walk in someone's shoes" as the first important behavior for creating "Moments That Matter" in remote collaboration.[151]

In terms of boosting the skill of empathy in the virtual and remote space, it can be valuable to understand:

- The needs, drivers, and preferences for the individual—what motivates them, what are their preferences. This is a major theme from this book.
- More about their context. The context in which we operate, in a hybrid and remote space, can be very different. What is important, is to note the other person's context.

As we will explore in Chapter 17 on emotional intelligence, empathy is a core skill. At the same time, we don't want to over-empathize. As Adam Waytz indicated in his article, *The Limits of Empathy*, "Empathy taxes us mentally and emotionally. It's not an infinite resource, and it can even impair our ethical judgement. That's why if we demand too much of it from employees, performance will suffer."[152]

#4: Relationships with Stakeholders

Internal and external stakeholders are a final category of key relationships to navigate. I explore this category more in depth in Chapter 20, Project Management, given that many times it is projects which shape our outreach and relationship building in the remote and hybrid space.

Consider the different stakeholders you work with. Who is internal to your organization? Who is external? Undertake the relationship-mapping exercise with them.

Given that we are regularly working together, and that "no person is an island," collaboration is also critical. The virtual space magnifies and amplifies things. Let's now turn our attention to Collaboration and Partnering.

COLLABORATION AND PARTNERING

"Good collaboration amplifies strengths, but poor collaboration is worse than no collaboration at all."[153] —Morten Hanson

In addition to building relationships, we also want to explore the topic of collaboration. In all of my books, I have had a chapter dedicated to the topic of collaborating and partnering, whether we are working with people to co-lead a program, working with a producer on a webinar, or looking to expand our network within another location.

Collaboration is the oxygen of highly effective teams and their leaders. In the virtual space we need to collaborate regularly with both internal and external partners. This chapter explores tips for collaboration and also elaborates on the acronym of LEAN IN WELL.

Collaboration in the remote space may be synchronous with people collaborating via meetings, or it may happen asynchronously through tools like Trello, Asana, and Slack.

Prior to the pandemic, it was estimated that "the time spent by managers and employees has ballooned by 50% or more over the last two decades."[154] This is an increasingly important area to focus on—a study pointing to 50% more need to use skills in collaboration.

In his book, *Collaboration*, Morten Hansen shares these three reasons why collaboration is important:

1. **Redefine Success:** define success as a bigger goal, farther than narrow agendas.
2. **Involve Others:** open to input, different viewpoints, debate, and working with others in the decision-making process.
3. **Being Accountable:** see themselves as responsible for reaching goals and accountable for decisions made.

In the virtual space, it is also important to:

- **Be able to offer something to the other.** The principle of reciprocity plays out.
- **Connect in with others.** We do not operate within a vacuum, and word-of-mouth recommendations are key.
- **Learn about the context in which they operate,** so that you can identify assumptions you might be making, and learn about the reality.
- **Ask for feedback.** How do others see you working in partnership?

Making virtual partnerships work is grounded in trust, clarity, and making sure things are a win-win.

What's Different about Collaboration in the Virtual Space?

Differences with virtual collaboration:

- You need to be even more intentional and proactive. Don't assume it will "just happen."
- Trust is a requirement. If there is no or low trust, people will not show up. They are likely to "ghost" you. Trust is one of the eight ingredients required for collaboration.
- Check out and name the assumptions.
- Consider the right platform for the connection.
- Keep collaboration focused. Leverage the Eight Essential Meeting Questions found in Chapter 19 on Meetings.
- Be specific with follow up, and follow up more frequently. Out of sight can mean out of mind.

When Do We Collaborate?

The 2016 *Harvard Business Review* article explored if Collaboration Overload was happening. A key part of virtual team success is knowing when to collaborate and when not to. It's also about knowing when you need to enroll others and when you don't.

As I wrote in *Effective Virtual Conversations*:

When to collaborate:

- When a group decision is important.
- Where groups are homogenous.
- When you are working with a team.
- When buy in and engagement are important.

When not to collaborate:

- When the group is very diverse and the focus is more on the individual level.
- When time is limited.
- When the issue is straightforward.
- When there is no shared purpose or end result.[155]

A 2012 article by Linda Stewart cited the following reasons as challenges for virtual teams: "Difficulty in building a shared sense of purpose; over-reliance on electronic communications; low team cohesion and trust; and the general sense that virtual team members are less satisfied with the team experience than team members in the same location."[156]

As we have explored throughout the book, avoiding these pitfalls by building shared purpose, using hybrid communications, and focusing on building trust and connection can serve to mitigate against some of the disconnection remote and hybrid workers experience.

INGREDIENTS FOR COLLABORATION

As I explored in *Effective Virtual Conversations*, there are a minimum of seven skills required for great collaboration: trust, candor, connection, flexibility and adaptability, self-awareness, the ability to work across differences, and relationship management.

Which of these skills are most important for you to develop?

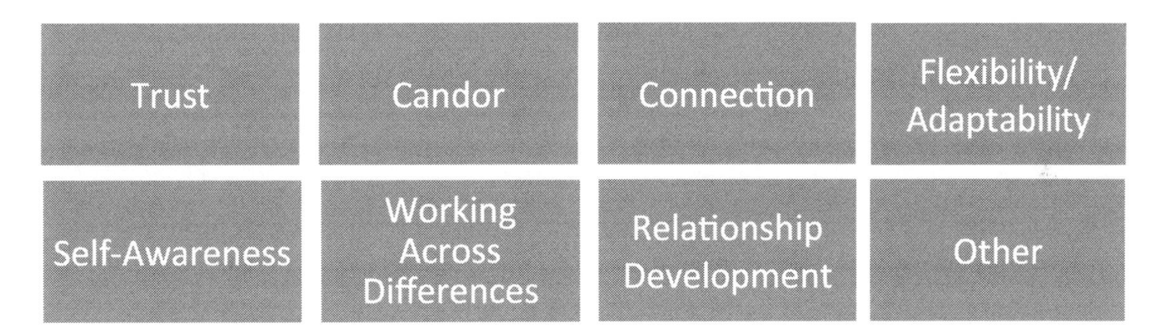

What Makes Collaboration Work—Essential Practices

Even with the best skills, it's important to create habits and practices around collaboration. Some of the more common pieces of advice include:

Communicate and create your alignment. Let people know when you are available. Be clear with what you can and cannot offer.

Respond regularly. Build time into your schedule to maintain and build relationships.

Adjust. Know their style preferences around how they want to communicate and make decisions, and adjust your style accordingly.

Listen! What are they really saying?

Making collaboration intentional. Schedule regular one-on-ones. Make meetings regular, and ensure there are feedback loops.

Bring people together or use streaming where possible.

Note what you bring to the table. Collaboration is about partnership. Partnership requires that we are willing to reduce ego to be in dialogue and relationship with another. What is it that you have to offer a partner?

Be able to see how things work in context with one another.

Check in along the way—bust assumptions. Ask for feedback and adjust.

Linda Stewart indicated that "people and process skills" made up 90% of the collaboration equation; "technology" rated only 10%.[157]

As you consider the current situation, what is the thing that you can help with? What do you want to ask from your partner?

SIX QUESTIONS FOR COLLABORATION

Six questions for you to consider as you enter into any new partnership discussion:

1. What do we both bring to the table as strengths? How are they complementary? Similar?
2. What is important for us individually? How do these values align? How are they similar? How are they different? How do we define these values? Where are they illustrated?
3. What is our shared vision for our work together?
4. What can we count on from each other?
5. What will we do if things go off the rails?
6. When and how will we check in around our progress? Provide feedback to each other?

PHASES OF A PARTNERSHIP

In establishing and maintaining partnerships, it can be useful to make sure to meet regularly and map out the relationship. Let's look at these four phases and the questions you and your partner can be asking along the way.

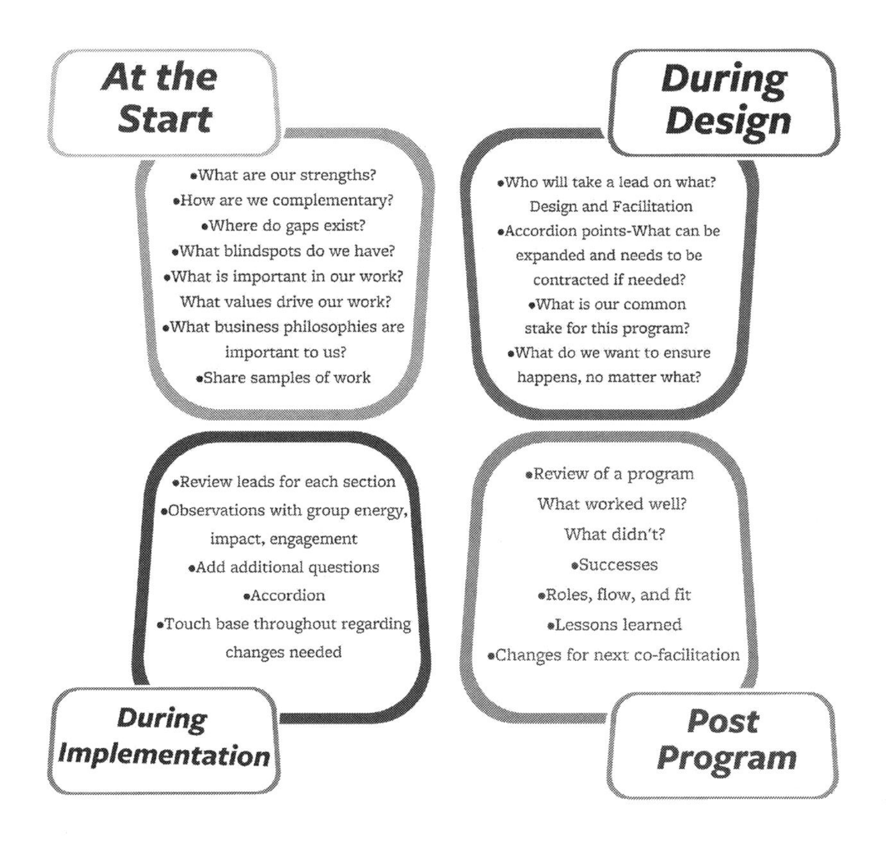

Essential Questions to ask of any partnership:

1. What do we each bring to the partnership?
2. What are the strengths of each person?
3. What are our weaknesses?
4. How are we complementary?
5. What blind spots might our strengths create?
6. How do we compensate?
7. What can we create together that we can't do alone?
8. How do we provide contrast for each other (short-term/long-term, or big picture thinker/granular perspective)?

9. What is our stake in this work?
10. What will success look like?
11. What do I need to do to really be present, and bring my best to this work?
12. What am I committed to, no matter what? What are we committed to, no matter what?

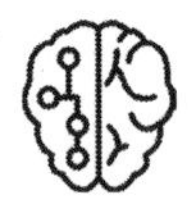

BRAIN TIP: MIRROR NEURONS, VIRTUAL HANDSHAKES, AND BONDING

Pre-pandemic, many assumed that virtual relationships could never be as strong or powerful as in-person relationships. In recent years there have been many studies which have debunked these myths. Consider the work around mirror neurons which posits that, just like a mirror, we are influenced by those around us. The notion of mirror neurons indicates that our brain will "fire" in ways that are similar to those we are in dialogue around. My brain will mimic the things that I am surrounded with. So, if everyone is up, I'll be up. If everyone is low, I'll be low. With this in mind, what is the environment you want to create for your groups?

For those who have wondered if people can't build as strong relationships in the virtual space, a 2013 study found that bonding does happen and can "reach levels present in face-to-face communication," even if it takes longer.

Third, consider how you create digital conditions similar to in-person gestures. A 2014 Harvard study found that "handshaking promotes cooperative deal-making." High fives are an important part of signaling encouragement. Consider how heart and celebration emojis have been used on Zoom calls you have been part of, as well as gestures like "love bombs" or "two thumbs up."

RECONNECTING THE WORKPLACE TIP: NO PERSON IS AN ISLAND

"No person is an island." In reconnecting the workspace, our relationships are a critical part of the equation. Relationships help us thrive in the remote space.

At any given time there are multiple relationships which are focusing on creating, building, or maintaining, internally and externally.

Partnering and collaboration are essential ingredients for helping people thrive and co-create the best solutions for the moment. What opportunities exist to expand your network and impact?

END OF CHAPTER QUESTIONS

- Which relationships need attention?
- What do you need to do to more effectively navigate your relationships?
- Collaboration—Who do you want to collaborate with? Why is this important? What do you want to note about the Collaboration Design Questions?

CHAPTER 11

LEARNING AND THE TALENT CYCLE– DEVELOPING YOUR PEOPLE (TALENT MANAGEMENT)

"The mind is not a vessel to be filled but a fire to be kindled." – Plutarch

Principle: People are the strongest link to any organization. Ongoing learning is absolutely essential in today's workspaces.

Myth: Team development and capacity building will happen naturally.

This chapter explores what is commonly referred to as capacity building, talent management, or developing your team.

In this chapter we will explore:

- Creating a culture of continuous learning
- What is talent management?
- What's different about talent management in the virtual space?
- What do you, as a leader, and team members need to know about learning and training and development?
- What skills are needed for teamwork?
- Tools for different team development
- Team Tool: Checklist of key activities to undertake to boost the capacity of your team
- Developing new team leaders

Other topics related to talent management are covered in greater depth, including coaching and mentoring (Chapter 15), onboarding (Chapter 12) and teamwork skills (Chapter 8).

CREATING A CULTURE OF CONTINUOUS LEARNING

Against the backdrop of VUCA and ongoing change, creating a culture of ongoing learning is essential not only for today but also for what we can't see down the road. Continuous learning helps us be successful today and anticipate what might lie ahead.

Learning occurs individually, as a team, and as an organization. Learning on these three levels is imperative for forward movement.

We know from a 2016 *CultureWizard* report that only 22% of virtual teams actually receive formal support in team development.[158]

In creating an ongoing culture of continuous learning, it can be useful to consider:

- What do people need to excel in teams?
- Psychological safety
- Edmondson's teaming: 3 pillars—curiosity, passion, and empathy
- Practices such as deep learning, deliberative practice
- Chunking

TALENT MANAGEMENT

Team leaders are usually responsible for the entire talent management cycle.

The talent management cycle can be broken down into:

1. Recruitment: identifying and hiring new team members. This may also involve job design.
2. Orientation: the initial days and months of helping people get settled, learn about the corporate culture, and connecting them with others.
3. Onboarding: defined here as the longer process of getting people settled. It is often said that the first 90 days of a new employee are critical.
4. Ongoing training and development.
5. Coaching and mentoring.
6. Performance management.

Subsequent chapters address different parts of the talent management cycle, including onboarding, coaching and mentoring, and performance management.

ATD, the Association for Talent Development, defines *talent management* as "a holistic approach to optimizing human capital, which enables an organization to drive short- and long-term results by building culture, engagement, capability and capacity through integrated talent acquisition, development and deployment processes that are aligned to business goals."[159]

For ATD, talent management is wider than this talent cycle. It also includes succession planning, or who is going to step next into certain roles. This may be wider than leadership roles and also focuses on key team functions:

- Retention: keeping key employees
- Organizational Development
- Rewards and Recognition
- Employee Engagement
- Culture
- Coaching and Mentoring
- Performance Support
- Career Development

In essence, talent management is about creating an enabling environment for your team and focusing on capacity development and strengthening individual team members. It is also about building engagement, capacity, capability, and culture.

WHAT'S DIFFERENT ABOUT VIRTUAL TEAM CAPACITY DEVELOPMENT?

Like many other topics in this book, virtual teams are often "out of sight and out of mind." In most organizations, resources and attention are not dedicated to virtual team development, making it appear to be an overlooked activity. We know that it is critical to build capacity in virtual and remote teams today.

Capacity building for virtual teams needs to occur at three levels:

1. The individual team member
2. The collective team
3. The individual team member and his or her matrix relationships

Key Considerations with Virtual Team Management

Be aware of the local legislation in place. Liaise closely with Human Resources. If they do not know what the local legislation is, you need to find out.

Address performance issues as they emerge. "Out of sight" does not mean "out of mind." Be proactive in keeping an open door. You want to create enough safety for team members to bring issues early on in the process. Chapter 13 takes a deeper dive into performance management and tools you may wish to use.

The Role of the Leader in Capacity Development

As it relates to capacity development, the leader of a virtual team is to:

- Help team members collaborate
- Support and/or lead development opportunities for the individuals of the team or the team itself; this usually means that they need to design and lead the training themselves

When helping team members collaborate so they can do their job better, it may involve creating a culture of collaboration. Josh Bernoff notes that talent management collaboration systems should do two basic things:

1. Help workers find answers to problems
2. Connect them with others capable of helping them[160]

RECRUITMENT: PUTTING YOUR TEAM TOGETHER

As a virtual and remote team leader, we may be involved in building the team. This may start as early as the beginning of the recruitment process, involving identifying the job description and also undertaking the interviews with others in the organization.

When we are looking to add new team members, we want to consider the following:

- What is the role? The job requirements? The major job tasks and responsibilities?
- Consider the essential skills of the job. What are essential and core job requirements? How does the role connect in with others on the team?

- Provide clarity around what is required. What level of autonomy? Self-direction? Innovation? Collaboration with others?
- What do you need to communicate about the team culture?
- As you consider the big picture, what does the team need? Who will complement the team?
- Be aware of the legislation and work practices that are part of the countries you are recruiting for.
- Clarify and be aware of the requirements. Have you personally vetted it yourself? What local level realities need to be taken into account?

Interview Questions

Interviewing itself is an art form. As a team leader, you may be looking for certain characteristics to help virtual team members excel, such as self-direction, the ability to work well with others, or past virtual experience.

Common questions used when hiring virtual and remote team members include:

- What is your experience in working remote or virtually?
- What did you find challenging when working remote? What did you enjoy?
- What helped you be productive when working remote?
- What strategies did you use to build connections with others on the team?
- Tell us about how you communicated while being a member of a virtual or remote team.
- Tell us about a time when you successfully moved a virtual project forward.
- What have you done to work across differences?
- Share a work example which illustrates a time when you were flexible and adaptable.
- What skills and characteristics would you bring to our team?
- What support needs do you have as a professional?
- As a team member/leader, consider this situation: What would you do if you were not able to reach your boss and you had a key issue that you were facing?

Three Questions to Ask about Learning and Development

As a virtual team leader, you are likely to be the one responsible for developing your team. This was the part of the work that I really enjoyed. Here are three questions you will be wanting to consider with learning and developing your team:

1. What do they **want** to learn?
2. What do they **need** to learn?
3. What's **worked** in the past?

There are many different ways to learn, as we explore next in the ecosystem, from microlearning and video-based learning to regular ongoing team development to mentoring and coaching.

THE ECOSYSTEM OF ONLINE LEARNING

In my book, *Effective Virtual Conversations*, I explore a wide range of different types of virtual learning spaces. As illustrated in the Ecosystem of Online Learning,[161] there is a range of different self-directed and peer-directed learning opportunities, from more informal ones, such as coaching, peer learning, and team development, to more formalized learning, such as e-learning, educational processes, and video-based learning.

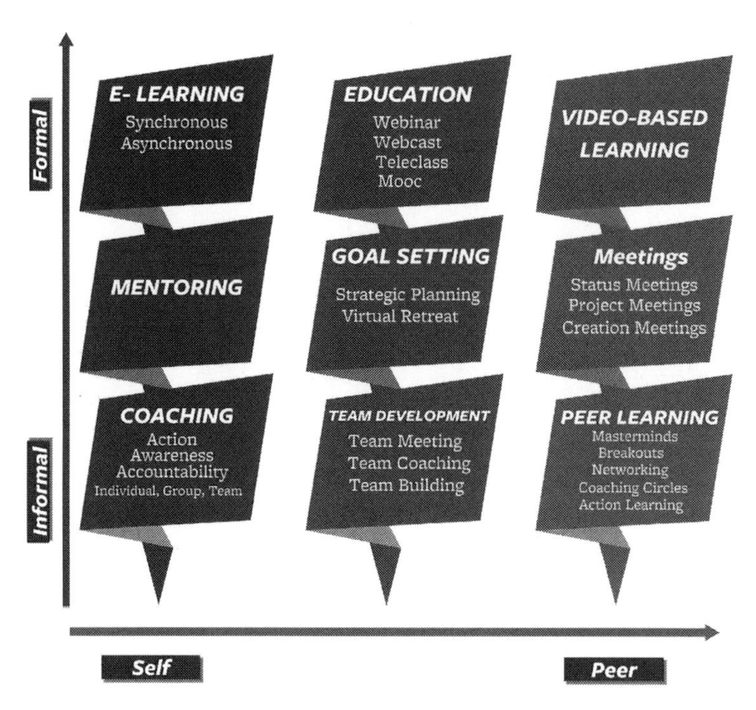

Keep in mind, it's not always about training. In building the capacity of our team, we want to make sure we are the right modality for the right topic. We often decide to throw training at people when we think of learning. In fact, there are many different elements that people can learn from. It could be:

- An in-house lunch and learn
- A virtual learning class
- Microlearning where we are exploring mini-modules
- A MOOC—Massive Open-enrollment Online Course
- An e-learning program
- Something you decide to put on yourself

Is training the right or only way to learn? Maybe someone would learn more from coaching and/or mentoring?

Microlearning in Action

Microlearning, or "short bites of training," can be a great supplement to other types of learning, in particular, a way to sustain or expand the learning to make it stickier. We are operating in a context where learning has significantly changed. With microlearning being shorter bites of learning (typically anywhere from three to ten minutes), there are several benefits:

Just-in-time consumption. Rather than having to block off one day for training, microlearning can be consumed in one sitting.

Opportunity for immediate application. Depending on design, microlearning can be a prompt for immediate application and action.

Expands the training time, to allow for more absorption. Consider the ROCK Learning Model of AGES[162] (Attention, Generation, Emotion, and Spacing), where S stands for spacing or sequencing. Microlearning allows for an expanded series of touchpoints which may support enhanced retention one week to one year later.

Bite size pieces which are easier to digest. Shorter is often better. Continue to think about things in threes: what are the three main points you want to cover in the process?

Seven Microlearning Possibilities

What's possible for you in your work? Consider these seven different ways microlearning is positioned:

1. **Group coaching support.** Many times, group members have content needs which are not appropriate to bring into the mainstream coaching process. Are there some microlearning opportunities to enhance content needs which you or a content expert could provide?

2. **Short emails or newsletter prompts.** Whether it's in text or video, short email prompts can keep things visible and alive. My 90-Day BizSuccess program included three-times-a-week questions or quotes which were sent out to group members as a way to keep the learning—and action—alive!

3. **Breaking down longer training programs into three- to ten-minute bites** which people can take on a daily or weekly basis. What are the mini-modules you could create?

4. **Videos to reinforce learning in the classroom**. For example, if you are meeting with a leadership cohort regularly, how could videos sent to learners or available on an LMS (learning management system), support learning reinforcement and application?

5. **Virtual work sprints.** What could get done in the moment, rather than waiting for longer windows of time to get it done?

6. **Consider developing a stand-alone video series** for some of the work you want to promote. This could be a series of short three- to five-minute videos on a topic you are passionate about.

7. **Repurpose content.** Content can be repurposed. What can you repurpose into a new output? If you have a one-pager, could it become a short demo video? If you have an article, could it become a checklist?

Activity:

- Take 10 minutes to brainstorm or Mind Map your ideas around microlearning.
- As you look at your ideas, what would have the greatest impact?
- What would be the easiest to implement?
- When you are ready, turn to the monthly template which will help you sequence and design your microlearning bites!

WHEN YOU ARE ASKED TO LEAD THE TRAINING YOURSELF

Most remote organizations don't have a head trainer. In deciding what you want to do for training, consider the following:

- How much time will it take?
- How do you connect people with what's important about the topic or training right away?
- What are the outcomes you are aiming towards (this should shape both content and the approach to training)?
- Does this have to be a one-off training, or can it be delivered over time?
- What's the nice to know/need to know, and where to go? Break down content into these three buckets. Need-to-know content gets incorporated. Nice-to-know content can be addressed in future sessions, and where to go gets moved into a directory or other log.

What other questions are really important for you to explore as you consider leading your training?

Most team leaders will come up against the question of "What can I do myself?" and "What do I need to outsource to others?"

Questions to consider with regard to these considerations are:

- What outcomes are you looking for?

- What skills and knowledge about these topics do you have?
- How important is it for you to be part of the conversation as an active participant?
- What additional skills are needed?
- How could a neutral person benefit the conversation?

CONSIDER THESE ELEMENTS TO POWERFUL PROGRAM DESIGN

The modular approach. How can you design something for one setting which can be combined and used for others? Like Lego pieces, the modular approach has things combine and come together.

Scaling training/support around topics, e.g., delegation. What is the short version? Where do people go for more information?

Capacity building and development need to have a focus. We want to make sure that we have a focus on helping team members also grow and learn and pass on their skills. This could involve peer learning and mentoring, as well as peer coaching.

Transferability—don't leave it on the screen. Make sure you provide learners with an opportunity to transfer their learning to their context. How can you transfer new insights onto others in the team? What application opportunities are available?

Provide space for consistent action. Building habits are important in the remote space. One of the more powerful learning experiences my community went through recently was the 21 for 21 Virtual Co-working Sprints. What can you do to create more space for consistent action?

Key skills to sharpen: listening and questions. Where are you listening? Are you listening for the solution? Are you listening for the outcome? Are you asking questions to help the person gain more awareness, or are you asking a question to have people indicate an outcome?

Deep work. What are the habits and practices that will help you with keeping a focus on this?

LEARNING FOR NEW TEAM MEMBERS AND LEADERS

Learning is ongoing, and it's likely that ongoing support will be needed to cultivate new practices and skills. Practices and skills are grounded in beliefs and mindsets—check the text box for these.

Beliefs and Mindsets around Remote and Hybrid Teamwork

We need each other, even if we don't see each other regularly.

Sharing information with each other and working together can make the end product a better outcome.

Coaching and mentoring and capacity development are important for our team.

Learning is ongoing.

We also need to consider these questions: What about learning new skills? How do we help others think for themselves? How can we partake in the work that we do? What else can we pass on to others? What systems will help onboard new team members?

Five key areas team leaders and team members need support around:[163]

1. Dialogue around what changes might be required regarding their new role.
2. Mentoring by someone experienced who can share best practices and their experience in leading virtual teams.
3. Budget to travel out to meet with their team and bring them together on a regular basis. "Out of sight" does not mean "out of mind"; just as we invest in co-located teams, investing in the development of virtual teams is also necessary.
4. Necessary tech support for the team in order to connect effectively, efficiently, and in real-time. This might involve using a combination of WebEx or Zoom for virtual meetings, and portals such as Slack for keeping people connected and sharing documentation/materials on a real-time basis.
5. Regular development opportunities and check ins with their peers and staff to share best practices and also to be able to enhance their skills.

IDEAS FOR JOB SHADOWING WITH A NEW TEAM LEADER OR TEAM MEMBER

- Share what your daily routine is
- Review job description
- Identify/review who you need to go to, to get things done
- Review the systems that help you in your work:
    - Resourcing—how to get things for your team
    - Budgeting—what is needed about budgeting?
    - Relationship building—what key contacts are going to help you? Internally? Externally?

    - Evaluation and impact—what do you want to do to evaluate?
    - Goals—key goals, tracking of goals
- Discuss relationship management—key relationships to get things done, working with your boss, network of professionals that you can tap into
- What impact could you have with others?
- Tracking of goals
- Managing up
- Mentoring—how things are really done in an organization
- What's the possibility for change? How do we support change in the team?
- Meeting management
- Skill transition
- Evaluation

DIFFERENT DEVELOPMENT FORMATS: SPRINTS TO VIRTUAL RETREATS TO GET IT DONE DAYS

Teams and organizations shift incrementally. It's the small steps which add up over time. In the virtual space, a plethora of different development formats exist which can be leveraged for different needs.

From the world of start-ups and small business development, there has been an opportunity for a number of more innovative virtual program ideas to emerge. We are going to explore three here:

- Sprints
- Virtual Retreats
- Get It Done Days

Reminder: *CultureWizard*'s 2016 study found that only 22% of teams had focused on any virtual team development. This is definitely an area team leaders will want to explore. There are many different models we can incorporate into developing our team.

Sprints

Sprints are short bursts to get work done virtually. These might run for minutes, hours, or days. My favorite program in this category is the 21 for 21 Virtual Co-working Sprints, daily 21-minute co-working sessions for a 21-day period of time where people get things done.

Sprints are a fixed period of time during which a project must be completed. Emerging out of the Agile landscape, sprints can now be found in many industries. They are ideal for experimentation, getting things done, and prototyping.

As Jake Knapp writes in his book *Sprint*, "Before the sprint begins, you'll need to have the right challenge and the right team. You'll also need time and space to conduct your sprint."[164]

Whether you are a marketing team or a solopreneur, we can all benefit from the deep focus created in a sprint series.

Ideas for your own team sprint:

- Development of a new special project: for example, building out and prototyping a new product or service
- Completion of projects: for example, writing a report or a book, creating a video, organizing your office

Having completed multiple sprint series as part of the 21 for 21 Virtual Co-working Sprint series, I have continued to hear how powerful it is for participants to get things done in an uninterrupted time block. Many times we premise it on Parkinson's Rule, that tasks expand to the amount of time we give them. For example, if I give myself four weeks to get something completed, it likely will take four weeks. If I give myself five days, I can likely get it completed in that time window.

Leaders might consider building out a development project for your team.

A marketing team might focus on the development of different ideas/pitches for a different product which you can then vote on and move forward with.

How else might you use a sprint?

Virtual Retreats

Just as retreats are a key part of the pause of organizations, so are virtual retreats. Whether we work face-to-face or virtual, we can all benefit from a brief pause and focus.

In virtual retreats you will want to design with the process in mind. Retreats typically include outcomes such as:

- Get to know the team
- Strengthen our skills in the areas of having courageous conversations, offering feedback, delegation, or other
- Develop a workplan for next year
- Explore what team and organizational really looks like

As you think about "Creating a Pause" for your team, ask yourself:

- What outcomes are you aiming for?
- What are the key elements for virtual retreats, e.g., team building, pause, getting to know each other, skill development, planning?
- What type of programming components do you want? Think offline work, paired work, breakout work, team time.

- What do you think you might need?
- What are the elements which will move the team forward?
- What is going to be the best blend of virtual retreat time for the focus on team results and relationships?
- What will you do to follow up with this?

Take something that normally would take six hours and iterate it to happen in only 45 minutes. This can include a collective or an individual hack. Several years ago I started planning program hacks, to move from program idea to a rough skeleton in only 45 minutes. Prior to this it took six hours. While the 45-minute version is not a complete version, it does allow for the skeleton of the program.

Get It Done Days

Get It Done Days are longer and focused co-working sessions where people bring a list of their things to do, individually or collectively. It helps people get things checked off their list. It can also be very useful for teams to engage in Get It Done Days as a team. These could include:

- A day to focus on getting project tasks completed
- Addressing key items you have been putting off, such as report writing, administrative tasks
- A day dedicated to planning for the quarter or year (for example, building out your marketing strategy or a program design)

The benefit of Get It Done Days, which may run for two to three hours, is that it is a dedicated time free from distraction for people to focus and get things done.

6 SIX QUESTIONS: TALENT MANAGEMENT

1. As you consider the entire cycle of talent management, what needs attention?
2. What do you need in order to do your best work?
3. Who do you need to do your best work?
4. What is going to be the best way to support you?
5. What is going to help the team and organization excel?
6. What else is important to note about people?

TEAM TOOL:

CAPACITY DEVELOPMENT CHECKLIST

USE THE FOLLOWING TO IDENTIFY THE DIFFERENT CAPACITY DEVELOPMENT OPPORTUNITIES IN YOUR WORK.

THREE THINGS/SKILLS I NEED TO DO MY JOB MORE EFFECTIVELY THIS QUARTER:

1. ____________________
2. ____________________
3. ____________________

OPPORTUNITIES:

- ☐ JOB SHADOWING
- ☐ TRAINING
- ☐ COACHING
- ☐ MENTORING
- ☐ INFORMAL LEARNING
- ☐ ONLINE COURSE
- ☐ MOOC
- ☐ OTHER

PEOPLE IN MY NETWORK	
AREAS IN WHICH I WANT TO GROW	
AREAS IN WHICH I WANT TO SHARE MY IDEAS	
INSIGHTS I HAVE HAD	
FEEDBACK I WANT TO ASK FOR	

I AM MOTIVATED TO GROW AND LEARN	1 ———— 10

©2021 - Jennifer Britton | PlanDoTrack.com | StandOutVirtually.com

BRAIN TIP: PRIMING

Priming is a psychological term which is used to describe the ability to set people up for success. Given the importance of this in talent management and onboarding, consider how you can:

- Shape expectations early on; co-create ways of working
- Model behavior
- Ask questions to let people "percolate" on things
- Create an environment of trust

As Judith Glaser writes, "Priming causes us to think in a different way and changes our mind about how we will approach a task." She continues, "Priming helps us set the stage to achieve great results with others."[165]

Practically, what do you want to do to prime others for a great experience?

RECONNECTING THE WORKSPACE TIP—TALENT MANAGEMENT

Talent management in the remote, hybrid, and virtual space often feels disjointed and not very clear.

In supporting others to do their best work, think about what you want to make more clear in terms of learning opportunities, career pathways, and growth across the entire lifecycle from recruitment to ongoing development opportunities.

It's difficult to communicate our culture in the virtual, remote, and hybrid space. This is one of the key elements which will help people recognize if they want to be part of it. In terms of creating a robust culture, we want to make sure things are visible. This is translated through our brand, our mottos, our mantras, and even our digital icons. Talent management can also be laid out visually in terms of different pathways, to make the journey from recruitment to onboarding to new employee and seasoned employee. Consider how you can also make your learning process more visual—how training, coaching, and mentoring all connect.

What are the things which need more visibility? When would people benefit by coming together under one roof (where possible), and what are the best elements done in person and virtually?

END OF CHAPTER QUESTIONS

- Which parts of the talent management cycle are important to note?
- Which parts of the Virtual Ecosystem of Learning are you operating within?
- What could you do to incorporate a sprint, Get It Done Day, or virtual retreat?
- What is important to note about the employee journey from recruitment to leadership or mentor?

CHAPTER 12

ONBOARDING FOR NEW VIRTUAL TEAM MEMBERS AND LEADERS

"In determining 'the right people,' the good-to-great companies placed greater weight on character attributes than on specific educational background, practical skills, specialized knowledge, or work experience."[166]
– Jim Collins

Principle: Set people up for success.

Myth: Will you sink or swim? New roles in the virtual space don't have to be a one-upmanship or survival of the fittest. An old mindset to leadership onboarding in many companies was "Who will sink and who will swim?"

In the remote space there is a tremendous amount of learning on the job and need for initiative. The more effort we put into supporting team members during the first few months of a team member's role, as well as their ongoing evolution, the more payoff we may see.

The first 90 days of a leader's experience has been noted as being critical for success. In a virtual team, this holds true for all team members. As we saw in the last chapter, the cycle of talent management encompasses recruitment to orientation to onboarding (the first 90 days), to regular team development support.

This chapter explores the front end of the talent management cycle and key activities of the often overlooked topic of onboarding, including:

- Recruiting for a good fit
- Building your "super team"
- Essential elements for the first 90 days for team leaders and team members
- Exploring stretch zones and assumptions
- Building capability to help your new team members
- Three essential skills: decision making, boundaries, and delegation
- Introductory team activities
- Brain Tip: Mental Models

This chapter's principle is, **Set People up for Success.** The start of any process is a critical time for laying the foundation for success. In many helping practices such as therapy and coaching, the notion of "fit" continues to be identified as an enabling, and essential, factor for success. It's less about the skills and more about the intangible relationships. As you move forward with your work, what are the things people need in order to be set up for success?

We will explore one of the most critical time windows for a team's success—the first 90 days. In fact, for some project teams, that process may be their entire lifecycle.

This chapter started out with a quote from Jim Collins, who studied companies that went from "good to great," sustaining their company performance through the ups and downs of many turbulent economic and political eras. In that research, Collins identified a number of factors which lead to sustained greatness, what is commonly referenced as, "you need to get the right people, on the right bus, in the right seat." As I wrote back in 2007:

Your team is your ally in the virtual and remote world.
Without being able to travel, your reach as a leader extends through your people.
The team's reach is through peers.

This chapter and Chapter 11 explore the talent management cycle. From recruitment to onboarding, orientation, and ongoing support and feedback, we can create a "super team." This chapter explores many of those facets.

The lifespan of teams has shifted dramatically from 1997 to 2007 to 2017. Think about the speed and churn of leaders and their teams in the last six to twelve months. With that in mind, it can be useful to think about things in a systems approach.

RECRUITMENT: GETTING THE RIGHT PEOPLE ON THE RIGHT BUS IN THE RIGHT SEAT

A significant part of the first 15 years of my career was about recruitment. During those years I led hundreds of interviews with national and international staff in the countries I was based in, recruiting for my teams as well as other projects. I was also attached to a special project which looked at the cost of, and reasons for, an early return of global assignments. Simply put, what led to people not being successful in an international assignment?

What I learned from all those hours of conversation was how important the right fit, the right mix of skills, *plus* flexibility and adaptability is. While this chapter is not meant to be a substitute for good recruitment, HR, and legal advice, it is geared to get you thinking about your own team and who you want on it.

Interviewing is probably one of the most important onboarding processes. As I always used to say, "Interviews are an opportunity for the organization/team to get to know the candidates, and the candidates to get to know the team and organization."

If you are a virtual team leader, you may be asked to get involved with recruitment. Consider this to be a first step in onboarding. It sets the tone and context for a person's entire engagement. Here are some of the questions you might consider asking if you are involved in recruiting and interviewing other virtual team leaders and team members. Again, fit is important for both, given the remote nature of the work.

Interviews with virtual team leaders:

- What are the skills you lead from regularly?
- What is the most exciting thing about being a virtual team leader?
- What do you find is the biggest challenge?
- What are the tools you use regularly as a virtual or remote team leader?
- What is the one thing you hear that your team members need?
- What resources do you tap into regularly?
- What are the top three communication tools you need every day?
- What advice do you have for team members?

Once you've found the right candidate and made the offer, it's time to bring those super-team members on board.

BUILDING YOUR "SUPER TEAM"

Teams are the engines for many organizations. Being able to harness the unique talents of a diverse group of professionals is a challenge for many. Refer to these tips for building your team:

1. Consider what experience might be useful. Learning from experience may be just as important as a degree or course taken.
2. Look for complementary skills. We know that teams which are diverse are often more productive and high performing.
3. Consider the training and development needed. What are the training and development needs for each team member? Take a look at the skill sets needed. What are people's capabilities for learning and growth? We operate in a context, fields and industries which didn't exist five or

ten years ago, which are changing the way we operate. Which skills can be taught and grown? Which areas such as flexibility and adaptability are harder to teach?

Getting the Right People on the Right Bus is a big part of the equation. Are they in the right seat as well? Jim Collins' analogy from his 2000 book, *Good to Great*, is just as relevant now as it was when first written. Thinking about the overall composition of the team, as well as their strengths, can help you explore roles.

ONBOARDING AND ORIENTATION

Onboarding is an essential part of the talent management process, which starts from when the job posting is read to recruitment to orientation and the first few days on the job. Often the one- or two-day orientation is confused with onboarding, which can last several months or, optimally, 90 days.

Think back to your current role. What was your first day on the job like? My guess is that there was an impetus for you to do work virtually. It may have been to have the independence to work from anywhere, or because there is not a revenue flow to visit your team.

There are varying reasons people work virtually. From reducing the carbon footprint to reducing office size, having an opportunity to work virtually can be lifechanging. For some it can be empowering working 6:00 a.m. to 3:00 p.m., whereas others enjoy not having the cost of commuting for several hours a day.

Orientation Topics

Topics you will want to include in the immediate orientation are:

1. The key facets of the job: job roles and responsibilities.
2. Job performance expectations: what work is required? What does success look like? What is expected in terms of hours of work, reporting, etc.?
3. Immediate needs around resourcing: who to go to, accessibility (where to go), communication (How to), performance issues (What to do).
4. Shared expectations: how to communicate, leadership, problem identification and solving.
5. Team culture and identity: who the team is and "how things are done here."
6. Key personnel and stakeholders to meet and connect with (internal and external).

I cover the range of these six key orientation topics more in-depth in the *90-Day Guide for Virtual, Remote, and Hybrid Work Success*. A different topic is explored each day over the course of 90 days.

NEW TEAM LEADER DEVELOPMENT

Many teams in today's business context are a mobile, distributed, or remote work force. Whether it's because the talent pool is dispersed or commute times are pressurizing employees, remote work can be as effective or even more so when virtual teams are set up for success. The following six elements are what new virtual teams need in order to thrive:

1. **Clarity regarding reporting relationships**: Who are they to report to on what issues? When is reporting required? If matrix reporting relationships exist, what do they report to whom? What issues need to be co-reported?
2. **Clarity regarding expectations regarding working**: hours, approaches, breaks, how to log and share work, etc.
3. **Technology and ability to connect with others** in the team and across the organization. Working remote can be a lonely endeavor; and just as social time is important for face-to-face teams, so is face-to-face for virtual teams.
4. **Regular check-ins and feedback** may revolve around the questions:
    a) How is it going?
    b) What's working? What's not?
    c) What support do you need?
    d) What are your current priorities?
    e) What resources do you need in order to get the results you want?
5. **Platforms so they can see each other and connect with their team:** This could include regular virtual potlucks where the team actually connects for a meal from each of their locations. It could also include face-to-face time on a quarterly or other regular basis.
6. **Clarity regarding how to flag issues**: what issues to raise and when. Who should they be flagging issues to? When is the team leader available and how?

Six Areas to Focus on during the First 90 Days

There are several core areas to be focusing on in your role during the first 90 days:

1. Understanding your role
2. Getting to know your team
3. Understanding the preferences of your team
4. Knowing your boss(es)—matrix management
5. Developing relationships with stakeholders
6. Getting a lay of the land—identifying a workplan, priorities

Let's take a look at each one of these.

Leadership Focus #1: Understanding Your Role[167]

As a virtual team member, you are likely to wear many hats: point person, relationship builder, go-to expert in that location, trouble shooter, person responsible for the budget, technical point person, relationship builder, project manager, etc. **What would you put on your list of roles?**

It is important to understand your role and the expectations from your different stakeholders—boss, peers, team members, internal and external stakeholders. This is a critical part of settling in and learning during the first 90 days.

Leadership Focus #2: Getting to Know Your Team[168]

As leader of a new team, you may want to ask these questions in individual one-on-ones and/or as a group:

1. What should I know about your work and role?
2. How do you like to be supported, or, what supports do you need?
3. What type of communication do you prefer? (phone/text/email)
4. What should I know about your learning style? (visual/kinesthetic/auditory)
5. Tell me about your work style. (If your team members have done a DiSC, MBTI, or other, get them to talk about this.)
6. What are your key priorities right now? What support do you need with these?
7. What's challenging about your role?
8. How does your role interface with others?
9. What do you enjoy about your work right now?
10. What works well with the team right now?
11. What hasn't worked so well in the past? (Be aware of levels of trust and team history when asking this one.)
12. What expectations do you have of me? (and share your expectations of them with them)
13. What would you like this team to be known as?

Leadership Focus #3: Understanding the Preferences of Your Team[169,170]

As a peer or leader, knowing the preferences of you team members is critical. It is likely you will be working through them, so being intentional in getting to know them is key.

Getting to know your team members is one of the most important things you will do in the first 90 days of a new team leadership role.

Understanding each team member's role and their preferences are key. Find out from each team member:

1. **What is their role all about?** How does it connect with others? What priorities do they have? What are the key crunch points of the year for theme?
2. **What are their key goals**, according to their role, and also the bigger picture?
3. **What are their preferences in terms of communication?** Some team members may prefer face-to-face conversations versus quick email replies. What are their expectations around your communication? What are your expectations around hearing from them?
4. **What do they find rewarding?** Each of us is motivated by different factors. How does this person want to be acknowledged or rewarded when they do a great job? Do they prefer public recognition in a meeting, or a mention in an email?
5. **What are their expectations of you?**
6. **What are your expectations of them?**[171]

Leadership Focus #4: Knowing Your Bosses[172]

Notice the plural here! As a virtual team leader or member, you may be reporting to a number of teams, e.g., one geographic, one functional.

As a team leader, you make your work much easier based on a strong relationship with your team, as well as with your boss. Each organizational culture will differ, and it is likely that you will need to interface regularly with your boss, even if you are on a virtual team, or in a different location than they are.

Questions to Consider:

1. What are the key priorities for your boss?
2. What do they prefer in terms of communication, information, quality, etc.?
3. What are their expectations of you? Of the team?
4. What do they see as key priorities for the team? For you?
5. What is their perspective on strategic issues facing the team? What are their priorities? How does your work, and the team's work, support their success? How does your leader want to be communicated to?
6. What information is most important for them to have, and *when*?

Leadership Focus #5: Developing Relationships with Your Stakeholders

Virtual team leaders and team members will interface with a wide variety of stakeholders and partners, both internal and external to the organization. Refer to Chapter 10 on relationship management for this.

Leadership Focus #6: Getting a Lay of the Land

In this final leadership focus area, it's important to identify the workplan, the priorities, and the systems through which you will get work done.

There can also be a number of new learning opportunities for both leaders and team members.

Stretch Zones for New Virtual Leaders

While ongoing learning is the norm, the following are ten common stretch areas for new virtual team leaders. What forums have you created for new leaders to ask these types of questions?

- How often should I stay connected?
- What can I do to learn more?
- How do I balance my workload?
- How do I support others who might be more of an expert than I am?
- Do you ever get comfortable with "not knowing"?
- What's important for me to know about virtual team leadership?
- What advice would you have for new team leaders?
- Managing up and down: What do I report up? What do I report down?
- How do I get to know and support my team members if I don't get to see them, or work with them?
- What can I do to ensure I continue to move my career forward?

Five Leadership Assumptions for New Team Leaders to Reframe[173]

Assumptions are the "kiss of death," especially in the virtual space. The following are important to examine and reframe into something more positive.

Here are five immediate assumptions which may be challenging for new team leaders and team members in the virtual space:

Assumption #1: Everyone needs and wants the same type of support.

Every team member will have their own strengths, styles, and personalities. Take time at the start of an engagement to learn who each person is and how they want to be supported. Areas such as how they want to be communicated with can vary tremendously from team member to team member.

If we don't bust this assumption, chances are that many of your team members will not connect with you. Trying to support everyone in the same fashion often leads to lower levels of engagement and trust.

Assumption #2: I need to do everything myself.

When you are a leader, delegation is key. It's important that we empower the team to do their work. Micro-monitoring is more important than micromanaging. While delegation is often considered an art form, mastering this skill early on can make the difference between flow and overwhelm.

Assumption #3: I always need to say yes.

From boundaries with your time to learning to say "no" (diplomatically to your boss and team), creating boundaries is a key skill for team leaders. When you lead from the middle—supporting those above and below you—being able to say "no" tactfully is an important skill to master, as are the skills of negotiation. If it's impossible to say "no" you may need to say, "I can do this, but it will mean I can't do that. What do you recommend as the primary focus?"

What might *you* need to say "no" to?

Assumption #4: This is going to be easy.

As leaders, we often need to make the hard calls and difficult decisions. Some naively step into leadership thinking that it will be a bigger paycheck and similar work. Not quite. While things won't always be easy, the learning curve does slow down. Your first leadership role may present you with the steepest learning curve. For those who enjoy challenge, successive leadership roles will usually provide additional challenge in different ways.

Rather than feeling like leadership is going to be hard, what's another perspective you can adopt?

Assumption #5: You are going to be just like the last person who filled the role.

Leaders can benefit from busting this assumption early on. As a new leader, you'll be bringing different skills, experiences, and a different personality to the table. Make your worklife easier by not putting additional pressure on yourself, trying to be just like the "other leader." Reminding your team and your boss and stakeholders about your unique strengths can create a win-win for all involved.

What other assumptions do you notice you hold around leadership? What needs to be reframed?

IMMEDIATE TRAINING AND CONTENT NEEDS FOR TEAM LEADERS AND TEAM MEMBERS

Ongoing learning is the norm for most virtual leaders. Take advantage of opportunities to develop leadership and teamwork skills. Training programs you may want to explore could include:

- Collaboration
- Emotional intelligence
- Virtual team leadership

Many of these are covered in subsequent chapters.

Other questions team members and leaders may be asking at the start are:

- What can I do to build connections across my team? This may include a variety of approaches including peer circles, buddies, or other informal events. They provide opportunities to build connections across the team. It's not just the team members who want to connect with each other, it may be other teams and stakeholders that you want to connect with.
- Who can help mentor me? Find a mentor who has the experience that you are looking for. Is it a particular set of skills and experiences you can benefit from?
- Where else do I get skills? Keeping skills relevant is critical in today's experience. Look to online courses, as well as other opportunities such as mentoring (formally and informally).

WHAT'S DIFFERENT WITH VIRTUAL TEAMS—TALENT MANAGEMENT AND DEVELOPMENT

As it relates to the virtual space, key differences include:

- The need to equip all team members with skill
- The ability to be able to make decisions "on the fly"
- The level of self-direction and initiative
- The need to focus on creating better balance

Team building capability can take on new meaning as team members take the role of the leader in the formal leader's absence. This is where we shift our attention now.

Developing Team-Building Capability in Our Own Teams

While capacity development is critical in many teams today, it is absolutely essential to high performance in virtual teams, given that people are working independently. In *Effective Virtual Conversations*, I write, "In virtual teams, it is also imperative that we build capability in the skills of new team members."

As a team leader, consider how you can be building capability within your team around:

- Goal setting
- Reporting
- Coaching skills, particularly peer coaching skills
- Feedback
- Business acumen (as appropriate to the work you do)
- Difficult conversations
- Relationship building
- Emotional intelligence

- Conflict management
- Influence

Many remote team members utilize these skills every day. What are you doing to build capacity in all team members in these areas?

Just as onboarding of new team leaders is important, the onboarding of new team members can be just as critical. Some of the areas you will want to focus on in the onboarding process for new team members are:

- Team culture: who are you as a team; agreements (how we do things); values (what is important to us)
- Who to go to: key resource people—other members of the team, internal resources, external stakeholders
- Reporting requirements: budget, resources, status updates
- Team meetings
- Understanding your role
- Key goals, KPIs (Key Performance Indicators) and corporate priorities
- Goal setting (whether you use a One-Page Plan or other framework)
- Feedback and performance management issues

Be sure to clarify expectations around:

- Surfacing important issues
- Availability (when you are on and when you are off)
- Quality and completion of tasks
- Addressing conflict
- Work-life (again, boundaries around when you are on and off)
- Reporting
- Collaboration with others on the team
- Meeting focus
- Communication

What other issues are important for you to brief new team members on?[174]

THREE ESSENTIAL VIRTUAL TEAM MEMBER SKILLS AND TOOL BUCKETS

There are several skills and tools that take on new significance when operating in a virtual or remote world, whether it is 24/7 or across one time zone. The need to empower the team members you are working with is unique to the remote space. Given that they work remote, skills such as decision making, delegation, prioritization, and troubleshooting are needed by all team members.

All team members will want to be equipped with tools in:

A. Decision making and prioritization

B. Creating boundaries

C. Delegation

This section takes a deeper look at skills and tools in these areas.

A. Decision Making

Equipping the team with skills and tools around decision making is critical. They are likely making decisions every day related to their work and the work of the team. There are several tools we can use when making decisions, including:

FIVE WHYS	The Five Whys comes from the Lean Six Sigma world and encourages a deeper dive by asking "Why" around the current situations you experience. Let's look at an example of customers providing poor feedback on a tool: The first time **WHY** is asked uncovers that the tool was late in arriving due to delivery issues. Asking **WHY** it was late for delivery uncovers there was no one there to receive it. Asking **WHY** a third time uncovers that parcels are being delivered to residences by a courier only during the workday. The fourth time **WHY** is asked, the answer is, because that's how we have always done it. This question leads to exploring who else could deliver it, resulting in exploration of other options. When the fifth **WHY** is asked around what's important for customer service and delivery, the company settles on the cheapest option—one that will deliver to residential locations after working hours. As seen in this example, the Five Whys help to uncover more issues, getting to a better root cause of a business problem, challenge, or situation.

ROOT CAUSE FISHBONE	When making a decision, we sometimes don't know why things happen. The Root Cause Fishbone is useful when we want to explore the various factors which impact or lead to a situation or business issue. Created by Kaoru Ishikawa, it helps to identify elements which lead to quality issues and is another way to look at cause and effect. This helps us look at varying factors impacting the bottom line. It is a very visual tool, that looks like a fishbone with different arms extending from the backbone of the fish, representing the causes that lead to an actual effect. Common offshoots include Environment, People, Materials, Method, Machine. Let's look at an example of the challenge of negative customer service. What are the factors that led to this experience? **Arm #1** is Environment, or context. What layers do people need to go through in order to reach out to the customer? What does the website look like? What happens when people call in to get customer service? **Arm #2** is People. We identify which employees are in contact with the customer. What was the experience of the customer/employee interface? **Arm #3** is the Method. What does customer service look like? Is it done online? Is it done face to face? In this part of the fishbone, we want to explore which elements are important. The fishbone diagram gives us a really good idea of how we want to explore the cause and effect, and it can incorporate many different labels, including properties, cost, culture, people, process, policy, platform, and proximity. How might a Fishbone diagram help you unravel a situation?
FORCE FIELD ANALYSIS CRITERIA	Force Field Analysis from Kurt Lewin is another decision-making tool which is often used in program design and development and change. It helps to uncover what are the forces moving things forward (encouraging change) and what are the forces moving things back (blocking change).
1-10 RATING	The 1–10 rating tool encourages scaling. On a scale of 1–10, with 1 being low and 10 being high, where are you on this continuum? This simple scaling can help to quickly identify where people are. The 1–10 rating tool is a quick way to create a baseline.
DOTMOCRACY	This is a tool to visually identify priorities. After listing out all the options (on a flipchart or whiteboard), provide your group 2–3 colored dots and ask them to dot their top 3. This provides a very visual way to explore what priorities are, and stimulates discussion around what decisions are important for the group to explore.
IMPACT/EFFORT	This gets people to consider a 2 x 2 matrix of impact and effort (*Low* to *High*) on both scales. It is useful when identifying and prioritizing different options. For example, if we were to enhance our social media presence, it would take low effort and yield low impact. If we targeted this through ads, it might be higher effort, but also higher yield. This tool provides a visual way to explore options and weigh them.
PRIORITIZATION MATRIX	A prioritization matrix can be created for instances when you need to weigh the costs and the benefits. Similar to impact and effort, this helps us determine what is going to be the best course of action.

POST-IT NOTE PLANNING	Provide each team member with a set of Post-it notes, and ask them to write out key activities, projects, or tasks in their area. On a flipchart or whiteboard, divide the page into quarters with an intersecting horizontal and vertical line. Each quarter represents the quarter of the calendar year when the activity or project is to be completed. Each team member then places their Posts-its in the relevant quarter, grouping any similar tasks. Dialogue then can follow around priorities, who is going to be responsible, and resources required. It may be determined that there are too many activities in each area. This exercise is excellent in providing a meta-view or big-picture view. This can also be explored one quarter at a time.
PROCESS FLOW	Process flow helps us to break down and lay out the exact steps needed to help a team move from A to B. Breaking down the exact steps can be useful in determining what needs to happen, when, and by whom. It can also identify the different decision-making points.
PERFORMANCE TREE	The Performance Tree is shared as a team tool and creates a more collaborative problem-solving and decision-making approach on performance-related issues.
VALUES WORK	Values create an anchor around what is important for us, thereby influencing decisions. Decisions which are grounded in values may be more sustainable.

B. Creating Boundaries

As indicated throughout this book, creating boundaries is an integral part of virtual work. From being pulled to work 24/7 to attend meetings of teams you are part of, to finding conflicts when you are part of multiple teams, setting boundaries is critical. Here's what I wrote more than a decade ago:

> What is the connection between boundaries and balance? Sit back and think about all the things you have to do today. Looking at this list, are there certain tasks you could have said "no" to? What would it be like to delegate or postpone some of these tasks? What are you aware of now?
>
> Setting boundaries is not just about saying no to things. It is about getting clear on your values and what is important to you (in both the short and long term) and making conscious decisions from this place of values. What do you want to say yes to? What are your priorities? What will not serve you in the short or long term? How could clearer boundaries support you? What would clearer boundaries change?[175]

More on the topic of boundaries can be found in Chapter 18: Personal Productivity and Time Management.

FOCUS IN TODAY'S DIGITALLY DISTRACTED WORLD

Keeping focused in today's digitally distracted world is a critical topic for virtual team members. Today's workspace is often called the Attention Economy. Focus is a key issue from a brain perspective and more. In the virtual space it also involves:

- Ensuring we build in periods of disconnection
- Minimizing interruptions
- Moving devices out of the way which might create distraction. For example, it's estimated that we touch our phones 2,617 times a day![176]
- Prioritizing what is important
- Being strategic and regularly asking the question, " What's the big picture?"
- Unplugging and practicing moments of digital detox
- Leveraging the power of the collective—creating peer accountability through buddies and peer partners

What is going to provide you with more focus and less digital distraction?

C. Tips for Delegation

Delegation is critical for virtual team success, yet a lot of team leaders are not confident with handing things over. The same may hold true for one team member delegating to another.

In the spirit of "keeping things simple" when it comes to delegation, keep in mind the Five Ws model. Here's what I have written about it:

What: What do you want to delegate? What are the specifics? What resources do they need to complete this?

Who: Who will you delegate to? Do they have the skills required? What support do they need along the way?

When: What are the major milestones along the way? How will you check in, and when?

Why: Why is this task important? Have you communicated the big picture?

Where: Where does the work need to take place?

How: What are the steps/actions required? How will it be measured? How will you all know it has been successful?

A lot of leaders fall into the trap of not delegating and doing it all themselves. What is the cost of this?

On the flipside, some leaders may over delegate, wondering why things are not done right.

Often, the questions flowing out of the Five Ws have not been taken into account. Perhaps the person being delegated to does not have the skills or resources to do the work, or doesn't have the authority to make it happen. Perhaps they've gotten things done, but there have been no checkpoints, so the actions taken really weren't the ones needed.

6 SIX QUESTIONS A DAY—DELEGATION[177]

1. What tasks/activities/things can you delegate to others?
2. Who on the team would benefit/thrive with this task?
3. What will they need to be successful with this?
4. What other information will be important to share, e.g., resources, success measures, why this task is important, what impact it has on other work, key milestones, others needed to be involved, etc.?
5. When, and how, will you check in on progress?
6. What will you do to capture lessons learned and celebrate completion?

INTRODUCTORY ACTIVITIES—TEAMS

A number of activities are really key in new (and experienced) teams during the introductory phase. During the first phase of team development we want to focus in on:

- Creating connection
- Building trust
- Learning about each other
- Creating ways of working or team agreements on how we want to operate together
- Navigating conflict, surface issues, and each other's expectations
- Exploring and creating common ground
- Making sure to integrate the Six Factors: Shared Vision, Shared Performance Measures, Shared Behavioral Norms, Team Roles, Team Practices, Shared Commitment

Because these are often areas that teams will cycle around, it is useful to revisit them regularly.

Key activities during the introductory phase:

- One-on-one with boss
- Job shadowing with others
- Creating a buddy/partner

- Focusing on these areas with your buddy/partner: Who's who, where to go, key resources, key reporting, team goals, getting things done on the team

What's Different:

With only 22% of virtual teams having benefited from formal team development, this is an open opportunity. Key things to keep in mind are:

- Build in time for team development
- Make it specific
- Be sure to focus on both relationships and results

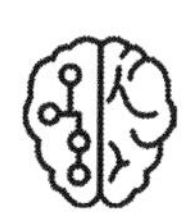

BRAIN TIP: MENTAL MODELS

We learn by building onto what we know already. Key to learning in a volatile context is ensuring that we are activating mental models.

Senge describes mental models as "deeply held internal images of how the world works, images that limit us to familiar ways of thinking and acting. Very often we are not consciously aware of our mental models or the effects they have on our behavior."[178]

In the team context, shared mental models are useful in creating common ground and shared understanding. We can create shared mental models through experience and practice. For example, if a team is struggling with difficult conversations, you may introduce a model such as Kerry Patterson's *Crucial Conversations*, or Kim Scott's *Radical Candor*.

The underbelly of mental models is that they provide us with bias and are grounded in possible assumptions, which, if unexplored, may create bias in how we operate and interface with others.

Creating shared mental models within the virtual teams helps people align their approaches consistently. In an environment of teaming, this is critical for consistency, especially as people may be part of one or more matrix teams.

For example, Kim Scott's *Radical Candor* encourages feedback from a place where you Care Personally and Challenge Directly. Without this type of feedback you will find yourself providing feedback from a place of Obnoxious Aggression (which might sound like being an A-hole), Ruinous Empathy (which is too kind, stepping over the feedback), or perhaps Manipulative Insincerity (making yourself look good at the expense of others).

Keeping things simple as a virtual team is critical. Part of this is priming people for experiences and creating shared mental models. When we have shared mental models, we have a shared approach, which allows us to create together and move forward together.

SETTING UP COVERAGE WHEN YOU TRAVEL OR ARE OFFLINE

In years gone by, team members would spell each other off when they were on holiday, on leave, or out at training. In the virtual space, it's harder to notice a colleague who has gone offline. It is important to consider who will look after your work when you, as a team leader or member, are on leave, or if you have taken on special projects.

Setting up coverage involves letting others know what you do. It may involve systematizing things so that others can step in and do your work. A remote and hybrid work challenge may be that people don't see you in action anymore, and work is more interdependent, so coverage needs to be more intentionally planned.

Virtual job shadowing is easy to do. Here are a few tips to consider:

- Who are the people you can job shadow with? Who would be able to fill your role quickly?
- What information would someone need in order to do your work?
- Where could they find the needed information?
- What systems would benefit in being established so others could step into your work?
- Who can you pass off to when you need to take some time away?

TEAM TOOL: 90-DAY CHECKLIST

Use the following to make sure you have covered some of the key elements of onboarding:

Key items to cover for this staff member are:

1. ______________________________
2. ______________________________
3. ______________________________

Key priorities for their role are:

1. ______________________________
2. ______________________________
3. ______________________________

Key contacts for the role are:

______________, ______________, ______________

My expectations are:

Team culture: who we are (values, mascots)	
Who to go to: key resource people—other members of the team, internal resources, external stakeholders	
Reporting requirements: budget, resources, status updates	
Team meetings	
Understanding your role	
Key goals, KPIs (Key Performance Indicators), and corporate priorities	
Goal setting (whether you use a One-Page Plan or other)	
Feedback and performance management issues	
Surfacing important issues	
Availability (when you are on and when you are off)	
Quality and completion of tasks	
Navigating conflict	
Work-life (again, boundaries around when you are on and off)	
Reporting	
Collaboration with others on the team	
Meeting focus	

RECONNECTING THE WORKSPACE TIP—ONBOARDING

In creating a robust remote and hybrid workspace, onboarding experiences create multiple opportunities for people to learn more about their roles and responsibilities and to meet key contacts from across the organization.

Onboarding should spend time to introduce your unique corporate culture—from mantras and mottos to your unique stories and heroes.

Who can support your new hires? What job shadowing opportunities will support them? What is important to communicate during the first 90 days of the onboarding experience?

For more on this topic, check out our *90-Day Guide to Virtual, Remote, and Hybrid Work Success.*

END OF CHAPTER QUESTIONS

- What are the topics which are important to cover in the onboarding process?
- What tools do you want to explore around decision making?
- What can you do to focus on delegation, focus on boundaries?

CHAPTER 13

PERFORMANCE MANAGEMENT AND FEEDBACK

"The single biggest problem in communication
is the illusion that it has taken place."
– George Bernard Shaw

Principle: Everyone owns performance management and feedback. It's not just a once-a-year activity. It is likely that it may also be a three- or more-way conversation, given that matrix relationships exist.

Myth: Feedback and performance conversations happen only once a year.

This chapter explores the important realm of performance management and feedback. The landscape of performance conversations continues to change rapidly in the business context, with many organizations moving away from a formal annual process to a just-in-time feedback culture. Performance conversations span the range from positive feedback to difficult conversations and courageous conversations. These related topics are covered in this chapter.

Teams exist to get results. In this chapter on performance management, we are going to explore:

- Performance management
- What's different about performance management in the virtual space
- What gets in the way of performance?
- Why performance may not occur

- Common challenges in a virtual team around performance management
- Goal setting
- Getting to root cause around performance
- The REVET model of performance management and feedback
- Tips for cultivating a feedback culture in your team
- Fostering peer-coaching approaches in your team

Feedback needs to be both positive and constructive, and it is very uncommon to hear from virtual, remote, and even hybrid teams who indicate they are lacking in feedback mechanisms.

Vicente Peñarroja, et al., wrote, "How Team Feedback and Team Trust Influence Information Processing and Learning in Virtual Teams: A Moderated Mediation Model." Key outcomes of their study are quoted here:

- . . . how team feedback influences information processing and learning in virtual teams.
- Group information is positively related to team learning in virtual teams.
- The direct effect of team feedback on team learning via group information elaboration is moderated by team trust.[179]

They further note that team feedback is effective to improve group information elaboration and learning in virtual teams when team trust is high.

As with other topics, it is important to stress that peak performance on virtual teams is supported by all team members having tools and know-how around topics of performance. Equipping just the team leader with this knowledge base is not going to support the entire team.

WHAT'S DIFFERENT WITH FEEDBACK IN THE VIRTUAL SPACE?

Many organizations (both in-person and virtual) have been making the move to a regular feedback culture, rather than hosting extravagant once-a-year performance reviews. Given the autonomous nature of much virtual and remote work, regular feedback can be overlooked. Savvy virtual and remote team leaders will know that regular positive and constructive feedback is essential for a high-performing virtual team.

There are three differences we want to keep in mind.

First, you may not be seeing team members regularly. As such, it is important to sift out hearsay (what you have heard) versus observable behaviors (what you have seen).

Second, matrix management is a regular part of virtual work. It is important to explore questions including:

- Who is evaluating and providing feedback and when?
- What does success look like from each leader's perspective?
- What three-way touchpoints are you having with the employee and the supervisors?
- Are there different feedback structures at play in both teams? Different legislative bases?

Third, the peer element also impacts feedback. Peers within a virtual team may be working closely with other peers, and may, in fact, observe the everyday performance activity of their peers. Peers who work together can provide critical feedback. As such, take time to build peer skills in this area as well. Be sure to explore the topic of peer coaching as an approach in Chapter 15 if you are interested.

PERFORMANCE MANAGEMENT AND WHY PERFORMANCE MAY NOT BE OPTIMUM

When we think about performance management, it is likely that the first thing that comes to mind is feedback and formal performance reviews.

Many organizations are now moving to an annual cycle of performance management. Here's how the University of Berkeley defines performance management:

> Performance management is an ongoing process of communication between a supervisor and an employee that occurs throughout the year, in support of accomplishing the strategic objectives of the organization. The communication process includes clarifying expectations, setting objectives, identifying goals, providing feedback, and reviewing results.[180]

There can be a myriad of reasons of why we don't see the performance we want in a team. It can be due to such factors as:

1. Lack of clarity around goals.
2. Lack of specificity around what success will look like.
3. Unclear expectations.
4. Lack of measurement or checkpoints to see how progress is coming.
5. Root cause of performance issues.

What is at the core of your performance challenges? Consider this as we explore the following challenges:

Performance Challenge #1: Developing Clarity around Goals

> Principle for Virtual Teams:
> Make sure that everyone is clear on what the goals are and how they will be measured.

An area that is often overlooked by leaders and team members is getting really clear on goals.

Goals in virtual teams occur on a myriad of levels, including long term and medium term, local-level office goals, regional team goals, and matrix goals. Clarifying goals is an inherent part of performance management and building a performance culture.

Clarity around goals includes:

1. What are the goals that are relevant?
2. How do my goals align with yours?
3. How do my goals support yours?
4. How do they overlap or feed into one another?

Are You Using OKRs or KPIs?

Differences in languaging across industries have become more pronounced in the remote space where we are all together. One difference you may be hearing about as it relates to goals is KPIs (Key Performance Indicators) versus OKRs (Objectives and Key Results).

Here is a quick overview (which could be an entire chapter in itself).

KPIs have been well integrated into the corporate space for several decades. A KPI for a team might be to "Increase sales by 50% in the next year." KPIs are important organizational indicators and often are created on a one-year time horizon.

OKRs are used by organizations including Google and Walmart. OKRs are based on more frequent goals and results. John Doerr's framework to writing good OKRs invites us to complete the following statement:

I will (insert OKR) as measured by (insert Key Result).[181]

What is the appropriate framework for you to be focusing on your goals?

Performance Challenge #2: Specificity around What Success Will Look Like

While many organizations are familiar with SMART goal frameworks, not everyone uses it. The SMART-E goal framework gets granular and very detailed, or specific, around what success will look like. In a virtual team, it is imperative that team members are clear about these specifics, rather than just assuming what success will look like.

Let's take a look at what SMART-E goals are (note my addition of the E).

We want to make sure our goals are:

S—Specific: What specifically do you want to achieve? What will it look like?

M—Measurable: How can you track progress?

A—Achievable: With some stretch, are these achievable?

R—Realistic: Again, with stretch, are these realistic and in range?

T—Timebound: What's the timeframe on this? Next week, end of June, early next year?

E—And most of all, are these goals **Exciting**? If they are not exciting, chances are they might not get done, or may get done only to get them checked off.

Principle: Over-communicate and over-specify your goals.
Get into a habit of doing this as a team. Assumptions occur when this does not happen.

Let's take an example of producing a report. If we sit down to discuss the production of a report with a virtual team member, we will want to get much more specific than saying, "I'd like you to produce a report."

We will first look at the following:

S—Specifics: What is the report on? Key successes this year for the team? Implementation of activities due to the funding received for the project?

Who is it for?

What parts or components should be included? How long is it? What should it include, e.g., photos, videos, case studies?

Will it be print and hard copy?

Once we get granular around the details, we also then want to be specific around M—Measurable.

M—Measurable: What are the measurements which will frame this activity or goal?

We know that it's got to be 60 pages—no more due to page size, no less because that would leave blank spots in the booklet.

A—Achievable: Is this possible?

At this point we want to confirm that this is possible, given time, skills, and resources. Who else might need to be brought into the project for support? What responsibility or authority might be needed so the staff can complete the task?

R—Realistic and/or Relevant: In further refining this goal, it is important to discuss the relevance of this project, or the *Why?* Why is it important for the project to look the way it will? Why is it important to have 60 pages, versus 59 or 61? What is important about capturing success stories? The staff member may now understand that these stories will be beneficial for future funders, as well as staff themselves.

T—Timebound: In looking at our second-to-last category, Timebound, we want to provide benchmarks so that we can check in around progress. While we don't want to micromanage projects, setting checkpoints for quick reviews and updates can provide a space to make sure things are progressing as planned, any resources needed are identified, and questions are answered as needed. It is often easier to set a time at the end of your meeting so you don't have to do a back and forth on email.

Finally, you will want to check in around the **E—Exciting**. How is this project/task/goal exciting? This speaks to motivation and what will help the staff continue to move through the ups and downs of the project. Perhaps the staff member has always wanted to focus on publishing, or writing, or maybe this is a way they see that they can leverage their past experience as a yearbook editor. Ask the team member why the project is important and how they find it exciting.

The SMART-E framework allows us to break down the goals we are working on into more manageable chunks, and it helps us connect with the bigger picture of why goals are important as we look at adding an E (Excitement).

While I have used an example with just one person here, you can use this same framework for breaking down team-based goals as well.

Team Leader Best Practice—Communication

When assigning tasks, consider the Is/Is Not framework before you assign a task, or build in a few minutes to have the team member identify their next steps.

Performance Challenge #3: Unclear Expectations

Unclear expectations are the "kiss of death" in the virtual space. Overcommunicate, and check that everyone's hearing the same message. Working through the SMART-E framework also helps.

Another great tool to further clarify expectations is the Is/Is Not framework. Consider this example: Juan is asked to do a presentation for the next team meeting. After a night of struggling with what his team leader, Sunitra, has asked for, he reaches back by IM to ask to have a quick chat.

One tool they have just been introduced to is the Is/Is Not framework. He asks Sunitra to help him work through what's expected with this upcoming team presentation.

They start off generating what the presentation *is* about:

It is:

- Ten minutes in length
- For the staff members
- Focusing on the best practices learned from his recent fundraiser (three is ideal)
- Addressing three things that did not work

It is not:

- Laborious—no video or extra elements needed
- To replace the upcoming more detailed report which will be generated
- Going to be shared outside of the team (*Whew!* Juan thought it might be recorded and shared with the Board of Directors)

Juan leaves the meeting feeling more confident and thanks Sunitra for her time.

Note how quickly the Is/Is Not framework can be utilized and how it helps with clarifying expectations.

Performance Challenge #4: A Lack of Checkpoints or Feedback Conversations

The fourth performance challenge is the lack of checkpoints or feedback conversations to see how progress is coming. This could be as simple as, "How's it going?" to "What feedback are you seeking?" It is important to be intentional and proactive in building in checkpoints and feedback conversations. Given that "what doesn't get scheduled, doesn't get done," it is important to put it in our calendars on a regular (weekly, biweekly, or monthly basis).

A final area to consider is how goals are being reported on and how the leader(s) and team members are meeting to discuss how progress is coming and what changes may need to be made.

This leads us to our next focus around feedback.

Performance Challenge #5: Getting to Root Cause around Performance

There are a myriad of reasons why performance does not happen. We often create assumptions around why things aren't working. In the virtual space, these can be pronounced because we are not seeing the person in action regularly.

Getting to root cause of issues is critical for virtual, remote, and hybrid team performance. Given that we may not see everyone in action, it is critical to be able to pinpoint performance challenges within the virtual space. Leaders and team members should be able to identify issues quickly.

One tool which is incredibly useful and lends itself to exploration and discussion, is Robert Mager's Performance Tree. This is a step-by-step decision tree which gets people to think through what might be at the root cause around common performance issues.

Let's take a look at the example of Sandra, who is having trouble balancing her work. She has been starting her work day late and is consistently running late for meetings. She has reached out to her team leader, Serge, to have a discussion about this. Serge decides it's a great opportunity to use the Performance Tree tool he heard about in training recently.

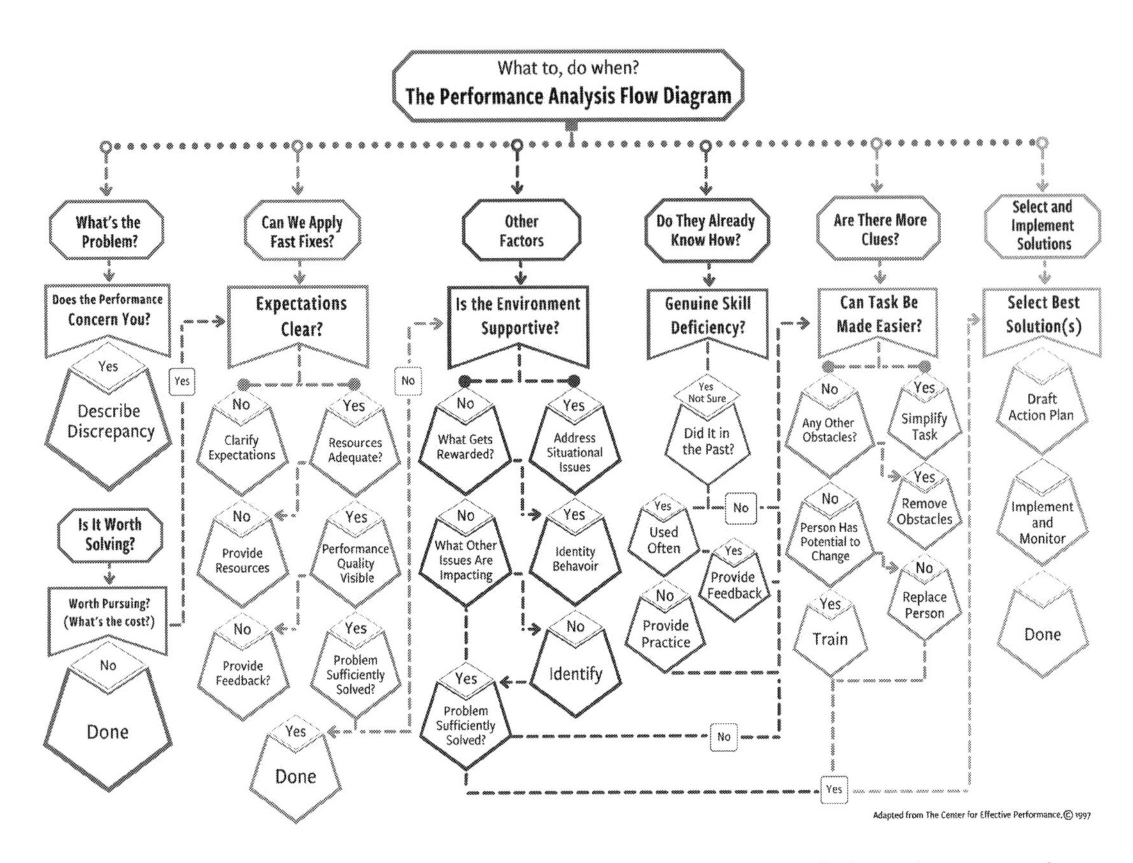

The Performance Tree consists of a series of yes/no questions we can work through to get to the core of an issue. Let's take a look at this:

Serge starts the conversation by asking: Is this issue important enough to be addressed? YES.

The cost of this challenge is that it is leading to a sense of resentment for other team members who are also having to juggle multiple demands. It's also led to the cancellation of a five-figure contract which an external partner did not think could be fulfilled because of the tardiness and lack of follow through.

The first category we want to explore is, **Is this an issue where the performance concerns you?**

Next question: Do we need to pursue it? Absolutely we do because the cost is that this is now holding up other staff members from executing their job.

If it was an issue that's not important to pursue, we can say no and we're done and we close off on a performance discussion.

In Sandra's example, we then want to continue down the tree, so our next question is: **Is there an opportunity to do something quickly or apply what we call fast fixes?**

So, the first line of exploration for Serge and Sandra is, are the expectations clear about what is expected around working hours and balancing personal demands? Are we explicit? And knowing that work starts at 8:30 a.m., it is not the case that expectations have been clarified for everyone on the team. We need to do that. We need to write that out. We need to have one-on-ones. We need to specify that the expectation is that you will be at work at 8:30, ready to start.

Once that's done, then we can see if the behavior changes, and that if we have not made expectations clear, we need to clarify them. If there's no change in performance, we need to continue on down the tree.

So our next line of questioning is, **are there adequate resources available for Sandra to be available at work for 8:30?** Well, perhaps they are getting stuck in accessing resources. Part of their role is that they need to pick something up each and every morning to start their job. Sandra is a hybrid worker, and the in fact that the other office is not staffed until 8:30 it means that Sandra arrives at her own workplace late every day.

So, the resources are not adequate for the person to do the job. Within that case, we need to then provide resources. Maybe we need to loop back to the other team and help that them get that out of the way.

If we do find that resources are adequate and that is not the issue, then we need to go to our next layer, which is asking, **is the performance quality visible?** Do they understand what work looks like at 8:30, at your desk, ready to start work? Do they understand the implications of *not* starting at 8:30?

If we have not really been specific on this, we need to provide feedback. If it is clear, however, that may not be the issue. Hopefully the problem is solved. If it is, we're done, and the person can make the necessary change.

If not, then we need to look into the layer of **the other things that could be at play**. For example, **is the environment supportive?** Very similar to the earlier situation, the environment is not supportive because Sandra has to get something before she can actually show up to work. Together, Serge and Sandra can brainstorm with others who might be able to pick up the item and whose work isn't as interconnected with others. They recognize that John might be able to help out.

So, if that is the case, we need to address a situational factor first. If John can't help, then we may ask the next question, **what's getting rewarded?**

As Serge and Sandra unpack this, they realize that what is actually being rewarded is a lot of "check-box activities"—doing things that are not impacting the bottom line.

As we're going through this process, we're actually dropping down into the next question, which is, **are there other issues that are impacting this situation?** And as we start to uncover this, we are getting quite clear that performance measures were not specified, not only to Sandra, but to everyone else.

As we continue down the tree, we then ask, **is there actually a genuine skill deficiency? Does the person not know how to do it?** Does this person need more information or more training on how they've done it in the past? If so, maybe they've forgotten about it. So we need to see if there's some new training, maybe as a refresher. Perhaps they're not using the skill regularly. If it is this, then we just want to provide feedback and hopefully they'll be able to pick that up.

If there's not a refresher, then we need to ask **is a skill set used?** Often we need to provide more practice. Perhaps they already know how to do it and the deficiency is that, in fact, it's not just about picking up a report, but it's actually completing a report which takes more time. This then leads to some of our final questions beyond whether they already know how.

The next category is**, are there some other ways to help this performance issue be rectified?** So, the next line of questions is, **are there any other obstacles?** If so, let's remove them. Once that is done and performance does not change, we need to ask, **does the person have the potential to change?**

Sometimes in performance issues, especially ones that are chronic, we want to remove the person from the role, as maybe they will not ever change. This is not a quick answer to get to, and would need to be explored in light of the appropriate human resource framework in your organization.

It could be, as you can see from this example with Sandra and Serge, there are so many different reasons why Sandra is not able to get to work or meetings on time. Because Serge can't see what's happening, it's really valuable to work through this series of questions together. Together the conversation is empowering rather than pointing fingers or making assumptions.

What might you use the Performance Tree for?

At the end of the day, we want to select the best solutions. It might involve training, it might involve job shadowing, it might involve changing the job responsibilities, or getting someone else to do it. From there, we would work with the employee to draft an action plan. In essence, that will answer the questions:

1. What are you going to do?
2. By when will you do it?
3. How will I know that you have done it?

Now it is up to the employee to make the change. It is up to the leader to circle back and make sure they have made the change. From there they can implement the change and together be monitoring how that solution is working.

Ultimately, we hope this process of working through the Performance Tree will lead to an agreed course of action where people are satisfied and happy with what has been achieved.

In working through this example, you've had a chance to see the Performance Tree in action. It is an invaluable tool for any performance conversation activity for you.

Think about a current performance issue you are facing on your team. Specify the issue and work down the tree.

Consider, what are the different questions you want to be exploring with your team member?

The beauty of the Performance Tree is that it can be a problem-solving tool which can be collaboratively used by both the leader and the virtual team members to start identifying and solving what the root-cause issues are.

When we don't see each other, many of these issues are implicit, and not clear unless we specify them. They're not visible to others when we can't see them every day.

This tool helps, in a very structured way, to identify what issues are at play with performance.

DEATH OF THE PERFORMANCE REVIEW?

Increasingly, organizations are retooling their performance review process, recognizing that feedback conversations need to happen all year long. In recent years there has been a shift away from form-based performance reviews and assessments to ongoing conversations, which are doing away with the performance review.

Lillian Cunningham references a study done by management research firm CEB that states, "the average manager spends more than 200 hours a year on activities related to performance reviews," (that's the equivalent of 25 business days—nearly a month of work). "When you add up those hours, plus the cost of the performance-management technology itself, CEB estimates that a company of about 10,000 employees spends roughly $35 million a year to conduct reviews."[182]

In the virtual and remote space, it's hard to provide feedback on behaviors, and performance is becoming much more measured on *results*. Key to providing feedback, we want to think about the *What, Why*, and *How*.

One option is to take a strengths-based approach.

A 2017 *workhuman* blog attributes Gallup's State of the American Workplace report with saying that "managers' ongoing performance conversations be:

1. Frequent: When employees have opportunities for improvement, address them immediately so they can apply lessons learned to their current work.
2. Focused: Address progress, successes, and barriers to current work.
3. Future-oriented: Traditional approaches to feedback tend to focus on evaluation and criticism of what employees did wrong—which feels judgmental and punitive."[183]

Performance management in today's context requires ongoing conversation in the team. Refer back to chapters on Essential Conversations to have within the virtual team and the role of Leader as Coach.

In a *Wall Street Journal* article titled, "How Performance Reviews Can Harm Mental Health," Chana Schoenberger references the Neuroleadership Institute, whose researchers found that when employees are given ratings, they go into fight or flight mode—"the same type of 'brain hijack' that occurs when there is an imminent physical threat like a confrontation with a wild animal."[184]

The study also shows that the element of surprise in annual ratings is detrimental to employee happiness and engagement. Half of all workers are surprised at the rating they receive, and of those, 90% are unhappy because they expected a higher rating. Their engagement also drops 23%.

WHAT TYPE OF FEEDBACK ARE WE OFFERING?

In their book, *Thanks for the Feedback: The Science and Art of Receiving Feedback Well*, authors Heen and Stone indicate that there are three reasons why we provide feedback:

1. **Appreciation**—feedback motivates and encourages staff
2. **Coaching**—helps to increase knowledge, skill, capability, growth, or raises feelings in the relationship
3. **Evaluation**—tells you where you stand, aligns expectations, and informs decision making

Think about an upcoming conversation. Why are you providing feedback? Is it to provide appreciation, coaching, or evaluation?

FOUNDATIONS AND ESSENTIALS FOR FEEDBACK

For effective feedback conversations to occur, we need to ensure that there is trust in the relationship. If trust is not there, it's likely that feedback will not be received as intended.

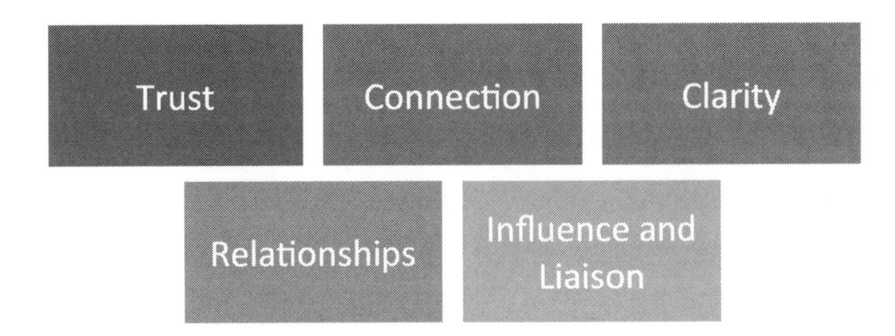

The way we connect is also important. Try to stream where possible, or undertake feedback face to face. Feedback needs to be frequent and current. If I receive feedback weeks after something has occurred, it's not useful. This is particularly true in the rapid workspace of remote and hybrid work where things change every hour or day!

Clarity includes a focus on what is expected. Foundational to building a strong feedback culture are our relationships and the skills of influence, particularly in the remote space where we cannot see each other.

The person providing feedback should also consider how they play the role of liaison, connecting the person receiving feedback to the resources (people or things) they need in order to do a better job.

WHY FEEDBACK?

> "Employees who report receiving recognition and praise within the last seven days show increased productivity, get higher scores from customers, and have better safety records. They're just more engaged at work."[185]
>
> – Tom Rath

Feedback Factoids to Consider

- A Towers Watson study found that "43% of engaged employees receive feedback at least once a week compared to only 18% of employees with low engagement."[186]
- OfficeVibe.com notes "14.9% lower turnover rates in companies that implement regular employee feedback."[187]
- According to business2community.com's infographic about feedback, "65% of employees say they want more feedback."[188]

6 SIX TEAMWORK QUESTIONS: FEEDBACK

1. How does each person prefer to receive feedback?
2. When did you last acknowledge each team member?
3. Around the task or project at hand, what does success look like?
4. What constructive feedback is needed individually?
5. What constructive feedback is needed collectively?
6. What's important to do in preparation for feedback?

Feedback needs may also be culturally shaped. While Canadians may prefer feedback in a more circular way, a German team member may expect that feedback is direct and clear.

There are several things that get in the way of feedback including:

Levels of trust: When trust levels are low, feedback can be viewed in different ways.

Frequency: When feedback is not frequent enough, it is challenging as we may have created new habits around those behaviors or the feedback may no longer be relevant.

Is it hearsay? It's harder to view employees in action, so feedback beyond results achieved may be perceived as hearsay.

Given the virtual nature of teams, feedback is often not provided because it is not scheduled. This topic can be related to tracking and scheduling key activities.

HOW TO PROVIDE BOTH POSITIVE AND CONSTRUCTIVE FEEDBACK

Earlier studies found that managers are uncomfortable with providing feedback. For example, 63% of executives indicated that their biggest challenge to performance management was that "managers lacked courage and the ability to have difficult performance conversations."[189]

Both positive and constructive feedback is important in a virtual team context. Given the sense that we operate in a vacuum, providing both positive and constructive feedback is useful.

An Appreciative or Team-Based Approach to Feedback

We all need feedback, both positive and constructive. Peers sometimes do not get a chance to provide feedback to each other. As a team, you may want to create a pause in a team meeting to share with one or two others:

1. The strengths I see you bring to work are:
2. What I appreciated about your approach/work is:
3. One thing I would like to see more of in our work together is:

Words to Use and to Avoid

> "Never promise more than you can perform."
>
> – Publilius Syrus

As Judith Glaser wrote, "Words create worlds." The way we say things has a tremendous impact. In the remote space, things get amplified. That includes the good and the bad. With that in mind, it is very important to think through *how* you are going to say things. Take a note of these words to avoid and reframe:

INSTEAD OF	USE
But	And
I can't do that	Here's what I can help you with
No way	Here's what's possible
No, I can't because	Sure, as soon as . . .
No, I can't because	Yes, right after . . .
You didn't do this right	Here's how to do this
You're confusing me	I'm confused
I don't know	I'll find out
You should have	Here's what to do next time
I can't	What I can do is
You never	This is often
This is done okay, **but**	This is done okay, **and**
What's your problem?	What's going on? *Or* Tell me . . .

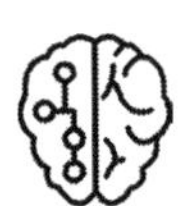

BRAIN TIP: HOW DOES FEEDBACK TRIGGER US?

Feedback is received by everyone in different ways. Feedback has the potential to significantly impact us, and will be seen through the lens of how we see the world. One interesting model to explore is David Rock's SCARF model.

Consider, how feedback triggers us in terms of our own needs as it relates to:

- **S**tatus
- **C**ertainty
- **A**utonomy

- **R**elatedness
- **F**airness

What do you notice about how you give feedback? Is it specific, short, in the moment? Does it need to be integrated with other conversations? What can you do to create regular and ongoing conversation touchpoints?

Focus feedback to the most important items. Ask yourself, what's urgent and important? What's the priority?

As you go to prepare for feedback, ask yourself,

- When are we having the feedback conversation?
- Are we both clear on the purpose of feedback?
- What will create a good environment for the feedback conversation?
- What feedback is considered valuable by the employee around feedback?
- As the leader, what feedback is important for me to provide?
- What specific examples do I have to share?
- What can I do to remember to follow up?

The REVET Model of Providing Feedback: Preparing for Feedback

A final piece that is critical to this puzzle is to have a common framework and approach for having more regular feedback. Aligned with the notion that teams are supported by shared mental models, teams I work with do find it challenging to have feedback conversations. Over the past few years, I have been sharing the REVET approach to feedback. This is a quick mnemonic which can help guide the conversation in the following five areas.

The REVET Model of Preparing for Feedback:

Roles, projects, and goals—What's important?

Expectations —What is expected?

Value—What does the person value? How do they want to receive feedback?

Examples—Provide specific examples.

Time—When is the most appropriate time to have the conversation?

In preparing for feedback, consider:

R—Roles, projects, and goals

As we start to prepare and lead the performance conversation, consider the person's roles, projects, and goals.

What are the Roles the person inhabits; what projects are they involved with? What are their goals?

Considering these questions helps us to make sure that feedback is relevant for the person.

E—Reflect on performance expectations

Feedback needs to be tied to what is expected of the person's role. What is required by the job?

What are the expectations set about performance? What does success look like? What are the key issues they are focusing on, and most likely value feedback around?

V—Value

What do they value?

Think about the style of the person you are speaking to. Some people value feedback delivered frequently and "off the cuff." Other team members may prefer feedback offered in a structured fashion, or in writing, with some time between receiving the feedback and then having the performance conversation.

If you have not yet thought about feedback, now is the time to do so.

E—Examples

When have you seen this occur? What examples do you have?

Providing specific examples is essential for an effective performance conversation. What have you personally witnessed in the virtual space? Feedback needs to be about observable behaviors and outputs. If you have not seen it, you may not be the right person to provide feedback in that manner. You could facilitate a peer feedback discussion with the person and those who see them every day, one-to-one.

T—Timing

What is the most appropriate time for the conversation? Is it a mid-morning? Evening? Lunchtime conversation? What distractions need to be minimized? What follow-up is needed?

A final consideration is follow-up. When will you follow-up and check in to see what action they have taken, and what you can do to follow-up?

After preparing for the conversation, you want to have the conversation.

GIVE IT WITH COURAGEOUS AND DIFFICULT CONVERSATIONS

As I reflect on the different team engagements I have had, a majority of teams have asked to focus in some way on difficult, or courageous, conversations.

Related to the topic of feedback is the topic of courageous and difficult conversations. Difficult conversations are usually performance related and often fall outside of the normal range of feedback.

Many teams struggle with their ability to have difficult conversations. We may call them candid conversations or courageous conversations. Part of the challenge for virtual teams is that fact that team members may not have enough connection with each other, or they may not feel they have enough connection or high-enough levels of trust to have these important conversations.

In any team there are a number of courageous conversations which need to take place including:

- I'm not happy with my work, my role, my tasks.
- One or more team members are not pulling their weight.
- I don't feel connected to others.
- There are competing priorities—which one do I focus on? If I do A and not B, how will my team leader react?

What are the courageous conversations your team needs to have?

To get some practice as a team, you may want to discuss these situations. Difficult conversations are like a muscle—we need to speak through them. For example, what would you say when:

- Someone drops the ball
- Providing feedback to your boss
- A presentation is not going well

Practice these and provide feedback about how they sounded.

6 SIX TEAMWORK QUESTIONS: DIFFICULT CONVERSATIONS

1. What's very important about this conversation?
2. What makes it difficult?
3. What are the different perspectives at play?
4. What is the common ground between the parties?
5. What outcome do we want?
6. What's important to consider about the other?

Key to having difficult conversations is making sure that you "GIVE IT":

G—Identify what **common ground** you both have.

I—Specify that it's an **important** conversation and clarify what the intent of the conversation is. Is it to resolve an issue, flag an issue?

V—Understand what the other person **values** (is it having discussions that are detailed or quick, pre-planned)?

E—Provide specific **examples**.

I—Discuss what's **important** about the issue.

T—Make sure that the conversation is taking place at the right **time**. Is it free from distractions? You also set a time for follow-up and check in.

It's important to take time to **prepare for the conversation**. In addition to preparing using the REVET model, there are other questions to consider before stepping into a courageous conversation:

1. What's your **intent**? As a result of the conversation, what do you hope will ensue?
2. How does the person **prefer** to receive feedback?
3. How can feedback focus on **observable** actions and not personality?
4. What are your **strengths** in offering feedback? What are theirs?

The answers to these questions will help you prepare for the conversation.

Key to having courageous conversations is practicing having these conversations so that you can see for yourself what is easy and what is challenging.

It can be beneficial to practice with people you usually work with. In practicing having a difficult conversation it may not be the "difficult issue of the moment"; but, going through the movements of having the conversation can provide valuable learning in terms of the other person's style and what they find important.

It's also important to **take time to have the conversation**. What will create a positive environment in which to have the conversation?

What Makes a Courageous Conversation?

Part of the challenge for virtual, remote, and hybrid teams is the fact that team members may not have enough connection with each other, or they may not feel that they have high-enough levels of trust to have these important conversations.

TEAM TOOL: VISUALS FOR DIFFICULT CONVERSATIONS[190]

Here's a short exercise to start working around difficult conversations:

Preparation needed: Create a slide with a range of photos or icons people can select from.

Time needed: 20 to 45 minutes (depending on team size)

Instructions: Show the slide with icons/images people can select from. An example I have used is this photo which I purchased from Adobe Stock[191]

Round #1: Ask people to share (hearing from each person at a time), which photo or icon did they select? What does that represent for them around difficult or courageous conversations?

After you have heard from everyone, ask, "What have you learned about others in hearing about their selection?" Note this down for yourself. Invite people to share if they would like.

Round #2: Ask people to select another icon which represents the stance/approach they would like to take going forward. Again, have them share which icon they selected, and have them share one practical thing they will do/have conversation around.

This is a high-trust exercise and it takes time to have the conversation. Ensure that you allocate enough time, and invite people to share at the level they feel comfortable.

In closing, consider courageous conversations in your team. What are they? What does the team need to have these more regularly? What frameworks are you using as a team to create a common language and approach?

RECONNECTING THE WORKSPACE TIP—MAKING THINGS VISIBLE

Managing performance in the virtual, remote, and hybrid space requires that we are even more explicit about observable behaviors. What can we make visible? What do we need to clarify? What is important to demonstrate? Feedback needs to be ongoing and delivered in different ways—verbally, written, and even visually.

Consider the results and feedback frameworks which will support ongoing communication, feedback, and growth.

END OF CHAPTER QUESTIONS

- What is important to note about performance management?
- Where could you use the Performance Tree?
- What can you do to prepare for feedback? How can REVET help you?
- What difficult conversations are necessary?
- When could you use the GIVE IT Process with the team?

CHAPTER 14

CONFLICT MANAGEMENT

"Nothing kills relationships more surely than issues left unspoken."
– Bob Wall

Principle: Address issues quickly and surely. "Molehills can become mountains." In virtual teams, being proactive around conflict is critical. When conflict is not addressed directly and quickly, issues fester and grow much larger than they need to be. Virtual teams are often more diverse than co-located teams, which often means more diverse perspectives, contexts, and opinions. Open communication is key.

Myth: Conflict is bad. In fact, conflict is often a signal that the team is gelling. Teams get stuck when they do not have common frameworks and shared tools to have a conversation.

This chapter explores the topic of conflict, an inevitable part of the virtual team experience. We will look at:

- The foundations of conflict
- What's different with conflict in virtual teams
- Different approaches to navigating conflict
- Four keys to navigating conflict—naming the elephant in the room
- Tips for working through conflict
- Brain Tip— Amygdala Hijack
- Team Tool

CONFLICT MANAGEMENT

The differences which exist in teams, from personalities to priorities and varying resources and skills, lead to conflict, both overt and covert. In fact, conflict is part of the healthy development of teams. What is not always healthy is *how* we address it.

Navigating Conflict

"Our ability to work through differences and conflict is a key skill for leaders and team members. What we know from research about teams is that complementary skill sets make a team strong."[192] Across a team it is likely we have different styles and values, shaping how we interrelate and engage. All of these create the potential for conflict. Developing skills in the area of conflict management is critical for team sustainability and functioning.

Conflict is present in many forms, and our ability to navigate conflict can mean the difference between thriving and dysfunction.

Take note of what Fons Trompenaars writes in *Riding the Waves of Innovation*: "When you look more closely at what type of diversity leads to creativity in teams, you find that the invisible, voluntary characteristics dominate. In particular, functional differences in skills, information, creativity, and expertise have been shown to improve performance because they give rise to stimulating debate, and this leads to creativity and improved problem solving. These findings fuel the view that diversity in teams creates a positive environment of constructive conflict—an environment in which ideas synergistically revolve into higher level outcomes than would be achievable in more homogenous teams."[193]

Conflict is a valuable part of team development. Where teams often get stuck is in how to harness conflict in their favor.

COMMON SOURCES OF CONFLICT IN A VIRTUAL TEAM

Conflict in a virtual team can emerge for many reasons, including these eight. Notice which ones are impacting your situation.

Information: Conflict can emerge around information when it is inadequate, is not detailed enough, has different bases of understanding, or lacks context.

Assumptions: Assumptions easily emerge due to different cultures, priorities, and contexts. When unexplored, they have the potential to create conflict.

Misunderstandings: Misunderstandings are possible due to context, culture, and language.

Resources: Availability, who has access, and amount of resources can cause conflict.

Conflicting priorities: This is a really important one to explore as a team. Whose work takes precedence when you are part of matrix relationships (i.e., you have a local supervisor and are part of a local team, but you also connect into a global team)?

Culture: Returning to the studies around culture, we know that different nationalities embrace culture in different ways. Some cultures embrace conflict, and others avoid it at all costs. For example, in Canada, we are more likely to avoid conflict than our American neighbors who are more likely to address conflict head on.

Perspectives: Multiple perspectives abound in remote work. Sometimes conflict is caused by different perspectives around an issue.

Lack of context: A lack of context or different bases of understanding can also lead to conflict. In essence, I can't see your context, and you can't see mine. Communicating regularly and sharing key points of information is critical in mitigating these types of conflict.

What do you notice about the sources of conflict in your team?

Principle: Address Issues Quickly and Surely

Virtual leaders lose the respect and trust of team members when issues are not addressed quickly and surely.

In getting the most out of the limited time you may have together as a remote team, it's important for leaders to keep a firm hand on process. Common issues which are easy to let slide include:

- Lateness/tardiness at meetings
- Gossip
- Lack of preparation
- Lack of follow-through
- Not sharing information with others
- Poor/sloppy attention to details
- Distraction during meetings
- Not flagging issues early enough, potentially leading to issues snowballing and impacting others
- Inappropriate behavior or comments
- Derogatory statements made about gender, religion, race, age, or other factors

A major challenge in working with a virtual team is the different legislation enshrined in national laws. For example, in the Caribbean, I might be given a "call name" such as "thick" or "chubby," appropriate in one cultural context, but completely inappropriate and against the legislation of my home country. As a team you will want to co-create shared agreements about **how** you, as a team, want to talk with, and operate with, each other. It is important to specify what behaviors are appropriate and inappropriate.

It is important to address all of these issues quickly, and/or create shared agreements as a team as to how they will address these.

This returns us back to the important component of co-creating expectations and revisiting them regularly to ensure that everyone is operating along the same lines.

Questions to consider:

- What conflicts exist on the team right now? What is at the heart of it (resources, priorities, information, trust, etc.)?
- How do team members react to conflict?
- What shared processes or models do you have for addressing conflicts?
- What is important to address within the team right now?
- What are next steps?

IN CONFLICT: WHEN ADDRESSING ISSUES OF IMPORTANCE OR LET THE PPT SLIP

One of the more challenging issues for teams is *how* to raise issues related to conflict. A quick reminder and frame around this is to remember the "PPT SLIP," or, in other words,

1. Be **prepared**: Think through implications, context, and how things may be perceived as equitable or not.
2. Consider any **policies or procedures** which may be contextual: For example, if a performance issue is being flagged, what needs to be communicated or documented? In a virtual or remote team, there may be different legislation which needs to be followed for each team member, given their location. Have you consulted the relevant persons (HR, talent management) to find out what the specific legislation, policies, and procedures are governing each staff member?
3. Make sure it is the right **time** to have the conversation: Is it private? Free from distractions?
4. Talk to **specifics.** In any performance conversation, we want to make sure we are talking to observable behaviors, not personalities. Avoid hearsay.
5. **Listen**. Do not interrupt. Listen for what the person is saying. Are you listening for what you are going to say next, or what the person is really saying?
6. Ask for their **interpretation**. To reduce defensiveness, ask the other person what they notice about the situation and their role in it. They may already be well aware of the issue.
7. **Problem solve** together and create an action plan of next steps. These next steps should be SMART-E:

   Specific: What are they committing to do exactly? What will this look like?

   Measurable: How will it be measured? What will success look like?

   Achievable: What resources does the person need?

Relevant: Is this relevant to the context, the situation?

Timebound: When will you check in with this?

Exciting: What is important about this for motivation?

Conflict needs to be addressed swiftly and firmly, especially when legislation is at play or when it is related to health and safety.

Sources of Conflict in Matrix Management[194]

A specialized type of conflict which exists in remote teams is conflict related to matrix management. The additional layer of membership in multiple teams creates the unique potential for conflict.

As I wrote in Teams365 #601, matrix teams are commonplace in the virtual, remote, and hybrid space. With that, it is important to explore where conflict may emerge. This could include:

- Conflict between local-level priorities and global or project priorities
- Conflict between direction and style of local leader and matrix leader
- Conflict due to styles in general
- Potential conflict on multiple levels around communication styles—direct versus indirect communication
- Conflict created by working across multiple time zones, which can impact meeting times and perceived favoritism
- Conflict around resourcing (perceived and real)
- Conflict around team membership—my "local" team and my "project" team
- Conflict around team culture—how things are done on different teams, what's acceptable and what's not

In approaching conflict, it is useful to explore where the conflict is stemming from. Conflict can be due to:

- Goals: Is there conflict over what end results the group is trying to achieve?
- Roles: Is there conflict over who should or can do what?
- Procedures: Is there conflict over the strategies, methods, or tactics used for doing something?
- Relationships: Is there conflict over how people relate to each other?
- Limits: Is there conflict over what is or isn't possible and what level of power the group has?
- Timing: Is there conflict over when something will be achieved?
- Information: Is there conflict over facts, figures, or data being used?
- Values: Is there conflict over what is right, wrong, fair, ethical, or moral?

What do you notice about the sources of conflict?

WHAT'S DIFFERENT WITH CONFLICT IN A VIRTUAL TEAM

As Michelle LeBaron writes in her online paper, *Culture and conflict*, "Cultures are like underground rivers that run through our lives and relationships, giving us messages that shape our perceptions, attributions, judgments, and ideas of self and other. Though cultures are powerful, they are often unconscious, influencing conflict and attempts to resolve conflict in imperceptible ways."[195]

It's very easy to put culture in a box and put it away in the corner. Unfortunately, this may lead to grievances, or disengagement, and/or people leaving the team. Due to the virtual nature of team relationships, issues can be heightened before they are dealt with.

Conflict is a very culturally influenced topic. From what we consider to be conflict to how we approach it, conflict can be perceived and navigated in different ways.

How to support teams during conflict:

Normalize it. Flag and openly discuss potential sources of conflict and how you want to deal with it.

Help people understand how they naturally approach conflict. Do they compromise, accommodate, compete? We may have natural approaches which may or may not be the best solution, for example, choosing competition when collaboration is needed. It may be an instance when the relationship is more important than the result.

Have a shared approach for dealing with conflict. Conflict can get very emotional. Create a common language and common framework to help provide structure and process around addressing conflict. Different teams may explore models including Susan Scott's Fierce Conversations or Kerry Patterson's Difficult Conversations.

Provide people with the space and tools to work through conflict. It takes time. Prioritize these conversations, dedicate time, and provide support when conflict needs to be addressed.

DIFFERENT STYLES IN APPROACHING CONFLICT

There are different styles which occur when we are faced with conflict. Much of this depends on how important the **relationship** is, and how important the **results** are.

Relationship factors may include any of these:

- Do I need to work with this person long term? If so, I may be more flexible and accommodate or collaborate.
- Do I have a connection with this person?
- Do I trust this person? If not, I may choose to adopt a win-lose approach like competition.
- Do I know this person?

In terms of results, we may be thinking about:

- What is our stake in the outcome (how it will impact us in the long term)?
- How important is getting the end result?

APPROACHES

What is your natural style in navigating conflict? Most conflict models point to these five types of approaches to conflict:

Accommodate: In accommodation, the other party wins, at our loss. When the relationship is important but the results are not, we may choose to accommodate, or let the other party "win" to enable the other party to have their preferred outcome.

Over time, when accommodation is overused, it can lead to resentment. In virtual teams, being aware of different power differentials is important.

Compromise: In compromise, I win some and you win some, but ultimately neither party really wins. Compromise may be important when the outcome or result is important for both of us, as is the relationship.

Over time, this is not a sustainable approach, as compromise may water down end results needed.

Avoid: There are instances where it makes sense to avoid conflict and sweep things under the rug. The challenge and danger with this over time is that the issue can fester, and the small minuscule issue can grow into an elephant. Where it may be appropriate to avoid conflict is when the issue is not important and the relationship is not important. **In avoiding, I lose and you lose.**

This is a very common approach towards conflict in virtual teams, often because teams do not know each other, or trust each other, as much. When trust levels are low, teams may choose to avoid or ignore conflict. In avoidance, the molehills become mountains over time. Issues that could have been addressed quickly, mushroom. At some point they may come to a breaking point where they are much bigger than they should have been.

Collaboration: **In collaboration, I win and you win.** While collaboration takes more time to come to a common ground, it can be the best outcome.

Collaboration takes time and may be the preferred approach when relationships and results are both important. Not every situation warrants collaboration. As Morten Hansen writes in his book, *Collaboration*, "Bad collaboration is worse than no collaboration."[196]

A virtual team will want to be very clear on when collaboration is the best strategy. What are the issues which are important for both relationships and results? Over time, collaboration can build trust and foster better results.

Compete: Finally, we may choose to compete to achieve an important outcome when the results are key and the relationship is not as important. **In competition, I win and you lose.**

When competing, we need to be aware of when it becomes too aggressive.

In the long run, this is not a beneficial strategy as not everyone will not want to move into a win/lose position.

As you consider these five different styles, what are examples of each one, and how would you and others benefit from adopting that approach? When might the approach be beneficial?

For those interested in learning about their own style or supporting team members in this area, one interesting online resource I found is Conflict911.com/resources.

When Conflict Emerges: Naming the Elephant in the Room

Here is what I wrote in Teams365 #511: Four Keys to Navigating Conflict:[197]

In general, what can you do when navigating conflict?

1. **Be proactive and address conflict early on.** While easier said than done, many view navigating conflict as very challenging, in part because issues may have escalated even more than at the start.
2. **Find the common ground.** Finding similar vantage points or even "slivers" where you can see "eye to eye" is a starting point in navigating conflict. These mini-windows are opportunities to open dialogue and mutual problem solving, rather than raising walls.
3. **Recognize that conflict can be a healthy thing when we have the tools to navigate it**. Where cultures do not recognize that conflict is a normal and natural part of human relationships, it may be minimized and swept under the rug. Conflict can also be seen as "abnormal" and "vilified" where something is wrong. What is the culture at your workplace around conflict? How does that help? Hinder?
4. **Invest in your skills in navigating conflict**. Conflict management is not always well modeled in our work places and families. If this has been your case, it can be useful to invest in professional development and/or mentoring so you have more phrases and even a model or process to follow. Where is conflict management well modeled? What tools and resources are people using?

Navigating differences is an important skill set for today's global environment. What actions do you want to take towards building your skills and capacity?

TEAM TOOL: QUESTIONS FOR WORKING THROUGH CONFLICT

Becoming curious about other people's perspective, context, and framework is an essential part of empathy and remote work.

There are many different approaches to working virtually, and it is likely that you will be in partnership with others many times during your work. It is critical that you take time to notice what's important about your end goals and the relationships you are involved in.

At the start, you will want to use some of the following questions to help you frame out your approach to conflict rather than jumping into a particular model or process.

Questions to Consider around Conflict

As team leaders and members, we may experience conflict on a couple of different levels.

As we approach conflict on an **individual** level, it can be useful to consider these questions:

1. In the bigger picture, what is important?
2. What is more important—the relationship or the results?
3. What is really important about the relationship with this person?
4. What is really important about the outcome of this goal?
5. What is the line in the sand you will not cross?
6. What can't you accommodate for, or compromise around?
7. What can you concede to?
8. What is your BATNA? (Best Alternative To a Negotiated Agreement)?
9. What is your walking-away point?

On a **team level**, when they are experiencing conflict, you may want to consider these questions:[198]

1. What are the main perspectives around this issue?
2. What does each perspective have to offer in terms of insights and value?
3. What are the pros and cons of each perspective?
4. Where is there common ground?
5. What is at stake if this issue is not resolved?
6. What is most important around this issue—result or outcome? (A reminder from the previous discussion around approaches that relationships versus results may help us determine what approach we want to take. Do we choose to avoid, compete, collaborate, etc.?)
7. Finally, what is it going to take to resolve this issue?

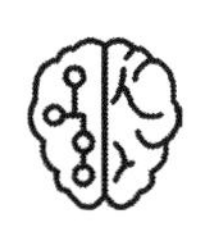

BRAIN TIP: AMYGDALA HIJACK

There is a whole brain science behind conflict, and to take us into this arena, let's look at the concept of the Amygdala Hijack. When we get angry or triggered (as we might in a conflict situation), we experience emotional flooding. This cocktail of neurotransmitters floods our bodies, literally sending our higher brain processes "offline for a short while." Our Amygdala kicks in, encouraging us to fight, flee, or freeze.

Even educators have explored what is possible to support children who get triggered. Here are the results of an interesting project which has incorporated puppets to help children understand what happens when they get triggered.

Puppets are used to help children understand that the "prefrontal cortex—the part of the brain responsible for thinking and executive function—goes offline when kids get angry and their amygdala—the part of the brain responsible for responding to threats and danger—takes over and begins making decisions for them."[199]

Understanding this helps us do better with self-regulation and getting our emotions in check. Rather than trying to "push through," it can help people understand what they may need in order to regain their center, which may mean going for a walk or engaging in some mindfulness practices.

RECONNECTING THE WORKSPACE TIP—CONFLICT

Conflict is a challenging topic in the virtual, remote, and hybrid world, given that there may be different preferences in terms of giving and receiving feedback. Additional challenges can be the sense of not knowing others well enough, or feeling like we don't "see them in action." Finally, in some workspaces there may be a sense that there are no channels available in which to raise issues.

What is your common ground and commitment to addressing and resolving the conflict? This can include asking questions like:

- What's your part of the equation?
- What's important?
- What's the connection to the bigger picture?

As you think about reconnecting the workspace, what is important to note about conflict?

END OF CHAPTER QUESTIONS

As you close out this chapter, consider these questions:

- What are the major/possible sources of conflict on your team?
- What is each team member's natural approach to conflict?
- What is at stake if this is not resolved? What questions should the team consider?
- What approaches, tools, or frameworks do you have as a team to work through conflict?

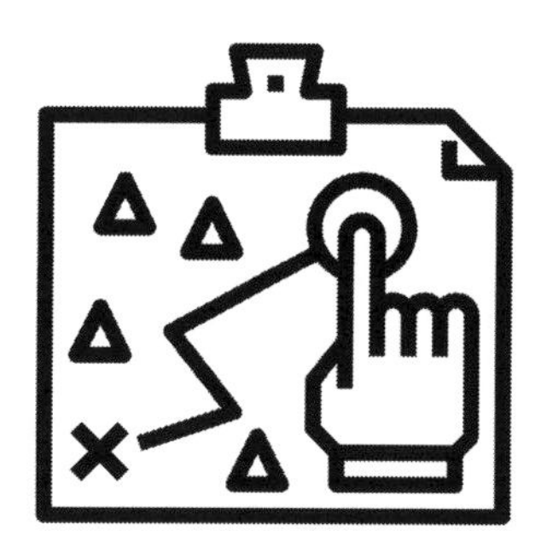

CHAPTER 15
COACHING AND MENTORING

"The mind is not a vessel to be filled, but a fire to be kindled."—Plutarch

Principle: Growth and development occur over time. Growth is a process of change, and coaching is not just a one-off conversation.

Myth: Coaching is just about the results and action. Coaching occurs over the dual axis of Awareness and Action. It can be as important to enhance our awareness about our biases, strengths, assumptions and beliefs, and mindsets, as it is around taking consistent action.

Developing our team and harnessing their capabilities are a key to success. This chapter explores the modalities of coaching and mentoring. Coaching and mentoring skills are essential for both virtual leaders and team members. Whether coaching is being used as a support to develop the entire team as a collective, or individuals in the team, coaching and mentoring play an important role in building **capability**, enhancing **results**, and strengthening **relationships**.

In this chapter we will explore:

- What is coaching?
- What is mentoring?
- How are they different?
- The lifecycle of coaching and mentoring conversations
- In Focus: Coaching
    - The four cornerstones of coaching: Goals, Action, Awareness, and Accountability
    - Fostering a peer coaching environment: building this capability
    - The variety of coaching conversations today

    - Tips for coaching your team
- In Focus: Mentoring
    - Building a mentoring toolkit
    - Questions for a robust conversation
    - Team tool: Mentoring Log

VIRTUAL LEADERS (AND TEAM MEMBERS) AS COACH

For decades, the most effective virtual leaders have known that the road to high performance within a virtual team is to invite and empower their team members. On issues where clear direction is needed, i.e., any corporate outputs, using many of the tools we've explored to facilitate dialogue is key. The leader as coach is not a new idea, but it is taking root in organizations globally. A joint study by the Human Capital Institute and the International Coaching Federation found that 80% of organizations use a coach approach to management and leadership. A 2017 study by the *Financial Times* found that one of the hardest skills to recruit for is the ability to coach and train others.[200] Another top-five skill required was understanding digital impact on businesses.[201] In their 2019 Global Coaching Study, the International Coaching Federation found 71,000 professional coach practitioners, with the number of leaders or managers who are using coaching skills having grown by 46% since 2016, of which approximately 15,900 were leaders as coach.[202]

So What Is Coaching?

The International Coaching Federation defines *coaching* as "partnering with clients in a thought-provoking and creative process that inspires them to maximize their personal and professional potential."[203]

GloboForce's 2017 study found that 93% of managers needed skill development in the area of coaching.[204]

Coaching is grounded in a series of skills, including Goals (covered Chapter 13 on Performance Management and Feedback), Action, Awareness, and Accountability. It's this focus on these four areas that makes it distinct from related disciplines such as training, facilitation, counseling, and organizational development. Another key distinction is the fact that the person being coached is the one who is shaping the process.

The benefits of coaching in the workforce range from enhanced productivity to better balance, stronger relationships, clearer goals, alignment across a team or organization, reduction of the silos that exist and stronger organizational culture. Coaching also provides an important reflective pause for people to stop, reflect, dialogue, and move forward with focus.

Coaching Defined

Coaching is a "conversation with intent." As a modality, is it about supporting the person we are talking to, to take action and/or expand awareness around their roles, work, and self. It's also a conversation grounded in accountability. The next section explores the four areas.

Regardless of the coaching model, foundational coaching philosophies include the following:

- At the heart of coaching is empowerment. Coaching is grounded in the beliefs that the person being coached, or the coachee, is creative, resourceful, and whole. They have the answers within themselves, and coaching provides the pause and process to discover, explore, synthesize, or connect around the answer. Coaching is founded in the philosophy that people are capable of change and have the answers themselves.
- In coaching, the client is the one responsible for shaping and moving the process forward. The client is the one who is at choice to make decisions, taking the action they want in order to support the goals and change they are seeking. The coaching client "drives the bus," sets the flow, and commits to the action they want to take, day to day, and week to week.
- Coaching is a process. It's about supporting change over time. Practically, this means that coaching is not usually a one-off conversation, but rather a series of conversations.

There has been an explosion of different coaching models and approaches. Coaching models connect with a core set of competencies (skills) and are grounded in similar cornerstones.

The coaching competencies, according to the International Coaching Federation, are:

- Demonstrates Ethical Practice
- Embodies a Coaching Mindset
- Establishes and Maintains Agreements
- Cultivates Trust and Safety
- Maintains Presence
- Listens Actively
- Evokes Awareness
- Facilitates Client Growth

In an organizational context, coaching conversations may take place between a team leader and his or her team member, with an entire cross-functional group (i.e., a group of new leaders being developed in the organization), as well as within a team. Whether we are coaching one or many, coaching is coaching.

As coaching is utilized, coaching cultures emerge and evolve. Coaching can be woven into many different types of development initiatives.

THE FOUR CORNERSTONES OF COACHING: GOALS, ACTION, AWARENESS, AND ACCOUNTABILITY

Coaching Cornerstone #1: Goals

Goals are at the heart of the coaching conversation. Coaching is about expediting, accelerating, or reframing a set of results.

A starting point for any coaching conversation is around goals. A = Where are you now? B = Where do you want to go or be around this issue? What are the steps that are going to get you from A to B?

In a virtual or remote team, we often work autonomously or as part of matrix relationships. Clarity around goals and roles can be key. Where things may get off the rails is when team members are focusing on different goals. In a coaching conversation, we may want to help people connect their individual goals to the collective team level.

Goals can be explored from several levels:

- Individual and collective goals
- Local, regional, and global
- 30,000 foot and granular or "in the weeds"
- Aspirational and real
- Short term, medium term, and long term

Earlier in the book, I focused on the SMART-E goal framework.

In addition to supporting your goals by exploring the SMART-E framework, other coaching goal frameworks include John Whitmore's PURE and CLEAR goal frames:

PURE goals are: **P**ositively Stated, **U**nderstood, **R**elevant, and **E**thical.

For example, in service to stakeholders, communities, and customers we support, we will host 15 focus groups during the next 12 months to better understand the changing market needs.

CLEAR goals are: **C**hallenging, **L**egal, **E**thical, **A**greed, and **R**ecorded.

In the virtual space, creating a way where goals can be recorded and shared is paramount when matrix relationships exist.

Making goals visible and simple—The One-Page Plan. As I wrote, in my former world of work as a virtual team leader, I was guided by a 30-page plan. Helping team members wean this down into manageable bite-sized pieces was crucial for success. This is where a One-Page Plan can be useful. Refer back to Chapter 3 for more information.

What's different about the coaching conversation virtually? Coaching conversations have been occurring globally for many decades now. Originating with phone conversations, it has not been uncommon for clients to meet with their coaches over a long period of time. While coaches and clients are embracing streaming technologies, it's not uncommon for coaching conversations to still take place by phone where people enjoy the deep focus, lack of distractions, and enhanced anonymity.

Trust is at the heart of a coaching conversation. Without trust, it's likely that the conversation will remain on a surface level, rather than digging into the "deep waters" of exploration, such as beliefs, assumptions, and mindsets. **Listening** skills are also paramount in coaching. Take some time to boost these and refer to Chapter 6 on Communication.

Given that coaching supports a process of change, there is an understanding that the client will take regular action in between the touchpoints. Pre-work and post-work or coaching assignments create opportunities for people to put ideas into practice.

IN FOCUS: THE COACHING SKILL OF QUESTIONING

Questioning forms the backbone of the coaching conversation. Questions are the mechanism to expand awareness, gain new insights, and create new connections.

Powerful questions usually are short (five to six words in length), and are open-ended (note how many start with *What*). Powerful questions may expand awareness, synthesize ideas, or help connect the dots.

Let's look at these examples:

- Where are you now?
- What's important?
- Where do you want to be?
- What will help you move from A to B?
- What's important about this end result?
- What's going to accelerate things?
- What will success look like?
- What might get in the way?
- What are you committed to doing, no matter what?
- What is it going to take to get there?
- What do you need to say "no" to?
- What learning are you having?

Mike Rother, in his article "Toyota Kata," shares these five questions for managers to use:[205]

1. What is the target condition?
2. What is the actual condition now?

3. What obstacles do you think are preventing you from reaching the target condition? Which one are you addressing now?
4. What is your Next Step? (next PDCA/experiment) What do you expect?
5. When can we go and see what we have learned from taking that step?

Note the variance in language. Key to the coaching process is adjusting the language to have greatest impact with the person being coached.

A final model which can be useful to keep in mind when you go about the coaching process is the GROW Model, created by Alexander, Fine, and Whitmore. GROW stands for:

Goals: What is important?

Reality: Where are you now? Where do you want to be?

Options: What will help you move from A to B?

Wrap-up: What will you do? By when? How will I know?

Coaching for innovation and creativity. Coaching is an important vehicle for innovation and creativity. Exploration of different perspectives around an issue is central to many coaching models, such as the Co-Active Coaching Balance Process.[206]

What's another way of looking at this?

Coaching for innovation and creativity is important when we are motivating teams to be creative.

Alternatively, we may be working with individuals and teams to generate new solutions:

Sometimes, we want to help our team explore different perspectives around an idea to foster a new perspective, a new solution, or new options. A valuable tool to use is the Six Thinking Hats from Edward De Bono. De Bono's Six Thinking Hats has become a famous OD (Organizational Development) tool, getting people to put on different "hats" to explore new perspectives around an issue.

In this activity, group members will explore a different perspective around the topic of discussion, as a way to generate new insights around the topic. Each of the six hats has a different color assigned. Each group will explore the topic through that lens. For example, if a team is looking at making a change to customer service, the red hat would focus on what that change would look like from an emotional level. Instead of creating *dread,* we want to create *fun*. Or, if we explore it from a *control* place, what plans and processes are going to help us get better customer service in place?

Coaching Cornerstones #2 and #3: The Dual Axis of Coaching—Action and Awareness (or Insight)

In introducing the foundations of coaching, it's important to explore the dual axis of coaching: *Action* and *Awareness*. Coaching conversations generally happen across the X and Y axis of **action** and **awareness** or **insight**; and just as in any scatter plot, each team member will have a different focus. some will be more focused on action (getting things done) and others on awareness (learning more about themselves, others, and issues). As we look to exploring awareness, we are helping our team members gain awareness in several key areas which impact their work and relationships that surround them.

Coaching for action usually takes us into the realm of:

- Results
- Goals
- Action
- Enablers—things that will help change or results
- Derailers—thing that will hinder change or results
- Resources
- Strengths and obstacles
- Knowledge
- Performance measures

In contrast, areas we may find we explore when coaching for awareness include:

- Belief systems
- Patterns
- Assumptions (critical for exploration)
- Perspectives (this is hard, I won't understand it)
- Mindset
- Values

In any conversation, we may find ourselves across the spectrum of supporting people to accelerate results or to enhance awareness. Like an X-Y axis, the balance of awareness versus action can vary. Coaching for awareness and action may feel different. Think about the difference of pace and breadth as it relates to action or awareness.

The Iceberg Model. In *PlanDoTrack* and *Coaching Business Builder*, I shared the framework of the Iceberg. The things above the waterline are those that are visible and observable. In a virtual environment, we want to make those things explicit.

It's the things which exist below the waterline—mindsets, habits, perspectives, assumptions, beliefs, and values—which do change results. These shape our behaviors, which then influence our results.

In today's business world, our focus is often on behaviors and impacts but not what's below the waterline. In fact, what's below the waterline may be the things which are misaligned, problematic, or leading to poor results.

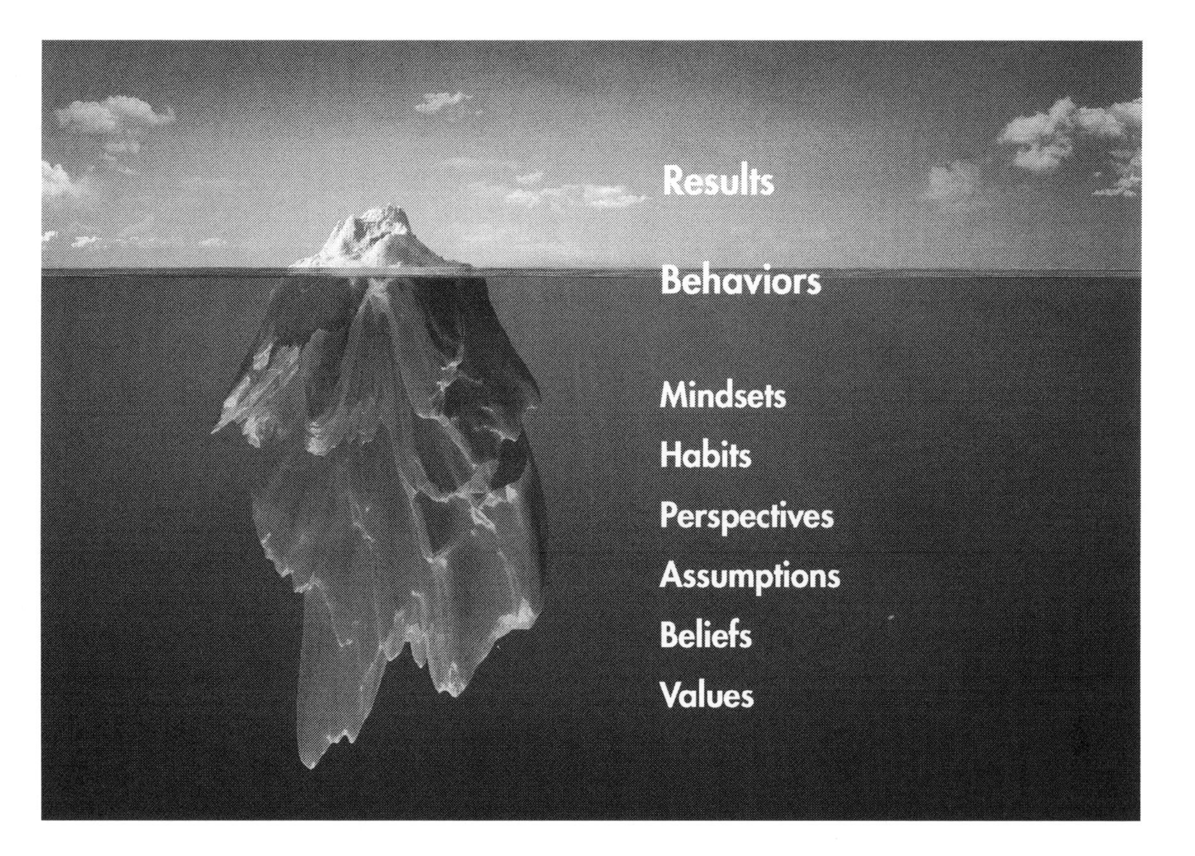

Working with the important metaphor of the iceberg, when coaching for awareness we want to help un-layer such things as:

- Values
- Perspectives
- Beliefs
- Mindsets

It's usually when we get to the "under the waterline" issues that we can start pulling the lever on things that have significant change. What do you notice?

Coaching is conversation tailored for the dialogue, what does the person believe in? What do they value?

I go more in-depth with the Iceberg in *PlanDoTrack*, Section 1.

There are many different coaching models which exist, and most have as a foundation, goals, action, awareness, and accountability. Coaching is not a one-off conversation but a sustained series of conversations.

Coaching Cornerstone #4: Accountability

Accountability is an essential part of virtual team success and the final cornerstone we will explore. Accountability closes the loop of results.

A critical part of the coaching conversation is having dialogue around *What's next?* A major challenge of many organizations today is that people are not clear on what accountability means or what it can look like.

We first need to define *accountability.* What does it look like? What does it sound like?

Questions we might be asking around accountability include:

- Who owns this task?
- What will success look like?
- What does it mean to be accountable?
- How do you want to be held accountable?
- What are your next steps?
- What will you do before we meet again?
- What's going to help you? What's going to hinder you?
- Who will do this? By When? How will I know?

Consider incorporating these tips into your team conversations and meetings this week:

Get specific: Accountability is enhanced when everyone leaves the table with a shared understanding about what next steps are. Make a focused effort to be specific in meetings you attend and lead around who is going to do what, by when, and how this will be tracked. Given the amount of meetings we attend, send a quick follow-up note highlighting key action steps, timelines, and those responsible. This should be brief.

Micro-monitor, not micromanage: At your team meeting this week or during your one-on-one sessions, ask the questions, "What are you focusing on this week? What results are you accountable for this week?" Being aware of what your team members are focusing on helps you to track all that is happening in the team. Note that it is to micro-monitor, not micromanage.

Partner team members together: Consider the idea of creating accountability partners on the team. This involves pairing team members together and having them meet on a weekly or biweekly basis to support each other in checking in around their major tasks and milestones.

Get clear: Make sure everyone is clear about what success looks like with the major tasks and activities being focused on this week. When we aren't clear about the end result, it's hard to be accountable.

Make check-ins a habit: Experiment with starting meetings with a check-in or status update on key activities, and tasks different team members are working on. Again, check-ins should be brief. Avoid the trap of their becoming the entire meeting!

Be curious and helpful: If follow-through is not happening, have a discussion with those involved. Adopt a coach's stance of "curiosity" using questions to help "tease out" or explore what is happening, or why follow-through has stalled. As leaders, we may automatically move to a more punishing approach, shutting people down rather than exploring what's at the root cause.

To boost the culture of accountability within our team, consider the following:

Focus on the end game: What are the goals you are working on? What does success look like?

Ask *What if?* What are the consequences if something is not done? For you? How does it impact the work and results of others? When we don't provide the big picture of how different tasks are connected it can detract from why follow-through is important.

Share the *Why?* Helping people understand the *What if*, along with *Why* these tasks and results are important, also helps to boost accountability. Help team members understand how their activities connect to each other, and to those you support.

Give feedback: We need to provide feedback on what's working, and what's not. Without a feedback loop, team members will be unclear as to how things are progressing.

Offer space for check-ins: We know it's important to check in, but we don't leave time, or create time, to do so. What will it take this week to dedicate time for these activities—providing clarity, making sure the team understands the *What if?* and *Why?* Creating time for feedback?

Offer resources: Finally, decide who needs to be involved and what resources are needed to boost accountability within your team.

What an Accountability Conversation Can Sound Like

Let's listen in to an accountability conversation between Sam, a business owner, and one of his key leaders in this quick one-on-one.

Hey Susan, do you have a couple of minutes to connect?

Sure Sam. Let's grab this area over here.

I just wanted to take a few minutes to find out how it is going with your actions this week.

Okay, I guess.

What is working well?

Well, actually I had an insight which has helped me get clear on the outcomes. The introductions you made also helped me to be more in dialogue with stakeholders.

What's the key learning been for you?

How important it is to build relationships.

What's helped?

Building in time in my schedule.

What else?

Focusing in on what they need. Listening.

Tell me a bit more about listening.

Well, like you have been reminding us, I'm trying to listen more for what they are saying rather than thinking about what I am going to ask them next.

Where else could these listening skills help you?

In my internal relationships.

Who else do you want to build relationships with?

I really need to build relationships with IT, HR, and Ops.

What else?

Well, I could also use some of those same connections to help me with the reports.

What specific help you do need?

Well, I need to learn more about certain areas. I'm not quite clear about it.

What areas?

On different perspectives around the issue. I think if I can frame it out, it will go really fast.

What else?

I think that's about it. This really helped me get clearer.

What are your next steps going to be?

I'm going to reach out to Ned, Olivia, and Max, as well as Dee.

When do you want to check in?

Let's meet again in a week. I should have made some good inroads by then.

How can you transfer these new insights onto others in the team?

I'd be happy to share this in the quarterly learning morning we have planned. I think others could benefit from this.

Notice the flow of the conversation and how Sam uses open-ended questions to open up the dialogue. He leaves time and space for Susan to answer.

Also note Sam's use of the *What else?* questions.

Many coaching models assert that the use of *What else?* questions helps take the conversation deeper. Inherent to these types of one-on-one conversations is that there is enough time for the response, and that trust levels are high, so that the conversation does not feel like a "grilling session." It invites the other person to explore and envision what is possible, while generating more options, and gaining more clarity about what's next.

THE COACHING ARC: UPDATE THE *FROM ONE TO MANY* ARC IN ILLUSTRATION

Note that coaching has a number of steps I call the Coaching Arc in *From One to Many: Best Practices for Team and Group Coaching*. Key steps include:

- Establish the coaching relationship—what is the purpose of our conversation?
- Build trust and rapport—without it, a conversation is unlikely to dip into the deeper waters of coaching.
- Create goals—where are you now and where do you want to go?
- Identify the focus areas which will take you from here to there.
- Engage in the conversations to get support for awareness and action.
- Identify your next steps and what you are committed to.
- Set up your next meeting. Check in to reflect on key learning and identify your next steps.

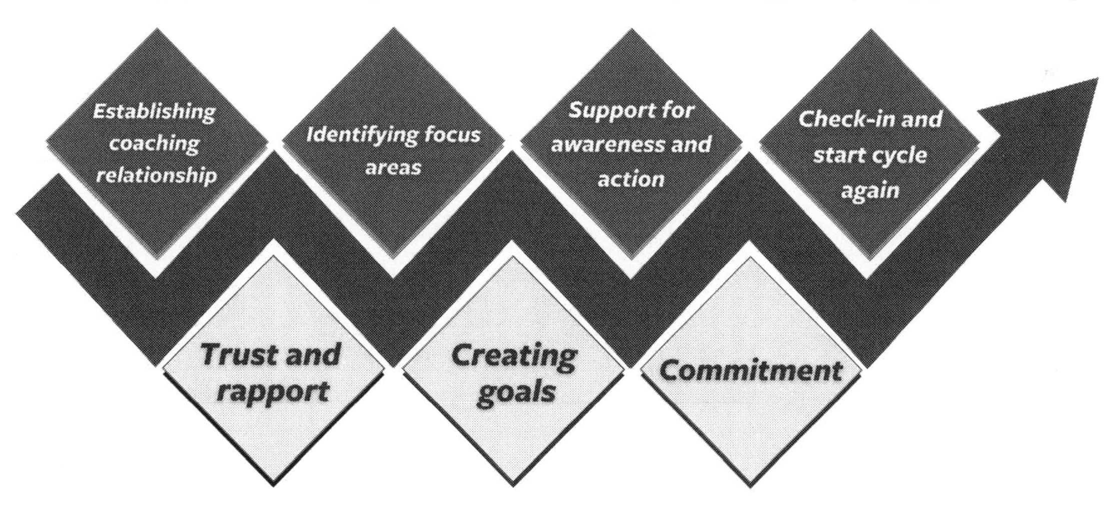

IN FOCUS: QUESTIONING

Support in today's ever changing environment often includes helping people think through what they are experiencing. This is one main benefit of coaching. Core to the coaching process is the use of powerful questions. Questions are often traced back to the ancient days of Greece and the use of questions by Socrates, to elicit deeper learning and insights on the part of the learner. During times of complexity, ambiguity, and uncertainty, helping people explore alternative perspectives, assumptions, and options is important. Central to the coaching process is the use of powerful questions to help the "client" uncover, or unearth, what they know. In general, the most powerful questions:

- Are open-ended and don't just elicit a yes/no answer
- Are short, i.e., five to six words in length
- Start with a *What*

Note that:

How questions put people into process orientation and will get them thinking about what they will do.

Why questions expand connection with vision.

We can ask questions to support ***action***, such as:

- What are your next steps?
- What has worked before?
- What will you do next time to avoid the challenges you faced last time?
- What's going to create momentum?
- What will help accelerate?
- What might get in the way?

We can ask questions to support awareness, such as:

- What beliefs underpin your approach?
- What's another way of exploring that?
- What assumptions are you making?
- What's important?
- What do you want to say no to?
- What could get in the way of success?
- Why?
- Why not?
- What else?

Coaching questions provide an opportunity to explore different perspectives. The value of this approach with individuals is that it taps into what people know, increasing engagement. For teams, it provides a conversation space for the best ideas to be harnessed.

BUILDING COACHING CAPABILITY IN THE VIRTUAL TEAM—PEER COACHING

In recent years, peer coaching has come more into focus. With virtual and remote teams, peer coaching skills are an essential part of the capacity development process. Formal and informal peer coaching opportunities provide a vehicle for coaching development for the team to work on. This might include exploration of these questions:

- What's your current business challenge?
- What do you need more of?
- What is the request you want to make of the team?
- What's the one thing you need support/brainstorming with, with the team?
- What else is important to communicate?

For many years we've asserted that a peer-to-peer conversation can be more impactful than a peer-to-leader conversation. This is backed up by research from Kelly Palmer and David Blake, and Stanford University.[207] Think about your own experience and what impact peers have had on your learning and insights.[208]

Building the Peer Coaching Muscle

Investing time in the development of peer coaching skills is important. The following section will explore several of the core skills you will want to develop. Note that coaching is not advising.

Essential skills for peer coaching include:

- Listening
- Questioning
- Suspending judgment
- Attention: Where are you paying attention?

Here are seven key skills to focus on as peer coaches:[209]

1. **Listening**: We listen at multiple levels in the coaching conversation. Listening is not about what am I going to say next. Rather, listening as a coach puts the emphasis on hearing the client and the context you are in. What do you notice about the pace and pitch of the speaker? What is being said and what is not being said? What is being said between the lines? What do you notice about the words and the tone? What is the energy behind the conversation?

2. **Questioning**: In coaching we want to use questions that are open-ended and are not inviting a yes/no response. In any coaching conversation (peer coaching, team coaching, leader as coach), it is important to use questions that expand **awareness**, prompt a new **perspective**, invite **discovery**, or support **action**. Powerful coaching questions often start

with *What* and are only five to six words in length. We also want to use language that is consistent with, and is impactful for, the person being coached.

3. **Curiosity**: Throughout the coaching process, the person being coached is the expert. This can be a 180-degree shift from our typical process where the leader is the expert. Fostering curiosity and a comfort in "not knowing" or not having all of the answers is important. A central philosophy in coaching is that the client has the answers that they need. The process of coaching will help them distill, clarify, and find focus.

4. **Assumption busting and perspective shifting**: Throughout the coaching conversation, it is likely that you will be exploring and "busting" assumptions as well as shifting perspectives. Helping peer coaches gain skills in this area is important for all kinds of conversations needing to take place in organizations today.

5. **Mirroring**: The skill of mirroring is similar to paraphrasing, but it is reflecting back what you have heard verbatim (word-for-word). In mirroring, it is important to reflect the words back exactly as you heard them. Mirroring often creates new insights for the speaker as they hear themselves in stereo.

6. **Support for goal setting and achievement**: Coaching is grounded in the core goals as set by the person. A starting place for any coaching process is to identify goals and the focus of the conversations. The peer coaching conversation should provide an opportunity to move towards those goals, as well as identify blockages.

7. **Creating accountability supports:** Creating support for accountability is essential. As John Whitmore wrote in his seminal *Coaching for Performance*, accountability is about getting people to specify, "What will you do? By when? and How will I know?" Holding people accountable for taking the action they have identified is foundational to the coaching approach. As peers, we know that accountability plays an even bigger role.

As coaching cultures mature, peer coaching will play an expanded role in expanding the conversation, and impact, of coaching.

20 Peer Coaching Questions:

- What's your biggest challenge right now?
- What's in conflict with each other?
- What's the outcome you want?
- If you were to change one thing, what would that be?
- If you were to recommend one thing, what would that be?
- Who do you need to enroll?
- Why?*
- Why not?*

*When trust levels are low on the team or in the relationship, these questions can be perceived as inflammatory and may put people on the defensive.

- What assumptions are you making?
- What's the one thing you are not thinking about?
- What's the fastest way to resolve this issue?
- What else?
- What perspective are you thinking about this from?
- What would success look like?
- What are the strengths you can lean into?
- What might be in the way?
- What could help?
- What do you need to say no to?
- How would a team approach help with this situation?
- What's possible?

Consider how you as a team want to incorporate coaching conversations in your work. Is it peer coaching, coaching skills development, team coaching, individual coaching, or other?

MENTORING: MAKING IT WORK– MENTORING APPROACHES

Mentoring is often confused with coaching but, in fact, it is different. Mentoring conversations occur when we focus on sharing what we know and what our experience has been. Mentoring used to be seen as pairing a more senior person with a junior person to "pass everything down." Today it is common to see many examples of reverse mentoring. In reverse mentoring everyone benefits; where the more senior person benefits from being mentored by juniors, particularly as it relates to technology and new ways of working.

Mentoring Defined

Mentoring once was considered a process in which younger professionals would benefit from older professionals. In today's VUCA world, both mentors and protégés can benefit from each other. For more experienced leaders, they may learn just as much from someone who is younger, particularly around different ways of working, technology, or latest applications or industry research. This is particularly important, given that the knowledge base is doubling every two years.

Mentoring plays an important role for new virtual team leaders. Research continues to find that more seasoned leaders' help is key to the process. Research continues to focus on the importance of exceptional virtual team leaders as those who are experienced already with mobile and virtual work.

Mentoring has its own lifecycle. Similar to in-person mentoring conversations, virtual mentoring can benefit from having:

- A fixed start and end point
- Core goals that the mentee or protégé (the person being mentored) wants to focus on

- A roadmap of where you want to go
- Regular touchpoints
- Ongoing feedback to know what works and what doesn't within the mentoring conversations

When establishing a mentoring program, consider:

- Official pairing is done based on mentoring requests
- Providing a selection of tools (note the mentoring log or mentoring worksheet)
- Measurement occurs at a macro-level/programmatic

Phases of the Mentoring Roadmap:

Just as in coaching, there are a number of key steps of the mentoring conversation.

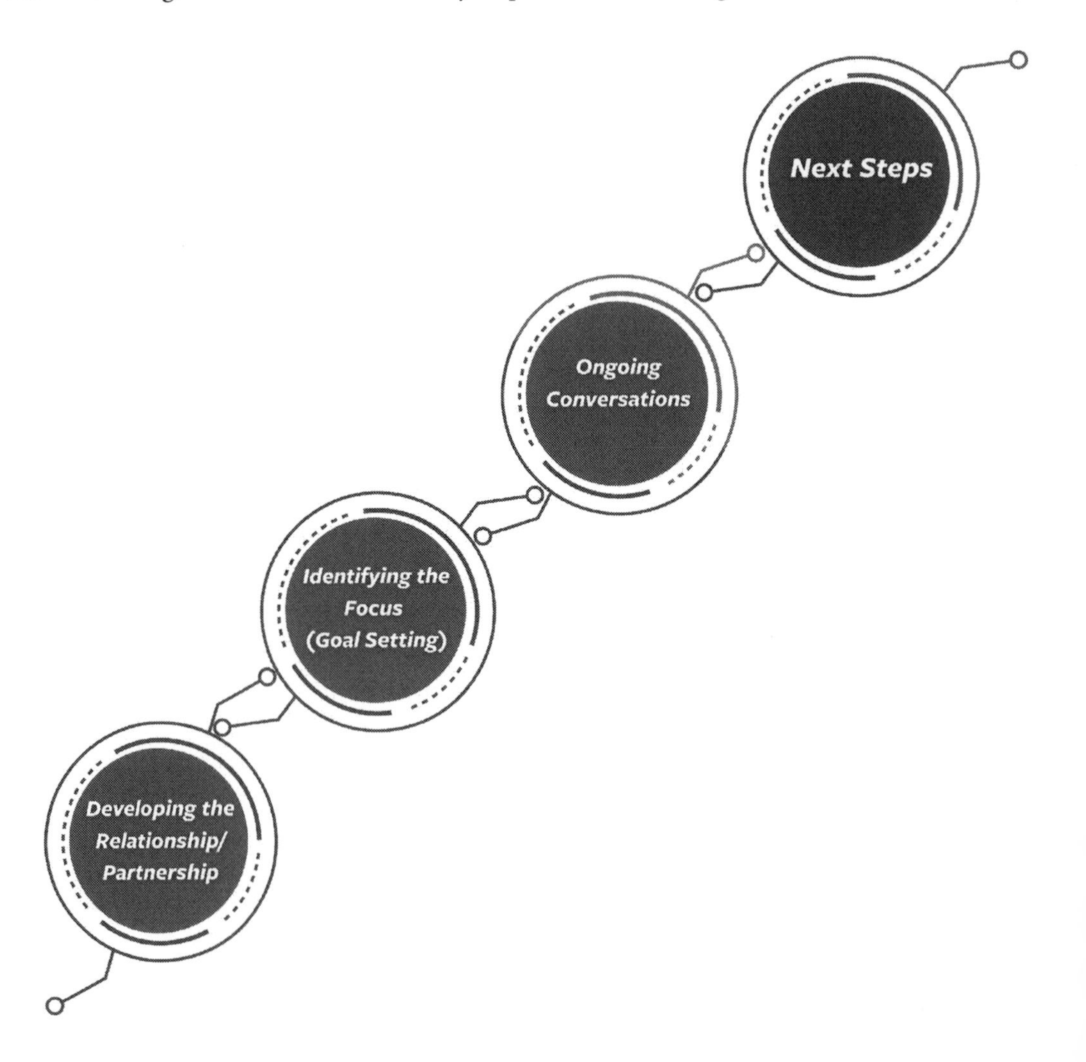

Tools for mentoring:

Supporting the mentoring journey can include tools such as the Mentoring log (see later in the chapter), where you can note what you focused on, and what actions came out of that.

SIX QUESTIONS: MENTORING—QUESTIONS TO GET THE MENTORING CONVERSATION GOING

1. What do you want to focus on today? What's going to be a good outcome for our call?
2. What have been your biggest successes as a virtual team leader/professional?
3. What were the ingredients that have shaped your success? What has gotten in the way?
4. What have been the most important moves you have made in your career?
5. What resources do you recommend I tap into?
6. What's the most important piece of advice you would have for new virtual team leaders?

Evaluating along the Way

Like other modalities, ongoing feedback cycles will help to shape, and reshape, the mentoring conversation. Asking these questions along the way can be useful:

- What's working well?
- What have you found most valuable so far?
- What have you put into action?
- What learning have you gleaned from our conversations? (both mentor and protégé)

Areas You Might Want to Explore With a Mentor

While every mentoring process is different, mentoring conversations will be customized by those who are being mentored. The following includes several questions you may want to explore in the course of your conversations:

Tell me how you:

- Approached conflict with your team
- Learned to explore assumptions
- Grew as a leader
- Learned to give better feedback
- Learned to have difficult conversations
- Fit in time for self-care/renewal
- Balanced work and life commitment

- Led others virtually
- Coached others virtually
- Tackled the isolation of being a virtual and remote leader
- Became an effective leader in the global context
- Managed performance

Tip: Creating a roadmap together of key topics you want to explore can be valuable in terms of having a plan.

Tips for Making Virtual Mentoring Work

Like in-person mentoring, virtual mentoring benefits from the following:

- Having a plan or roadmap of where you want to go.
- Creating clear roles and responsibilities. Know who is responsible to do what. Is the mentor creating the focus for the meetings? Or the protégé?
- Clarifying expectations: Who is doing what? When will you meet? How will you schedule? What is something that needs to get shifted?
- Leave it up to the mentee (person being mentored) to take action.
- Using visual channels where possible. Rather than a phone call, would a Zoom or Teams call work better?
- Using the mentoring checklist/log to capture key discussion items and what next steps have been agreed to. This can be a useful form for both mentor and protégé to refer to over time. A copy is included at the end of this chapter.

What's Different with Virtual Mentoring?

Some mentor partnerships have found that mentoring has been easier to fit in and schedule in the remote space. Challenges can include finding time to schedule, and navigating the fewer visual cues.

As with other virtual events, out of sight means out of mind, and creating some structure around your virtual conversation can be useful. Prioritizing this as an important event is also important. Remember, mentoring has a start and an end. It's not always a long-term relationship, so if energy around the conversations seems to be flagging, it may be signaling that it's time to wrap things up.

Streaming can help to minimize some of the lag that occurs, but it is also important to keep in mind the different visual contexts you operate within.

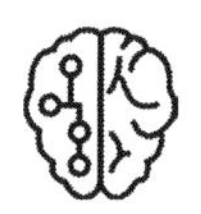

BRAIN TIP: PEA/NEA—OPENING THE SPACE FOR POSSIBILITIES

This chapter's brain tip explores how to expand the space for possibilities. Moving into a mindset of hope and possibility is key to thriving in a disrupted environment.

For many years, Richard Boyatzis has explored the impact of coaching on the brain. In his work he has isolated the impact of certain questions to what is known of the Positive Emotional Attractor network (PEA).

Asking questions like "What's possible?" and "What if you won 50 million dollars?" activates the PEA.

When the Positive Emotional Attractor network is activated, so is the parasympathetic network, which is the part of the brain responsible for compassion, flow, and thriving.

In contrast, questions that start with *Why* tend to activate the Negative Emotional Attractor network, or literally "close the mind."

What changes do you want to make to your questions with the PEA/NEA in mind?

TEAM TOOL: MENTORING LOG

Over the course of a mentoring pairing, you may have a multitude of conversation touchpoints. It is common to hear that in both mentoring and coaching conversations, it's unclear what was covered and agreed to over time. The Mentoring Log is a quick form to capture key learning, and identify focus areas for the conversation. This log can be reproduced as needed.

Log of Meetings and Other Activities

Date/Time/Location:____

Focus:

Comments During/After Meeting

Follow-up Steps

Mine:

Mentor/Protégé:

RECONNECTING THE WORKSPACE TIP—SUPPORT THROUGH CONVERSATION

Supporting others to do their best work in the virtual, remote, and hybrid workspace is an integral part of keeping organizations moving. Professionals at all levels of an organization can benefit from enhanced coaching skills in goal setting, questioning, listening, and accountability. What type of support will work best for you—coaching or mentoring?

What are the conversations you want to initiate? What can you do to connect team members with their vision, values, beliefs, and assumptions? How can the iceberg model support you to do your best work?

END OF CHAPTER QUESTIONS

Coaching:

- Take a look at skills needed. What skills are you good at?
- What hats do you wear as a leader? Coaching? Mentoring?
- Make a list of 20 powerful questions.
- What can you do to leverage coaching and mentoring to help people thrive? What can you do to activate the PEA?

Mentoring:

- What opportunities for mentoring (formal and informal) exist on your team?
- What supports would be useful for the mentoring conversation?
- Who is going to drive the mentoring conversation?

CHAPTER 16
STRENGTHS-BASED TEAMWORK

"Focusing on strengths is the surest way to greater job satisfaction, team performance and organizational excellence."
– Marcus Buckingham

Principle: Helping people connect with their strengths can lead to a more engaged, more productive workplace.

Myth: We all can do things equally well. Research has found you can develop strengths, but it takes more effort grow weaknesses and to complete tasks which are not in your arena. Research by Gallup indicates that helping team members leverage their strengths has an impact on productivity, engagement, reduced turnover, and increased sales.[210] Strengths-based leadership does not mean that people focus only on work that leverages their strengths; they find opportunities to lead from those strengths as often as they can, as they will find completing tasks easier, quicker, and better when able to do so.

This chapter explores:

- The business case for strengths-based teamwork
- Two different strengths frameworks you can use
- Five ways to cultivate strengths in your team
- Brain tip: Neuroplasticity

"Although individuals need not be well-rounded, teams should be."[211]
—Tom Rath

THE BUSINESS CASE FOR STRENGTHS

We have seen that there are far-reaching impacts on helping people bring their strengths to work every day.

As Gallup has found, employees who are encouraged to lead from strengths by their managers are six times more engaged, demonstrate 8.9% greater profitability, and have 12.5% greater productivity.[212]

Studies of more than 1.2 million employees (across 22 organizations, seven industries, and 45 countries) have shown that managers account for at least 70% of the variance in employee engagement across business units.[213]

The same study showed that 90% of the workgroups studied who received a performance intervention "had performance increases at or above the following ranges:

- 10% to 19% increased sales
- 14% to 29% increased profit
- 3% to 7% higher customer engagement
- 6% to 16% lower turnover (low-turnover organizations)
- 26% to 72% lower turnover (high-turnover organizations)
- 9% to 15% increase in engaged employees
- 22% to 59% fewer safety incidents"[214]

Workers who are able to lead from their strengths regularly report more satisfaction, energy, and *ease*. In a team context, strengths become an important area to explore. When partnering, something any team member does, strengths are also an important part of the conversation to ensure tasks are fully leveraged and people are placed in appropriate roles.

Like other development initiatives, senior level support is important, as is building a culture which focuses on strengths. This might include supporting everyone in an organization to explore what their strengths are, and encouraging teams to identify what the teams are.

LEADING WITH THE RIGHT STRENGTH

> "What great leaders have in common is that each leader truly knows what their strength is and can call on the right strength at the right time."
> —Tom Rath

As Tom Rath writes in his book, *Strengths Based Leadership*, we need to know which strengths to lead with at different times. At the same time, overused strengths become what many, including Hogan, term "blind spots." Given the demands of remote work, where we have to rely on ourselves for motivation and productivity, it can be important to note what your strengths are, along with where you may overleverage them and create blind spots.

If you and your team have undertaken a strengths-based assessment such as the StrengthsFinder 2.0, you may want to undertake a follow up by reading *Strengths Based Leadership*. This book provides a solid framework for looking at major leadership strengths in four key areas. On a team level, strengths are very important.

WHAT'S DIFFERENT WITH VIRTUAL TEAMS

Helping team members do their best work is important for both performance and results. Much has been written in terms of supporting teams through *peak* performance by helping them reach their flow state.

Originally identified by researcher Mihaly Csikszentmihalyi in his book *Flow,* he describes flow as "being completely involved in an activity for its own sake. The ego falls away. Time flies. Every action, movement, and thought follows inevitably from the previous one, like playing jazz. Your whole being is involved, and you're using your skills to the utmost."[215]

At times of flow we find ourselves lost in what we do best. Helping team members become more aware of, and be more open to, creating flow is an important part of creating a culture of high performance within a virtual team. It is important to help the entire team learn more about their strengths, as they likely will be creating the pre-conditions for this work.

In a virtual and remote work context, helping team members understand the skills and strengths they can naturally leverage is important, as work may be completed more individually than collectively.

At the virtual team level, create opportunities for team members to share their strengths with the different teams they are part of. Exploring how strengths can be leveraged across the team may support enhanced productivity, role fit, and satisfaction. It is an important part of the collaborative conversation as well.

Things to consider:

- Shifting from a deficit-based approach to a strengths-based approach is a paradigm shift.
- Strengths-based frameworks may not always have a cross-cultural appeal. This may go in contradiction to many cultural approaches.
- Some team members will find it challenging to "own" their strengths. This becomes an interesting conversation.
- Fostering a strengths-based culture takes time and may not always be a natural evolution.
- Some teams may find that their systems are not set up to be "strengths friendly." For example, rather than focusing on what you are doing well, feedback culture may evolve to focus only on the negative.

What adjustments do you want to make?

WAYS TEAM LEADERS CAN LEVERAGE THEIR STRENGTHS

We all have natural strengths. When we are able to use these strengths, it can create a "flywheel" where we enjoy our work, contribute more, and enjoy the after-effects of the work.

There are several avenues to approach for strengths-based conversations. Teams may find that they are exploring the 34 categories of the Gallup StrengthsFinder model, or the 24 Character VIA Signature Strengths. We know that strengths can remain quite stable over time. What are some ideas for supporting team members to bring these skills every day?

It provides team members with a common framework, and opportunity to learn more about **who is who** within the team, and where do they really excel.

VIA Strengths emerged out of the positive psychology movement and include six virtues (Wisdom, Courage, Humanity, Justice, Temperance, Transcendence), and 24 character strengths. As Niemiec and McGrath write, "Character is the part of your personality that people tend to admire, respect, and cherish."[216]

Three characteristics are common to Signature Strengths, making your combination very unique. Signature strengths are **Essential** (key to who you are), **Energizing** (you gain energy when able to use them), and **Effortless** (they are easy for you to leverage).

Consider these strengths and related roles:

VIA STRENGTHS	STRENGTHSFINDER2.0	WELL SUITED FOR:
Love of learning	Learner	Special projects where learning is a part of the process
Strategic	Strategic	Part of a task force responsible for strategic planning, and strategic direction; working on the big picture
	Maximizer	Peer coach or mentor role
	Relator	Social committee member/stakeholder engagement
	Ideation	Likes to see the big picture
	Input	Curator on the team; someone who loves to collect items

HELPING YOUR TEAM LEVERAGE THEIR STRENGTHS

What are some practical and tactical ways team leaders can support their team members in bringing their strengths to work every day? Consider these ideas:

#1: Help your team understand what their strengths are. Knowing our strengths is not an intuitive process for everyone. As a starting point, help team members understand what their strengths are.

There are several ways to explore strengths, including the VIA Character Strengths Survey and StrengthsFinder.

Without an assessment like VIA Strengths, get team members to consider the question, "When are you at your best?" to help them become more aware of their strengths.

#2: Get team members to share their strengths with others. A great team meeting conversation includes discussion around, "What are each person's strengths?" and "How do you use them every day at work?" Whether you make it part of a regular team meeting or a special event, conversations like these lay the foundation for effective team development.

#3: Pair people with different strengths. Teams which excel usually have complementary strengths. Pair people on the team together who may have complementary strengths.

#4: Pair people who have similar strengths. You may also want to pair people who have similar strengths so they can compare notes and get inspired from each other about how they leverage that particular strength.

#5: Find ways to utilize your strengths more regularly. When we are able to use our strengths more readily, engagement goes up, as do our satisfaction levels. If using strengths is not possible at work, have a dialogue with your boss about special projects/development opportunities which would leverage your strengths. Personally, my participation in many special projects and committees allowed me to bring my best to work. These projects permitted the further development of my own skill set and opened up new opportunities for the use of strengths in future roles.

What other ways do you see as possible for people on the team to leverage more of their strengths?[217]

TWO SETS OF LEADERSHIP QUESTIONS—STRENGTHS

Six questions to facilitate a strengths-based conversation individually:

1. What are your top five strengths?
2. What do they look like in action?
3. What are the strengths you are using every day at work?
4. What are the strengths you are not using?
5. How is your strength being overutilized?
6. What blind spot is that creating?

Six questions to facilitate a strengths-based conversation as a team:

1. What do we notice about our strengths across the team?
2. What areas do we have great bench strength in?
3. What are we lacking?

4. What blind spots does that create as a team?
5. What are we not aware of?
6. What do we need to do to overcome this?

TEAM TOOL—USING YOUR STRENGTHS WITH VISUAL CARDS

Summary: This activity provides the opportunity for individuals or teams to identify their strengths. This can be used in connection with other strengths-based profiles such as VIA Character Strengths Survey.

Purpose: To explore strengths individually or collectively.

Time: 10 to 120 minutes (combined with other strengths activities).

For Whom: Individuals, teams, groups

Instructions:

Create a layout of 10 to 12 images (or an equal number to those present). Go to Adobe Stock, Pexels, or Pixabay for photos you might incorporate.

If completing this on the individual or team level, use some of the sparker questions to get people thinking.

Have each person select at least three photos which represent what they see as their strengths, or their team's strengths. Reflect on what they notice about the photos and what they represent. Get them to identify an example of when they have used that strength.

If you have time, pair people in a breakout. Have another group/team member select up to three other photos which represent how they see that person's strengths. Have them share these one at a time, also providing their partner with a story of when they have personally seen that strength in action.

This activity is a great complement to such other strengths-based approaches and assessments as VIA Strengths or StrengthsFinder2.0.

Sparker questions:

- What three adjectives would you use to describe yourself?
- What adjectives would others use to describe you?
- What do you see as your top three strengths?
- When are you at your best?
- What do your strengths in action look like?

Questions to consider on a team level:

- According to *Strengths Based Leadership*, what areas are your strengths in? Which of the four are represented/covered?
- As you consider your team, where are your strengths?
- If you were to take a look across the entire team, where do your strengths lie collectively (which of the four areas)? What are the gaps?

Possible uses:

- To identify strengths to boost planning, support productivity, and expand awareness
- To support a team in getting to know each other and their strengths
- To boost engagement and productivity

COLLABORATION AND STRENGTHS

Practically, the strengths conversation may lead to an eagerness to explore the topic of partnership and collaboration. In a collaborative workspace, one plus one equals more than two. Collaboration is an additive approach.

While partnership and collaboration are things we often strive for, there are some important considerations in making them effective.

Is collaboration the right thing, right now?

Plan your collaboration. While partnerships are often evolutionary, spending time to intentionally design your partnership can help with alignment, synergy, and focus.

Conditions where partnerships may fall apart are when:

- Expectations are unclear, they are not shared, or clarified
- Values differ
- Approaches are not working
- Priorities differ
- Real issues are not addressed

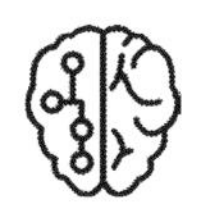

BRAIN TIP: STRENGTHS, HABITS, AND NEUROPLASTICITY

Research shows that people who think more positively and who use their strengths more live longer,[218] achieve a higher income,[219] and are more likely to flourish as individuals and teams.[220]

Gary Luffman, Director of think. change. Consulting, writes, "Estimates range from 40–80%+ of what we humans do is driven and controlled by habit. This highlights the effects of a fundamental process our brain carries out in order to 'help' us function in the world we live in. This process is called neuroplasticity and describes the brain's ability to re-wire itself to help us carry out activities we regularly do more efficiently, often without needing to tap into our very limited conscious processing reserves."[221]

Neuroplasticity is an area growing in empirical research. There are studies mapping the neuroplasticity of Taxi Drivers in London to the changes our brains have undertaken to manage remote work. As Jenifer Marshall Lippincott wrote in March 2020, "Even while working and learning remotely, we will find ways to connect, work and survive. We already have."[222]

In closing, strengths play a key role in high performance and also emotional intelligence. What are you doing to foster them?

RECONNECTING THE WORKSPACE TIP—MAGNIFYING STRENGTHS

Building a strengths-based culture helps people bring their best selves to work. In times of uncertainty, change, and disruption, we may lean more heavily into our strengths, even to the point of overuse. What strengths are getting overmagnified? Which ones need more attention?

Connect team members with their strengths through activities geared to magnify strengths, such as:

- Rolling out team strengths exploration sessions
- Matching project roles to strengths
- Providing peer feedback about a colleague's strengths in action

END OF CHAPTER QUESTIONS

- What are the strengths of individual team members?
- How do they use their strengths at work?
- What strengths don't they utilize?
- What are the strengths of the collective team?
- What's important about the strengths conversation for you as a team? What's present? What's missing?

CHAPTER 17

EMOTIONAL INTELLIGENCE

"The research shows that for jobs of all kinds, emotional intelligence is twice as important an ingredient of outstanding performance as ability and technical skill combined. The higher you go in the organization, the more important these qualities are for success. When it comes to leadership, they are almost everything."
– Daniel Goleman

Principle: Virtual and remote leaders need enhanced skills in EI (emotional intelligence) to know themselves, manage themselves, navigate relationships, and understand their colleagues. Given that things get magnified in the virtual space, so can our styles, including the good, bad, and not so great.

Myth: Soft skills aren't needed. In fact, non-technical skills like communication, relationship building, and influence are important and do contribute to the bottom line.

In this chapter, we explore the topic of Emotional Intelligence. Whether you are an IT expert, a medical technician, or a sales person, "soft skills" are critical, especially in the virtual space. It's not usually the technical issues which hinder growth, it's the ability to create solid relationships. As with other skills, it is imperative that we develop these competencies in our staff, not only in leaders.

As Colleen Stanley writes, "Emotional Intelligence (EI) is the ability to recognize your emotions, and to correctly identify the emotion you're feeling and know why you're feeling it. It's the skill of understanding what trigger or event is causing the emotion and the impact of that emotion on yourself and others; and then adjusting your emotional response to the trigger or event in order to achieve the best outcomes."[223]

For years we have known that leaders who excel are emotionally intelligent. In the virtual space, all team members can benefit from honing their EI skills.

This chapter explores:

- What is EI and why is it important?
- What's different with EI and virtual teams?
- The four dimensions of EI and core EI skills
- Ways to cultivate EI in your virtual team

EMOTIONAL INTELLIGENCE

In the virtual space, helping team members become more proficient in developing and utilizing emotional intelligence skills not only helps with **getting things done** but helps people in **self-management** (managing triggers and enablers), and in **building effective working relationships**.

Since the 1990s there has been a focus on building EI skills in leaders, and in today's workspace that needs to extend to the wider workforce.

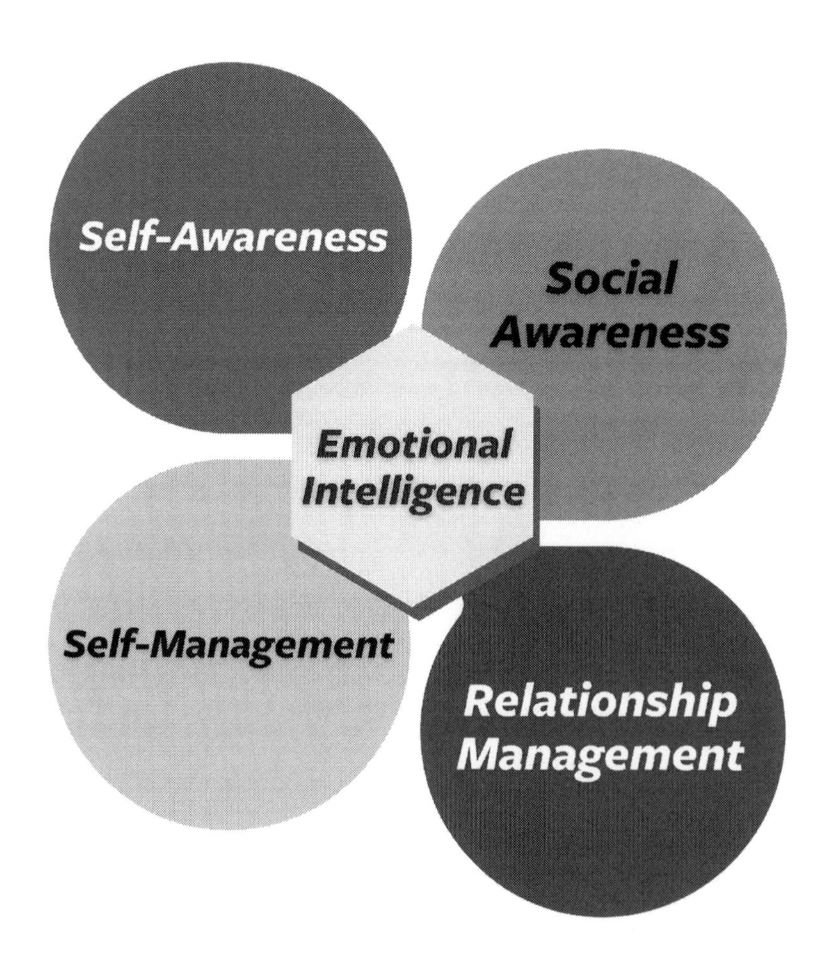

Under the umbrella of EI we have more than a dozen skill sets, from optimism to change catalyst to empathy and adaptability. Emotionally intelligent people bring skills from across the range of these four quadrants:

- Self-Awareness
- Social Awareness
- Self-Management
- Relationship Management

It can be useful to have the team take stock of where they are in each of the four domains of emotional intelligence. You may want to dedicate time throughout the year to this topic, perhaps addressing a separate skill in each quarter.

There are several different models which explore what emotional intelligence is, including the work of Goleman as well as Salovey.

"We define emotional intelligence as the subset of social intelligence that involves the ability to monitor one's own and others' feelings and emotions, to discriminate among them and to use this information to guide one's thinking and actions."[224]

In Salovey's work, the four branches include:[225]

1. Perceiving emotions
2. Facilitating thought
3. Managing emotions
4. Understanding emotions

WHY ARE EI SKILLS IMPORTANT TO TEAMS AND VIRTUAL TEAMS IN PARTICULAR?

Why is it important to build emotional intelligence in our team? There are a variety of studies which point to the varied benefits of enhanced EI in all members of the team.

Consider these studies:

Cross, Rebele, and Grant found that, "over the past two decades, time spent in collaborative activities has increased by 50 percent or more."[226]

Exploration of areas such as understanding emotions can help us with collaboration, navigating conflict, and understanding signals of stress so we can adapt our approaches for others.

At the team level, why build emotional intelligence for teams? Carolyn Stern of EI Experience indicates that EI allows for the following:[227]

- Open and honest group conversation
- Respect for others who may have different opinions

- More confidence gained by individuals
- Improved productivity
- Increased efficiency

Hillary Elfenbein undertook a study linking EI with team performance at work. It found:

- "Teams with greater average emotional intelligence have higher team functioning than [did] groups with lower emotional intelligence."
- "The ability to understand another's emotional expressions explained 40 percent of the variance in team performance."[228]

How do we understand emotional expressions in our virtual teams? In their research, Druskat and Wolff found "Group emotional intelligence is about small acts that make a big difference. It is not about in-depth discussion of ideas; it is about asking a quiet member for his thoughts. It is not about harmony, lack of tension, and all members liking each other; it is about acknowledging when harmony is false, tension is unexpressed, and treating others with respect."[229]

Emotional intelligence becomes an enabler and foundation for having difficult conversations. It's important to build skills in all four areas for high performing teams.

***Primal Leadership: Learning to Lead with Emotional Intelligence* sets out 21 skills across four areas.** In virtual teams we want to make sure we cultivate the skills in each of our team members, given their roles in interfacing with both internal and external staff. The following sections explore these different skill areas.

When Do You Know a Focus on Cultivating More EI Skills Is Needed?

Sometimes we notice when EI skills are not there. Some of the signals we might see or hear, or questions being raised, are:

- They are not listening to me.
- How come you don't see my perspective?
- She's so hard-headed.
- They just don't get it.
- No one wants to work with me.

Emotional intelligence, and what authors Goleman, Boyatzis, and McKee call *primal leadership*, helps to explore questions that include "What emotional resources do leaders need to thrive amidst chaos and turbulent change? How do leaders create an emotional climate that fosters creative innovations, all-out performance, or warm and lasting customer relationships?"[230]

THE FOUR AREAS OF EMOTIONAL INTELLIGENCE

Self-Awareness

The first of the four areas of emotional intelligence we will explore is self-awareness. Self-awareness is about knowing ourselves. According to Goleman, Boyatzis, and McKee's *Primal Leadership*, skills in this area include:

- Emotional self-awareness
- Accurate self-awareness
- Self-confidence

A quarterly activity you may want to undertake is to do a stock-taking or self-assessment around these skills. It can be as simple as asking people to rate themselves on a scale of one to ten around each of the skills. This provides an opportunity for the team to learn more about themselves, their natural style, and strengths. For example, some people are big-picture thinkers while others are small-picture thinkers.

In learning more about ourselves, we can understand:

- Our enablers—what helps us with our work relationships and results
- Our derailers—things that may get in the way of our work relationships and results
- Our triggers—things that may hit our buttons to either supercharge us or set us back
- What changes we need to make when working with others

Self-awareness is very important in the remote space, as we do not always have the same feedback mechanisms as we do face to face. Being able to focus on ourselves is important.

Social Awareness

Social awareness, the second of four EI areas, is all about understanding others' emotions. As Goleman et al. write, this includes skills in:

- "Empathy: understanding the other person's emotions, needs, and concerns.
- Organizational Awareness: the ability to understand the politics within an organization and how these affect the people working in them.
- Service: the ability to understand and meet the needs of clients and customers."[231]

Activities which can help to build skills in social awareness are to have conversations around what is your natural style so that you are able to adjust this when working with other team members. Social awareness is about knowing the emotions of those around you.

Empathy

Empathy is a core skill we want to foster in virtual, remote, and hybrid teams, especially given the range of team backgrounds; the fact that we operate from a different contexts. Empathy is defined in *The EQ Edge* as the "ability to recognize, understand, and appreciate the feelings of others."[232] Empathy has been defined by some as "putting yourselves in the shoes of others."

- What it looks like: Empathy has several components, including our ability to understand another person's feelings, as well as "read" where people are coming from. A third type of empathy is actually caring. Empathy is also important in terms of building rapport with others.
- What it sounds like: When we understand another person's feelings, it helps us more accurately adjust our approach. If someone comes to a call and says they are "fine" and you can see from their body language and tone of voice that something else may be happening, we can adjust our approach.
- When we can read where people are coming from, we are able to think through their needs and preferences. Learning to be more empathetic is part of the rationale behind working with teams and individuals to help them learn to adjust their styles.
- Building rapport in the virtual space is absolutely essential. What are the things you do to establish a connection, find common ground, and build trust?
- To really care can be seen in many instances, such as CEOs taking pay-cuts in lean times to freeing up resources, as well as people going the extra mile when needed.
- How we develop it: In his book, *The EQ Leader*, Stein shares several ways we can cultivate empathy, including focusing on listening skills and considering the other person's personal experiences or perspective. We can demonstrate more compassion by thinking about how business impacts affect others. He also encourages the support of global managers and notes "when working in new or different cultures, it's important to be empathetic."[233]
- Building rapport in the virtual space is something I cover extensively in *Effective Virtual Conversations*. Consider what you are doing to find common ground and connect people around the Six Layers of Connection™.

What is important about being empathetic? What are you able to help the other person connect with?

As a team, two other discussions you may want to have to help team members build self-awareness are:

1. Understanding our impact on others. What we do that positively impacts others, and negatively impacts others.
2. Understanding what your team members, clients, and customers need and how you may need to adjust your style.

All team members, not just virtual team leaders, can benefit from skills in organizational awareness, which is all about understanding the complex dynamics of an organization. This includes understanding power differentials, how things work formally and informally, and how to influence.

Finally, service is an important skill set, given that virtual team members may have more direct connections with internal and external stakeholders.

Self-Management

The third area of EI is self-management, namely, our ability to manage our emotions and motivate ourselves. Our ability to follow through, motivate ourselves, and adapt to change is part of this skill area and an essential requirement for virtual success. Self-management also includes helping team members understand why we get triggered by others.

Self-management is about building onto what we know about ourselves and being able to manage accordingly, based on our awareness. Given the autonomous nature of virtual work, it can be important to focus on this.

Skills in the areas of self-management, according to the *Primal Leadership* framework, include:

- Self-control
- Transparency
- Adaptability
- Achievement
- Initiative
- Optimism

As you consider the work of virtual and hybrid teams, note how important these skills are for all team members in terms of perseverance, motivation, and other levers.

Activities to help teams with self-management include:

- Becoming aware of your emotional range—what you may need to "dial up" and "dial back" when working with others
- Motivation, particularly internal motivation
- Self-management and controlling our emotions and mindset

Emotional intelligence—six questions to consider:[234]

- What does emotional intelligence mean for you?
- How do you define each of these skill areas? What's important?
- As you consider these areas, which ones are your strengths?
- What does each skill look like to you in your work? Your leadership? Your teamwork?
- If you were to put attention around one area, which would it be?
- What steps could you take to strengthen your skills and awareness in the area you have identified?

Relationship Management

The fourth category is relationship management. Most EI models refer to this as being able to navigate relationships and work effectively with others. Skills in this area include:

- Inspiration
- Influence
- Developing others
- Being a change catalyst
- Conflict management
- Teamwork and collaboration

As you will note, we have explored most of these skills already in different chapters.

No person is an island, and as most can attest from the working experiences of 2020, relationships are key in terms of keeping business moving.

Building Relationships

As we explored in Chapter 10, building relationships virtually is a key priority for all virtual, remote, and hybrid team members, perhaps to an even greater extent than with in-person teams. In the in-person realm, people are very close in proximity and spending time with peers and co-workers is an everyday occurrence. In the virtual space it's important to be more intentional in building relationships. The skill of influence becomes even more important. Business still occurs through relationships, whether you are virtual, work remote, or work beside someone else. The principle of reciprocity plays out on a regular basis (I help you and you help me).

Five ways to support the ongoing development of relationships in a virtual team:

#1: Relationship mapping. Creating a visual map of who is connected with whom, and who does what, helps to anchor and contextualize relationships in the remote space.

When people start a role, have them map out the different contacts or people they may work with. With a map in hand (global for global teams and regional for smaller remote teams), walk people through who some of their main contacts will be. In a face-to-face environment we may distinguish between internal and external stakeholders. In the virtual space we want to do that as well, although building relationships with people you are in contact with internally and externally may feel somewhat the same due to lack of proximity. Virtual team leaders will want to help team members map out key relationships they will want to foster, and schedule some of these meetings. Virtual team leaders can provide a virtual introduction.

On a team level, you can map out key relationships and have discussion around what you notice is important and where things are getting in the way.

Some other ideas for cultivating formal and informal relationships in the team include:

#2: Virtual potlucks. We all need to have lunch and, if we can't get together around the same watercooler, what about doing a regular virtual or hybrid potluck to allow for informal dialogue?

#3: **Encourage virtual networking** such as quiz shows or virtual scavenger hunts. Be sure to schedule it and build it into workplans. As I write, "What doesn't get scheduled, doesn't get done!"

#4: Mentoring. pair people together who can learn from each other. Mentoring is two way, and reverse mentoring has taken on significance with younger professionals providing significant value in the support they are offering to older professionals in areas such as technology, etc.

#5: Job shadowing. Provide an opportunity for people to learn from each other as they move through projects or other tasks.

WHY IS EMOTIONAL INTELLIGENCE IMPORTANT?

There are a number of reasons why emotional intelligence is important. From developing more cross-cultural competence to getting results, engaging others, navigating complexity and uncertainty, and boosting retention. Two underrated skills are influence and empathy, as explored earlier in this chapter.

One that is particularly important in today's global space is that of cross-cultural competence. Consider these research findings:

"Employees with higher Emotional Intelligence were rated by their colleagues as easier to deal with and more responsible for creating a positive work environment. Their supervisors rated them as more interpersonally sensitive, more tolerant of stress, more sociable and having greater potential for leadership."[235]

GETTING RESULTS

> "Emotions drive people, and people drive performance."
> —Joshua Freedman

As the 2020 Workplace Vitality Report from SixSeconds found, "Leaders who score high on emotional intelligence are 7x as likely to have high leadership performance outcomes."[236]

The 2017 Workplace Vitality Report found: "When emotional intelligence is a priority, organizations are 22x as likely to be high performing."[237]

A study by Gilkey, Caceda, and Kilts found that "strategic thought requires as much emotional intelligence as it requires IQ."[238]

Robert Johansen writes in *The New Leadership Literacies: Thriving in a Future of Extreme Disruption and Distributed Everything*, "If leaders are going to thrive in a future of extreme disruption, they must not only manage their own energy, they must encourage, model, and reward positive energy in others."[239]

"28% of productivity is predicted by the presence of useful feedback, choice in work, seeing the value of work, and having a positive climate"[240]

UNCERTAINTY AND COMPLEXITY

EI also helps us when we are facing uncertainty and complexity.

With the complexity of working across distance, culture, and time zones, in an environment which is always changing, and which we do not see, cultivating skills in areas such as Adaptability, Optimism, Initiative, and Organizational Awareness is important.

The Six Seconds Model to Emotional Intelligence is grounded in the KCG model, which invites people to consider: What am I feeling? What options do I have? What really matters?[241]

A study by Darvishmotevali, Altinay, and De Vita found "Emotionally intelligent employees are more likely to be able to predict environmental uncertainty, adapt to environmental changes, solve problems and show creative performance in dealing with colleagues and customers."[242]

What can you to do boost EI skills to support in uncertainty and complexity?

EMOTIONAL INTELLIGENCE AND CROSS-CULTURAL EFFECTIVENESS

Emotional intelligence skills are critical for cross-cultural effectiveness. Of particular note are skills in empathy, accurate self-assessment, self-control, and adaptability.

Reilly and Karounos published a paper, "Link Between Emotional Intelligence and Cross-Cultural Leadership" and found that "EI is a key component for a successful leadership and emotional intelligence traits have a widely applicability in different cultures. Especially, social skill, which comprising the ability of adjusting to a different cultural environment, is regarded as a crucial element of being a successful global sales manager. For the international sales managers, it is essential to know well the complexity of relationships between cultures so that they can identify the factors which contribute to form connections in a cultural setting."[243]

Think about this common situation:

You are having a business meeting in Buenos Aires and have scheduled the meeting close to your departure. In your haste you jump into business right away. You can tell very quickly that the leaders you are meeting with are not believing your story. What have you done wrong?

Taking time to build relationships is an important part of any business transaction in many South American cultures. Taking time to address the value of relationships by asking about family and getting to know one another is critical. It demonstrates respect and understanding of how things are done.

Consider these other priorities and drivers in business.

- Germany: punctuality, promptness, quality
- US: results, speed
- Canada: collaboration, having everyone on board, process
- China: promptness, detail
- Japan: tradition

Each business culture in which we operate is different, and understanding ourselves as well as our emotions is critical. In the virtual space, we may not be as attuned to the cultural differences of conversations if we have not traveled there.

What do you need to note about your work?

"Management is getting people to do what needs to be done. Leadership is getting people to want to do what needs to be done. Managers push. Leaders pull.
Managers command. Leaders communicate."
—Warren Bennis

> "Leaders enroll people to create a better future."
> —Marcus Buckingham

Teams with higher engagement are:[244]

- 50% more likely to have lower turnover
- 56% more likely to have higher than average customer loyalty
- 38% more likely to have above average productivity
- 27% more likely to report higher profitability

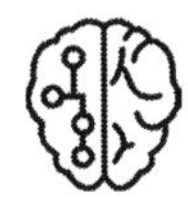

BRAIN TIP: EMOTIONAL CONTAGION

There's a saying that "one bad apple spoils the bunch." *Emotional contagion* is a term which has evolved to describe the impact of emotions on others. It's been well researched, including by Schachter (1959), Cacioppo and Petty (1987), and Levy and Nail (1993).[245]

The significance for virtual teams is that emotional contagion spreads across a Zoom room, just as it may in person. Given that our touchpoints are more magnified, the impact of a negative or positive affect may have an even greater impact.

In her article, "Faster than a Speeding Text: 'Emotional Contagion' at Work,"[246] Sigal Barsade cites her research around emotional contagion in the group context in a study entitled, "The Ripple Effect: Emotional Contagion and Its Influence on Group Behavior."[247]

The study found that "the positive emotional contagion group members experienced improved cooperation, decreased conflict, and increased perceived task performance."

Barsade writes, "In fact, executives can use their knowledge of the impact of mood contagion to create more positive team dynamics, increase performance, and decrease turnover by consciously managing their own emotions and the emotions they want to spread."

Given that the communication and culture of virtual teams can be magnified due to the lack of ongoing touchpoints, leaders and team members can benefit from becoming more sensitive to the tone and emotion behind their communications and how this can be construed.

TEAMWORK TOOL: JOHARI WINDOW

One of the first tools I was introduced to as a young professional in international development work was the tool of the JoHari Window. Created by Joseph Luft and Harry Ingham, the tool provides an opportunity for individuals to learn more about themselves and others. Our cultural lenses can also layer onto this. The notion is that a strong team and strong relationships will be created when we expand what is known to ourselves and others. The goal is to literally open the window of what is known, hidden, blind, or other.

	KNOWN TO SELF	NOT KNOWN TO SELF
KNOWN TO OTHERS	OPEN	BLIND
NOT KNOWN TO OTHERS	HIDDEN	UNKNOWN

In order to open the window panes, we use disclosure to share what is hidden. We can use learning to uncover what is not known to self or other, and we can use feedback to help expand awareness on those things we are "blind" to, but that others know, see, and experience with us.

RECONNECTING THE WORKSPACE TIP—EMOTIONAL INTELLIGENCE

With relationships and results being more diffuse and across cultures, emotional intelligence skills are key for professionals in the remote and hybrid world at all levels. Consider boosting emotional intelligence across your organization or business by:

- Undertaking an emotional intelligence assessment
- Creating opportunities for reflection and feedback on key projects and initiatives

END OF CHAPTER QUESTIONS

- Where do your strengths lie across the emotional intelligence skills?
- What is important to develop within yourself? Your team?
- Where might the Johari Window be useful to explore?

CHAPTER 18

PERSONAL PRODUCTIVITY AND TIME MANAGEMENT

"He who every morning plans the transactions of the day and follows out that plan carries a thread that will guide him through the labyrinth of the most busy life."
– Victor Hugo

Principle: Boundaries and balance are important for doing more with less. Time management and productivity is about being focused and strategic. "I am only one person, I can only do so much."

Myth: 24/7—It's about working around the clock. The Law of Diminishing Returns states that at a certain point, your inputs do not meet your output. In any project (writing a book, creating a presentation, writing out a new plan), there will be a point when things are "good enough."

One of the areas magnified for any virtual or remote professional (team member, leader, or worker), is that of personal productivity and time management. For years I have worked with team members struggling to figure out where their time is going and create boundaries so that their work across time zones does not become 24/7. The question of how to renew also emerges in this space.

This chapter provides you with tools around time management and personal productivity, as well as navigating the tricky waters of work-life.

In this chapter we are going to explore tips for time management and personal productivity for the entire team:

- What's different about time management and personal productivity in the virtual space?
- Creating boundaries
- Supporting work-life integration across the team
- Renewal as a remote team
- Time management principles and models
- Creating focus in the distracted space
- Tools for prioritization
- Managing interruptions
- The cost of distractions
- Team Tool: Action Priority Matrix/Time Tracking
- Brain tip: myth of multitasking and dopamine

A 2018 study by Gallup found that "Burned-out employees are 63% more likely to take a sick day and 2.6 times as likely to be actively seeking a different job."[248]

A June 2020 study mentioned by Michael Leiter found that with all licensed physicians in Canada, "the percentage experiencing burnout had risen to 23%, up from a pre-pandemic baseline of 14%. The engaged percentage fell from 36% to 27%."[249]

There is never enough time to get things done as a remote professional. Creating boundaries around your work is important so that it does not become all consuming.

It's not uncommon for remote workers to be juggling multiple projects, along with ideas and relationships, while receiving even more work.

Keeping at your peak is important. What do you notice about when you do your best work? What needs to be communicated to team members? How do you help them problem solve?

Proactively creating boundaries is critical for virtual work. Virtual workers are the ones who need to manage their calendars and time, which means that creating boundaries around time and priorities helps to avoid overwhelm and an overloaded in-box.

Letting others know what you are working on is critical so that they know what you are doing. Create a meta view or big-picture view connection with your *Why, How,* and *When.*

If you are needing to focus more on certain projects and are already overloaded, you may need to triage your work. While it's challenging to turn work away, some diplomatic negotiation pointers could include:

- If I focus on this (insert project), I may not be able to do that (insert other task). What would you recommend that I focus on?
- Who else may be able to help you with the task?

- Proactively share priorities and peak times of work so others know how you are doing
- Let perfectionistic techniques go

In their book, *Creating Intelligent Teams,* Fridjhon and Rød talk about the importance of Lands Work in their writing. This process helps team members share more about the context of their work, literally taking team members into their Land. This type of discussion can be incredibly valuable in sharing more about priorities, pitfalls, and others.

Tips for Creating a More Productive Workplace—Essential Elements

- Dedicated desk space or working area.
- The ability to stream—Webcam.
- Minimize disruptions and interruptions. Gloria Mark has found that there is a significant cost with interruptions, where it can take upwards of 28 minutes to get back on task.
- Help team members when they get demotivated. In a regular job we might move people into a job shadowing function. In a virtual team, it is hard to do this so we may look at doing some virtual job shadowing, where people are encouraged to work together.
- Look at changing work location—maybe there are distractions in the global space.
- Pair with a peer partner for a few hours. What can you learn from each other?
- Reorient work hours to accommodate a remote or hybrid rhythm which may need to take into account other family members' schedules who are also working from home, as well as a more global reach.
- Take some time off and away.
- Bring team members to core locations (like the main office or a departmental retreat, when possible) so they are more connected and have a bigger sense of the whole/bigger picture.

SUPPORTING WORK-LIFE INTEGRATION ACROSS THE TEAM

As Covey wrote decades ago, before virtual was known as virtual, ". . . driven by an addiction to the urgent and continually respond to the four Ps—those things that are Pressing, Proximate, Pleasant and Popular—leaving very little time to do those things that are truly important."[250]

In the virtual space, everything can take on an urgency that really is not grounded in your reality. What is most important for you to focus on right now?

In creating positive work-life:

1. Know what your triggers are. What creates stress?
2. Understand your priorities.
3. What does renewal mean for you?
4. What boundaries do you need to set for yourself?
5. What gives you satisfaction?
6. What creates chaos?
7. What gets in the way of success?

Five Areas for All Virtual and Remote Workers to Explore—Time Management and Personal Productivity Tips for the Entire Team

As indicated at the start of this chapter, everyone on virtual teams will benefit from enhanced skills and practices in the areas of time management and personal productivity. It is not only for leaders or business owners, but for everyone.

Here are five things which support accelerated work in the virtual space.

1. **Helping team members learn to leverage their own work:** Help team members become better with prioritization. Embrace tools such as sprints (working in shorter periods), time trackers, task lists, and Learning to Say No. It may also involve identifying collaborative partners.

   These tips should be read in line with tips around etiquette and systems in Chapter 7 which balance off the personal and technical side of time management.

2. **Circadian rhythms:** Know when you are at your best. Also known as the science of time, chronobiology studies the circadian rhythms of a person.

   At what time of your day are you at your prime? When is it important to downshift?

3. **Knowing where people are spending their time:** For many years I have supported individuals, teams, and groups exploring their time through an activity called the time tracker. It gives people a sense of how much time people really are spending on tasks. Many of us get surprised when we find out where our time actually goes. One of the first steps in time management is getting a sense of where you actually spend your time.

   In 15- to 30-minute blocks every day, note down what you are doing. This might include commuting, in meetings, taking the kids to tennis, meals, recreation, strategic work, one-on-ones with team members, etc. At the end of the week, tally up where your time has been spent.

   Questions to consider:

   - What do you notice about where your time is being spent?
   - Any surprises?

- What's significant?
- What needs to be changed?
- How does this week differ from other weeks?
- What would be one change you'd like to commit to for the next week? What impact could this have?

There are a number of different ways you can now track your time: old school using paper and pen, as well as apps. If you have a copy of *PlanDoTrack* or *Coaching Business Builder*, be sure to work through your trackers in the workbook/planners.

4. **Systematize:** There are many things we do in any given work day. Some tasks which are fraught with repetition could be automated (think bills), while others we do one way because we always have.

   What are the systems which could benefit the team? Areas you can explore which might need attention:

   - Planning times
   - Meeting times
   - Deep work times
   - Commute times
   - Reporting times
   - Times during which you are having to overwork for team meetings and team events
   - Email management—what really needs copying in
   - Translation times

   Check out Chapter 3 of *Coaching Business Builder* or *PlanDoTrack* for more on this topic.

5. **Getting active**, and not always being chained to the desk. It's commonly asserted in remote work that "sitting is the new smoking." A sedentary lifestyle can have many impacts.

   Regular movement for virtual team members is important. Make things active—our brains flourish when they are hydrated. We need to move as well.

   As Thoreau wrote, "Methinks that the moment my legs begin to move, my thoughts begin to flow."

   Studies on movement and the brain have seen that walking helps to boost brain connections and boosts memory and attention.[251]

   Exposure to nature also has been seen to have a boost, particularly in the first five minutes. The same article links to many global studies which have found that time spent in nature helps with focus, creativity, and longevity.[252]

Take a look at the February 2021 article in *HBR* titled, "Don't Underestimate the Power of a Walk," written by my colleague, Deborah Grayson Riegel:[253]

She writes, "By nature, working virtually and remote can feel like being chained to a desk, especially if you are streaming all day. Luckily, the advent of mobile phones and apps can allow us to participate while on the go or on the walking treadmill. Some professionals encourage the 20/20/20 process, switching between the screen and your context every 20 minutes, for 20 seconds, while looking at things 20 metres away. Another way to get rest is to switch between streaming and non-streaming platforms."

RENEWAL AS A VIRTUAL TEAM

Peak performance does not always mean that we are "on." Every team moves through a cycle of periods of peak productivity and periods of rest and renewal. While many of these are project driven, in a virtual team different team members may be running at different times, not leaving much time for renewal. In order to ensure that team members are having time to renew, you will want to check into these items:

- Meditation breaks
- Virtual events for play and connection; from Peloton to virtual escape rooms, virtual events can take many forms
- Establish a TOIL (Time Off In Lieu) policy. When teams need to push hard and may be working outside of normal working hours for stretches, TOIL allows team members to bank "time off" (unpaid) to compensate. These can be valuable periods for team members to recharge and catch up on other personal events.
- Have an away process so you can work offline
- Have a back-up person so switching off is easier. In many workplaces today, staff are cross-trained so they can easily step into the role of someone else. Consider how you can create back up for others: who would be able to receive and respond to emails while you are gone (planned and unplanned)? How do your systems allow for this?

ONE SIZE DOES NOT FIT ALL—TIME MANAGEMENT PRINCIPLES AND MODELS

One size does not fit all in the remote space, and time management can be grounded in several principles, including:

- Be ruthless with where your time goes (Note the 4-D Model on the next page)
- What doesn't get tracked, doesn't get activated
- Parkinson's Rule: Tasks expand to the time we give them. How much focused attention do you really give to tasks?
- Brian Tracy notes in *Master Your Time, Master Your Life*, that "There were three factors that accounted for more than 80% of business success: clear goals and objectives, clear measures and clear deadlines. Remember, you can't hit a target you can't see."[254]

Time Management Models

From Covey's Big Rocks, to the 4 D model of time management, one thing is sure—we can't get time back. Helping team members find a system for managing their time, as well as planning, is critical for smooth workflow.

Several different time management models exist, including:

- Covey's Big Rocks
- The 4 D model: Microsoft and other companies employ the 4 D approach to time management: do it, dump it, defer it, delegate it. Microsoft has also adopted this approach for email management. This can extend to other areas where we can make a list of everything we have to do and then start to bucket it into these four areas.[255]
- The Action Priority Matrix
- Starting in early 2021, I have been hosting the 21 for 21 Virtual Co-Working Sprints. These 21-minute sprints provide a focused burst of energy and attention.
- I shared a weekly time management hack over at *PlanDoTrack's* blog for about a year. Be sure to check out these quick activities you can undertake.
- Another time management process includes thinking about things as ABCDE: A–Must do; B–Should do; C–Nice to do; D–Delegate; E–Eliminate. What would you put in each category?

Ruthless Time Management

In addition to taking a concerted focus with time management, it is critical to spend time exploring where your time is going. Time is a non-renewable resource. We don't get it back. A great team project is to have each team member undertake a time tracker for themselves. In a virtual team, it can be very interesting to note:

- Where is everyone's time being spent?
- What are the main components of everyone's work day?
- How are team members' working hours getting disrupted by projects from across the team?
- What can be minimized, streamlined, or systematized?

What are the areas that need attention? What else?

Know Where Your Time Goes

As a team, look at what the overlap areas are, and what the areas are that aren't overlapping. What changes does the team need to make in terms of their processes?

Areas to consider incorporating as you explore what optimal time management can look like:

- Team meetings
- Lunch breaks
- Start and end times of the day
- Workout routines
- Regular learning opportunities
- Time with loved ones

These are all areas where we may be able to get "more margin" back so we can focus on what's important to us.

Email Management

Email management in a virtual team takes on new meaning. While some team members who have been accustomed to face-to-face work may expect an immediate response, when working on a global team it is important to re-shift your expectations around communication. Is it realistic to expect an email response by the end of the day?

What channels are you using for communication: email, Slack, IM, live streaming calls?

Core to this, is that systems are streamlined. The average worker receives an average of 121 emails a day. An HBR article by Matt Plummer indicates that there is a 37% delay in responding, which actually leads to more time spent. Email management is key for employees of all kinds, given that this, along with Slack and other digital channels, are the lifeline to communication.[256]

The issue for team leaders can be more complicated, especially given the fact that some of your team members will prefer to be communicated to *only* by email.

The challenge with email is not only the volume, but also the intrusion and constant interruptions it creates.

Another email management tip is to set up filters so that certain emails are filtered out of your direct in-box. Perhaps these are informational pieces, or communications (hopefully not our blog updates!).

Work in a way that works well for you. Consider color coding your email with different colors for different projects, urgency, or contacts. This may be really useful for those who are more visually inclined.

Finally, what would it be like to turn off email for even an hour so you could concentrate? What about unplugging on your weekends? According to a study by Randstad, quoted in Forbes, 42% of professionals feel compelled to check email while on holiday. What does that say?

This chapter should be read in alignment with Chapter 19's meeting management and communication.

CREATING FOCUS IN A DIGITALLY DISTRACTED WORLD

Creating focus in today's digitally distracted work is a core skill.

Digital distractions are created by a variety of things. Consider:

- The bing of your email
- An "urgent" email which isn't an urgent email, as you are bcc'd in
- An instant message that comes through via Slack
- Having to toggle back and forth through different screens instead of being able to lay things out in one way
- Having different people on your team using different frameworks/platforms for reporting

The cost of digital distractions is multi-fold:

- Work doesn't get done
- Projects are not completed
- People are frustrated because they are not able to finish tasks
- Motivation suffers in the short term
- Engagement levels drop
- Turnover occurs much more quickly

There are significant human and business costs for both.

So, what are some ways to reduce digital distractions? Consider these items *as a team*. They need to be team based so everyone is doing them.

Be intentional as a team (and possibly as an organization) as to what the expectations are in terms of being "on" and when people can be "off." It's not uncommon for some organizations to have a block of global working hours where everyone needs to be available and meetings can be called.

- Experiment with "offline" blocks of hours where people can engage in their deeper work projects. Deeper work projects might include proposals, new projects, addressing strategic issues, and working on systems to ensure process and people flow.
- Turn off the technology or close it off at certain times of the day (this will need to be discussed as a team/organization in terms of what is realistic and appropriate).
- Think twice with subject lines, cc'ing and bcc'ing (which really shouldn't be used widely, if at all).
- Consider when having an analog copy of paper/hard copy might make a task move faster or be completed at a greater depth of synthesis. Deeper thinking of work cannot be completed with just cut and paste.

- Provide workspaces and/or flex arrangements so people can work with less distraction.
- Consider the best platform for the work.

What can you do as an organization or team to create more focus in the digital space?[257]

TEAM TOOLS: PRIORITIZATION

> "The key is not to prioritize what's on your schedule, but to schedule your priorities."
> – Dr. Stephen Covey

Prioritization can be key to high performance, but what happens when priorities are constantly shifting? Helping team members identify where their time is going is a key part of effective time management. While there are several frameworks to use, in this chapter we are going to explore two:

1. The Pareto Principle
2. Urgency/Importance Matrix

Tool #1: Pareto Principle

Helping team members focus on what's important for giving them the greatest impact is another conversation which can be important to have. In order to explore this, take a look at the Pareto Principle. Here's what I also wrote in my Teams365 #941 post:

> The Pareto principle, most commonly known as the 80/20 rule, is also another useful framework to have in mind when you are considering prioritization. The 80/20 rule asserts that we get 80% of our results from 20% of our activities.
>
> Teams can benefit from undertaking some analysis of where they are getting the bulk of their impact (whether it is sales, key relationships, customer service, etc.). Getting clear on these will help us to prioritize them in the larger scheme of things. How do these link back to the collective team function and priorities?[258]

6 SIX LEADERSHIP QUESTIONS

- What activities is each team member spending 80% of their time on?
- Which activities are the entire team spending 80% their time on?
- What activities are giving the team the greatest results?
- What amount of time are they spending on these?

- What do they want their 80/20 to look like?
- What activities are going to give them the best focus?

Tool #2: Time Management—Action Priority Matrix (APM)

The Action Priority Matrix[259] is an important tool in helping team members decide what is important to focus on, as well as what activities may take time. It gets team members thinking about their activities along the continua of both effort and action (low to high) and priorities (low to high) or alternatively impact and effort. Steven Covey's work enshrined the Urgency/Importance Matrix.

If we look to explore the *Impact* and *Effort* framework, we can map ideas across these *x* and *y* axes. Consider your current tasks and lay them out and determine whether your actions are:

Quick Wins: Things that are high impact and low effort. Quick wins in a team may mean completing several tasks on your to-do list that you can blow right through. Quick wins are important in creating momentum.

Time Fillers: Time fillers are low priority and low effort. These activities are truly "time fillers" and might include short projects like filing or quick emails. Part of time efficiency is getting these to not take over too much of your calendar. They may also be tasks that are kept in a running list and checked off as and when you have time. Fill-in activities may cycle into activities which have more urgency and could move into quick wins or major projects.

Major Projects: Major projects are high effort and high priority. Like with Covey's matrix, we want to spend time focusing on these areas, ensuring that resources and time are dedicated to them. Check out Chapter 20 on project management for more on this. Major projects is an area we want to dedicate time and focus on, as it will help us in the bigger picture.

Must Dos: There are activities that are low priority but have to get done. They are things that usually take a lot of time. As important tasks, if they are not completed, team and organizational function may not work well. Activities in this category include administrative reporting or fixes to equipment. While they are important tasks in the bigger picture, due to the amount of time required, they may be activities which we look to delegate.

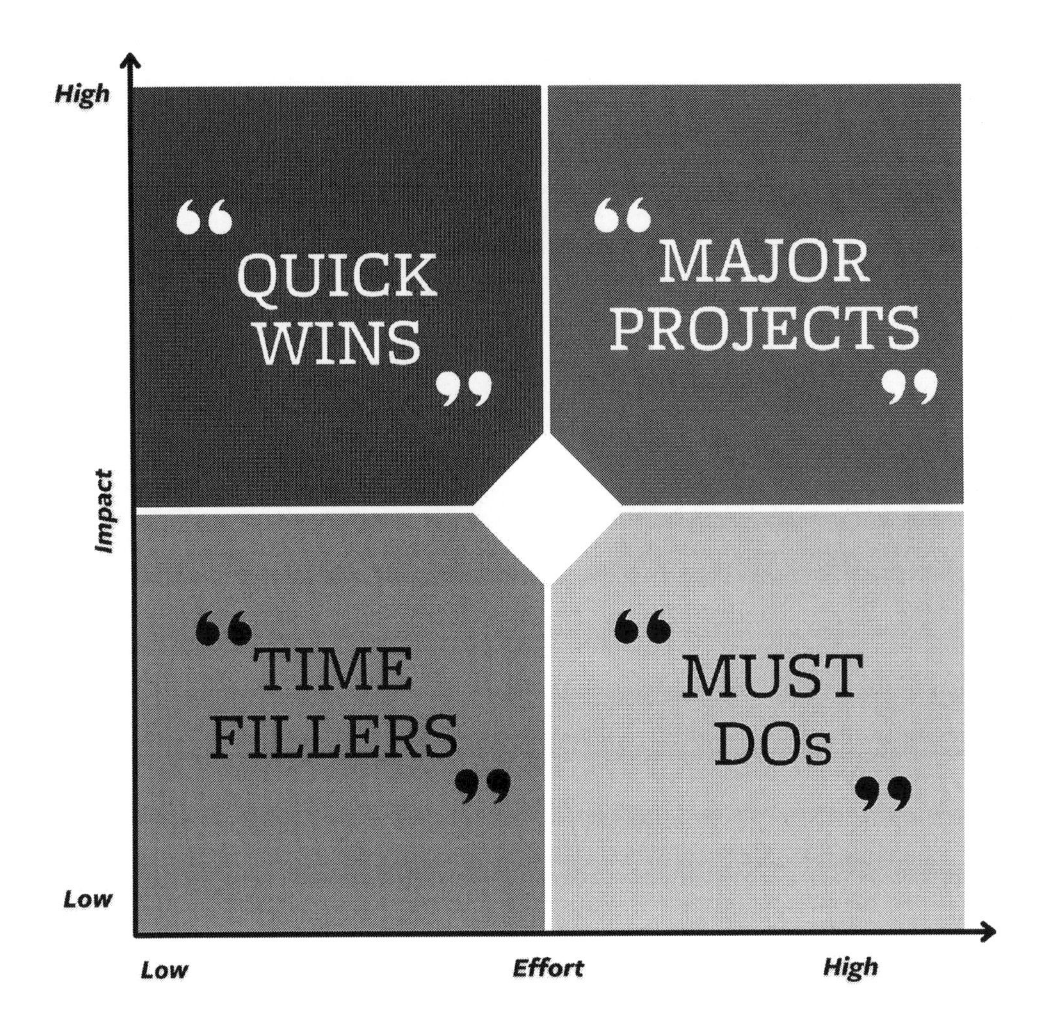

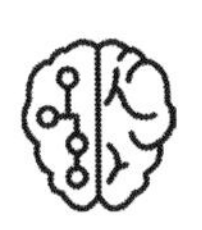

BRAIN TIP: MYTH OF MULTITASKING AND DOPAMINE

One of the fallacies of time management that has been debunked is that we can get more done when we multitask. In fact, it's estimated that when we multitask we may actually reduce our productivity by 40%. When we shift from one task to another, we experience a heavier cognitive load. Energy gets expended in order to switch tasks.

In order to get more done while working across projects, think about these principles. First, batch similar tasks. Instead of switching from numbers to conversations, batch things like accounting and budgets together. Likewise, earmark blocks of time for deep work and focus. Chunk larger tasks down so you can gain some momentum.

Consider the times of the day when you are at your best, and leverage your circadian rhythms. Sometimes time management means saying no, so notice when you are not getting things done as productively as possible.

Also consider your motivation. Dopamine plays a key role in motivation and gets released when:

- Things are unpredictable
- We are anticipating that a reward is coming
- We complete a task

The world of gaming is well known for its incorporation of this science of motivation and dopamine. Think about how your favorite game incorporates some or all of these principles.

As it relates to learning, motivation, and getting things done, consider how you can enact the flow of dopamine.

In multitasking we may feel like we are getting more done, when in fact we may not be completing tasks. Dopamine is released when we complete a task, thereby boosting motivation.

Consider these tips that are integrated into the 21 for 21 Virtual Co-working Sprints:

- Chunk things down into smaller tasks that you can complete and check off your list.
- Create uninterrupted focus by reducing notifications and other stimuli. 21 for 21 sprinters consistently note how surprised they are at how much they can get done without interruption.
- Reward yourself at key milestones, for example, at the end of the week.

THE COST OF DISTRACTIONS: TIME MANAGEMENT AND PERSONAL PRODUCTIVITY

Minimize Distractions

> "Growth depends on getting rid of the unwanted or superfluous."[260]
> —Dr. Henry Cloud

We know that interruptions and distractions play a key role in diverting focus. W. Edwards Deming says, "the average American worker has fifty interruptions a day, of which seventy percent have nothing to do with work."[261]

Research has found that the cost of interruptions is huge. Dr. Gloria Mark has found that it can take 20 minutes for an individual to get back on track after an interruption, but what about a team?

As a team, it is interesting to consider the question, "What interruptions take us off course?" Some additional questions you may want to consider as a team this week around this question are:

- What are the people, events, and things that interrupt us?
- What is the cost of these interruptions?

- What is the plus (or advantage) of these interruptions?
- What will minimize the interruptions?
- What interruptions actually help us?
- What will help us focus more?
- What times of day do I need to go offline?

In order to minimize distractions, consider:[262]

1. **Clear space for where you are going to work.** Whether our workspace is a small table which folds back into the wall when we are done, or we have dedicated office space, clearing the clutter can be an important step in creating space to focus and be productive.

2. **Consider your workspace—what needs to be cleared?** Spend 15 minutes this week clearing yourself more space.

3. **Make sure you have what you need in order to do your work**. Small issues can become big issues when working remote. An old laptop which crashes regularly, taking with it your hard work, becomes a liability. Slow internet speeds can also take a toll. While these issues might be minor pain when working remote once a month, if you need to work remote several days a week, the cost adds up. Consider what you might be tolerating in terms of equipment/ resources that just isn't cutting it. **What's the cost of replacing them? What's the cost if you don't?**

4. **Consider when you are at your peak for different types of work**. Some of us like the early morning to get our thoughts down on paper, while others like to tackle calls first thing in the morning. Consider your style and preferences in terms of when you would like to get different tasks accomplished, and *schedule it in*..

5. **Create Breaks.** Sometimes we get distracted because we don't allow ourselves time for a break, or we don't allow ourselves to get into the flow of one activity at a time. For focused bursts of work, consider the Pomodoro approach where you set a timer for a set amount of time (e.g., 25 minutes) and work until the alarm goes off. Other time management gurus recommend a 10-minute break every 50 minutes. **What is going to keep you focused and at your prime in terms of productivity?**

To support focus, ask:

- What should I start doing?
- What should I stop doing? Saying yes means saying no to something else. What do you want to say *no* to?
- What do I need to continue doing?

Many writers today note that we live in the Era of Attention, and that this is our most important resource. What do you want to focus on more?

What quiet time do you want to build in? As James Allen wrote, "Dream lofty dreams, and as you dream, so shall you become. Your vision is the promise of what you shall one day be; your ideal is the prophecy of what you shall at last unveil."[263]

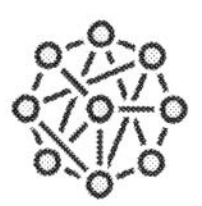

RECONNECTING THE WORKSPACE TIP— TIME MANAGEMENT AND PERSONAL PERFORMANCE

Time is a non-renewable resource; once it's gone we can't get it back. What's going to help team members be most productive?

With remote and hybrid work being more self-directed, encourage all team members to consider their peak times and what self-care can look like. With the cognitive load of virtual work being more, consider what team members can do to disconnect digitally and move in regular intervals. Use the option of work from home or work from anywhere to help with work-life integration, reducing role conflicts.

END OF CHAPTER QUESTIONS

- Where are you (individually and collectively) spending time?
- Prioritization: What are the key priorities for each team member?
- Where are team members getting their most impact?
- What are team members' biggest challenges in the area of time management?
- What can you do to minimize distractions?

CHAPTER 19

MEETINGS AND PRESENTATIONS

"There's no shortage of remarkable ideas,
what's missing is the will to execute them."[264]
– Seth Godin

Principle: Preparation makes perfect. Did you know that 10 hours of preparation goes into a 10-minute TED Talk? That's even after the presentation is written!

Myth: Just wing it! It's very hard to do things on the fly in the virtual space.

This chapter explores two related, yet distinct, topics: meetings and presentations. Both are critical in the virtual realm.

Meetings

On any given day, meetings have the potential to consume our time, especially in the virtual space where it can be common to be copied on everything. Estimates are that 40% of a professional's time is spent in meetings. Eleven million meetings take place every day, with a third noted as being ineffective. $37 billion is wasted every year on ineffective meetings.[265]

This chapter explores:

- The nuances of virtual meetings
- Five different types of virtual meetings
- Keeping meetings on track—8 essential questions

- Tips for follow-through
- Creating powerful presentations

Presentations

It is often said that one of the greatest fears of professionals is that of public speaking, which can include meetings and presentations. This chapter goes into some of the most important areas of presentations and meetings, as it relates to the virtual space. Note that tips included in each of these can be cross-fertilized to the in-person realm.

Virtual team leaders and members are likely to be responsible for leading a range of presentations, from stakeholder meetings to webinars, through to presentations on their area of expertise. This chapter explores:

- The three elements of any presentation: open, body, close
- Planning your presentation
- The accordion
- What's different with virtual presentations—flags/areas to keep in mind with virtual presentations
- Team Tool: Meeting Planner

WHAT'S DIFFERENT WITH MEETINGS IN THE VIRTUAL SPACE

Meetings in the virtual space are often plagued by Death by Conference Call.™ [266] Over the course of the day, we may be moving from virtual meeting to virtual meeting, Zoom room to Teams, and back to Zoom. One of the challenges is that everything looks the same. We rarely take time to bring it back off the screen.

As I explore in my book, *Effective Virtual Conversations*, there are several differences with virtual meetings, including:

- The pre-planning that's needed for a focused and supportive conversation
- The attention factor: The challenge of facing the multitasking mindset, where there is an allure for those streaming and participating to be turning their attention to responding to emails or updating documents
- The fact that it is harder to bring people together for the conversation (i.e., to run down the hall and bring them to you)
- There may be different devices involved—some calling in from a phone, with others calling in from a mobile, and others from a desktop.
- Some people may be calling in from one location as a group, while others are calling in individually.
- Follow up and tracking of results.

COMMON DERAILERS IN THE VIRTUAL SPACE

In addition to these differences, six different derailers for virtual conversations can be present in both virtual presentations and virtual meetings:

1. Lack of focus.
2. Different people and different platforms. One of the most challenging virtual realities is that people will be calling in on different platforms, creating inequity and different connection experiences. Let people know in advance what type of device they should be using to get the maximum out of the call.
3. Not having the right format in place.
4. Technical issues.
5. Making it all about the facilitator.
6. The facilitator's presence: How we show up and how we are perceived is very significant in the virtual realm. What energy are you bringing to the call?

Common virtual meeting faux-pas (or mistakes) include:

- Not having an agenda or not sticking to it
- Not starting and ending meetings on time
- Not calling on people you haven't heard from
- Not rotating meeting times
- Not being clear on what's been agreed to, next steps, and who is accountable

What are the mistakes you might make in your virtual meetings? (Refer to page 311 of *Effective Virtual Conversations.*)

DIFFERENT TYPES OF TEAM MEETINGS

Meetings are held for a variety of reasons, and it can be useful to identify why the meeting is being held. Is it to share information, make decisions, create alignment, strengthen the team, plan, coach, or share updates?

When you think of meetings, it is likely that you may think about:

- Check-in meetings. These are ideal for updates and troubleshooting.
- One-on-ones. One-on-one conversations with team members are critical for success in the remote space. Whether we are a sounding board, trouble-shooter, or liaison, making time for regular one-on-one conversations is critical.
- Decision-making meetings. These may involve prioritization of key issues for the team and parts of the team.

Several other chapters address these issues, including a section on one-on-ones, in Chapter 15 on coaching and mentoring.

Five common types of virtual meetings that team members will be a part of are:

1. Team meetings
2. Project meetings
3. Matrix meetings
4. Team building meetings
5. Planning meetings

Let's look at each one of these in turn.

Team Meetings

Virtual team meetings can take several forms and are important in that they provide:

- A touch point for people to share projects, opportunities, obstacles, etc.
- An opportunity to create team cohesion
- An opportunity to focus on any of the Six Factors, particularly in support of shared team practices

Formats could include:

- Daily huddles at 2:00 p.m. if team members are across one geographic location remotely, and are working towards an end-of-day deadline
- Weekly team meetings
- More extensive quarterly team retreats (half day)
- Get It Done Days for smaller teams (two- to three-hour blocks where team members focus on getting things done)
- Team hacks—sprints for 45 minutes to two hours to move quickly through prototyping or program design issues

Proactive leaders and teams know how important regular team meetings are. Meetings can be a team builder as well as important information conduit. While they may not be convenient, meetings should be scheduled regularly. For some, this may mean weekly, while for global teams this could mean monthly, with more frequent meetings scheduled depending on projects on the go.

Teams struggle when team meetings are not held consistently, and this can be a quick way for virtual and hybrid teams to create more alignment, traction, and results.

Tips for keeping team meetings moving include:

- Keep them focused—use an agenda
- When teams are spread across time zones, find a time that works for everyone, or rotate times so the same people do not have to compromise each time
- Consider what outcomes you want
- Be sure to review the Eight Essential Meeting Questions (see text box)

Eight Essential Meeting Questions

A quick way to get virtual meetings under control is to prepare for the session. Before you step into any virtual meeting you will want to ask yourself eight questions. Here are Eight Essential Meeting Questions I posed in *Effective Virtual Conversations*:

1. What's the purpose?
2. What takeaways do we want?
3. Who needs to be on the call?
4. What preparation is needed for us to be most effective?
5. What pace do we want to keep it engaging?
6. What will help keep the focus?
7. What is absolutely essential to cover?
8. What follow-up might be required?

Project Meetings

Virtual team members are likely to be part of multiple projects. An essential communication vehicle for projects is the status meeting. This is critical to getting things done and bringing projects in on time, scope, and budget. Check out Chapter 20 on project management.

While many different types of project meeting formats are possible, more common types of project meetings are:

- Written reports—when projects are centralized, everything may be reported through a dashboard or written report
- Weekly feedback through one-on-ones
- Regular feedback through status update reporting and meetings
- Huddles or daily meetings when teams are using an Agile process

IN FOCUS: STATUS UPDATE MEETINGS AND REPORTING

Status updates are usually the heart of any project management process. These meetings help to identify or "flag" what needs attention and what can continue as is.

Most status updates use a color coding of RED, YELLOW, and GREEN. Things that are going well are flagged green and some additional detail may be requested/required around actual work undertaken.

Yellow issues are those which require some attention and further discussion. This might include something that is starting to go out of scope or budget. While this does not require immediate attention, yellow issues are important to note, as they can easily become red.

Red issues indicate issues that require immediate attention. These are things that could derail a project or process.

In virtual teams, it is important to be clear about roles and responsibilities around projects. Who is going to do what? What should be flagged, and when?

One significant pitfall with status meetings is that they become a verbal channel for reporting. Rather than becoming a meeting that touches on each piece of information and updates from each team member which can take hours, use regular status update reporting to provide this level of detail. The status meeting then can focus on synthesis of items and decision-making around different points.

Matrix/Three-Way Meetings

One of the most important meetings virtual team members will be part of are the regular three-way meetings. This is especially true if you are part of any matrix management arrangement, where a team member may report to a local level supervisor as well as a more regional or global supervisor.

Given the complexity of leadership, these meetings will likely occur throughout the year. If these are not scheduled regularly (i.e., once a quarter), be proactive in scheduling one.

Team Building Meetings

In virtual team building meetings, we want to focus in on helping the team boost their **relationships and results**. Teams which excel have strong interpersonal relationships so that they can work across differences, raise and talk through challenging topics, and know each other's strengths and styles. Virtual teams which excel also are very clear on results by having clarity and knowledge around goals, their input, how goals intersect, and so on. Throughout the book, I have included several different tools which cover the relationship and result areas of team development.

Team building meetings can be used to:

- Strengthen connection
- Get to know each other better
- Incorporate other elements such as planning
- Understand how the team combines what each other does, strengths, and roles
- Create a series of common frameworks for the team, from having a common set of skills to approach conflict, to talking about difficult issues

Given that only 22% of team members may have participated in any virtual team building, it is important to look at what virtual team development can be like.

Team development might involve the facilitator's being at one site and the team's being in their conference room. This can be a great supplement or follow-on to training being undertaken in longer bursts.

It might involve virtual sessions held quarterly on topics of interest identified by the team (i.e., providing feedback, learning about our strengths, etc.).

Virtual and remote teams may also be coming together for annual, biannual, or quarterly face-to-face meetings. These could run for one or two days. Again, providing focus on both relationships and results can go a long way.

The following are ideas for building relationships and results in the team building context:

- 21 Activities for Virtual and Remote Teams, at PotentialsRealized.com
- SessionLab
- BusinessBalls.com
- MindTools.com

Planning Meetings

It is important for virtual teams to know what lies ahead and create alignment and a bigger picture of what they are working on. Holding quarterly planning meetings and/or strategic planning sessions is important.

Planning sessions for virtual teams can be virtual and/or in person. From half-day to full-day or one-hour blocks, planning meetings provide an opportunity to discuss and co-create your roadmap for the quarter, the year, or five years.

To facilitate virtual planning meetings, consider these tips:

- Provide an opportunity for everyone to feed in their insights and priorities and understand how they connect with the plan

- Use breakouts to have team members explore different parts of the plan
- As a strategic planning advocate, undertaking a SWOT or Strategic Issues Mapping sessio regularly is a "must-have" for a team. It helps the team create a common map of their issue and a vision of where they want to go. Another tool is the SOAR, which explores the SWOT from the Appreciative Inquiry perspective.

IN FOCUS: STRATEGIC ISSUES MAPPING

Planning and exploring strategic issues is a key issue for high performing teams. High performing teams in the virtual, remote, an hybrid world know where they are going and have a shared sense of what those key performance targets are. Spending time to visualize this map this can go a long way. This In Focus explores one of the tools: Strategic Issues Mapping.

The Strategic Issues Mapping tool can be useful in facilitating and mapping key issues facing the team/organization at several levels: short term, medium term, long term, or geographic—local, national, and international. Each circle can be labeled with an appropriate label. Have team members brainstorm the factors facing the team at each one of these levels.

The value of this exercise for remote, virtual, and hybrid teams is that we will all see this from a different perspective. The Strategic Issues Map will allow for us to visually share our insights and work with it.

Keys for a Successful Meeting

Are you making your meetings as successful as they could be? In *Effective Virtual Conversations*, share these eight things that can help you create the foundation for a successful meeting:

1. **Do you have all the right people at the table?** It's hard to bring someone in mid-call, s think about if you have everyone on the line or around the virtual table. Is there anyone els who could provide information, and/or the authority and responsibility to get things done
2. **What can be done pre-meeting vs. post-meeting?** In the virtual space most things tak more time, and we want to set people up for success. What can people do before they com to the call? How clear is communication around pre-work and what participants need t bring to the call?

   What needs to be done post-meeting? Consider these questions: What commitments aroun next steps and agreements have we made? Who will follow up? When?
3. **Keep the pace moving and engaging to avoid multitasking and Death by Conferenc Call**. As I wrote in *Effective Virtual Conversations*, "We have all been there! There's nothin worse than hearing someone having a conversation in the background. Where possible use streaming to avoid the Death by Conference Call mentality and multitasking. Creat

agreements around focus and/or presence during the calls." Check out the later part of this chapter on Moving the Needle on Engagement.

4. **Watch for and expect technology glitches.** Know your platform and practice it so you know how to keep going if technology issues happen.
5. **Get out of the rut with roles.** Having a job to do on a call can boost engagement. Provide opportunities for equal participation by rotating roles. Roles include that of note-taker (or scribe) and timekeeper. If you are on a web-based platform, set a timer. Assign times to each action or agenda item. Have a scribe/note-taker capture the minutes and circulate them.
6. **Be strong on process.** Again, from *Effective Virtual Conversations*, "In the virtual realm, it is really important to have a strong focus on process. This includes:
    - Letting people know what they can expect from the process.
    - Is there an agenda you will be following? (A meeting template is included at the end of this chapter.)
    - How will you be working with time?
    - What level of engagement do you expect?
    - Will you be going around the room?
7. **Set a clear focus for the meeting**. Have strict timeframes in mind. This includes sending out agenda items and agreeing on and sticking to time frames. It is likely that different group members will be in different time zones, so going overtime in virtual meetings is usually not respectful. Have a game plan on what absolutely needs to be covered and what can wait.
8. **Create ways of working and shared agreements.** Just as in team meetings, have agreements about how you will operate, especially around focus, etc.
9. **Consider multiple feedback loops.** Ask for feedback as you go. Take a "temperature check" or have people identify what they have learned so far.
10. **Consider the best platform.** Is a conference call the best way to go, or should you consider a more robust platform like Zoom, where you can see each other and have people move into breakouts? The type of meeting you are hosting will influence the platform. Consider the various options. Make sure it is easy so people don't spend their entire day getting into the call. (Refer to the August 2017 Community Call on Platforms for more on this topic.)
11. **Make things visual.** From having a place to take notes (if you are on a conference call) to using a virtual whiteboard, to having a photo to anchor the conversation, making things more visual boosts engagement and avoids the Death by Conference Call mindset where people automatically disengage. What visual anchors can you create in your work?

TEAM TOOL: VIRTUAL CALL AGENDA

Meeting Planner—Use this meeting planner to keep your meetings on track.

Template: Virtual Call Agenda

VIRTUAL MEETING DATE:		TIME (ACROSS TIME ZONES):	
Participants (Who needs to be there? Consider information, roles, and decision making ability)			
Pre-work before the meeting			
Date agenda sent out			
Key Takeaways—List Top 3			
1.		3.	
2.			
Time	Agenda Item	Agreements	Who/When
Follow up needed:			

One of the most overlooked areas with meetings can be who is going to do what. The team tool for meetings is a simple one-page action plan follow-up so people can track key steps and action items. A major meeting time-sucker can be the meeting minutes needed after a meeting. Sometimes this is a legal requirement and sometimes it is an antiquated reporting structure carried over.

Another consideration in virtual meetings is that you have a "ready-made" recording function which could serve as a legal record of the proceedings (hence no need to create copious notes). Automated transcription can quickly be generated to serve as minutes.

Finally, capturing to dos, agreements, and next steps in the chat log as you go, also provides a quick way to capture these important ideas, maximizing time.

POWERFUL VIRTUAL PRESENTATIONS

Creating Powerful Virtual Presentations

Presentation skills are essential for both team leaders and team members in the virtual realm. Whether they like it or not, team members will need to present to others. Consider these scenarios:

1. It's budget time, and your boss asks you to come in and present to the executive team, as you have been the one leading the project.
2. The team leader is away this week and you have been asked to "step in" and represent the team at an important department meeting.
3. The team leader is on the road and can't attend a key stakeholder meeting in your region. You have been asked to represent the organization.

In all instances, every team member needs to have well developed presentation skills. While this is not intended to be a replacement for a more experiential, hands-on set of training, I felt it was important to highlight several key practices for creating more engaging virtual presentations.

What's Different about Virtual Presentations

There are several things that are important to keep in mind about virtual presentations, namely:

- Pace
- Creation of an environment of active participation
- Connection—the Six Layers of Connection™
- Approaches, including the Five Engagement Levers™
- Key differences and tips for powerful virtual presentations

Pace

Most of us have suffered through the Death by Conference Call™ phenomenon, or experienced the meeting that drones on without a pause and through a monotone. In creating a more interactive and stimulating virtual presentation, our pace, pitch, and word choice create the environment for the call.

Pace change every few minutes is absolutely critical. While some authors indicate that a pace change through slides every couple of minutes is needed virtually, there will be instances where you will want to engage in dialogue and decision making with each other. Change pace by asking questions, polling the audience, and using breakouts or annotation.

If we do not change the pace regularly, it is likely that our team members are going to disengage. What will create a compelling focus for the team itself? What are the things that they will benefit from? How often do you want to change the pace?

For many years, we've been using the litmus test of every 7 to 10 minutes to be mixing things up, to be changing pace. In the virtual domain, we want to move that needle even more quickly. Now, this is where your group members are really going to be your best test, or feedback mechanism, in terms of how much faster that is. We hear from some e-learning designers that you want to do it every 30 to 60 seconds. For a lot of my learners, that's a little too long; they want to stop, hear a story, and then keep moving.

Create an Environment of Active Participation

Creating meetings which actively engage people is critical for any virtual meeting. As passive recipients, we are likely to turn back to the multitasking.

Some ways to actively engage people and create their active involvement includes:

Have the group shape the agenda and focus of the conversation before you even get in the virtual room. Consider these questions together:

- What is the purpose of the meeting?
- What are the outcomes you are looking for?
- What is your stance/perspective on the topic?
- What do you hope to learn?

Create shared expectations. Effective meetings have a shared set of operating principles. Keep focused, come prepared, minimize distractions. What are the standard operating procedures you want to create? Is there an expectation or communication around the notion that active participation is expected?

Make it interactive. Use breakouts and annotation throughout your presentation. Refer to the Five Engagement Levers™ later in this chapter.

Helping people connect early on with their WIIFM. Even if people have shaped the meeting, helping people connect early on in their What's In it For Me (WIIFM) creates an environment where people feel connected to the issues you are discussing. Questions you can use at the start of the meeting or presentation include:

- What's important about this topic for you?
- Think about your last week/month. What was the state of X in your work?
- What are the questions that will capture your attention?
- How will you be applying what we are exploring today?

Use media-rich sources. Include photos and slides in your presentation, as our brains process visuals faster than text. You may also want to use visual cards and video as other ways to create more active involvement of group members. This could include the use of video by tapping into apps like Lumen5 or Biteable.

Six Layers of Connection™

Connection in a virtual conversation often means the difference between a call that *stands out* and one that just bleeds into the rest of the day. Ultimately, we want to create calls which are memorable.

In my Stand Out Virtually Challenges, I talk about the Six Layers of Connection on virtual calls which includes connection:

- To you, the host
- To each other
- To the content you are offering
- To the context in which you are having the conversation
- To the technology
- To the application of what they are learning and what they will do next.

Consider these 12 different possibilities for creating more connection:

1. Doing a pre-call with each participant to learn more about them.
2. Sharing a welcome video message instead of/or in tandem with a welcome email.
3. Having group members share a welcome video introduction.
4. Using breakouts to connect people.
5. Assigning an accountability partner or buddy during the process.
6. Taking a poll to see where everyone is thinking around a topic.
7. Using annotation to have people stamp where they are in agreement around a question or topic.
8. Doing a scavenger hunt during the call.
9. Using an icebreaker like Bingo during the call to find things in common.
10. Using Kahoot to connect people into the content you covered.
11. Using MentiMeter to take a poll.
12. Using MURAL to help people connect and share ideas.

Approaches—Five Engagement Levers™

Using a variety of approaches to engage with your groups is critical. It helps us to activate and connect with different members of the group.

Having a variety of techniques and approaches to keep the call and presentation moving is key.

In addition to having a variety of approaches, you want to make sure that you are incorporating different approaches for different learning styles. It is important in the virtual realm, to be meeting the different learning styles—visual, auditory, and kinesthetic. We want to have the visual learning, which, of course, on a video-based or a streaming system like this, is so important.

We also want to have auditory approaches. Chances are, you may be meeting with your virtual groups for multiple touch points. What are those auditory ways that you can engage with podcasts, with short audio recordings, with dialogue-based approaches through breakouts, or in between sessions of peer partners? These are really critical in getting people into different sets of dialogue, and different sets of learning.

One area that is completely overlooked in a lot of virtual programming today is kinesthetic approaches. As an experiential educator at heart, I find it's very much all about getting people's bodies and minds into action on the calls. I'd like you to think about the activities you tend to go to in your work. Maybe one of your defaults is, "I'm going to send people out into a breakout." Or, maybe another approach is, "I'm just going to keep on talking."

Is there a way that you can get people to connect through the different channels, visual, auditory, kinesthetic, in a way that mixes things up? Maybe between sessions, or if you're doing a longer program, during a break, you might give people instructions like, "I want you, over the course of the next few minutes, to go and find a pad of paper, and bring it back with you, along with a pen, or find some Post-it notes," whatever the instructions are. We do want to always have different approaches to really keep things fresh and keep things moving.

Other approaches to creating more engagement is the use of breakouts, annotation, or media, as well as having a variety of approaches to use.

Breakouts

Breakouts are another critical engagement technique, providing the space for group members to connect and share in a group way. It's a powerful way to harness the peer process in a virtual call.

What's the ideal size of a break out? If break out size is too large, people will tend to get lost in the anonymity. **Social loafing** is the term that we use. And so, that typically will happen in virtual breakouts, where people can't see each other and are groups of five plus. Breakouts are usually effective when they are about two to four people. Two is great if you know that the technology is going to work, people are connected, and you have time and space for that deeper dialogue. Three or four is also a good number.

In breakouts, make sure that you're setting people up for success by assigning roles. Perhaps there's a facilitator, a note taker, and a timekeeper.

Also, be clear within instructions—How long? What are the instructions about returning back to the room? Are people expected to report back on what they've just said, or other?

With peer interaction, there is a lot of learning here; I think it's an under-tapped area, especially in the virtual domain. It doesn't have to just be all about the facilitator.

Annotation

Annotation is an under-utilized mechanism in many virtual contexts, and can be very appealing for those learners/group members who are more experientially and kinesthetically inclined. In other words, those who like to learn through doing, and learn hands-on.

Annotation is simply getting people to mark up the screen during a call. Most platforms have this as an option which you can "add on" or activate with an account.

Curious as to how you might be able to use it? Consider these ideas and related questions you might ask your group:

- Where are you? Map yourself on the map
- Where are you on the continuum? Have people mark where they are on any continuums you are speaking about
- Which one represents . . . . Show photos related to your topic and get participants to mark up which one they connect with
- What do you think? Pose a question and get people to turn to annotation (pen or text) to share their thoughts
- Select your choice. Provide different choices and have people mark their selection (great alternative to polls, which can be bulky to insert)

What other ways might you use to incorporate annotation into your work?

Media

Many participants *love* media-rich presentations. Being cognizant of copyright and intellectual property, how can we direct people to others' articles, TED Talks, or videos that they've done; keeping it aligned with this notion of, "How do we access the visual auditory kinesthetic?" Is there a way for you to bring a TED Talk into your conversation, or have as pre-work?

One final note on activities because I think, virtually, we are always thinking through how much time is this going to take.

Consider the 2:1 ratio. In the 2:1 ratio, we want to leave as much time, or double the amount of time, for dialogue after the process to reflect on the experience. And very much, think about powerful learning experiences you have facilitated or attended. Chances are, you move through an experience, whether it's putting puzzles together with team members or designing a process. And, after that, we want to leave a pause point; a pause point for reflection, for dialogue, for connection with others in our group, or even just individual writing. If you are trying to fit too much into a call, we may lose the end of the learning loop which anchors-in the learning.

What are the key messages which need to be transferred from the team leader to the virtual team members? What are the things that need to be communicated upwards?

Key Differences and Tips for Powerful Virtual Presentations

As I wrote in *Effective Virtual Conversations*, in *virtual presentations*, key differences are pace, energy, and the need for visual anchors. To keep things moving, remember:

1. **Capture attention quickly.** We have a limited time window—0.07 seconds according to Judith Glaser in *Conversational Intelligence* "to capture people's attention and help them differentiate between the fight or flight."[267] Other authors say you have half a minute or so. Regardless, we want to get people into the virtual room very, very quickly. And whether it is showing icons, or a visual, or a map, we want people to connect in with the topic quickly.
2. **Remember that people remember the start and end of things.** The "latency and recency effect" describes how our brains remember how you start your presentation and how you end it. The mid-point is likely to be fuzzy. Ensure that you reinforce key messages at the start and end of your presentation. It may be as simple as indicating "Three areas we are going to explore today are . . ." and at the end, "Three of the key themes we explored today were . . ." or "To highlight key decisions made . . . ." Consider how to create memorable impact by showing a video, an illustration, or something else to anchor thinking in the "messy middle."
3. **Less is more.** Trying to fit too much into your presentation may lead to a sense of overwhelm and lack of clarity. Consider the key messages you want people to remember and/or take action on. As you go to prepare, consider:

    - The key messages you want to communicate. What are the three key bullet points?
    - What elements of the presentation are essential? At the core, what is essential to cover?
    - What needs further reinforcement? What key ideas need reinforcement? When and how will you reinforce these?
    - What needs to be pruned? Yes, sometimes we do need to cut out a chunk!

    To distill through your content, you may want to ask yourself, "What is a *need to have*? A *nice to have*? And where can people go to learn more?" This can help to sift out information.

4. **Make it about the participant's experience.** Leading from the WIIFM, What's In It For Me, helps people connect early on to how the presentation connects with their world. This puts them in the driver's seat right away. What can you do to help people connect with the WIIFM?[268]
5. **Use the power of three.** Three things to remember and three elements of a presentation: the open, body, and close.

6 SIX TEAMWORK QUESTIONS—PRESENTATIONS

1. Who is your audience? What do they prefer and value?
2. What are the top three messages you want to communicate?

3. What is going to give you a strong start? Finish?
4. What do you notice about the transitions from one segment of your presentation to another?
5. What is going to engage the audience throughout the presentation?
6. As a result of the presentation, what do you want people to do? (Your call to action)

The Skeleton of a Great Presentation—Open/Body/Close[269]

In structuring your presentation, it can be useful to keep in mind a simple structure—open, body, close.

The **opening** of any presentation should not only capture people's attention but also encourage people to connect with the topic. Helping your audience consider, "What's in it for me?" or the connection point, will engage people right away. In the opener, you will also want to highlight where you are going and, possibly, your main points. The opening generally takes about 10% of the presentation time.

Different ways to open a virtual presentation include:

- Getting people to indicate where they are calling in from on a map
- Asking a question such as, "What's important about this topic?" and having people respond with what's important about the topic using chat or annotation
- Having a photo or a visual map of where you are going in your presentation
- Having a photo which people can connect with, along with a question like, "What's important about [topic] for you?"

The **body** of the presentation is the core. Consider the use of visuals to support what you have to say, and make sure your points are crisp and relevant. Given that we often try to fit too much in, what are the three main points? Stick to these. What graphics will support this? In presenting information, you may move through topic, example, application. Less is more.

The **close** of any presentation should summarize where you have been and reinforce what the main points were. In virtual presentations, you will also want to get people to think about, and note, their next steps, their actions, and/or what's different now. In order to "bring things off the screen," it's important to help people connect with what their next step is. The close should take about 10% of the overall presentation.

Notice how people have now had the main points reinforced three times: during the open, throughout the body, and during the close. Remember, people will be more apt to remember the start and close, so end it with a punch! What is your call to action, and what action do you want people to take?

In terms of how much time to spend on each one, consider the 10/80/10 rule. A maximum of 10% of your presentation time should be spent on each of the open and close, and 80% spent on the body.

Tips for Memorable Presentations

What are the top three messages you want to get across?

Integrate the Six Layers of Connection™. Make sure people connect with their WIIFM (What's in it for me?) in the first few minutes of the call.

Make it hands on. Leverage the Five Levers of Engagement™ to boost interactivity.

Watch pace! Pace in virtual presentation is much faster, and switching the pace every 7–10 minutes by using a different engagement lever can be critical for interactivity, involvement, and inclusivity of all voices.

If you can, get people in breakouts and share with their partners.

Leverage the Accordion.

The Accordion

A final tip around presentations is to incorporate the metaphor of the accordion. It's hard to know before a presentation what is going to have the greatest impact. Therefore, pre-session, consider what can be expanded if the conversation is moving quickly and what can be collapsed if people are enjoying a certain section. The accordion metaphor is invaluable to help you have a game plan for fluidity without constraining the conversation.

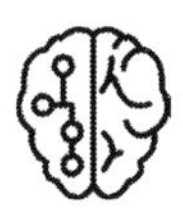

BRAIN TIP: VISUAL ANCHOR POINTS

Visual anchor points help to anchor a conversation, boosting the memorability factor.

As Geoffrey James writes in this *Inc.* article, "8 Ways Neuroscience Can Improve Your Presentations, "The latest neuroscience research has revealed that human beings process words and pictures i different physical areas of the brain. If your presentation includes pictures alongside text, people ar twice as likely to remember your message.

Combine text and graphics in your slides whenever you need to make an important point. A vide clip can create a burst of movement that accesses additional areas of the human brain, making you presentation (literally) more memorable."[270]

Images could include photos, illustrations, iconographs, or videos.

There are a number of resource sites which you may find useful in exploring for dynamic stoc photos. Always note copyright usage, and some sites will offer you a commercial license for a cost. I you have not found these sites already, check out:

- Pixabay.com
- AdobeStock
- Unsplash
- Pexels
- iStock Photos

I use many of these personally in my work, including a monthly subscription to AdobeStock.

Here are some recent examples of how visuals have supported virtual conversations.

1. **Photos** are a great doorway into the conversations of feedback, difficult conversations, and courageous conversations. Choose a different icon-rich photo around these topics (available at AdobeStock) to prompt a sharing and articulation of what each topic means for group members. Icons can be a more comfortable way to stretch into giving voice to what is difficult to talk about.
2. **Visual cards** are plentiful. For years I have incorporated decks such as Points of You or Conversation Sparker™ (my deck), for conversations of all kinds:
    a. to facilitate a visioning session for a team
    b. as a year-end close off where group members choose the photo which represents their learning from the year
    c. as an intention-setter for the new year
    d. to stimulate a conversation about how the team members would like to receive and give feedback

How might you incorporate more visuals into your work?

TEAM TOOL: VIRTUAL MEETING PLANNER

Presentations: Virtual Meeting Planner—Open/Body/Close (3 points for each)

Name of presentation:

Top 3 outcomes:

1.

2.

3.

Length: ______________________________

Platform: ______________________________ Contact Details: ______________________

Audience	What's important for them:
Open	Top 3 points
Body	Top 3 points
Close	Top 3 points
How will I create more engagement?	

RECONNECTING THE WORKSPACE TIP—PRESENTATIONS AND MEETINGS

Over the course of a given day we may engage in multiple conversations, moving from one meeting to another. What are you doing to connect people along the way?

In the virtual, remote, and hybrid world, you can help team members navigate the Six Layers of Connection™, namely, connection to:

- You
- Others
- Their context
- The content of their meetings
- The technology
- Application of their learning beyond the screen

What are the specific activities you can undertake throughout your presentation or meeting to connect people?

END OF CHAPTER QUESTIONS

Meetings:

- What key outcomes are you aiming for?
- Who needs to be at the table?
- What needs to go onto the agenda?

Presentations:

- What are the top three points you want to reinforce?
- Which of the Five Engagement Levers™ do you want to incorporate?
- What can you do to boost the Six Layers of Connection™?
- What visuals do you want to incorporate?

CHAPTER 20
PROJECT MANAGEMENT 101

"A good plan today is better than a perfect plan tomorrow."
—Proverb

Principle: Projects and programs are living, breathing entities. They have a lifecycle of their own.

Myth: A plan always stays the same. Adjusting and iterating plans has become the norm for projects large and small across many industries.

This chapter explores the field of project management. From traditional project teams to those who have embraced Agile, project management and the related skill sets are likely needed by all virtual and remote team members.

Projects are an ecosystem of everything we have talked about in this book. From Tuckman's model of the different stages of group and team development (forming, storming, norming, performing, and adjourning), to conflict, emotional intelligence, meetings, and project teams, projects provide a living and breathing laboratory for work.

This chapter explores:

- Project Management 101: Key best practices of projects and the project cycle
- What's different in the virtual space
- A shift to Agile—From Waterfalls to Post-its
- Six challenges for project management teams

- Key processes to keep projects moving:
  - Kick off
  - Project reviews
  - Closure
- Program development and management—projects on steroids
- Project sustainment and change

PROJECT MANAGEMENT 101

For many professionals today, their day is a series of projects. It is likely that team members are going to need to know how to manage their own projects. As a former program manager myself for many years, I learned there were several rules of thumb in making sure that projects are successful, starting with the foundations of keeping them on time, on scope, and on budget.

This triple constraint of time, scope, and budget creates a boundary around projects. A regular question any great project manager will ask is, "What is outside of project scope? Is scope creep happening?" In the virtual space, helping the team understand scope and budget issues, as well as time requirements, can make a big impact on time, productivity, and efficiency.

Phases of Any Program or Project Cycle

Projects can run for weeks or years. From the traditional ADDIE model (Analyze/Assess, Design, Develop, Implement, Evaluate) to SAM (Successive Approximate Method), project phases are similar at the core. As we shift from waterfall methods to Agile approaches, or from projects where all phases need to feed into each other to more rapid successive approaches, core elements of projects are similar. Let's look at them now.

PHASE	WHO AND WHAT	TOOL
Analyze/Needs assessment	Determining project requirements based on who the project is for	Design Thinking Tools—Empathy Maps Knowing Your Client
Design	Design sessions or sprints	Design Matrix
Implementation	Program development pitfalls	PERC Engagement Levers Six Layers of Connection
Evaluation	Program evaluations	Mid-point Reviews Retrospectives
Sustain	Sustainable change management	Learning

Needs Assessment

Key lessons learned from managing many six- and seven-figure projects over the years include:

Be clear on who is doing what, when, and how. Clarify assumptions. Overcommunicate using all channels available. Just because you "think" everyone understands, say it again. For years, successful projects have been measured by the Triple Constraint: coming in on time (at the deadline proposed), on scope (as they said they would), and on budget (at the dollar amount estimated). Just like a triangle, a change to one of these will impact the others. In order to stay "on task" we want to be clear with roles, goals, and milestones. Taking a look back at the Six Factors of High Performing Teams is a good reference in this area.

What are your communication channels? How will communication flow about what's working, and what's not? Set up regular communication touch points.

Institute regular project status meetings. For most projects, meetings are weekly or, potentially, daily. Hear from everyone on the team in a way that is meaningful. Encourage them to share their ideas about what is working and what is not.

Facilitate project post-mortems or debriefs. Every project has a multitude of learning points. It is important that that learning is carried forward into new tasks and projects so that mistakes are not multiplied and successes are integrated in future projects. Build in time for project status meetings and reviews during the project and after. Consider what other projects can benefit from the learning on current projects. Encourage team members to review the project status questions on their own. Refer to the evaluation questions which follow.

Make it visual. Be sure that everyone has access to the plan and focus areas, and can see what it looks like. In today's world of project management, Post-it notes abound, brought into the virtual space via platforms such as Miro and Mural. Others may still use the traditional Gantt charts. Ask a team to consider what is going to make the project and current focus visible and visual to all.

Under the umbrella of project management, we want to focus on many areas including:

- Planning
- Risk management
- Stakeholder management
- Performance management
- Organizational change management
- Communication management and governance

WHAT'S DIFFERENT FOR VIRTUAL, REMOTE, AND HYBRID TEAMS

There are several things that are different for projects in the virtual space:

Keep it in front! As mentioned, "out of sight" does not mean "out of mind." As we will see in this chapter, keeping things visual is important for project teams of all kinds.

Keep communication channels open. Communication is at the heart of any successful project. Know what others are working at, real-time. Chat, Slack, and Instant Messaging provide nonverbal channels to keep the conversation going.

Consider the shift to Sprints. Given that times of day may be different, timing can be compressed in the world of virtual teams. Rather than having six hours, you may find that you need to achieve things in the 45 minutes to two hours you have overlapping.

Be clear with what the focus is. All teams will benefit from being clear on what the focus is. As we will see in the next section on the shift to Agile, helping teams keep things visual is critical for project success. Having clarity on what the current task is and what the deliverables are, set the team up for success. When one person starts at 5:00 a.m. their time, 2:00 a.m. for another team member, and 11:00 a.m. for another, it's important that we have processes and procedures to:

- Know what we are working on
- Know what success is looking like
- Share our work and current thinking
- Update others

THE SHIFT TO AGILE—FROM WATERFALLS TO POST-ITS

Many organizations have moved to an Agile framework, emerging out of the IT development world. Agile as a methodology is grounded in team process. Scrum encourages the question, "how can we do what we do better?" Priorities and focus are just as important as is the principle of "everything is important—do it all at once."[271]

Key characteristics of Agile include periods of rapid iteration where teams are "failing fast" and learning from the process. Agile is also grounded in the philosophy of "inspect and adapt." It started with the questions, "How do you build autonomy, transcendence and cross-fertilization into a scrum team and from that combination activate hyper productivity?"[272]

Work occurs in Scrum, grounded in the principles of:

- Transcendent: "Have a sense of purpose beyond the ordinary . . . the very decision to not be average, but to be great, changes the way they view themselves, and what they are capable of."[273]
- Autonomous: Teams are self-managing and self-organizing.
- Cross-functional: Team members bring all the skills they need.

Scrum is also based in the planning cycle of Observe, Orient, Decide, Act, and then Plan, Do, Check, Act.[274]

Team Size Matters

Team size is important, and this is something we have noticed for years. Over a certain size, it's likely that a team is no longer one team but a series of nested teams. Sutherland writes in *Scrum: The Art of Doing Twice the Work in Half the Time*, "Groups of 3–7 people required 25% of the effort of groups of 9–10 to get the same results."[275]

As shared in an earlier chapter, as group size grows, the interaction touchpoints become exponentially larger. The impact of social loafing, or what is also known as the Ringelmann effect, is also significant.[276] You can view a short video on this in the Audiopedia on YouTube.[277]

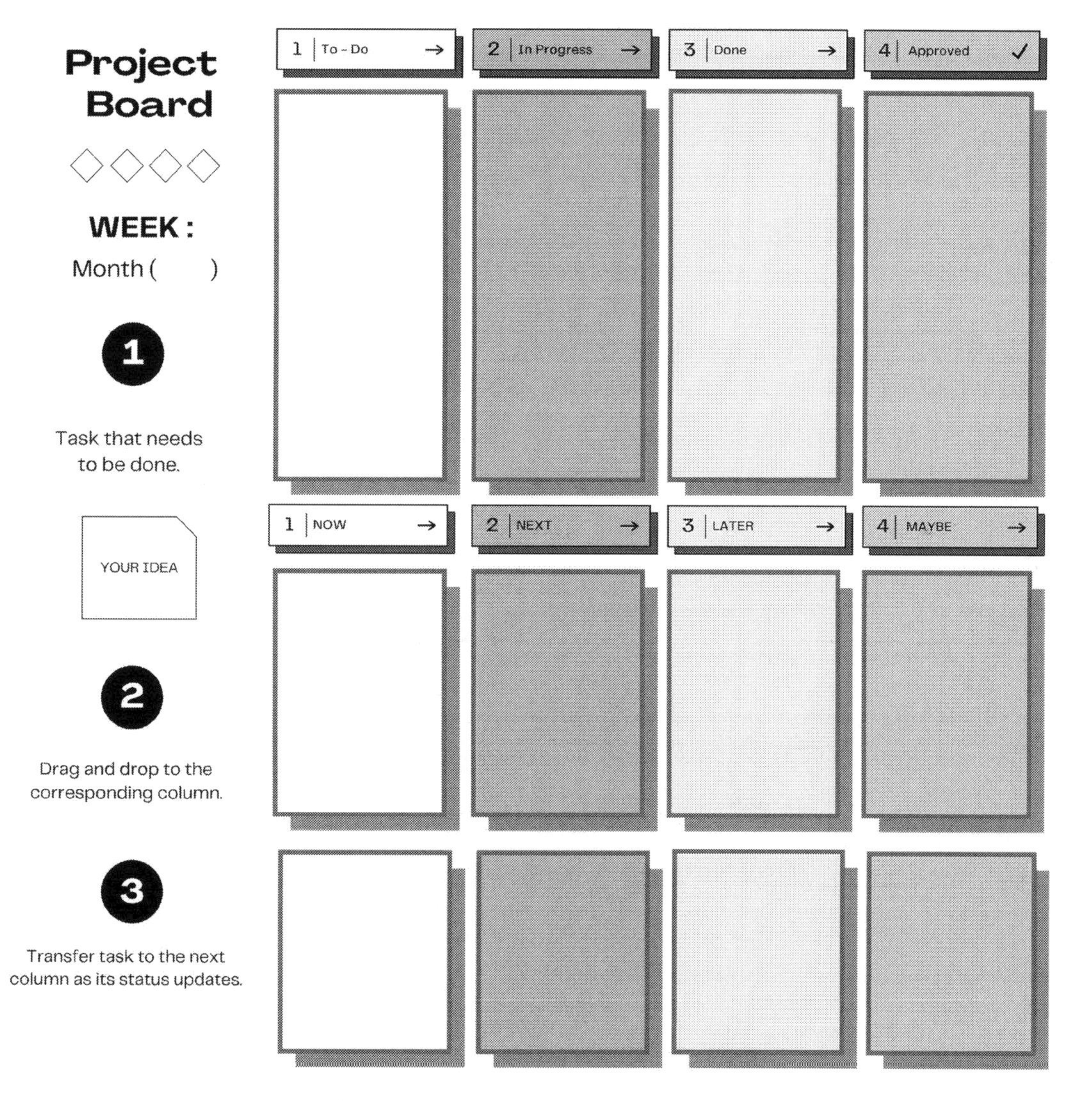

As a starting point, team members identify the buckets of work. Agile makes things visible. Project boards (physically and virtually) are dotted with Post-it notes indicating all of the Items for the project, and break them out to categories such as To Do, In Progress, Done, and Approved. A separate category of testing or validation may also be present. Moving tasks across these categorie keeps projects moving. It is also a very visual way to keep everyone in the loop in terms of what stag all tasks are in.

Focus is at a premium in the world of Agile, and teams move through "rapid sprints" to complet each project section. As Agile co-founder Sutherland writes, "Scrum accelerates human effort—i doesn't matter what the effort is."[278] Agile is now being embraced by organizations of all sizes an types, from education to financial services.

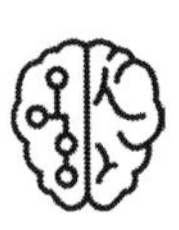

BRAIN TIP: DOPAMINE, QUICK WINS, MOMENTUM, AND MOTIVATION

Dopamine is a key neurotransmitter related to pleasure, learning, and motivation. It's also somethin that has been found to be triggered by "Small Wins." When we plan, and achieve those goals, releases more dopamine. Given the way our brain works, we then want to do it again to get anothe "hit of dopamine." This helps strengthen the loop of "self-directed learning." As it relates to plannin and projects, when we can get more hits from dopamine to fuel the quick wins with smaller goals, w can then start building some momentum as the goals start to stack together.

Dopamine is a powerful component of motivation and is crucial in boosting our effects.

On projects, notice how dopamine is released when milestones are created. Whether it is the gree checkmark of a completed task, or Xperiencify's *cha-ching* after completing a task, motivatio learning, and action go hand in hand with dopamine.[279]

Also consider the brain tip in Chapter 18, where we explored dopamine from a time managemer perspective.

SIX TEAMWORK QUESTIONS ON PROJECT MANAGEMENT

1. How is this project within budget, on time, and in scope? What needs attention? (The tripl constraint of project management focuses us on making sure we are within budget, on time, an in scope. If not, one of these three needs attention/change/modification.)

2. What involvement do the different internal/external stakeholders need? Consider the RASC framework—who is responsible and accountable versus those who need to be consulte and involved?

3. What are the key successes from this week (month or quarter)?

4. What are the top three to five upcoming milestones we need to place attention around?

5. What lessons have we learned this week? Where can they be applied?

6. What risks do we need to mitigate? How do we do this?

THE FLIPSIDE: THE CHALLENGES AND PITFALLS OF PROJECT MANAGEMENT TEAMS– SIX TEAM CHALLENGES FOR PROJECT MANAGEMENT TEAMS[280]

By their very nature, project management teams are unique, and they face unique opportunities and challenges. There are a number of challenges which face project management teams, along with some questions project managers may want to consider with respect to their teams.

Challenge #1: The Team's Finite Timeline

Project management exists for a finite period of time, with a fixed beginning and end period. This may be days, weeks, months, or sometimes years. Teams outside of the project world, theoretically, are forever.

Questions: What challenges does your team's finite timeline pose? What do you notice about the team process and their needs as you move from kick-off to implementation and finish?

Challenge #2: Different Roles and Responsibilities of Different Team Members

Project teams often involve a fluid mix of different team members coming in and out of the project.

Questions: How much time have you spent clarifying the different roles and responsibilities of the different team members in your project? Where is the overlap? What are the gaps?

Challenge #3: Different Team Members Belong to a Series of Different Project Teams

It is common for staff members to belong to multiple project teams at one time.

Questions: How strong is the association/membership to your team? What steps can you take to boost team member's association to your team?

Challenge #4: Possible Virtual Nature of the Project Team

A very common challenge within project teams is their virtual nature, where members of the team are mobile, or located in different venues. Virtual teams can pose a wide range of challenges, as they may operate across time zones, distance, and cultures.

Questions: If we have a virtual component to our team, who is on it? What obstacles exist due to our nature of the virtual team? What steps can we take to ensure that those needed are involved in our team process and communication?

Challenge #5: Unclear Vision for the Team

Unfortunately, it can be common for the vision of a project to be held tightly by a few members of a project management team, and not widely shared by all.

Questions: Who has contributed to the overall vision of the project? Who shares this vision? Wha steps can you take so that all team members share the vision?

Solution: Spend time with the team creating a common vision of the end result.

Challenge #6: Unclear on the Strengths of the Team

Given the often transient nature of project teams, it is quite common for the time together to b spent on action (which can often be unfocused) rather than preparation and planning. Remembe every 10 minutes of planning can save 60 minutes of unfocused effort.

Questions: What strengths does each team member bring to your team? What are the strengths c your team system as a whole?

Solution: Look for an assessment to measure the strengths of your team system, or StrengthsFind 2.0 to look at the strengths of individual team members.

KEY PROCESSES IN KEEPING PROJECTS MOVING

Projects are living, breathing entities, and it is important to keep things moving and be in communicatio with each other to share what you are working on, any changes made, and any learning as you go. I this section we will explore three critical components to keep projects moving along:

1. Kickoff meeting
2. Status updates
3. Project close-outs

The Kickoff Meeting[281]

We usually remember the start and end of things. This is known as the latency and recency effec Setting the stage for a successful project typically starts at the kickoff meeting. Beyond mere formalit the kickoff meeting sets the tone and foundation of the team process. Reminder: At this stage the tear is usually at the start of Tuckman's model, forming, and will inevitably move quickly into storming

A large part of my professional work has focused on program management which I describe as "proje management on steroids." As a former leader, director, and manager who worked at the UN, an within other international development organizations, a large part of my work focused on creatin leading, and managing multidisciplinary programs from disaster management through to health ca and education. Typically programs would consist of a multitude of discrete projects, involving dozer of experts, generalists, and other stakeholders. I realized very quickly in my career that one of th most important activities for a new project, program, or initiative was the kickoff meeting.

Some considerations in pulling together effective kickoff meetings are the following:

1. Who needs to be at the table or involved in the kickoff? Make a list. The RASCI framework of stakeholder analysis can provide us with a useful framework to think through the multitude of potential players, partners, and stakeholders. What happens if they are not represented from the start?

   The RASCI framework stands for:

   R—Responsible: Who is responsible for executing the project?

   A—Accountable: Who is accountable for results?

   S—Supporting: Who needs to support this project?

   C—Consulted: Who needs to be consulted and perhaps involved through the provision of knowledge, information, and expertise?

   I—Informed: Who needs to be informed about the project, outcomes, and results?

   How are you involving a representation of these different players? What's the most effective channel for communication?

2. What needs to be communicated at kick-off?
3. What roles and responsibilities need to be identified or clarified? What other expectations need to be clarified?
4. What ongoing communication, reporting, and evaluation processes will you create? Who needs to be involved and when? What are the major milestones going to be?
5. Check in on accountabilities: Accountability in today's business environment has become a Pandora's box at times. What are the specific accountabilities each person/party has? How will this be measured? Who are they accountable to? What's expected in terms of reporting? What happens if things go off course? Failure to discuss this from the start can set a slippery slope for any project or initiative.
6. Goals and outcomes: Of course, clearly defining goals and outcomes is another critical factor of success. What is the common vision across all stakeholder groups?

What components do you want to make sure you include into your next kickoff meeting? Anything else that you would add?

TEAM TOOL: STAKEHOLDER ANALYSIS—RASCI[282]

One of the most important tools for relationship building can be stakeholder analysis. This is enshrined in a tool known as RASCI. RASCI stands for Responsible, Accountable, Supporting, Consulted, and Informed. This helps us determine who needs to be involved at what project stage.

When I was a program manager and director managing multidisciplinary programs from disaster management to health care and educational curriculum redesign, stakeholder analysis was a key part of project, and program, success. It was probably the early 1990s when I first heard of RASCI, which really changed the way I looked at accountability and at who needed to be at the table.

For those who have heard of RASCI, what might immediately come to mind is stakeholder analysis. We often think that everyone needs to be involved all the time for accountability to happen, when, in fact, in any project there are multiple players, or stakeholders, each of whom need to be involved in different ways.

Consider one of your current projects. Who is involved? What level of involvement do they have?

Let's use the example of the roll out of a new team tracking tool for expenditures. Consider what needs to be communicated to whom, and who needs to be involved at what level. Who is:

> **Responsible**: Who needs to do the work? This might be the team leader who has to gather the expense information in the new format and submit it.
>
> **Accountable**: Who has ownership of this? Typically, the "responsible one" is accountable to this person. The accountable person might be the general manager, the team leader's boss. This person is accountable for decision making and the process and the quality of the project. This person is going to have high influence and high involvement for the project.
>
> **Supporting**: Who is supporting the initiative?
>
> **Consulted**: Who needs to be involved and asked for input? Those consulted may involve other team leaders who have gone through the change, and team members. Those in this category typically provide information, resources, and support needed for success.
>
> **Informed**: Who needs to be told about the change or kept informed along the way? Individuals who are not part of teams may need to be informed so they know what changes are happening.

Activity

As you consider a current change which is happening, apply the RASCI framework. Who is part of each of these different categories? Have you been communicating to them in the right way and frequency? What changes are needed?

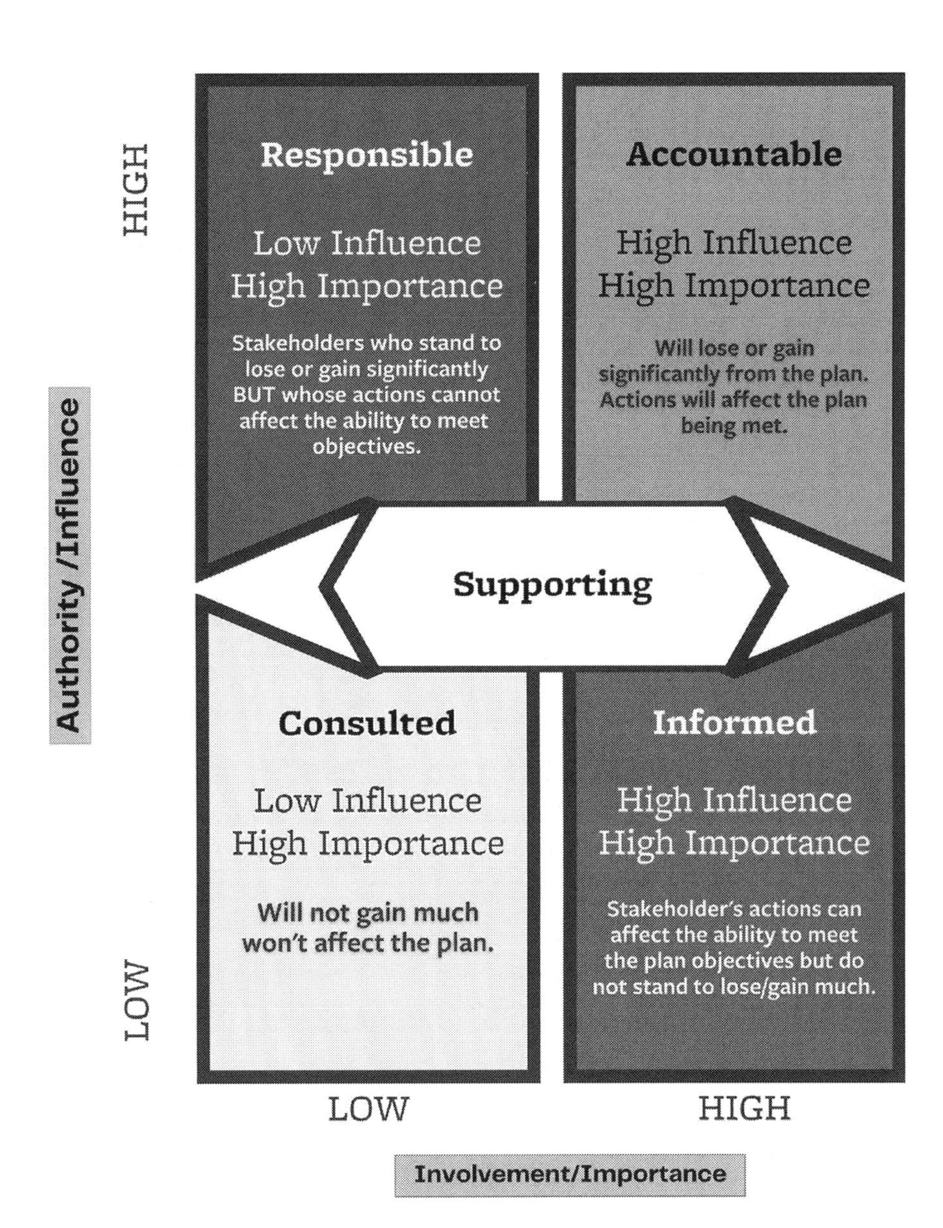

Status Meeting

Status meetings are intended to be a vehicle to update the project manager (and team members in the virtual space) on how things are going.

Status meetings can be virtual, in person, short, or long (e.g., 15 minutes a week to hours at a time).

In general, status meetings explore the questions:

- Where are you now?
- What's working?
- What's completed?
- What needs attention?

The project dashboard may signal things that are working (green), things that need attention (yellow), and things that are urgent (red). This visual can go a long way in keeping things moving.

In the Agile world, from Scrum we may find ourselves borrowing these questions:

1. What did you do yesterday to help the team finish the sprint?
2. What will you do today to help the team finish the sprint?
3. What obstacles are getting in the team's way?

The beauty of these questions is that they provide future focus and actionable, practical steps.

Accountability—Plan Regular Program Reviews

Reviewing the status of projects regularly is an important part of project success. As virtual teams, you will want to plan regular program review touchpoints, especially at the start, mid-point, and end of projects. During these meetings, you may want to review such questions as these:

- What is the progress toward the key program objectives and indicators?
- What major opportunities exist? How can these be leveraged?
- What problems exist? What is needed to address them?
- How are the actual costs comparing to the planned costs?

Project Close-Outs[283]

As important as the start of things is, so is the end. Project close-outs provide an opportunity for celebration and identifying lessons learned and specifying ideas and actions that can be taken forward.

As you move into a project close-out you will want to:

1. Identify lessons learned specific to this project.
2. Identify lessons learned which can apply to future projects.
3. Identify roles played by each team member. What worked? What didn't?
4. Undertake reflection on the stakeholder analysis and engagement process.
5. Celebrate!
6. Provide a formal close-out and formal acknowledgement of all those who participated in making the project what it was.

Questions you could use include:

- What lessons learned should be taken forward?
- What were project enablers (things that helped)? Derailers (things that hindered)?
- What would you do differently about the program if you could do anything?

- What limitations are holding you back from what you would ideally do?
- What are you learning from the program implementation so far?

PROGRAM MANAGEMENT—PROJECTS ON STEROIDS

Zinn, in the November/December 2008 edition of *Canadian HR Reporter*, said, "The emerging discipline of program management gives professionals the knowledge and skills necessary to think big picture and understand the benefits of leveraging the interdependencies between projects."

Within the frame of complexity, large scale problems, and global focus, it's likely that an increasing number of professionals will need to expand their focus from projects to programs.

"Program management is the coordinated management of interdependent projects over a finite period of time to achieve business results."[284]

Program management:

- Is strategic
- Provides a focal point for ownership and accountability for business results
- Enables horizontal collaboration across a business or industry
- Is cross-project and multidisciplinary[285]

Zinn identified four core skill areas for program management:

- A head for business
- Communication
- Critical thinking
- Collaborating

Program development pitfalls:

- Proper stakeholder relationships not developed and maintained
- Programs operate within a vacuum and are seen as static
- Lessons learned in earlier programs do not cycle through
- Risks are not identified and managed

Additional program management pitfalls (adapted from the field of project management):

- Unrealistic timeframes
- Lack of human resources
- Planning in a fixed mentality—failure to see the shifting priorities
- Lack of financial resources
- Lack of stakeholder support

MOVING THROUGH THE CHANGE PROCESS

This book would not be complete without reference to the ongoing face of change. Within a virtual and global context, some of our fellow team members may be at the doorstep of global changes we see on our TV. It provides us with the firsthand opportunity to hear about different perspectives and what impacts are happening on the ground.

While I am not aware of any studies of this nature (and if you find one let me know), it's likely that those attracted to virtual and remote teamwork thrive because they are open to, and excited by, change. Operating in a virtual team means ongoing change at multiple levels—if it's not change in our backyard, it may be change in another's.

Rogers' change model[286] identified six different stages or ways people may approach the change process. You may have members on your team who are:

- Innovators (those who are eager to create change)
- Early adopters (those who embrace the change early on)
- Early majority (those who get on the bus relatively early)
- Late majority (those who slowly adapt/get on the bus with change)
- Laggards (those who resist change)

Being aware of who will be advocates for change on the team is just as important as recognizing those who might need more support and conversation/attention throughout any change process.

What do you recognize in yourself about how you respond to, and initiate, change?

Change Management: Moving through Change—the ADKAR® Model

There are several different stages to any change process. Prosci's ADKAR® model is one of the best known, recognizing that in the change process we will move through the phases of:

A—Awareness. At this phase we recognize that change is needed.

D—Desire. At this phase we explore why change is important.

K—Knowledge. At this phase it is about developing the knowledge for change.

A—Ability. At this phase it's about assessing and building our capabilities for change.

R—Reinforcement. At this phase it is about reinforcing the changes.

Whether we are moving through it individually or collectively as a team, it can be important to note where people are at, and what type of support they want.

What's Different with Virtual

There are several layers around change which are different in the virtual, remote, and hybrid space. In addition to our individual perspectives and approaches to change, different members of the team may have different realities as they relate to change—some are impacted, some are not—given the dispersed nature and that things outside of the screen are different.

There also may be different cultural approaches to change. Depending on our geographic culture, some may embrace change and some may resist it. For more on how different nationalities approach change, check out the long-term orientation data on different countries from Hofstede's research.

Given the fluidity of work in this space, it can be beneficial to build change muscles across your entire virtual, remote, or hybrid team.

DEVELOPING A SUSTAINABLE CHANGE MANAGEMENT ENVIRONMENT

Interesting factoids:

- 80% of change management initiatives fail.
- We are in a period of unpredictable, ongoing change.
- *Alonovo* is Latin for "sustainable change."

Barriers to Change

In her book, *Thriving Through Change*, Elaine Biech identified the following barriers to change:

- Corporate culture
- Lack of resources
- Limited executive support
- Employee resistance
- Poor planning or lack of planning
- Lack of credibility

While a decade has passed since she wrote her book, we are still experiencing the following:

- Complexity
- Lack of clarity
- Fear of not knowing what to do

What are the barriers you want to consider and be aware of?

Supporting Your Team through Change

We all approach change in a different way. Regardless of how people approach change, it's important that we cultivate new skills in the areas of:

- Curiosity
- Focus
- Experimentation

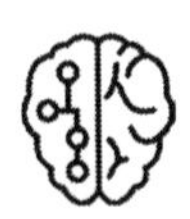

BRAIN TIP: SPRINTS AND HACKS

One way to build muscle in change is to shorten the program cycle. This can involve undertaking quicker bursts of work in sprints and hacks. Sprints provide focused bursts of attention and action. As demonstrated in the 21 for 21 Virtual Co-Working Sprints which began in January 2021, participants found they were able to build their muscles around focus over time, shortening the length of time needed to drop into deep focus and get things done.

In his book, *Working Relationships: The Simple Truth about Getting Along with Friends and Foes at Work*, Bob Wall shares that problems with teams can emerge due to ambiguity, incompatibility, overload, and disagreement. Each one of these leads to a different outcome.

Ambiguity is caused on multiple levels for teams, from lack of clarity around agreements on the team (what needs to be done, by whom, and when) to ambiguity in the context (changes to regulation, resourcing, people, etc.). This leads to uncertainty. Teams of all kinds need leaders to ensure that there is clarity around things that can be controlled, i.e., team agreements, and that the feelings of uncertainty and emotion are normalized. Ambiguity has the potential for trust to become eroded. Brain science also has shown that confusion is created when there is lack of clarity.

The second area Wall points us to is that of **incompatibility**. As he writes, "Some of the team's goals, roles, and procedures may be incompatible or inconsistent with other goals, roles, and procedures."[287] This is a common challenge for teams moving to a remote or virtual space. Consider the questions:

- What incompatibility exists between our goals, roles, and procedures?
- What is working well?
- What additional resources are needed?
- What processes need to evolve?
- What changes are needed around goals, roles, and procedures?

The third area he flags is **overload**. In a virtual team, it is essential that we are supporting ou team members with tools for enhanced productivity, prioritization, and workload management Chapter 18 on personal productivity and time management explores this topic further.

TEAM TOOL: VISUAL MAPPING OF A PROCESS

One of the principles we have explored throughout this book is making things visual. Our last Team Tool is that of virtual mapping of a process.

Virtual mapping of a process is understanding what needs to get done, by whom, and when.

Visual Literacy, as defined by Sunni Brown, is "using visual materials in various contexts" so that we can "Identify, Understand, Interpret, Create, Communicate, and Compute."[288] As she continues to share, "Group doodling lets people see a more accurate and bigger picture, simultaneously."[289]

Whether it is due to overload or other, taking time to visually map out processes along with our vision and goals is an important, and often overlooked, element of remote and hybrid work.

In 2011, Patti Dobrowolski introduced the world to the Draw Your Future™ process in her TED talk. This process makes a vision visible.

As Dobrowolski said, "Research shows 9 out of 10 of us who set goals every year never achieve them! Why? We know exactly what to do, but we live in a highly distracting world, and it's easy to lose track when you don't have a clear picture to help you stay focused. Draw Your Future™ is a simple, visual process to help you and your clients quickly understand where they are now, the Current Reality, where they want to be a year from today, the Desired New Reality, and identify the 3 Bold Steps they can take to get there."[290]

Learn more about Patti's work at UpYourCreativeGenius.com

Some other examples of processes you may visually map:

- The Stoplight—Red, Yellow, and Green—of the project status report
- Process maps
- The customer journey
- Your origin story (how you came to be as a team or organization)

The final area Wall flags is that of **disagreement.** Consider this common scenario:

"Disagreement about teamwork can also result in covert resistance to resolving the uncertainty. For example, a team member may have a fixed idea about what role she wants to play on the team. However, she may fear that a discussion of this matter will result in an answer she doesn't want to hear. She prefers to let the question linger unexamined, giving her the latitude to continue to do what she wants to do anyway, all the while trying not to draw the kind of attention that will result in a more open resolution of the matter. After a while, this kind of subtle sabotage of the team's developmental process results in resentment from the rest of the team that affects overall morale."[291]

BEING A CHANGE CATALYST

Whether you are a team member or team leader, being a change catalyst can be an important role. As I wrote in Teams365 #504:[292]

Change catalyst is another key skill in leadership today. Today the norm for most leaders is working in ever changing contexts, and needing to adapt "on the fly."

According to Goleman, Boyatzis, and McKee, leaders high in this competency "are able to recognize the need for change, challenge the status quo, and champion the new order. They can be strong advocates for the change even in the face of opposition, making the argument for it compellingly. They also find practical barriers to change."[293]

As you think about your skills, where do they reside in this area of being a change catalyst?

Part of being a change catalyst is also recognizing how people go through change. Rogers' change model identified six different stages or ways people may approach the change process. You may have members on your team who are innovators (those who are eager to create change), early adopters (those who embrace the change early on), early majority (those who get on the bus relatively early), late majority (those who slowly adapt/get on the bus with change), and laggards (those who resist change). Being aware of who will be advocates for change on the team is just as important as recognizing those who might need more support and conversation/attention throughout any change process.

What do you recognize in yourself about how you respond to, and initiate, change?

6 SIX TEAMWORK QUESTIONS—CHANGE

1. What are people's approaches to change?
2. What are the barriers to change?
3. What is driving change?
4. What is the hardest part of change?
5. What type of support do people need as they move through change?
6. What's going to reinforce the change process?

RECONNECTING THE WORKSPACE TIP—PROJECT MANAGEMENT

Projects are the vehicle of many teams in the hybrid and remote space. Projects really are a microcosm of larger initiatives. Consider what's going to help teams keep connected and keep their work within scope, time, and budget.

As it relates to connection, consider how projects can integrate many of the concepts covered throughout the book and in the Reconnecting the Workspace Tips.

END OF CHAPTER QUESTIONS

- What is important to note about project management?
- What do you notice about change in your team?
- What different types of programming can you use to move ideas and projects forward?

CHAPTER 21
SUMMARY AND WHAT'S NEXT

"Disruption isn't about what happens to you.
It's about how you respond to what happens to you."[294]
–Jay Samit

Principle: Ongoing learning, embrace the chaos, expect the unexpected.

Myth: Things will stay the same. In fact, it is likely that the pace of change will continue to be explored. Learning how to embrace the chaos and expect the unexpected is key. Our ability to become continuous learners may become the next wave of Darwinism, or survival of the fittest.

This chapter includes:

- A look at some of the emerging themes and related topics to what we've explored throughout the book
- Top 100 takeaways from different sections of the book
- An overview of the principles, myths, metaphors, and brain tips from across the book

My intent in pulling this book together was that it would be focused on practical, tactical ideas that you, as a remote, digital, or online professional, could implement right away. Whether you are a team leader, business owner, or individual contributor, it is my hope that you will put these ideas into practice, leverage the team tools, and consider how the brain tips can help to harness the best of your team.

In operating in a context that changes so rapidly, it's important to have a "go to" place to find information. With that in mind, this chapter focuses not only on the "what's next," but on summarizing some of the key ideas from each chapter. Rather than an appendix, this chapter pulls the top ideas out of each chapter to synthesize what we have covered.

A challenge when writing in a space which is ever-changing is to distill things down to the core, and leave them as platform-agnostic as possible. I hope that you will find that this book continues to be a valued resource even as things continue to evolve.

This book wraps up with a short focus on what's next. With virtual reality, AI, asynchronous leadership, and other factors becoming the norm, what are some of the themes teams may be impacted by going forward?

DESIGN THINKING

Teams today are being impacted by many new influencers, including the emerging disciplines of Design Thinking, Agile, Virtual Reality, and Change. While I would have loved to have included more on these disciplines and approaches, it would have made this book even longer. Given that some of these will be of interest, here's a quick overview of some of them:

Design Thinking is being embraced by organizations of all kinds, from humanitarian organizations to financial services. Design Thinking starts with the end user in mind.

Sharon Boller offers this definition: "Design thinking evolves solutions through an iterative process of observation, insight, ideation, experimentation, and testing. Its goal is to produce solutions that find the 'sweet spot' between human needs, business viability, and technical feasibility. The end user of the solution is the focal point. Any solution devised through the process must be designed with this user top-of-mind and involved in the formulation, design, and testing of the solution."[295]

Design Thinking involves these five main stages:

1. Empathize
2. Define
3. Ideate
4. Prototype
5. Test

Often, a sixth step is added: Implement.

There are many useful tools which we can incorporate, from Rapid Prototyping to Empathy Mapping to Journey Mapping to thinking about innovation to even using Mind Mapping to draw connections

Why it's important:

- It's about the end user
- It gets us moving: sprints and hacks

Disciplines and Approaches

Agile: Agile approaches have been embraced in recent years across industries and organizations of all sizes. It is likely that it will continue to be an influential approach for organizations or all sizes.

Agile has been referenced throughout the book. Whether it's the team-based approach or rapid iteration, many elements of Agile are embraced outside of the IT world it grew from. Other key elements which Agile has given us are:

- Getting things done
- Learning from experience quickly
- Adjusting as we can

Moving closer to the speed of change, the context is likely to change in the frame of longer projects, so these rapid cycles of prototyping help us to not invest as much and to design as we go.

Rapid Prototyping: Another current business driver is around getting things done quicker, faster, and in less time. One methodology which Agile has provided to us is the notion of rapid prototyping. While time has always been a pressure, as has getting things to market quickly, economics are encouraging this to be embraced across industries and nations. Rapid prototyping is emerging in all kinds of areas—from 3 D printing, to course design, to consumer products.

Sprints: One popular form of rapid prototyping is that of sprints. As Jake Knapp, author of *Sprint: How to solve big problems and test new ideas in just five days*, writes in "The Design Sprint," "On Monday, you'll map out the problem and pick an important place to focus. On Tuesday, you'll sketch competing solutions on paper. On Wednesday, you'll make difficult decisions and turn your ideas into a testable hypothesis. On Thursday, you'll hammer out a high-fidelity prototype. And on Friday, you'll test it with real live humans."[296]

In my work with business owners, this has meant collapsing design programs which used to run over the course of several hours into 45 minute sprints. It's amazing to see how we can do things.

Another format is to build out momentum in our work. Earlier this year I hosted the 21 for 21 series of Virtual Co-working Sprints, which had people coming together for 21 days at a time to work through 21 minutes of co-work together, where they brought projects that were important, and often, stuck. The results were amazing, and this experimentation continues. Experimentation can be large or small in the world of virtual. It's about quality, not quantity, given that scale can occur quickly once you've got it right!

NOW WHAT?

What are the core activities you want to put into practice?

As Aristotle wrote, "Learning is one thing, action is another."

What are you committed to doing?

This book could provide you with a 20-week cycle of learning, even if you focused on one of the chapters each week. Consider what you want to incorporate into your work. As you read through the Top 5 of 20 of the core areas this book has touched on, be sure to distill your key learning down, and highlight what you have learned.

TOP FIVES

This chapter is all about making things easier. In the spirit of capturing ideas and notations, and helping you remember all the different things that might be important, here is a list of 100 things.

MEETINGS (Chapter 19: Meetings and Presentations)

1. Make meetings regular.
2. Have a plan. What kind of meeting is it—for updates? To share information? To problem solve? Brainstorm? Other?
3. Keep to time. Keep them brief.
4. Make them interactive. Use engagement strategies of polls, breakouts, and annotation.
5. Rotate roles: timekeeper, note taker, facilitator.

Resource: Use the Eight Essential Meeting Questions.

COACHING QUESTIONS (Chapter 15: Coaching and Mentoring)

1. Short and concise: five to six words in length.
2. Questions can expand thinking and focus, gain awareness, and support people into action.
3. Start questions with *What* and *How*.
4. Avoid questions starting with *Why* unless there are high levels of trust.
5. Listen to what the person is saying, not the next question you are looking to formulate.

Resource: 20 questions for your next coaching conversation (+ Video)

LISTENING (Chapter 6: Communication and Conversations)

1. What are you listening for? Tone, pace, pitch, word choice?
2. What are you paying attention to? Are you listening to understand or figure it out? *Or* ar you listening 100% to what the person is saying?
3. What is the person *not* saying? What is the meaning behind the word?

4. What is getting in the way of listening?
5. How does body language align with what is being said?

Resource: Three levels of listening

FEEDBACK
(Chapter 13: Performance Management and Feedback)

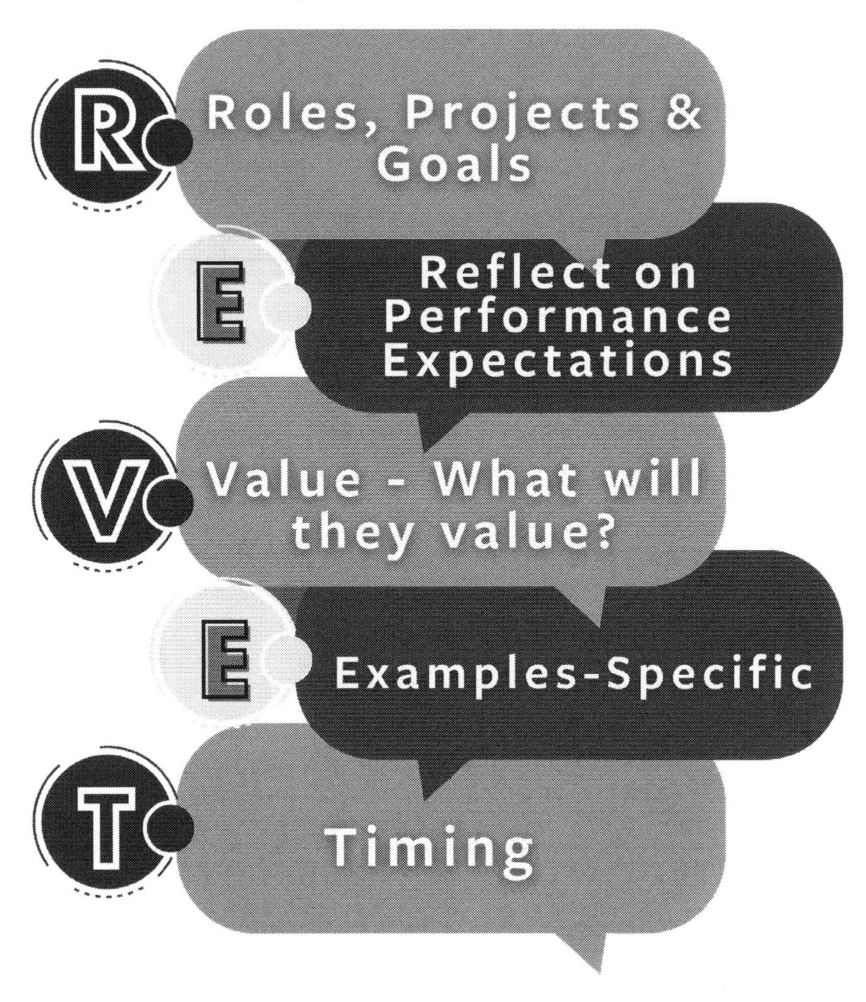

1. Make feedback regular and get everyone involved.
2. Make feedback constructive and positive.
3. Make feedback specific and based on observable behaviors. What happened? What was the impact?
4. REVET Model: Consider the needs of the person and what they value (verbal, written, time to reflect, in the moment).
5. Follow up with feedback given. What are you doing to put it into practice?

Resource: REVET Checklist

COACHING PROCESS
(Chapter 15: Coaching and Mentoring)

1. Where is the person at with this topic right now? Where do they want to go?
2. What does the person you are speaking with want—clarity, expansion of thinking, planning, brainstorming, new perspectives, a road map, other?
3. What will success look like at the end of the conversation?
4. How are you using the conversation to support goals, action and awareness, accountability?
5. What are the next steps? What does accountability look like?

Resource: Four cornerstones of coaching

MENTORING
(Chapter 15: Coaching and Mentoring)

1. Mentoring is about sharing experience with another person.
2. Mentoring helps with understanding the political context of a situation.
3. Mentoring should benefit both parties (mentor and protégé).
4. What does the mentee want to focus on? What would they benefit from hearing?
5. Incorporate the lifecycle of mentoring.

Resource: Mentoring Questions

TALENT MANAGEMENT
(Chapter 11: Learning and the Talent Cycle—Developing Your People)

1. What focus is needed around recruitment?
2. What can orientation and onboarding include to help new members understand the culture, learn how we do things, and find the people and resources they need to be successful?
3. What onboarding activities are there for the first 90 days for leaders and team members?
4. What training and development needs are there?
5. Take time getting to know your team.

Resource: Talent Management Checklist

ONE-ON-ONES
(Chapter 9: Leadership Practices)

1. Make one-on-ones regular.
2. Schedule them in.

3. What does the person want to focus on? Need from the leader and team members?
4. What is the follow through you need to check in on?
5. What frequency of conversations and type of conversations are valued?

Resource: One-on-one 20 Questions

TEAM CULTURE—CREATING ONE (Chapter 4: The Tapestry of Teams)

1. Team culture is about "how we to things here."
2. Team culture is made up of our values, practices, artefacts, slogans, mantras and mottos.
3. Team culture may be different than organizational culture.
4. What are the three adjectives which describe our culture?
5. Systems theory indicates that there is an "essence" of a team culture. Even if team members leave, the culture will remain the same.

Resource: Team Culture Checklist

TEAM CULTURE—CREATING OUR OWN (Chapter 4: The Tapestry of Teams)

1. What are the three adjectives that describe the team?
2. What are our values?
3. What are the behavioral norms that shape us?
4. How do we do things on the team?
5. What's important for other teams to know about us?

Resource: Team Culture Checklist

MATRIX RELATIONSHIPS (Chapters 9: Leadership Practices and 10: No Person Is an Island)

1. Three-way meetings are an important structure and process for updates, alignment, and work planning.
2. What are the priorities of the different parties?
3. What are the values and organizational culture of the different parties?
4. What needs to be shared with each leader/team (i.e., what issues should be surfaced)?
5. What is important for each of the three parties?

Resource: Matrix Management Three-way Meeting template

PROJECT MANAGEMENT
(Chapter 20: Project Management 101)

1. What does on time, in scope, and within budget mean?
2. What channels exist to keep others updated (i.e., meetings, knowledge sharing, etc.)? Is everyone clear on the milestones, success measures, roles, and overlap?
3. How does your work contribute to others? What are the success measures? How are you tracking and following progress?
4. When are you scheduling status meetings and updates?
5. What is the best approach to manage your project?

Resource: Project Management Status Report

CHANGE MANAGEMENT
(Chapter 20: Project Management 101)

1. Not everyone moves through the change process in the same way.
2. What are you doing to not only introduce the change but reinforce it along the way?
3. What's In It For *Me* Around Change?
4. What's the big picture of change?
5. What's the little picture of change?

Resource: Rogers' Model of Change

ONBOARDING
(Chapter 12: Onboarding for New Virtual Team Members and Leaders)

1. Onboarding goes beyond the initial orientation program. Think 90 days.
2. What are the essential elements which are important to communicate about the team, role, work etc.?
3. Who can provide support to new team members?
4. How clearly have expectations been shaped?
5. Share information about roles, culture, and communication channels.

Resource: Onboarding Checklist

TEAM EFFECTIVENESS
(Chapter 3: Team Effectiveness)

1. Review the Six Factors of High Performing Teams.
2. What is our vision for the team? How is this communicated and visible to us?
3. What are we doing to build relationships and focus on our results?
4. What does the team need in order to move ahead?
5. What are the team practices that are important for connection, information sharing, and focus?

Resource: Six Factors for Team Effectiveness checklist

RELATIONSHIP MANAGEMENT
(Chapter 10: No Person Is an Island—Relationship Management and Collaboration)

1. What are your most important relationships internally? Externally?
2. What do you bring to the table with each relationship?
3. What are the needs and values of the people you are in connection with?
4. What needs to be communicated to different stakeholders? When? At what level?
5. What "value add" do you bring to each relationship?

Resources: Relationship Map

MANAGING UP
(Chapter 9: Leadership Practices)

1. What does your boss(es) value?
2. What are their priorities?
3. What do they need from you?
4. What do you need to communicate upwards?
5. What issues does your boss want to share with others?

Resource: Checklist for Items to Go Up and Go Down

MEETINGS
(Chapter 19: Meetings and Presentations)

1. Ask the Eight Essential Meeting questions before each meeting.
2. What type of meeting is this? Is this the right platform for our type of meeting?
3. What pre-work needs to take place to make the most of the meeting?
4. What are the top three focus areas? What results do we want?
5. What follow-up is needed?

Resource: Eight Essential Meeting Questions

PRESENTATIONS
(Chapter 19: Meetings and Presentations)

1. Connect early on with the WIIFM.
2. Consider your open, body, and close.
3. Consider your visual anchor points.
4. What are you doing to connect in with the Six Layers of Connection™?
5. What Five Engagement Levers™ have you planned?

Resource: Presentation Checklist

EMOTIONAL INTELLIGENCE
(Chapter 17: Emotional Intelligence)

1. EI skills are more important than technical skills, the further you go up the leadership ladder.
2. We need skills in relationship management.
3. Self-awareness helps us know ourselves.
4. Self-management: What are your triggers?
5. Social Awareness: What do others need?

Resource: EI Checklist

CONFLICT MANAGEMENT
(Chapter 14: Conflict Management)

1. Everyone approaches conflict in different ways.
2. It is important to have a common approach to addressing conflict on a team.
3. What's at stake if this issue is not resolved?

4. What's important about the results of this conflict and the relationship at stake?
5. What are the most important things to communicate?

Resource: Conflict Styles

EMAIL ETIQUETTE
(Chapter 6: Communication and Conversations)

1. Use the subject lines effectively, requesting response as appropriate.
2. Make a specific request for reply (i.e., by the end of the day).
3. Use CC and BCC conservatively.
4. Reply in due course.
5. Use Out of Office—who is covering?

Resource: Sample email

LEADERSHIP PRACTICES
(Chapter 9: Leadership Practices)

1. What can you do to provide clear direction?
2. What is important about rewards and recognition?
3. One-on-ones are a critical part of team success.
4. The role of the team leader: list your top five things.
5. Which hats does the team leader wears?

Resources: Team Leader Hats or One-on-One Questions

TEAMWORK PRACTICES
(Chapter 8: Teamwork Practices and Skills for Results and Relationships)

1. Focusing on *results* and *relationships*.
2. Busting assumptions.
3. Knowing and not knowing.
4. Keeping connected as a virtual team member.
5. Building relationships.

Resource: Appreciations

PERSONAL PRODUCTIVITY AND TIME MANAGEMENT
(Chapter 18: Personal Productivity and Time Management)

1. Consider the Pareto principle—from what 20% of your time do you get 80% of your results?
2. What do you need to say no to?
3. Time tracker—where is your time really going?
4. Tap the power of renewal.
5. What is urgent versus what is important?

Resource: Time tracker

STRENGTHS
(Chapter 16: Strengths-Based Teamwork)

1. People who use their strengths every day at work are more engaged.
2. We all have unique strengths. When allowed to use them, we may move into flow.
3. What does the team require? What are their strengths?
4. What's missing on the team?
5. How are strengths being overused and creating a blind spot?

Resource: Strengths-based activity

BRAIN TIPS AND TOOLS

Over the course of the book we have covered 20 different Brain Tips and Tools, Principles, and Myths. This chart summarizes the different components of each chapter for easy reference.

CHAPTER	PRINCIPLE	MYTH	BRAIN TIP	TOOL	METAPHOR
Chapter 1: Workspaces in Today's Virtual, Hybrid, and Remote World	Keep it simple	We physically need to be together	Make It Visual	Mind Map	VUCA
Chapter 2: Today's Workspace—The Digital World	Expect the unexpected	It's all the same	Motivation and Color	Ladder of Inference	Chaos
Chapter 3: Team Effectiveness	Take time to co-create	I can do it all alone	Oxytocin	Six Factors	Link
Chapter 4: The Tapestry of Teams	Meet people where they are at	Everyone wants the same	Synchrony	Working with Styles	Different Styles
Chapter 5: The Triad of Trust, Safety, and Connection	It's reciprocal	Leader as driver	Growth Mindset and Amygdala Hijack	Trust Indicators	Triad
Chapter 6: Communication and Conversations	It's all about the conversation	We all want to communicate in the same way	Priming for Listening	Ask Better Questions. Have a Better Conversation and Results	Speech Bubbles
Chapter 7: Making it Scalable—Systems, Platforms, Tools	Lowest Common Denominator	I need to have all the answers	The Importance of a Social Network	Relationship Mapping	Practices
Chapter 8: Teamwork Practices and Skills for Results and Relationships	Ensure all voices are included	Everyone is the same	Zoom Fatigue is Real	Appreciation: At Your Best/ Prioritizing	Innovations

CHAPTER	PRINCIPLE	MYTH	BRAIN TIP	TOOL	METAPHOR
Chapter 9: Leadership Practices	Empower others	It's all about the leader	Neural Pathways and Habits	Is/Is Not	Leadership
Chapter 10: No Person Is an Island—Relationship Management and Collaboration	Relationships are an important part of high performance	I work in isolation *or* No person is an island	Mirror Neurons, Virtual Handshakes, and Bonding	Relationship Map	Relationships
Chapter 11: Learning and Talent Cycle: Developing Your People (Talent Mangement)	Teams which excel invest time and effort	Team development and capacity building happen naturally	Priming	Capacity Development Checklist	Connected Lightbulb
Chapter 12: Onboarding for New Team Members and Leaders	Set people up for success	Will you sink or swim?	Mental Models	90-Day Checklist	Checklist
Chapter 13: Performance Management and Feedback	Everyone owns performance managment and feedback	Feedback is only once a year	How Does Feedback Trigger Us?	SMART-E REVET Performance Tree	+/– Speech Bubble
Chapter 14: Conflict Management	Address issues quicky and swiftly	Conflict is bad	Amygdala Hijack	What's Important?	Conflict
Chapter 15: Coaching and Mentoring	Growth and development occur over time	Coaching is just about results and action	PEA/NEA	Arc of Coaching Conversation Mentoring Log	Roadmap
Chapter 16: Strengths-Based Teamwork	Connection with strengths = engagement and productivity	We can do all things well	Strengths, Habits, and Neuroplasticity	Strengths with Visual Cards	Superpower
Chapter 17 Emotional Intelligence	Emotional intelligence is critical for success	Soft skills are not needed	Emotional Contagion	Johari Window	Window

CHAPTER	PRINCIPLE	MYTH	BRAIN TIP	TOOL	METAPHOR
Chapter 18: Personal Productivity and Time Management	Boundaries and balance are important for doing more with less	We can work 24/7	Myth of Multitasking	Time Tracker	Productivity and Clock
Chapter 19: Meetings and Presentations	Preparation makes perfect	Just wing it!	Visual Anchors	Virtual Meeting Planner	Meetings and Presentations
Chapter 20: Project Management 101	Projects are living, breathing entities	A plan always stays the same	Dopamine Hits, Quick Wins, and Momentum	Virtual Mapping of a Process	Projects
Chapter 21: Summary and What's Next	Ongoing learning is essential.	Things will stay the same	No Brain Tip	Top 100 List	Next Arrow

RECONNECTING THE WORKSPACE TIP—ONGOING LEARNING

The world of remote and hybrid work requires ongoing flexibility and learning. What do you want to keep learning about? What new horizons exist? What's going to continue to help you bring your best self to work?

END OF CHAPTER QUESTIONS

As we wrap up our journey:

- What are the top 3–5 learnings you are taking from this book?
- Which myths have been shattered for you?
- Which principles are you going to embrace?
- What are you going to put into practice right away?

ENDNOTES

1. Ray Wang, *Disrupting Digital Business: Create an Authentic Experience in the Peer-to-Peer Economy* (Boston: Harvard Business Review Press 2015).

2. Eric Schmidt, "Every 2 Days We Create as Much Information as We Did Up to 2003," *Techonomy: Extra Crunch,* (August 4, 2010), https://techcrunch.com/2010/08/04/schmidt-data/?guccounter=1.

3. Klaus Schwab, "The Fourth Industrial Revolution," *World Economic Forum* (2021), https://www.weforum.org/about/the-fourth-industrial-revolution-by-klaus-schwab.

4. Amy Edmondson, "Psychological Safety and Learning Behavior in Work Teams," *Administrative Science Quarterly* 44, no. 2 (June 1999): 5, http://www.jstor.org/stable/2666999?origin=JSTOR-pdf.

5. Clint Witchalls, "Managing Virtual Teams: Taking a More Strategic Approach," *Economist Intelligence Unit,* (2009): 4, http://graphics.eiu.com/upload/eb/NEC_Managing_virtual_teams_WEB.pdf.

6. Ibid.

7. Ibid.

8. Ibid.

9. Jasmine Whitbread, as quoted in "Managing Virtual Teams: Taking a More Strategic Approach," *Economist Intelligence Unit,* (2009): 12, http://graphics.eiu.com/upload/eb/NEC_Managing_virtual_teams_WEB.pdf.

10. Gary Woodill, *The Mobile Learning Edge: Tools and Technologies for Developing Your Teams* (New York, NY: McGraw-Hill Education, 2010), 13.

11. Claire O'Malley, Giasemi Vavoula, Jp Glew, Josie Taylor, and Mike Sharples, et al., *Guidelines for Learning/Teaching/Tutoring in a Mobile Environment* (2005), https://hal.archives-ouvertes.fr/hal-00696244/document.

12. D. Keagan, "The Incorporation of Mobile Learning into Mainstream Education and Training" (October 2005), as quoted in Nilgun Ozdamar Keskin and David Metcalf, "The Current Perspectives, Theories and Practices of Mobile Learning," *TOJET: The Turkish Online Journal of Educational Technology* 10, no. 2 (April 2011): 1, https://files.eric.ed.gov/fulltext/EJ932239.pdf.

13. Simon Geddes, "Mobile Learning in the 21st Century: Benefit for Learners," Abstract, *Knowledge Tree e-journal* 30, no. 3 (2004): 1, https://webarchive.nla.gov.au/awa/20051201070451/http://pandora.nla.gov.au/pan/33606/20050928-0000/www.flexiblelearning.net.au/knowledgetree/edition06/html/pra_simon_geddes.html.

14. Jennifer Britton and Michelle Mullins, "Remote Pathways—Introducing the Remote Pathways Podcast and the Digital Dozen," Episode 1, Nov. 23, 2019, in *The Remote Pathways Podcast*, 25:07, https://www.buzzsprout.com/705708/2117871.

15. Carson Tate, "Pay Attention: Because It Impacts Your Productivity," *Huffpost*, posted December 6, 2017, https://www.huffpost.com/entry/pay-attention-because-it-impacts-your-productivity_b_10025996.

16. Sophie Nicholls Jones, "Working Remotely: It Does the Environment, Body and Business Good," *Chartered Professional Accounts Canada* (February 10, 2020), https://www.cpacanada.ca/en/news/canada/2020-04-20-remote-working-environment-impact.

17. Firstbase, "The Cost of the Office vs. Remote," https://www.firstbasehq.com/post/the-cost-of-the-office-vs-remote.

18. WSP, "How Will Covid-19 Change Demand for Office Space?" https://www.wsp.com/en-MY/insights/how-will-covid-19-change-demand-for-office-space.

19. Christopher Pappas, "Top 10 e-Learning Statistics for 2014 You Need to Know," *eLearning Industry* (December 1, 2013), https://elearningindustry.com/top-10-e-learning-statistics-for-2014-you-need-to-know.

20. Daniel Crow and Ariane Millot, "Working from Home Can Save Energy and Reduce Emissions. But How Much?" *IEA* (June 12, 2020), https://www.iea.org/commentaries/working-from-home-can-save-energy-and-reduce-emissions-but-how-much.

21. Gloria Mark, Daniela Gudith, and Ulrich Klocke, "The Cost of Interrupted Work: More Speed and Stress" (2008), Abstract, https://www.ics.uci.edu/~gmark/chi08-mark.pdf.

22. Larry Alton, "7 Tips for Dealing with Constant Interruptions," *Huffpost,* posted December 18, 2017, https://www.huffpost.com/entry/7-tips-for-dealing-with-constant-interruptions_b_5a376e9be4b02bd1c8c60831.

23. David Ulrich, "HR Interrupted," *HRProfessional Now* (July 2017), http://hrprofessionalnow.ca/leadership-matters/457-hr-interrupted.

24. Manpower Group, *Canadian HR Reporter* (September. 4, 2017).

25. Gary Woodill, *The Mobile Learning Edge: Tools and Technologies for Developing Your Teams* (New York: MGraw-Hill Education, 2010), 248.

26. Jack Nilles, *The Telecommunications-Transportation Tradeoff*, as quoted in Vicky Gan, "The Invention of Telecommuting," *Bloomberg CityLab* (December 1, 2015), https://www.bloomberg.com/news/articles/2015-12-01/what-telecommuting-looked-like-in-1973.

27. Jack Nilles, "MIS and Telecommuting: Friends or Foes?" Online article for UniForum Association, Annapolis, MD, http://www.uniforum.org/news/html/publications/ufm/feb96/friends.html.

28. "Latest Work-At-Home/Telecommuting/Mobile Work/Remote Work Statistics," *Global Workplace Analytics* (2020), https://globalworkplaceanalytics.com/telecommuting-statistics.

29. Ibid.

30. Lori Ioannou, "1 in 4 Americans Will Be Working Remotely in 2021, Upwork Survey Reveals," *CNBC* (February 6, 2021), https://www.cnbc.com/2020/12/15/one-in-four-americans-will-be-working-remotely-in-2021-survey.html.

31. Lin Grensing-Pophal, *Managing Off-Site Staff for Small Business* (Vancouver, BC. Canada: Self-Counsel Press Ltd., 2012).

32. Stephen Schilling, "The Basics of a Successful Telework Network," *HR Focus,* 76, no. 6, 9–11 (June 1999), as quoted in Elizabeth Hamilton, *Bringing Work Home: Advantages and Challenges of Telecommuting,* The Center for Work & Family, https://www.bc.edu/content/dam/files/centers/cwf/research/publications/researchreports/Bringing%20Work%20Home_Telecommuting.

33. Tom Joseph, as quoted in Emily Courtney, "Emphasize Outcomes over Hours for Remote Team Success," *Flexjobs*, posted September 2, 2020, https://www.flexjobs.com/employer-blog/work-outcomes-impact-over-hours-remote-team-success/.

34. Emily Courtney, "Remote Work Statistics: Navigating the New Normal," *Flexjobs*, posted December 21, 2020, https://www.flexjobs.com/blog/post/remote-work-statistics/.

35. Mark Murphy, "While Working from Home, People with This Personality Trait Have Experienced the Greatest Increase in Work-Life Balance," *Forbes* (September 18, 2020), https://www.forbes.com/sites/markmurphy/2020/09/18/while-working-from-home-people-with-this-personality-trait-have-experienced-the-greatest-increase-in-work-life-balance/?sh=4a368cb73d0d.

36. Lin Grensing-Pophal, *Managing Off-Site Staff for Small Business* (Vancouver, BC, Canada: Self-Counsel Press Ltd., 2012).

37. Stephen Schilling, "The Basics of a Successful Telework Network," *HR Focus,* 76, no. 6, 9–11 (June 1999), as quoted in Elizabeth Hamilton, *Bringing Work Home: Advantages and Challenges of Telecommuting,* The Center for Work & Family, p. 114, https://www.bc.edu/content/dam/files/centers/cwf/research/publications/researchreports/Bringing%20Work%20Home_Telecommuting.

38. Lin Grensing-Pophal, *Managing Off-Site Staff for Small Business* (Vancouver, BC, Canada: Self-Counsel Press Ltd., 2012), 115.

39. N. Fredric Crandall and Marc J. Wallace, *Work and Rewards in the Virtual Workplace: A "New Deal" for Organizations & Employees* (New York: AMACOM, 1998).

40. Kenneth Blanchard, Drea Zigarmi, and Robert Nelson, "Situational Leadership® after 25 Years: A Retrospective," *Journal of Leadership & Organizational Studies* 1, no. 21 (November 1, 1993), https://journals.sagepub.com/doi/abs/10.1177/107179199300100104.

41. Sunni Brown, *The Doodle Revolution: Unlock the Power to Think Differently* (New York, NY: Penguin Random House, 2014), 145.

42. Jennifer Britton, "Teams365 #794: Six Leadership Questions—Remote Workforce," *Potentials Realized*, posted March 4, 2016, https://www.potentialsrealized.com/teams-365-blog/teams365-794-six-leadership-questions-remote-workforce.

43. Jennifer Britton, "Teams365 #787: Six Leadership Questions—Remote Teams," *Potentials Realized*, posted February 26, 2016, https://www.potentialsrealized.com/teams-365-blog/teams365-787-six-leadership-questions-remote-teams.

44. 3M, "Polishing Your Presentation," Brochure, *3M Visual Systems Division* (1997), http://web.archive.org/web/20001102203936/http%3A/3m.com/meetingnetwork/files/meetingguide_pres.pdf.

45. Crockett, as quoted in "Why Visual Content Has Become the Single Most Important Way to Communicate," *Leapfrogging Success* (April 20, 2020), https://leapfroggingsuccess.com/visual-content-become-single-most-important-way-communicate/.

46. Jennifer Britton and Michelle Mullins, "Remote Pathways—Team Effectiveness in the Remote and Virtual Space," Episode 15, June 17, 2020, in *The Remote Pathways Podcast*, 15:55, https://www.remotepathways.com/podcast/ep015-team-effectiveness-in-the-remote-and-virtual-space.

47. Jennifer Britton, "Teams365 #1177: Common Mistakes Made by Virtual and Remote Team Leaders," *Potentials Realized*, posted March 22, 2017, https://www.potentialsrealized.com/teams-365-blog/teams365-1177-common-mistakes-made-by-virtual-and-remote-team-leaders.

48. Trina Hoefling, *Working Virtually: Transforming the Mobile Workplace* (Sterling, VA: Stylus Publishing, 2017), 219.

49. Jennifer Britton, "Teams365 #1163: Virtual Team Mistakes," *Potentials Realized*, posted March 8, 2017, https://www.potentialsrealized.com/teams-365-blog/teams365-1163-virtual-team-mistakes.

50. Paul Petrone, "How to Calculate the Cost of Employee Disengagement," *LinkedIn*, posted March 24, 2017, https://www.linkedin.com/business/learning/blog/learner-engagement/how-to-calculate-the-cost-of-employee-disengagement.

51. T. W. Malone and M. R. Lepper, "Making Learning Fun: A Taxonomy of Intrinsic Motivations for Learning," *Pressbooks* (1987), Chapter 27, https://learningenvironmentsdesign.pressbooks.com/chapter/malone-lepper-making-learning-fun-a-taxonomy-of-intrinsic-motivations-for-learning/.

52. Jennifer Britton, "Teams365 #736: Motivation and Your Team," *Potentials Realized,* posted January 6, 2016, https://www.potentialsrealized.com/teams-365-blog/teams365-736-motivation-and-your-team.

53. Jennifer Britton, "Teams365 #522: 6 Leadership Questions a Day-Virtual Teams," *Potentials Realized,* posted June 6, 2015, https://www.potentialsrealized.com/teams-365-blog/teams-365-522-6-leadership-questions-a-day-virtual-teams.

54. Adam Akers, et al., "Visual Color Perception in Green Exercise: Positive Effects on Mood and Perceived Exertion," Abstract, *ACS Publications* (August 2, 2012), https://doi.org/10.1021/es301685g.

55. Ibid.

56. Jennifer Britton, "Teams365 #1316: Leadership Practice—Rewards and Recognition," *Potentials Realized,* posted August 8, 2017, https://www.potentialsrealized.com/teams-365-blog/teams365-1316-leadership-practice-rewards-and-recognition.

57. Amy Edmondson, "The Three Pillars of a Teaming Culture," *Harvard Business Review* (December 17, 2013), https://hbr.org/2013/12/the-three-pillars-of-a-teaming-culture.

58. Ibid.

59. Ibid.

60. Amy Edmondson, "Creating Psychological Safety in the Workplace," January 22, 2019, in *HBR IdeaCast,* Episode 666, 27:36, https://hbr.org/podcast/2019/01/creating-psychological-safety-in-the-workplace.

61. "Agile Alliance Agile101" page, *Agile Alliance,* https://www.agilealliance.org/agile101/.

62. Cherissa Newton, "Plan vs Strategy: Is There a Difference?" *Center for Management & Organization Effectiveness,* https://cmoe.com/blog/a-plan-versus-a-strategy-is-there-a-difference/.

63. Ibid.

64. Jennifer Britton, "Teams365 #707: Leadership Myth V—Vision is not important," *Potentials Realized,* posted December 8, 2015, https://www.potentialsrealized.com/teams-365-blog/teams365-707-vision-is-not-important.

65. Jennifer Britton, "Teams365 #891: Visualization," *Potentials Realized,* June 9, 2016, https://www.potentialsrealized.com/teams-365-blog/teams365-891-team-building-tip-87-visualization.

66. Jennifer Britton, "Teams365 #1071: Team Development A–Z: F Is for Foil Modelling," *Potentials Realized,* posted December 6, 2016, https://www.potentialsrealized.com/teams-365-blog/teams365-1071-team-development-a-z-f-is-for-foil-modelling.

67. Jennifer Britton, "Teams365 #1113: Team Development Activity: V is for Vision," *Potentials Realized,* posted January 17, 2017, https://www.potentialsrealized.com/teams-365-blog/teams365-1113-team-development-activity-v-is-for-vision.

68. Google Team, "Understand Team Effectiveness," *re:Work*, https://rework.withgoogle.com/print/guides/5721312655835136/.

69. Belbin, "The Nine Belbin Team Roles," *Belbin.com*, https://www.belbin.com/about/belbin-team-roles/.

70. Glenn Parker, adaptation from "Team Players and Teamwork" (1990), https://brandmanvirtualteam1.weebly.com/uploads/7/5/8/7/7587559/12_characteristics_of_effective_teams_706.pdf.

71. Andrew Carnegie, *Goodreads,* https://www.goodreads.com/quotes/251192-teamwork-is-the-ability-to-work-together-toward-a-common.

72. Bruce Tuckman and Mary Ann Jensen, "Stages of Small-Group Development Revisited," Review, *Group & Organization Studies,* 2, no. 4, (December 1977), 419–427, http://faculty.wiu.edu/P-Schlag/articles/Stages_of_Small_Group_Development.pdf.

73. John Coleman, "Six Components of a Great Corporate Culture," *Harvard Business Review* (May 6, 2013), https://hbr.org/2013/05/six-components-of-culture.

74. Jennifer Britton, "Teams365 #226: Team Culture: Values, Practices and Habits," *Potentials Realized,* posted August 14, 2014, https://www.potentialsrealized.com/teams-365-blog/teams365-226-team-culture-values-practices-and-habits.

75. Jan Stanley, "Routines: The Unexpected Power of Habits, Practices, and Rituals," *TEDxBeloit,* (October 7, 2015), https://www.youtube.com/watch?v=O8PTQNDfdnU.

76. Jan Stanley, "Instead of a Resolution, Try a New Year Routine (Part 1)," *Positive Psychology News* January 4, 2016, https://positivepsychologynews.com/news/jan-stanley/2016010435265.

77. Mark Fields, as quoted in Jeffrey McCracken, "'Way Forward' Requires Culture Shift at Ford," *The Wall Street Journal* (January 23, 2006), https://www.wsj.com/articles/SB113797951796853248.

78. Irving L. Janis, *Groupthink: Psychological Studies of Policy Decisions and Fiascoes* (Boston: Wadsworth Cengage Learning, 1982).

79. Claudia Fernandez, "Creating Thought Diversity: The Antidote to Group Think," *Journal of Public Health Management & Practice,* 13, no. 6 (2007): 670–671, https://journals.lww.com/jphmp/fulltext/2007/11000/creating_thought_diversity__the_antidote_to_group.21.aspx.

80. Geert Hofstede, *Hofstede Insights*, https://www.hofstede-insights.com/.

81. Andy Molinsky, *Global Dexterity: How to Adapt Your Behavior Across Cultures without Losing Yourself in the Process,* (Boston: Harvard Business Review Press, 2013), 9.

82. Ibid.

83. Ibid., 13.

84. EHS Today Staff, "What Does Generation Z Value?" *EHS Today,* December 4, 2019, https://www.ehstoday.com/safety-leadership/article/21920499/what-does-generation-z-value.

85. Jennifer Britton, *Effective Virtual Conversations: Engaging Digital Dialogue for Better Learning, Relationships, and Results* (Newmarket, ON, Canada: Potentials Realized Media, 2017), 45–47.

86. Inside Small Business, "Gen Z Revealed as the 'Entrepreneur' Generation" (July 8, 2020), https://insidesmallbusiness.com.au/featured/gen-z-the-most-likely-generation-to-become-entrepreneurs.

87. Ryan Jenkins, "12 Surprising Generation Z Insights on Their Work Attitudes and Behaviors," *Ryan Jenkins,* https://blog.ryan-jenkins.com/2016/11/03/12-surprising-generation-z-insights-on-their-work-attitudes-and-behaviors.

88. Karim Ansari, "5 Ways to Prepare Your Workplace for Generation Z," *Undercover Recruiter,* https://theundercoverrecruiter.com/generation-z-workplace/.

89. EY, "Failure Drives Innovation, According to EY Survey on Gen Z," *Cision PR Newswire,* September 18, 2018, https://www.prnewswire.com/news-releases/failure-drives-innovation-according-to-ey-survey-on-gen-z-300714436.html.

90. Ryan Jenkins, "Generation Z Versus Millennials: The 8 Differences You Need to Know," *Inc. 5000* (July 19, 2017), https://www.inc.com/ryan-jenkins/generation-z-vs-millennials-the-8-differences-you-.html.

91. "How it Works" page, *Herrmann,* https://www.thinkherrmann.com/how-it-works#core_idea.

92. Jennifer Britton, "Teams365 #1393: Virtual and Remote Team Activity #9: Styles," *Potentials Realized,* posted October 24, 2017, https://www.potentialsrealized.com/teams-365-blog/teams365-1393-virtual-and-remote-team-activity-9-styles.

93. Sally Blount and Sophie Leroy, "The Synchronous Leader: How Social Synchrony Impacts Teams," *Human Synergistics International* (November 29, 2016), https://www.humansynergistics.com/blog/culture-university/details/culture-university/2016/11/29/the-synchronous-leader-how-social-synchrony-impacts-teams.

94. Simon Sinek, *Find Your Why: A Practical Guide for Discovering Purpose for You and Your Team* (New York: Portfolio/Penguin, 2017), 104.

95. Stephen Covey, "The Business Case for Trust," *Chief Executive* (June 4, 2007), https://chiefexecutive.net/the-business-case-for-trust/.

96. Towers Perrin, "Engaged Employees Drive the Bottom Line," http://www.twrcc.co.za/Engaged%20employees%20drive%20the%20bottom%20line.pdf.

97. Amy Edmondson, "Psychological Safety and Learning Behavior in Work Teams," *Administrative Science Quarterly* 44, no. 2 (June 1999): 354, http://www.jstor.org/stable/2666999?origin=JSTOR-pdf.

98. Laura Delizonna, "High-Performing Teams Need Psychological Safety. Here's How to Create It," *Harvard Business Review* (April 24, 2017), https://hbr.org/2017/08/high-performing-teams-need-psychological-safety-heres-how-to-create-it.

99. Barbara Fredrickson, "The Broaden-and-Build Theory of Positive Emotions," *NCBI,* 359, no. 1449 (September 29, 2004): 1367–1378, https://dx.doi.org/10.1098%2Frstb.2004.1512.

100. Jennifer Britton, "Teams365 #774: Six Leadership Questions—Trust," *Potentials Realized,* posted February 13, 2016, https://www.potentialsrealized.com/teams-365-blog/teams365-774-six-leadership-questions-trust.

101. Jennifer Britton, *Effective Virtual Conversations: Engaging Digital Dialogue for Better Learning, Relationships, and Results* (Newmarket, ON, Canada: Potentials Realized Media, 2017), 103.

102. Cuban Proverb, *Leading Thoughts*, https://www.leadershipnow.com/listeningquotes.html.

103. Peter Senge, *Leading Thoughts,* https://www.leadershipnow.com/listeningquotes.html.

104. Lizet Pollen, "6 Ways to Improve the Leadership Skill of Active Listening," *LinkedIn*, November 9, 2017, https://www.linkedin.com/pulse/6-ways-improve-leadership-skill-active-listening-lizet-pollen/.

105. Chip Bell, *Leading Thoughts,* https://www.leadershipnow.com/listeningquotes.html.

106. Jennifer Britton, "Teams365 #1146: *LinkedIn* Post: 12 Keys to an Effective Accountability Strategy," *Potentials Realized,* posted February 19, 2017, https://www.potentialsrealized.com/teams-365-blog/teams365-1146-linkedin-post12-keys-to-an-effective-accountability-strategy.

107. Abigail Johnson Hess, "Here's How Many Hours American Workers Spend on Email Each Day," *make it* (September 22, 2019), https://www.cnbc.com/2019/09/22/heres-how-many-hours-american-workers-spend-on-email-each-day.html.

108. Matt Plummer, "How to Spend Way Less Time on Email Every Day," *Harvard Business Review* (January 22, 2019), https://hbr.org/2019/01/how-to-spend-way-less-time-on-email-every-day.

109. Heinz Tschabitscher, "19 Fascinating Email Facts," *Lifewire,* March 15, 2020, https://www.lifewire.com/how-many-emails-are-sent-every-day-1171210.

110. Michael E. Gerber, *The E Myth Revisited: Why Most Small Businesses Don't Work and What to Do About It* (New York: Harper Collins, 1995).

111. Rob Cross, Reb Rebele, and Adam Grant, "Collaborative Overload," *Harvard Business Review* (January 1, 2016), 74–79, https://store.hbr.org/product/collaborative-overload/R1601E.

112. Jennifer Britton, "Teams365 #532: Systems to Support Your Work as Leader," *Potentials Realized,* posted June 16, 2015, https://www.potentialsrealized.com/teams-365-blog/teams365-532-systems-to-support-your-work-as-a-leader.

113. Jennifer Britton, "Teams365 #211: Meeting Management Faux-Pas," *Potentials Realized,* posted July 30, 2014, https://www.potentialsrealized.com/teams-365-blog/teams365-211-meeting-management-faux-pas1.

114. Jennifer Britton, "Teams365 #121: What Is Your Priority This Month?" *Potentials Realized,* posted May 1, 2014, https://www.potentialsrealized.com/teams-365-blog/teams-365-121-what-is-your-priority-this-month.

115. Jennifer Britton, "Teams365 #792: Making Remote Work for You," *Potentials Realized,* posted March 2, 2016, https://www.potentialsrealized.com/teams-365-blog/teams365-792-making-remote-work-work-for-you.

116. Jennifer Britton, "Teams365 #1870: Productivity Tip 18—What Doesn't Get Scheduled Doesn't Get Done." *Potentials Realized,* posted February 12, 2019, https://www.potentialsrealized.com/teams-365-blog/teams365-1870-productivity-tip-18-what-doesnt-get-scheduled-doesnt-get-done.

117. Jennifer Britton, "Teams365 #979: Gearing Up for Back to Work," *Potentials Realized,* posted September 5, 2016, https://www.potentialsrealized.com/teams-365-blog/teams365-979-gearing-up-for-back-to-work.

118. Vanessa Druskat and Steven Wolff, "Building the Emotional Intelligence of Groups," *Harvard Business Review,* 79, no. 3 (March 1, 2001): 80–90, 164, https://store.hbr.org/product/building-the-emotional-intelligence-of-groups/R0103E.

119. Keith Ferrazzi, "Getting Virtual Teams Right," *Harvard Business Review* (December 2014), https://hbr.org/2014/12/getting-virtual-teams-right.

120. Kim Scott, *Radical Candor: How to Get What You Want by Saying What You Mean* (London: Pan Macmillan, 2019), 217.

121. Robert Bruce Shaw, *Extreme Teams: Why Pixar, Netflix, Airbnb, and Other Cutting-Edge Companies Succeed Where Most Fail* (California: AMACOM, 2017).

122. Jennifer Britton, "Teams365 #1478: Working with Goals: The One-Page Plan," *Potentials Realized,* posted January 17, 2018, https://www.potentialsrealized.com/teams-365-blog/teams365-1478-working-with-goals-the-one-page-plan.

123. Jennifer Britton, "Peer Coaching: An Opportunity for Capacity Development," *LinkedIn,* posted February 28, 2018, https://www.linkedin.com/pulse/peer-coaching-opportunity-capacity-development-jennifer/.

124. Joseph Grenny, "The Best Teams Hold Themselves Accountable," *Harvard Business Review* (May 30, 2014), https://hbr.org/2014/05/the-best-teams-hold-themselves-accountable.

125. Carl Robinson, "How to Be an Authentic Leader: Why It Is Important and 75 Things Your Employees Need from You," *Advanced Leadership Consulting,* http://leadershipconsulting.com/authentic-leader-important-75-things-employees-need/.

126. Kim Scott, *Radical Candor: How to Get What You Want by Saying What You Mean* (London: Pan Macmillan, 2019), 9.

127. Ibid.

128. Robert Cialdini and Steve Martin, "Secrets from the Science of Persuasion," *Influence at Work* (November 26, 2012), https://www.youtube.com/watch?v=cFdCzN7RYbw.

129. Jack Zenger and Joseph Folkman, "The Ideal Praise-to-Criticism Ratio," *Harvard Business Review* (March 15, 2013), https://hbr.org/2013/03/the-ideal-praise-to-criticism.

130. Mariana Pascha, "The PERMA Model: Your Scientific Theory of Happiness," *Positive Psychology.com,* January 21, 2021, https://positivepsychology.com/perma-model/.

131. Gretchen Spreitzer, Christine Porath, and Christine Gibson, "Thriving at Work: Why It's Important and How to Enable More of It," *Harvard Business Review* (January 1, 2013), https://store.hbr.org/product/thriving-at-work-why-it-s-important-and-how-to-enable-more-of-it/ROT186.

132. J. J. Sutherland, *Scrum: The Art of Doing Twice the Work in Half the Time* (New York: Crown Business, 2014), 153.

133. Sonja Lyubomirsky, Laura King, and Ed Diener, "The Benefits of Frequent Positive Affect: Does Happiness Lead to Success?" *APA PsycNet,* 131, no. 6 (2005): 803–855, https://psycnet.apa.org/doi/10.1037/0033-2909.131.6.803.

134. J. J. Sutherland, *Scrum: The Art of Doing Twice the Work in Half the Time* (New York: Crown Business, 2014), 157.

135. Jennifer Britton, "Teams365 #990: Difficult Participants in the Virtual Realm," *Potentials Realized,* posted September 16, 2016, https://www.potentialsrealized.com/teams-365-blog/teams365-990-difficult-participants-in-the-virtual-realm.

136. Jennifer Britton, "Teams365 #1387: 20 Focus Areas for Virtual and Remote Team Development, #8: Strengths," *Potentials Realized,* posted October 18, 2017, https://www.potentialsrealized.com/teams-365-blog/teams365-1387-20-focus-areas-for-virtual-and-remote-team-development-8-strengths.

137. Jennifer Britton, "Teams365 #2388: Back to the Basics—Feedback," *Potentials Realized,* posted July 14, 2020, https://www.potentialsrealized.com/teams-365-blog/teams365-2388-back-to-the-basics-feedback.

138. Vignesh Ramachandran, "Stanford Researchers Identify Four Causes for 'Zoom fatigue' and Their Simple Fixes," *Stanford News,* February 23, 2021, https://news.stanford.edu/2021/02/23/four-causes-zoom-fatigue-solutions/.

139. Ibid.

140. Jim Whitehurst, as quoted in Glenn Llopis, "How to Lead in Times of Uncertainty," *Forbes* (January 5, 2017), https://www.forbes.com/sites/glennllopis/2017/01/05/how-to-lead-in-times-of-uncertainty/?sh=2faa6aa774a6.

141. Jennifer Britton, "Are You an Intrapreneur?" *Business Toolkit,* posted April 3, 2007, http://biztoolkit.blogspot.com/2007/03/are-you-intrapreneur.html.

142. The American Heritage Dictionary, def. *intrapreneur*, https://www.ahdictionary.com/word/search.html?q=intrapreneur.

143. Joyce A. Thompsen, "Leading Virtual Teams," *Quality Digest,* September 1, 2000, https://www.qualitydigest.com/magazine/2000/sep/article/leading-virtual-teams.html.

144. Jennifer Britton, "Teams365 #1231: 10 Questions for your Next Virtual Meeting," *Potentials Realized,* posted May 15, 2017, https://www.potentialsrealized.com/teams-365-blog/teams365-1231-10-questions-for-your-next-virtual-meeting.

145. Gary Hamel, *Brainy Quote,* https://www.brainyquote.com/quotes/gary_hamel_528674.

146. Marc Effron, *Leading the Way: Three Truths from the Top Companies for Leaders* (New Jersey: Wiley & Sons, 2004), 208.

147. Claire Pomeroy, "Loneliness Is Harmful to Our Nation's Health," *Scientific American* (March 20, 2019), https://blogs.scientificamerican.com/observations/loneliness-is-harmful-to-our-nations-health/.

148. Nasreen Khatri, "Being Alone Together: The Social Pandemic of Loneliness during COVID-19," *Lifespeak,* https://lifespeak.com/being-alone-together-the-social-pandemic-of-loneliness-during-covid-19/.

149. Jennifer Britton, "Teams365 #594: Matrix Management—4 Keys to Making It Work," *Potentials Realized,* posted August 17, 2015, https://www.potentialsrealized.com/teams-365-blog/teams365-594-matrix-management-4-keys-to-making-it-work.

150. Kronos, "Physical Safety, Psychological Security, Job Stability: Employees Worldwide Share Top COVID-19 Concerns for the Workplace of Today and Tomorrow," *The Workforce Institute* (September 15, 2020), https://www.kronos.com/about-us/newsroom/physical-safety-psychological-security-job-stability-employees-worldwide-share-top-covid-19-concerns.

151. Deloitte, "Remote Collaboration: Facing the Challenges of COVID-19," March 2020, https://www2.deloitte.com/content/dam/Deloitte/de/Documents/human-capital/Remote-Collaboration-COVID-19.pdf.

152. Adam Waytz, "The Limits of Empathy," *Harvard Business Review* (January 1, 2016), 69–73, https://store.hbr.org/product/the-limits-of-empathy/R1601D.

153. Morten Hansen, *Collaboration: How Leaders Avoid the Traps, Build Common Ground, and Reap Big Results* (Boston, MA: Harvard Business Publishing, 2009).

154. Rob Cross, Reb Rebele, and Adam Grant, "Collaborative Overload," *Harvard Business Review* (January 1, 2016), 76, https://store.hbr.org/product/collaborative-overload/R1601E.

155. Jennifer Britton, *Effective Virtual Conversations: Engaging Digital Dialogue for Better Learning, Relationships, and Results* (Newmarket, ON, Canada: Potentials Realized Media, 2017), 387.

156. Linda Stewart, "Building Virtual Teams: Strategies for High Performance," *Forbes* (March 30, 2012), https://www.forbes.com/sites/ciocentral/2012/03/30/building-virtual-teams-strategies-for-high-performance/.

157. Ibid.

158. Adam Schell, "Trends in Global Virtual Teams," *CultureWizard*, posted April 26, 2016, https://www.rw-3.com/blog/trends-in-global-virtual-teams.

159. Terry Bickham, *ATD Talent Management Handbook* (Alexandria: ATD Press, 2016).

160. Josh Bernoff, *Empowered: Unleash Your Employees, Energize Your Customers, and Transform Your Business* (Boston: Forrester Research Inc., 2010).

161. Jennifer Britton, *Effective Virtual Conversations: Engaging Digital Dialogue for Better Learning, Relationships, and Results* (Newmarket, ON, Canada: Potentials Realized Media, 2017), 104.

162. Education and Training page, Australian HR Institute, https://www.ahri.com.au/continuing-professional-development/education-and-training/.

163. Jennifer Britton, "Teams365 #1246: Five Things New Virtual Team Leaders Need," *Potentials Realized*, posted May 30, 2017, https://www.potentialsrealized.com/teams-365-blog/teams365-1246-five-things-new-virtual-team-leaders-need.

164. Jake Knapp, *Sprint: How to Solve Big Problems and Test New Ideas in Just Five Days* (New York: Simon & Schuster, 2016), 19.

165. Judith E. Glaser, *Conversational Intelligence: How Great Leaders Build Trust and Get Extraordinary Results* (New York: Bibliomotion Inc., 2014), 107.

166. Jim Collins, *Good to Great: Why Some Companies Make the Leap . . . And Others Don't*, (New York: Harper Collins, 2001), 51.

167. Jennifer Britton, "Teams365 #301: First 90 Days: Understanding Your Role and Developing Key Skills," *Potentials Realized*, posted October 28, 2014, https://www.potentialsrealized.com/teams-365-blog/teams365-301-first-90-days-understanding-your-role-and-developing-key-skills.

168. Jennifer Britton, "Teams365 #293: First 90 Days: Getting to Know Your Boss," *Potentials Realized,* posted October 20, 2014, https://www.potentialsrealized.com/teams-365-blog/teams365-293-first-90-days-getting-to-know-your-boss.

169. Jennifer Britton, "Teams365 #288: The First 90 Days: Knowing the Preferences of Your Team," *Potentials Realized,* posted October 15, 2014, https://www.potentialsrealized.com/teams-365-blog/teams365-288-the-first-90-days-knowing-the-preferences-of-your-team.

170. Jennifer Britton, "Teams365 #923: New Team Leader Foundations, Tip #1," *Potentials Realized,* posted July 11, 2016, https://www.potentialsrealized.com/teams-365-blog/teams365-923-new-team-leader-foundations-tip-1.

171. Jennifer Britton, "Teams365 #288: The First 90 Days: Knowing the Preferences of Your Team," *Potentials Realized,* posted October 20, 2014, https://www.potentialsrealized.com/teams-365-blog/teams365-288-the-first-90-days-knowing-the-preferences-of-your-team

172. Jennifer Britton, "Teams365 #589: First 90 Days for Global Team Leaders—Additional Considerations," *Potentials Realized,* posted August 12, 2015, https://www.potentialsrealized.com/teams-365-blog/teams365-589-first-90-days-for-global-team-leaders-additional-considerations.

173. Jennifer Britton, "Teams365 #958: Five Leadership Assumptions for New Leaders to Reframe!" *Potentials Realized,* posted August 15, 2016, https://www.potentialsrealized.com/teams-365-blog/teams365-958-five-leadership-assumptions-for-new-leaders-to-reframe.

174. Jennifer Britton, "Teams365 #1406: Effective Virtual Conversation Tip #20: Capacity Development," *Potentials Realized,* posted November 6, 2017, https://www.potentialsrealized.com/teams-365-blog/teams365-1406-effective-virtual-conversation-tip-20-capacity-development.

175. Jennifer Britton, "Work-Life Balance Tip #11," *Your Balanced Life Blog,* posted January 29, 2007, http://yourbalancedlife.blogspot.com/2007/01/work-life-balance-tip-11-set-boundaries.html.

176. Patrick Nelson, "We Touch Our Phones 2,617 Times a Day, Says Study," *Networkworld,* July 7, 2016, https://www.networkworld.com/article/3092446/we-touch-our-phones-2617-times-a-day-says-study.html.

177. Jennifer Britton, "Teams365 #738: 6 Leadership Questions a Day—Delegation," *Potentials Realized,* posted January 8, 2016, https://www.potentialsrealized.com/teams-365-blog/teams365-738-6-leadership-questions-a-day-delegation.

178. Peter Senge, *The Fifth Discipline: The Art and Practice of the Learning Organization* (New York: Currency, 2006).

179. Vicente Peñarroja, Virginia Orengo, Ana Zornoza, Jesús Sánchez, and Pilar Ripoll, "How Team Feedback and Team Trust Influence Information Processing and Learning in Virtual Teams: A Moderated Mediation Model." *Computers in Human Behavior,* Vol. 48 (July 2015); 9–16, https://www.sciencedirect.com/science/article/abs/pii/S0747563215000485.

180. Ibid.

181. John Doerr, quoted in Felipe Castro, "What is OKR?" *Felipe Castro,* https://felipecastro.com/en/okr/what-is-okr/.

182. Lillian Cunningham, "Accenture: One of World's Biggest Companies to Scrap Annual Performance Reviews," *Independent,* July 28, 2015, https://www.independent.co.uk/news/business/news/accenture-one-world-s-biggest-companies-scrap-annual-performance-reviews-10421296.html.

183. Sarah Payne, "Survey: 93% of Managers Need Training on Coaching Employees," *workhuman* , posted March 21, 2017, https://www.workhuman.com/resources/globoforce-blog/survey-93-of-managers-need-training-on-coaching-employees.

184. Chana Schoenberger, "How Performance Reviews Can Harm Mental Health," *The Wall Street Journal* (October 26, 2015), https://www.wsj.com/articles/how-performance-reviews-can-harm-mental-health-1445824925?xid=nl_powersheet.

185. Tom Rath, *Brainy Quote*, https://www.brainyquote.com/quotes/tom_rath_609414.

186. Stephen Young, "What's Trending in Employee Engagement," *WillisTowersWatson,* February 7, 2019, https://www.willistowerswatson.com/en-CA/Insights/2019/02/whats-trending-in-employee-engagement.

187. Officevibe Content Team, "Statistics on the importance of employee feedback," *Officevibe,* posted October 7, 2014, https://officevibe.com/blog/infographic-employee-feedback.

188. Jeff Fermin, "11 Remarkable Statistics about the Importance of Employee Feedback," *Business 2 Community,* October 7, 2014, https://www.business2community.com/human-resources/11-remarkable-statistics-importance-employee-feedback-infographic-01030460#iSoBSGsjVgL7PPPB.97.

189. Ibid.

190. Jennifer Britton, "Teams365 #1394: 20 Activities for Virtual and Remote Teams #10: Difficult Conversations," *Potentials Realized,* posted October 25, 2017, https://www.potentialsrealized.com/teams-365-blog/teams365-1394-20-activities-for-virtual-and-remote-teams-10-difficult-conversations.

191. Adobe Stock, Magele-Picture, File #142443954.

192. Jennifer Britton, "Teams365 #1403: Flashback Friday: Navigating Conflict," *Potentials Realized,* posted November 3, 2017, https://www.potentialsrealized.com/teams-365-blog/teams365-1403-flashback-friday-navigating-conflict.

193. Fons Trompenaars, *Riding the Waves of Innovation: Harness the Power of Global Culture to Drive Creativity and Growth* (USA: McGraw Hill, 2010), 75.

194. Jennifer Britton, "Teams365 #601: Potential Sources of Conflict in Matrix Teams," *Potentials Realized,* posted August 24, 2015, https://www.potentialsrealized.com/teams-365-blog/teams365-601-potential-sources-of-conflict-in-matrix-teams.

195. Michelle LeBaron, "Culture and Conflict," *Beyond Intractability,* July 2003, https://www.beyondintractability.org/essay/culture_conflict.

196. Morten Hansen, *Collaboration: How Leaders Avoid the Traps, Build Common Ground, and Reap Big Results* (Boston, MA: Harvard Business Publishing, 2009), 1.

197. Jennifer Britton, "Teams365 #511: Four Keys to Navigating Conflict," *Potentials Realized,* posted May 26, 2015, https://www.potentialsrealized.com/teams-365-blog/teams365-511-four-keys-to-navigating-conflict.

198. Jennifer Britton, "Teams365 #515: 6 Leadership Questions a Day—Conflict Management," *Potentials Realized,* posted May 30, 2015, https://www.potentialsrealized.com/teams-365-blog/teams355-515-6-leadership-questions-a-day-conflict-management.

199. Sarah Gonser, "What Brain Science Teaches Us about Conflict Resolution," *Edutopia,* February 5, 2020, https://www.edutopia.org/article/what-brain-science-teaches-us-about-conflict-resolution.

200. Jonathan Moules and Patricia Nilsson, "What Employers Want from MBA Graduates—and What They Don't." *Financial Times* (August 31, 2017), https://www.ft.com/content/3c380c00-80fc-11e7-94e2-c5b903247afd.

201. Ibid.

202. International Coaching Federation, "2020 ICF Global Coaching Study," https://coachingfederation.org/app/uploads/2020/09/FINAL_ICF_GCS2020_ExecutiveSummary.pdf.

203. "About ICF" page, International Coaching Federation, https://coachingfederation.org/about.

204. Sarah Payne, "Survey: 93% of Managers Need Training on Coaching Employees," *workhuman,* posted March 21, 2017, https://www.workhuman.com/resources/globoforce-blog/survey-93-of-managers-need-training-on-coaching-employees.

205. Mike Rother, "Toyota Kata—Habits for Continuous Improvements," *Methods and Tools.com,* https://www.methodsandtools.com/archive/toyotakata.php.

206. Karen Kimsey-House, Henry Kimsey-House, Phillip Sandhal, and Laura Whitworth, *Co-Active Coaching: The Proven Framework for Transformative Conversations at Work and in Life* (Boston: Hachette Book Group, 2018).

207. Kelly Palmer and David Blake, "How to Help Your Employees Learn from Each Other," *Harvard Business Review* (November 8, 2018), https://hbr.org/2018/11/how-to-help-your-employees-learn-from-each-other.

208. David Boud, "What is Peer Learning and Why Is It Important?" *Stanford University,* no. 418, https://tomprof.stanford.edu/posting/418.

209: Jennifer Britton, "Peer Coaching: An Opportunity for Capacity Development," *LinkedIn,* posted February 28, 2018, https://www.linkedin.com/pulse/peer-coaching-opportunity-capacity-development-jennifer/.

210. "Learn about the Science of CliftonStrengths," *Gallup,* https://www.gallup.com/cliftonstrengths/en/253790/science-of-cliftonstrengths.aspx.

211. Tom Rath, *Strengths Based Leadership: Great Leaders, Teams, and Why People Follow* (New York: Gallup Press, 2008), 23.

212. Jim Asplund, "Seven Reasons to Lead with Strengths," *Gallup,* September 12, 2012, https://www.gallup.com/workplace/236930/seven-reasons-lead-strengths.aspx.

213. Brandon Rigoni and Jim Asplund, "Strengths-Based Employee Development: The Business Results," *Gallup,* July 7, 2016, https://www.gallup.com/workplace/236297/strengths-based-employee-development-business-results.aspx.

214. Ibid.

215. Mihaly Csikszentmihalyi, as quoted in Kendra Cherry, "The Psychology of Flow," *verywellmind,* January 13, 2021, https://www.verywellmind.com/what-is-flow-2794768.

216. Ryan M. Niemiec, *The Power of Character Strengths: Appreciate and Ignite Your Positive Personality* (USA: VIA Institute on Character, 2019), 12.

217. Jennifer Britton, "Teams365 #1240: Five Ways to Work with Strengths and Your Team," *Potentials Realized,* posted May 24, 2017, https://www.potentialsrealized.com/teams-365-blog/teams365-1240-five-ways-to-work-with-strengths-and-your-team.

218. Becca Levy and Martin Slade, "Longevity Increased by Positive Self-Perceptions of Aging," *Journal of Personality and Social Psychology,* 83, no. 2 (2002): 261–270, https://doi.org/10.1037//0022-3514.83.2.261.

219. Jan-Emmanuel De Neve and Andrew J. Oswald, "Estimating the Influence of Life Satisfaction and Positive Affect on Later Income Using Sibling Fixed Effects," Abstract, *PNAS,* 109, no. 49 (2012): 19953–19958, https://doi.org/10.1073/pnas.1211437109.

220. Barbara Fredrickson and Marcial Losada, "Positive Affect and the Complex Dynamics of Human Flourishing," *PMC,* Abstract, June 29, 2011, https://dx.doi.org/10.1037%2F0003-066X.60.7.678.

221. Gary Luffman, "Strengths and Neuroscience: Developing a Strength Focused Habit," *Strengthscope* (July 25, 2016), https://www.strengthscope.com strengths-and-neuroscience-developing-a-strengths-focused-habit/.

222. Jenifer Marshall Lippincott, "Your Brain on Remote Work: Managing the New Normal," *training industry* (April 1, 2020), https://trainingindustry.com/articles/professional-development/your-brain-on-remote-work-managing-the-new-normal/.

223. Colleen Stanley, *Emotional Intelligence for Sales Success: Connect with Customers and Get Results* (New York: AMACOM, 2013), 4.

224. J. D. Mayer, P. Salovey, and D. R. Caruso, "The Mayer-Salovey-Caruso Emotional Intelligence Test (MSCEIT)," *Consortium for Research on Emotional Intelligence in Organizations,* http://www.eiconsortium.org/measures/msceit.html.

225. Ibid.

226. Cross, Rebele, and Grant, as quoted in Relly Nadler, "10 Reasons Why Teams Need Emotional Intelligence," *Psychology Today,* posted July 6, 2017, https://www.psychologytoday.com/ca/blog/leading-emotional-intelligence/201707/10-reasons-why-teams-need-emotional-intelligence.

227. Carolyn Stern, "How to Engage Your Virtual Team Using Emotional Intelligence," *EIExperience,* posted September 1, 2020, https://eiexperience.com/blog/how-to-engage-your-virtual-team-using-emotional-intelligence/.

228. Hillary Elfenbein, as quoted in Relly Nadler, "10 Reasons Why Teams Need Emotional Intelligence," *Psychology Today,* posted July 6, 2017, https://www.psychologytoday.com/ca/blog/leading-emotional-intelligence/201707/10-reasons-why-teams-need-emotional-intelligence.

229. Druskat and Wolff, as quoted in Relly Nadler, "10 Reasons Why Teams Need Emotional Intelligence," *Psychology Today,* posted July 6, 2017, https://www.psychologytoday.com/ca/blog/leading-emotional-intelligence/201707/10-reasons-why-teams-need-emotional-intelligence.

230. Daniel Goleman, Richard Boyatzis, and Annie McKee, *Primal Leadership: Unleashing the Power of Emotional Intelligence* (Boston: Harvard Business Review Press, 2013), xi.

231. Ibid., 255.

232. Steven J. Stein and Howard E. Book, *The EQ Edge: Emotional Intelligence and Your Success* (Mississauga, ON, Canada: John Wiley & Sons Canada Ltd., 2011), 22.

233. Ibid., 115.

234. Jennifer Britton, "Teams365 #490: Emotional Intelligence: Self-Management," *Potentials Realized,* posted May 5, 2015, https://www.potentialsrealized.com/teams-365-blog/teams365-490-emotional-intelligence-self-management.

235. Marc A. Brackett and Peter Salovey, "Measuring Emotional Intelligence with the Mayer-Salovery-Caruso Emotional Intelligence Test (MSCEIT)," *Psicothema,* 18, no. 1, (2006): 34–41, http://www.psicothema.com/psicothema.asp?id=3273.

236. Joshua Freedman and Tommaso Procicchiani, "Emotional Intelligence Fuels Vital Leadership: Three Essential Skills for High Performing Leaders," *Sixseconds,* July 6, 2020, https://www.6seconds.org/2020/07/06/three-essential-skills-for-high-performing-leaders/.

237. Joshua Freedman, Tommaso Procicchiani, and Paul Stillman, "Vitality 2017: Finding the Value of Emotions in the Global Workforce," *Sixseconds,* 2017, https://www.6seconds.org/2020/07/05/workplace-vitality-research/.

238. Roderick Gilkey, Ricardo Caceda, and Clinton Kilts, as quoted in Steven J. Stein and Howard E. Book, *The EQ Edge: Emotional Intelligence and Your Success* (Mississauga, ON, Canada: John Wiley & Sons Canada Ltd., July 5, 2011), 30.

239. Bob Johansen, *The New Leadership Literacies: Thriving in a Future of Extreme Disruption and Distributed Everything* (Oakland: Berrett-Koehler, 2017), 119.

240. Joshua Freedman and Carina Fiedeldey-Van Dijk, "Speaking Out: What Motivates Employees to Be More Productive," *epsychology.com* (2004), http://www.epsyconsultancy.com/resources/Speaking%20Out-productivity.pdf.

241. Six Seconds, "How to Cope with Uncertainty: Practicing Emotional Intelligence During Coronavirus," *sixseconds,* December 3, 2020. https://www.6seconds.org/2020/12/03/practicing-emotional-intelligence-during-covid/.

242. Mahlagha Darvishmotevali, Levent Altinay, and Glauco De Vita, "Emotional Intelligence and Creative Performance: Looking through the Lens of Environmental Uncertainty and Cultural Intelligence," *International Journal of Hospitality Management,* Vol. 73 (July 2018): 44–54, https://doi.org/10.1016/j.ijhm.2018.01.014.

243. A. H. Reilly and T. J. Karounos, "Link Between Emotional Intelligence and Cross-Cultural Leadership," *Bartleby Research,* Vol. 1 (Feb. 2009): 1–13, https://www.bartleby.com/essay/Link-Between-Emotional-Intelligence-and-Cross-Cultural-FKJ3M3ZNBC.

244. Waterford, Inc., "EQ Business Case: Bottom-Line Results That Are Real," *Waterford, Inc.,* 44, https://www.waterfordinc.com/eqbusinesscase.

245. S. Schacter, J. T. Cacioppo and R. E. Petty, and D. A. Levy and P. R. Nail, as quoted in Sigal Barsade, "Faster than a Speeding Text: 'Emotional Contagion' at Work," *Psychology Today,* posted October 15, 2014, https://www.psychologytoday.com/ca/blog/the-science-work/201410/faster-speeding-text-emotional-contagion-work.

246. Sigal Barsade, "Faster than a Speeding Text: 'Emotional Contagion' at Work," *Psychology Today,* posted October 15, 2014, https://www.psychologytoday.com/ca/blog/the-science-work/201410/faster-speeding-text-emotional-contagion-work.

247. Sigal Barsade, "The Ripple Effect: Emotional Contagion and Its Influence on Group Behavior," *Sage Publications Inc.,* 47, no. 4 (December 2002): 644–675, http://www.jstor.org/stable/3094912?origin=JSTOR-pdf.

248. Ben Wigert and Sangeeta Agrawal, "Employee Burnout, Part 1: The 5 Main Causes," *Gallup,* July 12, 2018, https://www.gallup.com/workplace/237059/employee-burnout-part-main-causes.aspx.

249. Dave Lievens, "How the Pandemic Exacerbated Burnout," *Harvard Business Review* (February 10, 2021), https://store.hbr.org/product/how-the-pandemic-exacerbated-burnout/H066FF.

250. Stephen Covey, nb. quote from mbadepot.com; site no longer available. Search Covey's Four Quadrants for Time Management for other sources.

251. JRB, "Why Walking Helps Us Think?" *The New Yorker,* August 4, 2020, https://myexcerpts.com/2020/08/04/magazine-the-new-yorker-why-walking-helps-us-think/.

252. Philippa Fogarty, "Why Walking Makes You a Better Worker," *Worklife,* March 3, 2019, https://www.bbc.com/worklife/article/20190304-why-walking-makes-you-a-better-worker.

253. Deborah Grayson Riegel, "Don't Underestimate the Power of a Walk," *Harvard Business Review* (February 2, 2021), https://hbr.org/2021/02/dont-underestimate-the-power-of-a-walk.

254. Brian Tracy, *Master Your Time, Master Your Life: The Breakthrough System to Get More Results, Faster, in Every Area of Your Life* (New York: Penguin Random House, 2016), 26.

255. Jennifer Britton, "Teams365 #241: Check It Off 4: Become Ruthless with Email," *Potentials Realized,* posted August 29, 2014, https://www.potentialsrealized.com/teams-365-blog/teams365-241-check-it-off-4-become-ruthless-with-email.

256. Matt Plummer, "How to Spend Way Less Time on Email Every Day," *Harvard Business Review* (January 22, 2019), https://hbr.org/2019/01/how-to-spend-way-less-time-on-email-every-day.

257. Jennifer Britton, "Teams365 #2051: Effective Virtual Conversations 106: Minimizing Digital Distractions and Creating More Focus," *Potentials Realized,* posted August 12, 2019, https://www.potentialsrealized.com/teams-365-blog/teams365-2051-effective-virtual-conversations-106-minimizing-digital-distractions-and-creating-more-focus.

258. Jennifer Britton, "Teams365 #941: New Team Leader Tip #13," *Potentials Realized,* posted, July 29, 2016, https://www.potentialsrealized.com/teams-365-blog/teams365-941-new-team-leader-tip-13.

259. MindTools, "The Action Priority Matrix: Making the Most of Your Opportunities," *MindTools,* https://www.mindtools.com/pages/article/newHTE_95.htm.

260. Henry Cloud, *Necessary Endings: The Employees, Businesses, and Relationships That All of Us Have to Give Up in Order to Move Forward* (New York: Harper Collins, 2010), 15.

261. W. Edwards Deming, *Brainy Quote,* https://www.brainyquote.com/quotes/w_edwards_deming_390810.

262. Jennifer Britton, "Teams365 #797: Four Ways to Minimize Distractions with Remote Work," *Potentials Realized,* posted March 7, 2016, https://www.potentialsrealized.com/teams-365-blog/teams365-797-four-ways-to-minimize-distractions-with-remote-work.

263. James Allen, *Goodreads,* https://www.goodreads.com/quotes/92409-dream-lofty-dreams-and-as-you-dream-so-shall-you.

264. Seth Godin, *Quotefancy,* https://quotefancy.com/quote/1208279/Seth-Godin-There-s-no-shortage-of-remarkable-ideas-what-s-missing-is-the-will-to-execute.

265. Drake Baer, "These 12 Meeting Mistakes Cost Companies $37 Billion a Year in Lost Productivity," *Insider,* November 20, 2014, https://www.businessinsider.com/common-meeting-mistakes-2014-11.

266. Jennifer Britton, "Teams365 #611: Team Building Tip #52: Death by Conference Call," *Potentials Realized,* posted September 3, 2015, https://www.potentialsrealized.com/teams-365-blog/teams365-611-team-building-tip-52-death-by-conference-call.

267. Judith E. Glaser, *Conversational Intelligence: How Great Leaders Build Trust and Get Extraordinary Results* (New York: Bibliomotion Inc., 2014), 103.

268. Jennifer Britton, "Teams365 #643: Three Keys to Strong Presentations," *Potentials Realized,* posted October 5, 2015, https://www.potentialsrealized.com/teams-365-blog/teams365-643-three-keys-to-strong-presentations.

269. Jennifer Britton, "Teams365 #644: Structuring Your Presentations," *Potentials Realized,* posted October 6, 2015, https://www.potentialsrealized.com/teams-365-blog/teams365-644.

270. Geoffrey James, "8 Ways Neuroscience Can Improve Your Presentations," *Inc.,* April 14, 2014, https://www.inc.com/geoffrey-james/8-ways-neuroscience-can-improve-your-presentations.html.

271. J. J. Sutherland, *Scrum: The Art of Doing Twice the Work in Half the Time* (New York: Crown Business, 2014), 34.

272. Ibid.

273. Ibid., 44.

274. Ibid., 39.

275. Ibid., 60.

276. Alan G. Ingham, George Levinger, James Graves, and Vaughn Peckham, "The Ringelmann Effect: Studies of Group Size and Group Performance," *Journal of Experimental Social Psychology,* 10 no. 4 (July 1974): 371–384, https://doi.org/10.1016/0022-1031(74)90033-X.

277. Audiopedia, "The Ringelmann Effect," *YouTube,* February 4, 2017, https://www.youtube.com/watch?v=RdcNkg4V594.

278. J. J. Sutherland, *Scrum: The Art of Doing Twice the Work in Half the Time* (New York: Crown Business, 2014), 203.

279. Lauren Marchese, "How Checklists Train Your Brain to Be More Productive and Goal Oriented," *Trello,* posted April 23, 2019, https://blog.trello.com/the-psychology-of-checklists-why

setting-small-goals-motivates-us-to-accomplish-bigger-things.

280. Jennifer Britton, "Six Team Challenges for Project Management Teams," *Business Toolkit,* posted June 12, 2008, http://biztoolkit.blogspot.com/2008/06/six-team-challenges-for-project.html.

281. Jennifer Britton, "Leadership A–Z: K Is for Kick-Off Meeting," *Business Toolkit,* posted November 28, 2013, http://biztoolkit.blogspot.com/search/label/leader%20a-z.

282. Jennifer Britton, "Teams365 #890: Raci and Accountability," *Potentials Realized,* posted June 8, 2016, https://www.potentialsrealized.com/teams-365-blog/teams365-890-raci-and-accountability.

283. Jennifer Britton, "Teams365 #554: Team Building: Project Close Out," *Potentials Realized,* posted July 8, 2015, https://www.potentialsrealized.com/teams-365-blog/teams365-554-team-building-project-close-out.

284. Dragan Milosevic, Russ Martinelli, and James Waddell, *Program Management for Improved Business Results* (Wiley, 2007): Chapter 1, Demystifying Program Management, https://doi.org/10.1002/9780470117897.ch1.

285. Russ Martinelli, Dragan Milosevic, *Project Management Toolbox: Tools and Techniques for the Practicing Project Manager* (Wiley 2008), 8.

286. Dragan Milosevic, Russ Martinelli, and James Waddell, *Program Management for Improved Business Results* (2004), 20–23.

287. Bob Wall, *Working Relationships: The Simple Truth about Getting Along with Friends and Foes at Work* (Davies-Black Publishing, 1999), 73.

288. Sunni Brown, *The Doodle Revolution: Unlock the Power to Think Differently* (New York, NY: Penguin Random House, 2014), 5.

289. Ibid., 26.

290. Patti Dobrowolski, "Draw Your Future," *TEDxRainier,* 10:35, https://www.upyourcreativegenius.com/draw-your-future.

291. Bob Wall, *Working Relationships: The Simple Truth about Getting Along with Friends and Foes at Work* (Davies-Black Publishing, 1999), 73.

292. Jennifer Britton, "Teams365 #504: Emotional Intelligence—Change Catalyst," *Potentials Realized,* posted May 19, 2015, https://www.potentialsrealized.com/teams-365-blog/teams365-504-emotional-intelligence-change-catalyst.

293. Daniel Goleman, Richard Boyatzis, and Annie McKee, *Primal Leadership: Unleashing the Power of Emotional Intelligence* (Boston: Harvard Business Review Press, 2013).

294. Jay Samit, "*Disrupt You!* Quotes," *Goodreads,* https://www.goodreads.com/work/quotes/42798988-disrupt-you-master-personal-transformation-seize-opportunity-and-thr.

295. Sharon Boller, "Design Thinking: Level-Up the Learner Experience," *Bottom-Line Performance,* October 11, 2017, https://www.bottomlineperformance.com/design-thinking-level-up-learner-experience/.

296. "The Design Sprint," *GV.com*, https://www.gv.com/sprint/.

BIBLIOGRAPHY

Biech, Elaine. *Thriving Through Change: A Leader's Practical Guide to Change Mastery.* Danvers: ASTD Press, 2007.

Britton, Jennifer. *Effective Virtual Conversations.* Newmarket: Potentials Realized Media, 2017.

Covey, Stephen M. R., and Rebecca R. Merrill. *The SPEED of Trust: The One Thing That Changes Everything.* New York, NY: Free Press, 2006.

De Bono, Edward. *Six Thinking Hats.* New York, NY: Back Bay Books, 1999.

Edmondson, Amy C. *Extreme Teaming: Lessons in Complex, Cross-Sector Leadership.* Boston, MA: Emerald Group, 2017.

Fisher, Rogers. *Getting to Yes: Negotiating Agreement Without Giving In,* New York, NY: Penguin Books, 2011.

Gallup. *Strengths Based Leadership: Great Leaders, Teams, and Why People Follow.* New York, NY: Gallup Press, 2008.

Gelb, Michael J. *The Art of Connection: 7 Relationship-Building Skills Every Leader Needs Now.* Novato, CA: New World Library, 2017.

Goleman, Daniel, Richard Boyatzis, and Annie McKee. *Primal Leadership: Unleashing the Power of Emotional Intelligence.* Boston, MA: Harvard Business Press, 2013.

Gregersen, Hal. *Questions Are the Answer: A Breakthrough Approach to Your Most Vexing Problems at Work and in Life.* New York, NY: Harper Collins, 2018.

Hansen, Morten. *Collaboration: How Leaders Avoid the Traps, Build Common Ground, and Reap Big Results.* Boston, MA: Harvard Business Publishing, 2009.

Hofstede, Geert, Gert Jan Hofstede, and Michael Minkov. *Cultures and Organizations: Software of the Mind.* New York, NY: McGraw Hill, 2010.

Knapp, Jake. *Sprint (How to Solve Big Problems and Test New Ideas in Just Five Days).* Avon, MA: Simon & Schuster, 2016.

Lencioni, Patrick M. *The Advantage: Why Organizational Health Trumps Everything Else in Business.* San Francisco, CA: Jossey-Bass, 2012.

Lieberman, Matthew D. *Social: Why Our Brains Are Wired to Connect.* New York, NY: Crown, 2013.

Loehr, Jim, and Tony Schwartz. *The Power of Full Engagement: Managing Energy, Not Time, Is the Key to High Performance and Personal Renewal.* New York, NY: Free Press, 2003.

Marston, William Moulton. *Emotions of Normal People,* Redditch, UK: Read Books Ltd., 2013.

Molinsky, Andy. *Global Dexterity: How to Adapt Your Behavior Across Cultures without Losing Yourself in the Process.* Boston, MA: Harvard Business Press, 2013.

Patterson, Kerry, Joseph Grenny, Ron McMillan, and Al Switzler. *Crucial Conversations: Tools for Talking When Stakes are High.* New York, NY: McGraw Hill, 2012.

Pink, Daniel H. *Drive: The Surprising Truth About What Motivates Us.* New York, NY: Riverhead Books, 2009.

Pink, Daniel H. *When: The Scientific Secrets of Perfect Timing.* New York, NY: Riverhead Books, 2018.

Putnam, Robert D. *Bowling Alone: The Collapse and Revival of American Community.* New York, NY: Simon & Schuster Paperbacks, 2000.

Rod, Anne, and Marita Fridjhon. *Creating Intelligent Teams.* Johannesburg, South Africa: KR Publishing, 2016.

Rother, Mike. *Toyota Kata: Managing People for Improvement, Adaptiveness and Superior Results.* New York, NY: McGraw Hill, 2010.

Sandler, Len. *Becoming an Extraordinary Manager: The 5 Essentials for Success.* New York, NY: AMACOM, 2007.

Scott, Kim. *Radical Candor: Be a Kick-Ass Boss without Losing Your Humanity.* New York, NY: St. Martin's Press, 2017.

Shaw, Robert Bruce. *Extreme Teams: Why Pixar, Netflix, AirBnB, and Other Cutting-Edge Companies Succeed Where Most Fail.* New York, NY: AMACOM, 2017.

Stone, Douglas, and Sheila Heen. *Thanks for the Feedback: The Science and Art of Receiving Feedback Well.* New York, NY: Penguin Books, 2014.

Sutherland, Jeff, and J. J. Sutherland. *Scrum: The Art of Doing Twice the Work in Half the Time.* New York, NY: Crown, 2014.

Wall, Bob. *Working Relationships: The Simple Truth about Getting Along with Friends and Foes at Work.* Mountain View, CA: Davies-Black Publishing, 1999.

Wang, Ray. *Disrupting Digital Business: Create an Authentic Experience in the Peer-to-Peer Economy.* Boston, MA: Harvard Business Publishing, 2015.

Whitmore, Sir John. *Coaching for Performance. GROWing Human Potential and Purpose: The Principles and Practice of Coaching and Leadership.* Boston, MA: Nicholas Brealey Publishing, 2009.

INDEX

A

B

C

D

E

F

G

H

M

N

O

P

Q

R

S

T

U

V

W

X

Z

CONNECT WITH US!

The Book: ReconnectingWorkspaces.com

Our Services: PotentialsRealized.com

For Coaches: GroupCoachingEssentials.ca

Planner and Productivity: PlanDoTrack.com

Remote Pathways Podcast: RemotePathways.com

@ReconnectingWorkspaces

@RemotePathways

Virtual and Remote Visionaries Hub, Effective Group Coaching

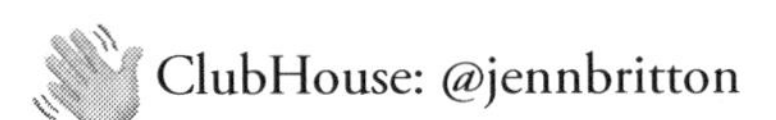
ClubHouse: @jennbritton

Email: info@potentialsrealized.com

Phone: (416) 996-TEAM (8326)

Set up a 15-minute conversation about your coaching, consulting, or training needs at

calendly.com/jennbritton

ABOUT THE AUTHOR

A trusted ally to thousands of coaches, business owners, teams and organizations since 2004, Jennifer Britton has dedicated her professional work over the last three decades to enhancing conversations and supporting results for businesses, teams, and organizations in the virtual, remote, and hybrid space.

An expert in group and team coaching and a performance improvement specialist, Jennifer founded her company, Potentials Realized, in 2004. Since 2006, her Group Coaching Essentials program has supported thousands in scaling the coaching conversation beyond the one-on-one coaching modality.

A former leader in the international humanitarian sector, she spent most of the 1990s and early 2000s leading geographically dispersed teams across countries and regions of the world that took five days to traverse. These experiences shaped her passion and insights around what is possible in the remote, hybrid and virtual space.

Over the last few years, her *PlanDoTrack* and *Coaching Business Builder Workbook and Planner* have been used by hundreds. The work is also rolled out by PDT and CBB Facilitators.

Jennifer is also the creator of the 21 for 21 Virtual Co-working Sprints.

An award-winning program designer, Jennifer is dedicated to supporting groups, teams and organizations in the areas of leadership, teamwork, and performance. Since the late 1980s, she has supported professionals across a wide sector with a global client list that spans government, corporate and non-profit sectors, from financial services to education to healthcare.

Jennifer is a thought leader in the field of group and team coaching. Her first book, *Effective Group Coaching*, was the first book ever to be published on the topic of group coaching. It has been used as a text and/or recommended resource for many coach-training programs for the past decade. She is a well-known international speaker on topics related to coaching, leadership, teamwork, virtual conversations, and capacity building.

Credentialed by the International Coaching Federation, Britton was originally trained and certified by the Coaches Training Institute. She has also completed advanced coaching training in multiple areas including Organization and Relationship Systems Coaching, Conversational Intelligence, and Shadow Coaching. She is a Draw Your Future™ Certified Facilitator.

A Certified Performance Technologist (CPT) and Certified Human Resource Leader (CHRL), Jennifer also holds a Masters in Environmental Studies (York University) and a Bachelor of Science in Psychology (McGill).

A typical day in Jennifer's work takes her around the world, as she gets to connect with professionals and organizations with Zoom from before dawn to early in the afternoon. She physically divides her time between just north of Toronto, and beautiful Muskoka, where she enjoys time spent in nature with family.

Printed in Great Britain
by Amazon